Reengineering Health Care

The Complexities of Organizational Transformation

TERRY McNULTY
and
EWAN FERLIE

OXFORD
UNIVERSITY PRESS

OXFORD

UNIVERSITY PRESS

Great Clarendon Street, Oxford OX2 6DP

Oxford University Press is a department of the University of Oxford.
It furthers the University's objective of excellence in research, scholarship,
and education by publishing worldwide in

Oxford New York

Auckland Bangkok Buenos Aires Cape Town Chennai
Dar es Salaam Delhi Hong Kong Istanbul Karachi Kolkata
Kuala Lumpur Madrid Melbourne Mexico City Mumbai Nairobi
São Paulo Shanghai Singapore Taipei Tokyo Toronto

with an associated company in Berlin

Oxford is a registered trade mark of Oxford University Press
in the UK and in certain other countries

Published in the United States
by Oxford University Press Inc., New York

British Library Cataloguing in Publication Data
Data available

Library of Congress Cataloging in Publication Data
Data available

ISBN 0-19-924084-1

1 3 5 7 9 10 8 6 4 2

Typeset by Newgen Imaging Systems (P) Ltd., Chennai, India
Printed in Great Britain
on acid-free paper by
Biddles Ltd., *www.biddles.co.uk*

For My Family
Terry

For Luis
Ewan

Acknowledgements

We acknowledge those organizations and individuals whose interest, support, and encouragement have enabled us to write this book:

Ian Bowns
Alan Brennan
John Hayes
Gerard Hodgkinson
Susan Lonsdale
John McGee
David Musson
Andrew Pettigrew
Kate Thomas
David Wilson

The Research and Development Directorate, Department of Health, for funding the study.

All those associated with reengineering at Leicester Royal Infirmary who cooperated with this study.

Contents

List of Tables

List of Figures

List of Appendices

Abbreviations

A&E	Accident and Emergency
BBC	British Broadcasting Corporation
BP	British Petroleum
BPR	business process reengineering
CD	clinical directorate
CEO	chief executive officer
CCSC	Centre for Corporate Strategy and Change
CQI	continuous quality improvement
DoH	Department of Health
DMU	Directly Managed Unit
EBM	evidence-based medicine
ECG	electrocardiograph
ENT	Ear, Nose, and Throat
GP	general practitioner
GUM	genito-urinary medicine
HA	Health Authority
HNA	Health Needs Assessment
HRM	human resource management
HSR	Health Services Research
ICI	Imperial Chemical Industries
ICT	Information Communication Technology
IT	information technology
LRI	Leicester Royal Infirmary
MIS	minimally invasive surgery
MIT	Massachusetts Institute of Technology
MLSO	medical laboratory scientific officer
NED	non-executive director
NHS	National Health Service
NHSCRD	National Health Service Centre for Reviews and Dissemination
NHSME	National Health Service Management Executive
NPM	new public management
OD	organizational development
PAS	patient administration system
RCT	randomized control trial
RHA	Regional Health Authority

ScHARR   School of Health and Related Research
            (University of Sheffield)
SSD   Social Services Department
TQM   total quality management
UK   United Kingdom
USA   United States of America

1

Introduction and Key Themes

Can large and complex organizations implement a strategy of 'Big Bang' change that seeks to move them from one configuration to another over a short period? While this strategy of organizational transformation is tempting for organizations under severe pressure to deliver ambitious performance improvements, is it wise or indeed even achievable?

This book describes and reflects on the experience of a major UK public sector organization (the Leicester Royal Infirmary, a large NHS teaching hospital) which in the mid-1990s undertook a serious and sustained effort to achieve such transformatory change, using the change model of Business Process Reengineering (BPR). This NHS Trust was coming under external and environmentally driven pressure to achieve ambitious performance improvements but needed to retain the support of doctors and other health care professsionals in doing this. This particular change programme was sustained, resourced, managed, and supported by stable top-level leadership: in other words it demonstrated a number of supporting conditions for achieving transformatory change. There was also a well-developed pattern of cooperation between managers and doctors in the site, and 'hybrid' or crossover roles had emerged which linked the two traditionally separate arenas of management and medicine (FitzGerald and Ferlie 2000). This hospital thus emerged as a high-profile national pilot site for BPR implementation to which others might look for guidance and lessons.

However, the impact of BPR-led change was less decisive and more locally variable across the many clinical settings in the hospital than was hoped for at the outset of the change programme: second order rhetoric gave way to first order impact. The process of change was highly contested and the outcome of change uneven. This was in large measure because doctors retained a high degree of control over work practices that the reengineers found difficult to reshape over very short time scales. These local behaviours reflect the sectoral context of UK health care, with its distinctive assumptions, strategic recipes, and regulating institutions. The pattern of professional dominance (Freidson

1970, 1994) was still observable at the clinical level and was not effectively challenged at least during the course of the BPR programme.

Management was anxious to form partnerships with clinicians in
order to implement the programme more effectively. Cooperation was
the desired strategy, rather than conflict or confrontation, reflecting an
assessment by senior management of the underlying power dynamics.
Doctors, especially those encouraged to move into management and
adopt a mixed clinico-managerial perspective, thus proved crucial to
the implementation of reengineering within clinical settings. Interestingly and unexpectedly, doctors' ability to shape the reengineering
agenda was often informed by their relations with middle managers
within the hospital. There were some signs of an accommodation
between clinicians and managers with responsibilities for particular
clinical service domains that served to fend off the transformational
ambitions of reengineering. This finding runs counter to the much
espoused view that relations between doctors and managers are necessarily conflictual in nature. So, the old had a powerful role in shaping
the emergence of the new (Denis et al. 1999), with the implication that
change proved to be less than transformational in nature.

The power base of professional workers—here doctors—remains a
crucial factor in the organizational context of change within the health
care sector. Behind this continuing pattern of professional dominance
lies a historic alliance between the UK State and elite professions that
may be under threat but has not yet broken down. The restructuring of
fundamental governance relations within the health care sector is proceeding at a much slower pace in the UK than the USA (Caronna and
Scott 1999), where professional groupings lost their dominance much
earlier, first to an expansionist federal government and then to market
forces and aggressive third-party payers (such as Health Maintenance
Organizations).

This conclusion as to the empirical impact of a BPR experiment in
this national pilot site is important because a number of stakeholders
and interest groups promote Big Bang change strategies. Management
seeks to develop a reputation for 'turnarounds' and 'transformational
leadership'. Each new group of ministers proclaims its vision for the
future, especially within public sector organizations, where political
control remains at its most direct. This often underplays implementation questions (or 'delivery' in the current New Labour formulation) at
least in the initial stages of reform programmes. The danger is that the
implementation lessons of the past will not be fully drawn given an
over-optimistic belief that this time the pattern could be different. This

is despite a well-known literature on implementation deficits within social policy programmes that goes back to Pressman and Wildavsky (1973). Thirdly, change management has become a major area of business for management knowledge producers. So management gurus, the popular business press, and management consultants act as idea carriers and product diffusers between sectors (Abrahamson 1991, 1996), talking up the impact of change products at the front end of each change process. These knowledge producers typically diffuse these products into the public sector once the market in the private sector has peaked. Finally, management scholars must also take some blame as we loudly produce a series of ever brasher conceptual models (here of organizational transformation) in order to grab attention in what is an overcrowded field. The promise and allure of so-called 'organizational transformation' strategies may attract many managerial practitioners beyond the results it delivers in practice. The failure to recognize this overreach is an interesting question, and suggests that many organizations deny or forget more than they learn.

So, our overall theme is organizational transformation and its limits. We will not only present our empirical case-study work, drawing out lessons for practice, but also seek to emplace it within the broader academic literatures to promote systemic learning as well as site-specific learning. In particular, aspects of organizational change theory (namely, organizational transformation, its limits, and process-based organizations) and the literature on the New Public Management (NPM) and public sector restructuring and on the changing role and nature of the health care professions all need to be considered. These three organizing motifs will be developed throughout the monograph. These core themes will be introduced in this introductory chapter, along with the overall design of the empirical study. They will be developed further in later chapters.

1.1 Organizational transformation, its limits, and process-based organization

Until the 1980s, many of the received models of organizational change were incrementalist (Lindblom 1959) in nature, and reliant on piecemeal, gradual, and even linear forms of change. Other models stressed 'muddling through with a purpose', using continuous and evolving consensus-building approaches (Quinn 1980). This same approach continues today in change models such as the Continuous Improvement

techniques (often associated with Total Quality Management programmes, TQM) which typically generate very many suggestions for
small incremental changes rather than a few radical changes (Joss and
Kogan 1995).

Starting in the 1980s and accelerating in the 1990s, there was a switch
of scholarly, consulting, and practitioner interest to more ambitious
and synoptic forms of organizational change. Various conceptual models of organizational transformation were produced (Levy 1986;
Dunphy and Stace 1988; Blumenthal and Haspeslagh 1994; Romanelli
and Tushman 1994; also Eisenhardt and Bourgeois 1988 on 'high velocity' environments), all of which reflected this change of interest. Other
authors (Tichy and Ulrich 1984; Schein 1985) stressed the role of transformational leadership in revitalizing mature organizations. This new
literature paved the way for the development of consultancy change
products that promised the delivery of rapid, transformational change.
The concept of an occasional radical and rapid 'paradigm shift'—interspersed with long periods of inertia—was invoked in Pettigrew's
(1985) study of strategic change at ICI, which applied Kuhn's (1962)
notion of a paradigm shift first developed within the sociology of science to the field of organizational analysis. Here was an alternative to
the usual evolutionary models of organizational change that instead
highlighted short periods of 'frame-breaking' change.

Within the field, an increasing number of UK organizations in the
1980s undertook large-scale or strategic change efforts, as traditional
markets dried up (in the private sector) or government pressure for
performance intensified (in the public sector). Such change efforts
included the delayering of management structures and ambitious culture change programmes (as in BP under Robert Horton). One set of
performance-related questions concerned who was doing well and
why in such strategic change efforts. Sets of favourable factors were
identified within research undertaken at the Centre for Corporate
Strategy and Change (CCSC), University of Warwick, both in the private sector (Pettigrew and Whipp 1991) and in health care (Pettigrew,
Ferlie, and McKee 1992). Later work (Ferlie et al. 1996) introduced the
theme of organizational transformation within the restructured public
sector, although it was too early to come to conclusions about its success at that stage.

The Warwick group was of course only one research centre in what
was a growing field. An important academic development internationally—and especially in the USA— was the growth of institutional theory from the late 1970s onwards (Meyer and Rowan 1977; Di Maggio

and Powell 1983). Important regulating forces (notably the State and the professions) were here seen as constraining permissible patterns of organizational behaviour, nowhere more so than in the public sector, where these regulating forces were strongest. Greenwood and Hinings (1993) wrote of organizations as being based on an 'archetype' or consistent set of interlocking properties which was difficult to shift. They defined an organizational archetype as 'a set of structures and systems that reflects a single interpretive scheme' (Greenwood and Hinings 1993: 1052). This included an awareness of the importance of the underlying organizational ideology as well as more evident structural factors. Another important development within sociology that affected organizational change theory was Giddens's (1984) concept of structuration, where organizational change is seen as a result of the interplay between human agency and context. Context affects agency and vice versa. A recurrent interest within structuration theory is with social practices and their transformations so that tracing the nature of interactions between agency and structure within major social (and organizational) change processes is an important research task. Child's (1972, 1997) model of strategic choice similarly combined an awareness of the organizational context as well as the possibility of managerial action.

From these perspectives, reproduction of organizing and work processes appears as least as likely as change. Any mature discussion should consider the limits as well as the promise of organizational transformation. An important weakness is empirical as there is as yet very little rigorous empirical evidence to assess the long-term impact of these planned transformation initiatives, so that much of the discussion of organizational transformation remains vague, normative, or coloured by special interest (such as consultant product development or organizational image projection). What happens when organizations launch these change processes? Do they achieve initial objectives? Do the benefits outweigh the considerable costs (as these change programmes may be very costly in time and money)? Given that the effects may well be lagged, do we have good longitudinal data that can assess the experience of the organization over a considerable time period?

There is also an important work of theoretical development to be undertaken. There increasingly appear to be intermediate effects between total success and total failure within organizational transformation efforts. Concepts of partial transformation and of unanticipated hybrid forms emerge as important findings (Oliver and Montgomery 2000).

Cooper et al. (1996) examined professional organizations (in this case, Canadian law firms) and concluded that sedimented rather than transformed organizations emerged, where there was a layering of one archetype on another rather than simple replacement. Kitchener's (1999) study of the potential transition from a professionally based archetype to a more market-based archetype in the UK health care system also found that formal structures and decision-making processes indeed changed, but that basic values, ideas, and practices persisted. The pattern of change was uneven and inconsistent, as underlying shifts to professional belief systems lagged behind formal structural changes. Indeed, established professional elites themselves actively engage in trying to reshape the reform agenda to fit their own purposes and beliefs (Denis et al. 1999).

BPR is an approach to organizational change that promises dramatic improvements in business performance. Its characteristic feature is the radical (or 'blanksheet') redesign of all key processes and systems within an organization, with implementation leading to discontinuous improvements in key measures of performance such as service or product quality or cost effectiveness (Hammer and Champy 1993). It stands in contrast to other change strategies that concentrate on making modest, incremental, improvements to existing processes over a long period. BPR is thought to be more likely to succeed if redesign and implementation are rapid (that is, completed within two years), otherwise prevailing inertia will lead to regression to the status quo. It requires a number of change leadership roles such as dedicated people organized in teams and sustained top-level support (Hammer and Champy 1993). However, the failure rate appears to be high and one estimate suggests that perhaps only 50 per cent of serious BPR initiatives achieve the type and scale of benefits intended (Caron, Jarvenpaa, and Stoddard 1994). It has also been criticized as very technically focused and as unable to handle the human, social, and political aspects of complex organizational change (Buchanan 1997; Willmott 1995). How are we to understand this bold rhetoric and approach to change management? We would already argue that it fails to take adequate account of underlying organizational contexts and dynamics: it is uninformed organizationally and too prescriptive, managerialist, and rationalistic in nature. These theoretical debates about 'organizational transformation' and its limits will be considered in more detail in Chapter 2, using some of the theoretical developments in structuration, strategic choice, and neo-institutionalist theory briefly mentioned here.

1.2　**BPR as an exemplar of process organization**

It is also helpful to conceive of BPR as one example of a larger family of organizational interventions. BPR is not merely a time-limited 'managerial fad' but is another variant on the theme of the 'process-based organization'. In an important article, Denison (1997) argues that the 'process perspective' on organizing is emerging as a major challenge to the functional principles of organizing adhered to for almost a century. Denison argues that the classical functional approach has been dominated by a concern to achieve forms of coordination that can enhance the scale of production and achieve economies of scale. Such control-dominated thinking about organizational design manifests itself in layers of hierarchical control and complex chains of command.

By contrast, a process perspective is more concerned with the value creation process itself, rather than mere control over the value creation process. In changing market conditions—such as the development of global scope, distributed control systems such as IT, and the shift from a sellers' to a buyers' market—value creation can be seen as a relatively non-hierarchical process that involves the lateral coordination of a chain of events taking place inside and outside the boundaries of formal organizations. Many recent management innovations superficially appear disconnected (quality; lean production; BPR; network or virtual organizations), yet at a deeper level they are united by a common concern to redefine or recreate the value chain. The organization is here understood not as a series of vertically integrated functional units but as a collection of interrelated processes that add value. Strategic choice is less about which business to compete in and more about how to create value in a chosen business. The emphasis within BPR on process redesign across (in the case of health care) patient pathways is a clear exemplification of an attempt to move to a more lateral mode of organizing.

This is an interesting conceptual ideal type, although there is a recognized paucity of high-quality empirical evidence (Pettigrew and Fenton 2000; Denison 1997) to ground the discussion. Denison's identification of BPR as the process perspective that has had greatest impact on business practice lends additional interest to the results of the present study as we can contribute to the limited stock of independently produced knowledge about process models of organizing within real world organizations. Chapter 2 considers this organizational literature on novel process-based models of organizing in greater depth.

1.3   Changing contexts of health care

1.3.1   *The new public management and public sector restructuring*

We argue that change management models are not generically applicable but their impact may well vary by the organizational context in which they are launched. Analytically, there is a need to define this notion of 'context' and bring it effectively into the discussion. A first dimension is the macro-context of the public sector as a whole. The NHS is a publicly funded organization where there are few markets, customers, or prices as would be conventionally understood. So one question is whether the shift to process-based organizations is dependent on drivers which are particular to the private sector (such as market pressure or assertive customers), or whether such (or analogous) forces could also exert pressure within public sector contexts. This relates to a well-developed debate on the problems and possibilities of intersectoral diffusion. Hammer and Champy (1993), for instance, argue that BPR is applicable to public sector organizations in principle, but that the public sector poses special implementation challenges that explain why it is that governmental agencies are often 'laggards' in reengineering terms.

A second question is whether those public sector settings are themselves changing and whether in particular they are becoming more 'firm-like' in their nature. The greater intersectoral convergence becomes the less valid the argument of public sector exceptionalism. How might we analyse such high-level changes across public sector agencies (which may be broad ranging in nature rather than narrowly confined to the health care subsystem)? We start by asserting that changing models of organization and management in public sector agencies—where the government is a monopoly funder—are likely to be highly sensitive to shifts in the political economy and high-level political and ideological ideas about how public services should be managed. So, a second high-level theme that will be explored throughout the book is the influence of this changing public sector context on the fate of the BPR change programme. Change exercises (such as BPR) are introduced within a changing public sector context and further contribute to those changes.

To do this, we need to characterize the large number of changes that have been apparent in UK public sector agencies over the last twenty years at a higher level of analysis. Ideas for the strategic restructuring of the public sector slowly emerged within the NPM umbrella. The NPM was an international movement that influenced public sector restructuring in a number of jurisdictions (Pollitt 1990; Hood 1991), but the UK can be seen as a 'high-impact' case (Hood 1995) and within the UK health care was a high-impact sector (Ferlie et al. 1996). Within the NPM movement, markets and management represent two mobilizing themes that were applied to the old public sector agencies that had grown up under the previous social democratic state as a reform programme. There was here increased pressure for public sector producers to demonstrate performance. Managerial roles were expanded in order to provide a countervailing force that could dilute traditional patterns of professional dominance and autonomy. Quasi-markets were also introduced in the NHS and other settings in the early 1990s in order to mimic the operation of market forces and sharpen incentive structures. Chapter 3 will discuss the development of the NPM in further detail and relate it to the changing sectoral context within which the case-study site operated during the BPR programme. Three NPM-related contextual forces stand out as of particular importance.

Strength and impact of quasi-market forces. The first theme relates to the strength and impact of internal market forces. One of the reasons that BPR was introduced was the expectation that accelerating market forces would place more pressure on the hospital to perform and that incremental improvements would be inadequate. Yet, the policy rhetoric also stated that the market would be a 'managed market'. The key question is: were internal market forces of a significant enough scale to act as a driver for organizational transformation or were they increasingly contained?

The growth of managerial and clinico-managerial roles. The second theme refers to changing managerial and clinico-managerial roles and relationships. A strategic objective of NPM reform efforts has been to introduce more visible and assertive managerial roles and to incorporate professional groupings within the managerial block to reduce the traditional divide between professionals and managers. This has led to the elaboration of managerial roles and capacity throughout the various tiers across hospitals, and not merely at the most senior levels where general management was initially confined. An important effect of the BPR programme in the site was the reduction of traditional professionally orientated middle management (such as nursing middle managers), but the creation of a smaller but more developed operational management cadre that could link strategic and operational change.

There have also been attempts to draw clinicians further into the management process. Indeed, the rapid diffusion of so-called clinical director roles in the 1990s was a marked feature of quasi-market restructuring (Kitchener 1999) and was strongly developed within the case-study hospital. Some important questions emerge. What happens to the relationships between clinico-managerial hybrids, general managers, and reengineers? Again, there is a debate about the significance of any shift towards clinico-managerial roles. In an American context, Freidson (1994) argues that much more active managerial roles are emerging at senior levels of professional groupings, with responsibility for performance management. Within the UK, some accounts (Ferlie et al. 1996) stress the role of clinical directors in dealing with 'thorny issues' such as underperforming colleagues, but Ackroyd (1996) argues that such changes are cosmetic, as reorganization is taking place round 'encapsulated' professional groups rather than reconstructing them.

The growth of strategic management. A third NPM-related theme is the extent to which there has been a growth of corporate identity and strategic management capacity within the hospital. Traditionally, management in the health care sector has been decentralized to individual clinical settings rather than being corporate or strategic in nature (Mintzberg 1979). The extended range of different stakeholders, competing objectives, and presence of many professional groups may impede the development of a strategic management capacity.

In this case study, however, we see the use of a sophisticated strategic management intervention that aimed to reconfigure the hospital as a whole. The corporate core designed and monitored an implementation strategy for a hospital-wide change programme aimed at achieving important organization-wide effects. This was linked to the renewal of the clinical directorate cadre within the hospital and the use of education and training interventions to promote a greater corporate identity amongst clinico-managerial hybrids. The change programme was strongly supported by the use of dedicated internal and external change agents as another implementation resource. One question is whether this strategic activity at the corporate level was able to effect change within the clinical settings. An analytic history of the strategic management of the BPR change programme is contained within Chapter 5, suggesting that there were important shifts in the course of the programme from an intended Big Bang strategy to an emergent more gradualist strategy as some of the implementation difficulties became increasingly prominent.

1.3.2   *Hospitals as organizations*

A second level at which context can be analysed is the meso-context of the whole population of hospitals. This can be construed as a collective organizational field (while the third or micro-level of context refers to the history and dynamics of the particular hospital under study). So, what kind of organization is a hospital? What are the implications of the dominant organizational form for process redesign efforts such as BPR?

A first assertion is that hospitals should be seen as a highly politicized type of organization. Organizations vary in the extent to which they are politicized: a central government department may be seen as highly politicized; while a small business is typically less politicized. Most obviously, there is a party political element to such politicization in publicly funded health care systems such as the NHS as elected politicians set the overall policy framework, which may well shift along with political control. Thus, Conservative governments promoted the internal market model between 1991 and 1997, which was largely abandoned by the New Labour government after 1997. But the health care system can be seen as highly politicized in a more subtle sense of bargaining between many different stakeholders. How do we conceive of this politicization process? We argue that there are many different occupational and interest groups within the health care system with competing goals and agendas. Change processes are not neutral between such groups, but produce winners and losers—and it may be entirely rational for the victims of change to put up resistance. These different groups bargain and negotiate between themselves, trying to form dominant coalitions. However, some groups have much more power than others, so that power inequalities may affect the outcome of change efforts. These are also institutions that are increasingly affected by the exercise of State power rather than micro-level 'negotiated orders'. We use a boundedly pluralist frame of political analysis, rather than a purely pluralist or a radical frame of reference. Chapter 3 will develop the argument that health care organizations should be seen as 'boundedly pluralistic' politicized systems, in which there are many interest groups but that some are much more powerful than others, including the State.

Secondly, we need to discuss the distinctive conditions produced by underlying high professionalization as well as high politicization. So, we distinguish in Chapter 3 between two alternative principles for the structuring of clinical work, whose coexistence within hospital organizations forms an important basis for the micro-politics of health care (Watson 1995). The first is the occupational principle of work organized by profession and then by clinical specialty. The second is the organizational principle of blocks of service organized along managerial lines, as seen in the diffusion of clinical directorate model within UK health care. The coexistence of the traditional occupational principle with an increasingly assertive organizational principle provides ample scope for political behaviour (in the wider sense) around attempts to alter or protect the historic division of labour. So, any analysis of the impact of a strategic change programme within health care will need to engage with the division of roles and power balance between clinical professionals, clinical directors, and health care managers.

While medicine has traditionally been seen as an extreme case of professional dominance (Freidson 1970, 1994), there have more recently been recurrent cycles of attempts to managerialize health care organizations (Harrison et al. 1992; Harrison and Pollitt 1994). So, should the NHS now be seen as a conventionally 'managed' organization? We argue that while there is evidence of some loss of autonomy on the part of UK doctors, there remain some important power bases on which they can call, particularly at the micro-level of the clinical setting. We suggest that the capacity of doctors to influence the fate of change programmes within hospitals remains considerable, and that a lack of professional ownership would still be a predictor of low impact. We also need to be mindful of the processes of negotiation for work 'jurisdictions' (Abbott 1988) that exist between different health care professions (such as doctors and nurses) or even between segments within the same profession (such as physicians and surgeons). Chapter 3 argues that this picture of high politicization and high professionalization poses considerable challenges to process redesign efforts within health care organizations that have not been adequately considered in much of the process redesign literature.

1.4   A process study: overall principles of design

While the detailed research design will be discussed in Chapter 4, broad principles of method can be outlined here. We believe that organizations—and the formal and informal processes that go on within them—exert important effects on the ability of any change programme to effect change. An implication is that qualitative and field-based research is needed which can get inside the black box of the organization to capture these effects, many of which will not be easily observable on the surface. This is reflected in the growing interest in qualitative research within health care organizations (Pope and Mays 2000) that should be seen as large, complex, and internally segmented. As institutions, they exert powerful effects on the behaviour of the groups and individuals within them. Our theoretical stance that change programmes are highly contextually sensitive implies the use of methods that can investigate context in a finely grained manner.

Some social scientists are currently calling for a return to the 'scientific' principles of quasi-experimentation in order to produce an evidence base for policy (Oakley 2000). We do not share this position and are closer to the stance of 'realistic evaluation' (Pawson and Tilley 1997) as appropriate to messy and naturally occurring settings. This is another implication of a preference for qualitative, field-based approaches. While Randomized Control Trials, quasi-experiments, and input/output studies are valuable in addressing some well-defined research questions, they are in our view being overextended into fields in which they are frankly unhelpful, such as change management. The influence of the Evidence-Based Medicine movement on some approaches to research into health care organizations has been apparent. Triallists' current search (Bero et al. 1998) for discrete change levers that exert generic effects on all health care organizations is unlikely to bear fruit even in the long term because of an inability to control either for the nature of the intervention (BPR may in fact take very different forms in different hospitals) or the organizational context (so American or French results may be very different from UK results). Their methodological stance reflects the over-dominance of the biomedical research paradigm within Health Services Research which has traditionally crowded out alternative methods, using what is in this field an inappropriate hierarchy of evidence model at the apex of which stands the RCT. Within the change management field, such quantitative methods need to be succeeded by more qualitative approaches better able to examine patterns of behaviour within complex real world organizations at a holistic level.

Reflecting this overall methodological position, we are interested in how and why questions at least as much as what questions. The 'what' measure is a rather modest and indeed qualitative one: the amount of change experienced within the clinical settings sampled. We were not interested in establishing statistical patterns across whole populations of organizations, but rather in undertaking an in-depth analysis of the experience of one organization. Thus we used qualitative methods well adapted to the study of organizational process, behaviour, and interactions. Such methods are well established in British organizational research and there is growing interest in them within HSR (Pope and Mays 2000), as it broadens out from its narrow biomedical base.

Given this overall decision to adopt a qualitative approach, it was then necessary to specify methods that were appropriate for the tracking of change within a large organization rather than (say) gathering qualitative data on a relatively contained group of patients' experience of their use of health care services. This was an organizational process study. Keen and Packwood (2000: 51) argue that within empirical and evaluative forms of analysis 'case studies are valuable where policy change is occurring within messy real world settings, and it is important to understand why such interventions succeed or fail'. In such settings, experimental designs are neither feasible nor likely to answer the why and how questions posed. The basic design chosen was an intensive case study of the whole organization. This fits with a generic methodological orientation in much of our work that can be defined as a longitudinal, contextual, and comparative case study-based method for studying organizational change (Pettigrew 1990). As is common within organizational research, the analysis operated at the levels of organizational structure and process and also the assessment of some intermediate change-related outcomes (such as evidence of shifts in throughput, waiting times, or interdepartmental coordination) rather than an analysis of final clinical outcomes. The analysis is longitudinal rather than cross-sectional in nature, as we wish to plot the whole career of the BPR intervention over time. The intervention also needs to be understood in the light of local antecedent conditions and earlier small-scale interventions upon which BPR built. The analysis is contextual because the change outcomes can only be understood in the light of local and sectoral contexts (such as continuing professional dominance over work practices). While this is a study of one organization, there are comparisons offered between different clinical settings within the organizational case study in order to expose and explain variation in change. We have in fact a nested set of case studies within the one organization. In addition, Chapter 9 also reviews the results of other studies into BPR in health care organizations to test our findings against a wider body of literature.

Finally, our analysis is systemic and holistic rather than highly focal in nature: we wanted to plot the experience of change across the organization as a whole. Multi-tier analysis was needed (FitzGerald et al. 1999) to access interactions across different tiers within this complex organization. As an intervention, BPR is highly diffuse rather than contained in nature, directly spawning a large number of different projects and indirectly creating further 'knock-on' interventions. As we were working in an organizational laboratory over which we had no power, we could not of course 'control' for the effects of other confounding interventions in a way that would be normal within an RCT type design. Change may indeed have multiple causes—some of them quite unexpected—so that the challenge is to identify within an inductive analysis of the hospital system various possible causal agents and how they interact. Disentangling the effects of the BPR programme from other possible causal agents is indeed difficult, although we have tried to address this problem of identifying and discussing alternative causes within interviews and the writing of the case studies.

Another objection may be that we have produced local rather than systemic knowledge. Although this is a study of a single hospital, it adds to a wider body of knowledge, apparent in the study of corporate change programmes in health care (Joss and Kogan 1995 on TQM) and even the impact of BPR in other hospitals (Buchanan 1997; Packwood, Pollitt, and Roberts 1998). It is also related to a body of organizational theory, permitting conceptual rather than empirical generalization. Goffman's (1961) case study of a single psychiatric hospital, for example, produced the theoretical construct of the 'total institution' that had wide relevance not only to other psychiatric hospitals but other organizational classes (such as prisons and medical schools).

We undertook a series of nested case studies at three interacting levels: the corporate core (Chapter 5); the intermediate divisional level (Chapter 7); and the clinical setting (Chapter 6). There was a purposeful approach taken to the selection of cases at the level of the clinical settings to assist our exploration of possible sources of variation. This inter-setting comparison helped us develop an inductive model of the change process across the settings (Chapter 8). Such identification of low-level patterns represents the beginnings of middle-range theory-building (Eisenhardt 1989).

1.5 Concluding remarks

Three organizing themes (organizational transformation and its limits; BPR seen as a vehicle for a possible shift to a novel process-based organization; and the influence of the changing context and political economy of UK health care organizations on such change efforts) have been presented in this introductory chapter and will be worked through in more detail in later chapters. The use of qualitative methods is defended as appropriate given that this is a process-based study of organizational change within a natural setting. The potentially powerful role of professional groups in shaping the outcomes of transformational change strategies was also highlighted.

Our empirical analysis will suggest that partial change was apparent in the hospital, but not radical transformation: there were important limits to the achievement of Big Bang change. As an empirical study of the fate of a corporate change programme, it is a valuable addition to the literature, providing learning material for reflective managerial practitioners. It illuminates a naturally occurring attempt to secure organizational transformation within a large and complex public sector organization. This experiment included a sophisticated attempt to generate a strategic management framework and to think about different approaches to implementation so that this local experience of change management provides lessons that are more general. We seek in this monograph to produce an empirically based and theoretically informed analysis of the experience of BPR implementation by a leading public sector organization. Just as managerial fashions can spread out from such high-profile early adopters, so we hope that our production of evaluative knowledge will more usefully diffuse to the practitioner as well as the academic communities, provide a base for learning, and influence managerial behaviour in the future (Abrahamson 1991, 1996). In the next chapter, we explore the BPR phenomenon in more detail and relate it to the literature on organizational transformation and its limits. We also consider BPR as one example of a possible shift to a wider new process-based form of organizing.

2

Understanding Business Process Reengineering as Planned Organizational Transformation

2.1 Introduction

Greater environmental turbulence and attention to organizational change as a core organizational capability are apparently informing a widespread interest in more transformational approaches to organizing and strategizing in contemporary organizations. Transformation represents a relatively recent emphasis within organization theory and practice directing attention to matters of scale, pace, and impact of change processes in and around organizations. Until the 1980s much work centred on change at the team, unit, or divisional levels (Greiner and Barnes 1970; Mumford 1972; Partin 1973; Ottoway 1976). Models of organizational change were incremental in nature and stressed 'muddling through with a purpose' through consensus and evolution (Quinn 1980; Lindblom 1959). Change theories implicit in early quality approaches to production and total quality management continued to emphasize small incremental changes rather than radical changes (Denison 1997; Joss and Kogan 1995). A recent scholarly, consulting, and practitioner interest in more ambitious and transformatory forms of organizational change coincides with perceptions of intensifying industrial competition on a global scale, technological innovation, and changing patterns of consumer demand and behaviour (Dunphy and Stace 1988; Blumenthal and Haspeslagh 1994; Romanelli and Tushman 1994; Eisenhardt and Bourgeois 1988; Pettigrew 1987; Tichy and Ulrich 1984; Schein 1985). For individual firms, transformation is projected as critical to survival and leadership within volatile organizational environments. Business Process Reengineering is promoted as a contemporary prescription to guide and accomplish organizational transformation (Hammer and Champy 1993). What is business process reengineering, and how should we examine the possibilities and progress of reengineering in practice? With these key questions in mind, Chapters 2 and 3 develop the conceptual 'lens' through which the implementation and impact of reengineering in the case-study site will be described, analysed, and explained throughout the remainder of the monograph.

This chapter introduces business process reengineering as an important example of a new perspective of organizing—the process perspective (Denison 1997). While business process reengineering may be itself a relatively short-lived managerial change programme, the signs are that it is related to change efforts that are consistent with the underlying process perspective of organizing (Denison 1997). The full adoption of a process perspective might indeed be seen as an organizational transformation. The radical spirit of organizational transformation can be clearly observed in the idealized image of the 'process organization' and the rhetoric of business process reengineering promising dramatic change and improvement in organizational processes and performance (Hammer and Champy 1993).

Diverse commentaries observed about reengineering are labelled classical, incremental revisionist, and critical. Classical and incremental revisionist writers are shown to exude great confidence in the capacity of organizational leaders to effect transformation through interventions based on ideas of business process reengineering. Critical writers are sceptical, expressing concern about assumptions of organization and change employed by classical and incremental writers, as well as results of BPR in practice. They encourage deeper questioning of the link between BPR and organizational transformation.

What is organization transformation, and how can we empirically assess a BPR-inspired attempt at organizational transformation? These questions are addressed in the second half of the chapter wherein several theoretical schemes are presented as helpful to the challenge of assessing and explaining the process and impact of BPR. Organizational transformation is viewed as a complex process involving challenge and change to established structure, action, and performance. It is doubtful that organizational transformation can realistically be characterized as either a single event or a time-limited linear process unfolding in an even-paced and sequential manner. A more sustained and scholarly literature about organizational change and transformation suggests a complex link between the ambition, intent, and outcomes of managerial change initiatives (Pettigrew 1987). Developments in sociology and organization theory point to simplistic notions of transformation implied in much of the BPR literature and a need to attend to the relationship between human agency and context within any explanation of organizational change (Child 1997, 1972; Greenwood and Hinings 1996; Giddens 1984).

Child's (1972) influential theory of strategic choice was originally advanced to avoid overlooking organizational leaders' influence over organization form, process, and purpose. In contrast to much of the BPR literature, strategic choice is socially contextualized. As action in context, strategic choice is to be understood by locating the agency of organizational actors within the mutually pervasive relationship between organizations and relevant environments. Strategic choice appears as an example within the organizational domain of a more generally observable process of structuration (Giddens 1984). For Child (1997), the choices and actions of managerial agents are mediated by the very same cognitive and relational structures that such choices and actions are designed to modify. Organizational and institutional environments may thus enable or constrain agency. For this study of BPR, an implication of strategic choice theory is that any assessment of the impact of BPR needs to look for continuities as well as change, as the organization or its environment may provide restraining forces which blunt the impact of managerial interventions. We are right to be wary of highly subjective concepts of 'leadership' that ignore contextual conditions. Indeed, more successful styles of leadership will be those that recognize the limits of permissible action, while perhaps trying to change them in the longer run.

In moving between assessment and explanation of the impact of BPR it is necessary therefore to study the interaction between intra-organizational and extra-organizational dynamics. The neo-institutional model of radical change proposed by Greenwood and Hinings (1996) is helpful in this regard. More accommodating of agency and choice than institutional theory, Greenwood and Hinings's (1996) theory of radical change is much more attuned to the organizational and institutional dynamics of change than models of change that underpin much BPR and change management prescription. Possibilities for radical organizational change are adjudged to lie in interaction between 'exogenous' dynamics (market context and institutional context) and 'endogenous' dynamics of interests, values, power dependencies, and capacity for action.

The concept of 'capacity for action' facilitates a deeper discussion of managerial approaches, actions, and skills for accomplishing transformation in the closing part of the chapter. BPR's Big Bang approach to change through high investment in a pre-packaged product and prescribed technology stands in stark contrast to the other studies that characterize major organizational change to result from longer-term processes of learning, conditioning, and influencing. Critical related managerial skills and actions include recognizing and sensing a need for change; conditioning the organization for change; leading and visioning change; energizing and influencing people; and linking strategic and operational levels of the organization (Pettigrew and Whipp 1991; Child and Smith 1987; Pettigrew 1985). Whilst acknowledging the perceived necessity for accelerated and radical change in contemporary organizational conditions BPR appears a risky strategy for accomplishing transformation in the light of existing evidence.

2.2 A process perspective on organizing

For future performance, organizations are being urged to experiment with new organizing structures and processes. A whole host of concepts have been prescribed including business process reengineering (Hammer and Champy 1993). Whilst some argue that the diversity of organizing models and prescription represents no clear paradigm of future organization (Djelic and Ainamo 1999), others observe a 'process perspective' on organizing emerging as a major challenge to 'functional' principles of organizing adhered to for the best part of a century (Denison 1997).

Denison's thesis is that the classic functional approach to organizational design assumed value creation and has as its principal concern resolution of coordination problems associated with enhanced scale of production and attainment of economies of scale. Organizational design is thus seen as a discipline that has addressed control of the value creation process, but not the underlying value creation process itself. Control-dominated thinking about organization design is manifest in layers of hierarchical control and complex chains of command. This approach suited what Denison terms 'a sellers' market'. By contrast, a process perspective of organization is more concerned with the value creation process itself, rather than merely the control of the value creation process. In changing market conditions—such as the development of global scope, distributed control systems via IT, and the development of a buyers' market—value creation is seen, for the most part, as a relatively non-hierarchical process that involves the lateral coordination of a chain of events taking place inside and outside the boundaries of formal organizations.

For Denison (1997) most recent innovations, both practitioner and scholarly inspired, are process oriented in their inclination to organizing, managing, and (re)designing the value chain—a linked system of inter-dependent activities that are used as building blocks for competitive advantage. 'Quality', 'kaizen', 'benchmarking', and 'lean production' are seen to be early process initiatives focused primarily upon managing and improving efficiency of the existing value chain. 'Customer focus', 'cycle time', 'lateral or horizontal organization', 'de-jobbing', and 'reengineering' are seen as later process perspectives concerned with organization and reorganization of the existing value chain. 'Mass customization', 'network organizations', 'virtual organizations', and 'organizational learning' are more recent process perspectives distinguished by a primary concern with creating and redefining the value chain.

Denison's (1997) characterization of the ideal-typical 'process-organization' is therefore one wherein the primary issue of organizational design is creating value. Organizing is understood not as a series of functional units, business units, or national organizations but as a collection of interrelated processes that create value. Strategic choice is less about which business to compete in and more about how to create value in a chosen business. Maximum value creation is created when concerns with quality and efficiency are coupled with flexibility to respond to customer needs. Dynamics of industry structures usually mean that any particular value chain is a relatively short-lived construction in need of constant revision. The primary control system in the process organization is the market. Hierarchy is present at three levels serving the operation and improvement of an existing value chain, matching resources and dynamics of the value chain and designing value creation processes of the future.

A paucity of empirical evidence associated with this ideal-type organization is recognized (Pettigrew and Fenton 2000; Denison 1997). Denison's identification of business process reengineering as the process perspective that has had greatest impact on business practice makes this study's interest in the process and fate of reengineering a potentially important contribution to the very limited stock of empirical knowledge about process views of organizing. The following discussion of business process reengineering therefore looks more closely at the ideas of BPR, the linkage of BPR to a process theory of organization, the transformation rhetoric associated with BPR, and evidence of BPR effects in practice.

2.3   Business process reengineering

Business process reengineering is defined as 'the fundamental rethinking and radical redesign of business processes to achieve dramatic improvements in critical contemporary measures of performance such as cost, quality, service and speed' (Hammer and Champy 1993: 32). Some see the origins of BPR to lie with learning by management consultants from a decade's experience of observing and assisting high organizational performance through the development of a process approach to organizing and managing (Hammer and Champy 1993). Others locate the origins of the concept more within the realm of academe, suggesting its roots lie in MIT's research programme 'Management in the 90's' which focused on the impact of information communication technology (ICTs) on organizations (Burke and Peppard 1995; Peppard and Rowland 1995).

As a concept business process reengineering soon gained in influence diffusing quickly from its American, manufacturing origins to Europe and non-manufacturing settings. Why this piece of 'technology transfer' happened as fast as it did has been the subject of some discussion. BPR champions and advocates are inclined to attribute the appeal of BPR to practitioners' recognition of the importance of the BPR as a business philosophy to create dramatic performance gains (Hammer and Champy 1993). Others explain the appeal of BPR by referring to enabling processes in the wider context of BPR, for instance, the revolution in information technology (Vankantraman 1991) and the failure of preceding management innovations to deliver promised improvements in organizational performance, including total quality management and culture excellence (Thackray 1993). Others attribute the rise of BPR to its resonance with contemporary discourse about organizational transformation and the changing nature of work and organization, for instance, the advance of information technology, delayering and downsizing, empowerment, and team-working (Grey and Mitev 1995; Grint 1994; Grint and Case 2000). Fincham (2000) suggests that the appeal of BPR has been to inspire confidence in practitioners operating with great uncertainty and insecurity. BPR is seen as the latest management fad, whose 'bandwagon' has been fuelled by evangelical texts, disciples and converts, and the push of management consultants.

Early influential articles which helped diffuse the concept and spawn the vast literature now associated with BPR include Davenport and Short (1990), who observe that successful companies were using information technology in ways which were more advanced than their traditional application. Vankantraman (1991) elaborates on these observations, identifying BPR as the third of five levels of information technology-induced transformation. However Hammer (1990), followed by Hammer and Champy's *Reengineering the Corporation: A Manifesto for Business Revolution*, first published in 1993, has played the most prominent role in the diffusion of BPR ideas to a wide managerial readership (Hammer and Champy 1993). Hammer and Champy (1993) is reasonably seen as the key text that evangelized the BPR idea through its enormous sales. Other texts have followed in the wake of this, further outlining, refining, and revising core ideas for practitioners (Peppard and Rowland 1995).

2.3.1 *BPR organizational form and process*

The vast literature about BPR that has accumulated ensures the task of capturing the essence and progress of BPR is not straightforward. Aside from the critical commentary of BPR emanating largely from writers in academe (Knights and Willmott 2000; Grey and Mitev 1995), literature primarily written from a stance of advocacy and interest in prescription has developed internal differences. Grint and Case (2000) distinguish between 'radical' or 'classical' BPR proponents, such as Hammer and Champy and 'incremental revisionists', such as Davenport (1993) and Heygate (1993, 1994). For the purpose of this discussion, Hammer and Champy's original text is used as the main reference point in outlining key ideas of BPR. It has preserved its position as the seminal BPR text and later in this monograph it is revealed how those leading BPR in the case-study site espoused, at least initially, the classical version of BPR. Indeed, they allegedly went as far as to obtain Hammer's advice and public support for the initiative.

Denison's (1997) identification of BPR with those process perspectives interested primarily in managing and improving the existing value chain suggests a middle-level ambition of BPR that contrasts sharply with the radical image and rhetoric that accompanied the introduction and popularizing of business process reengineering. In Hammer and Champy (1993), BPR is promoted as a 'new business model' to transform performance, productivity, and profit in the 'the post industrial business age'. Decline in industrial competitiveness and performance at national and firm levels is attributed to organizing arrangements that foster a division of labour and task specialization. Approaches to organizing, dating back to the ideas of Adam Smith and Scientific Management are cast as 'artifacts from another age' to be rejected. BPR is presented as a head-on challenge to the organization of work into functional, departmental, specialist boundaries that encourage people to pursue sectional goals and lose sight of the overall work process and the objective of getting goods to customers. As the key idea of BPR, Hammer and Champy (1993) promote organizing around core business processes as the antidote to such dysfunctional segmentation. The primary organizational design task is viewed to be identification of core business processes within organizations and construction of complementary information and reward systems to support these particular processes. Hammer and Champy define a business process as 'a collection of activities that takes one or more kinds of input and creates an output that is of value to the customer' (Hammer and Champy 1993: 35).

In the ideal of the reengineered organization, structural and ideological changes occur to transform organizational form and process for value creation in a market context. Employees and managers are driven by organizational objectives of value creation and customer service rather than sectional goals and interests that contradict overall organizational performance. Employee efforts and performance evaluation are oriented to the performance criteria of customer and the 'market' over and above internal inspired standards, values, or measures of performance. Previous failings of horizontal and vertical organizational boundaries are eradicated in favour of a way of organizing characterized by seamless, highly integrated 'end-to-end' processes of organization and production that result in eradication of waste, inefficiencies, high costs, poor customer response time, and defective quality. Delayering of bureaucracy and top-down hierarchies occur as departmental structures are dismantled and replaced by process teams. Jobs change from narrow simple tasks to become multi-dimensional tasks involving a broader range of value-adding skills. Old routine work is eliminated in favour of high-involvement work fostering innovation, growth, and learning. Power relations and dynamics in the workplace change as a reengineered work environment is an empowered, high-involvement work environment, wherein employees are permitted and required to think, interact, use their judgements, and make decisions to create outputs that meet customer needs and values. Flattened or delayered organization using process teams promotes less centralization and greater involvement of lower-level workers in the business and greater self-management. Greater self-managed involvement facilitates managerial work becoming more a process of coaching than supervision. Information Technology (IT) is seen as a critical enabler of BPR-inspired organization form and process (Hammer and

Champy 1993). The preceding commentary provides a sense of the anticipated form and process of a reengineered organization. Such ideals are returned to when we endeavour to describe and analyse the impact of a transformation initiative in this case-study site.

2.3.2 *BPR change method and practice*

How does one create the reengineered organization? The other key theme of reengineering literature and prescription addresses the creation of this form of organization. Reengineering method as it is termed here is clearly relevant to an analysis of reengineering as a process of organizational change within the case-study site.

Commentary about BPR method below is informed by three different strands of the BPR literature, each displaying important differences on key matters relating to reengineering as a change process. The observation of these three strands of BPR literature owes something to an accumulating interest in the theory and practice of BPR. Revealing some of the dynamic of BPR literature, it is apparent that whilst some difference in opinion was present from the outset of reengineering, for instance between initial proponents Davenport and Hammer, different strands of BPR literature have emerged and crystallized in the light of reports about the performance and practice of BPR over the 1990s. First, there is BPR method as portrayed in the classical BPR literature of Hammer and Champy (1993). This differs from the second category of writing including that of so-called 'incremental revisionists' such as Davenport and Stoddard (1994) and Burke and Peppard (1995). This is now a large, practitioner-dominated literature prescribing BPR change management and how best to succeed at BPR. Typically, issues covered include: how to identify business processes; how to identify skills and resources needed to reengineer; how to build reengineering teams; and how to use consultancy approaches when reengineering (Peppard and Rowland 1995; Teng, Grover, and Fiedler 1994; Dixon et al. 1994). A third category of writing about BPR method represents a more critical consideration of BPR as a managerial technology. Emerging from those operating with primarily scholarly concerns and interests, this critique scrutinizes theoretical premises of BPR literature in respect of organization and change.

Competing performance claims and a lack of substantiated empirical evidence ensure that the picture about the practice and performance of BPR is conflicting and uncertain. Since the promise of big gains in performance (Hammer and Champy 1993), proponents have continued to proclaim its dramatic impact (Hammer 1996; Caron, Jarvenpaa, and Stoddard 1994). Simultaneously, a more sceptical and critical view of BPR has gathered momentum suggesting unfulfilled promise and other unwelcome effects of BPR. Survey evidence reporting failure rates of 70–80 per cent and short-term gains as well as cases of process improvement and simplification rather than dramatic transformation, are cited to argue that BPR has not proved so radical and impacting on the bottom line of the organization as promised (Grint and Willcox 1995). Wider unwelcome effects of BPR within and beyond firms include work intensification and redundancies, loss of working expertise and knowledge, greater stress, and more intensive working conditions for those that remain in employment after reengineering (Knights and Willmott 2000).

These criticisms bring into sharp focus the usefulness of the following prescription of BPR change method by Hammer and Champy (1993). Namely, that the promise of BPR can only be realized by taking an approach to organization transformation that is: objective and outcome focused; a fresh start; holistic; radical and rapid; driven from the top down using a process team infrastructure. It is worth considering further this prescription and subsequent reaction to it.

2.3.2.1   *A fresh start*
To achieve business improvements in cost, quality, service, and speed, Hammer and Champy (1993) prescribe that BPR must represent a break with past work processes and arrangements. Improvements in business performance, it is argued, can only be achieved by the redesign of 'core' business processes, starting only with a 'clean sheet of paper' and objectives for the business. Reengineering a company means tossing aside old systems and starting over. It involves going back to the beginning and inventing a better way of doing work (Hammer and Champy 1993: 31).

Subsequently, Davenport and Stoddard (1994) adjudged this 'clean sheet' approach to be part of reengineering mythology that has created unreasonable expectations and impractical advice for those interested in reengineering. They suggest that in practice a 'clean-slate change' is rarely found and a 'blank sheet of paper' used in design usually requires a 'blank cheque' for implementation. Excepting instances of BPR on greenfield sites, these authors suggest firms make a distinction between clean-slate design and clean-slate implementation or alternatively design with a 'dirty slate' to yield more realistic implementation. Critical management scholars have also taken issue with the clean-slate rhetoric.

Grint and Case (2000) note the 'institutional amnesia' implied by the BPR rhetoric of starting over. They are scornful of the assumption that the uprooting of organizational norms and traditions is a prerequisite of radical increases in productivity. The 'act of deracination' implied by BPR suggests politics will be eradicated in a depoliticized, reengineered organization governed by an overarching rationality. Eloquently stated, using a horticultural metaphor, their counter-argument is that organizational politics is a hardy perennial plant not to be forgotten by shearing off the top. Neither can one remove a culture or invoke the institutional amnesia implied in the heavy rhetoric of starting over.

2.3.2.2 Radical holistic change

BPR is also prescribed as a total change solution or an 'all or nothing proposition' (Hammer and Champy 1993: 5). The possibility of achieving discontinuous performance by partial and piecemeal change is rejected. Rather, the blank page has to be filled with core process redesign that is radical, holistic, disregards existing ways of working, and invests in completely new ways of accomplishing work. Hammer and Champy draw a distinction between BPR and other change initiatives, including total quality management to make the case for radical as opposed to incremental change.

Counteracting such advice is the view of Davenport and Stoddard (1994), who do not see BPR as synonymous with organizational transformation and antithetical to quality or continuous improvement approaches. Rather, they observe the practice of BPR to be part of a portfolio approach to organizational change embracing in a contingent fashion more incremental and continuous approaches to change. Indeed, they suggest that BPR when approached with the intent of rapid wholesale business transformation is unlikely to succeed. Peppard and Rowland (1995) also employ a more accommodating stance toward the relationship between BPR and incremental improvement. Keleman, Forrester, and Hassard's (2000) analysis of BPR and TQM in the case of Mailcom, a UK service organization, concludes that the gap between BPR and total quality management (TQM) is greater in theory than practice. In Mailcom, reengineering was found to be an adjunct to quality management initiatives already established in the organization.

For Hammer and Champy (1993), the pace of BPR-related change must also be rapid. Further making the case against total quality management and its incremental approach to change, Hammer and Champy caution against dragging the effort out, suggesting a twelve-month period as long enough to prepare the case for reengineering and 'release' a reengineered process. A longer time scale is seen as a recipe for impatience, confusion, and distraction. For Hammer and Champy capturing hearts and minds is not considered a priority condition of the change process (Knights and Willmott 2000). They suggest that whilst a case for reengineering must be made it is a futile exercise trying to make reengineering happen without upsetting people. Vested interests in preserving current operations, fear of job losses, or discomfort with the prospect of jobs post-reengineering cannot be allowed to be the organizational inertia that is a barrier to success (Hammer and Champy 1993).

2.3.2.3 *Leadership of a top-down change initiative*
BPR has been characterized as a top-down change process relying heavily on qualities of individual leadership. BPR requires a 'leader' who 'makes reengineering happen'. The leader is a senior executive who acts as authorizer, visionary, and motivator. Hammer and Champy write:

the push for reengineering must come from the top . . . people near the frontline lack the broad perspective that reengineering demands. . . . any business process inevitably crosses organizational boundaries, so no mid-level manager will have sufficient authority to insist that such a process be transformed. Furthermore, some of the affected middle managers will correctly fear that dramatic changes to existing processes might diminish their own power, influence and authority. Only strong leadership from above will induce these people to accept the transformations that reengineering brings. (Hammer and Champy 1993: 207–8)

Reengineering failures are attributed to a breakdown in leadership. They repeatedly stress leaders taking personal responsibility for creating and 'selling' key messages.

Most reengineering failures stem from breakdowns in leadership. Without strong, aggressive, committed and knowledgeable leadership, there will be no one to persuade the barons running functional silos within the company to subordinate the interests of their functional areas to those of the processes that cross their boundaries. (Hammer and Champy 1993: 107)

Since Hammer and Champy, BPR's projection as a top-down change process has been subject to criticism. Davenport and Stoddard (1994) challenge this approach to change as ignoring much of what we have previously learned about the value of participative work design. They go as far as to suggest that gains in ownership of change compensate for shortcomings of participative work design principles such as a more cumbersome change process and the need to tolerate variations in detailed work processes. Others push the critique of the BPR approach to people even further. Willmott (1995) suggests an inconsistency between BPR ideas about empowerment and a dictatorial approach to change. Advocacy of delayering and empowerment is seen as contradicted by hierarchical and authoritarian methods of implementing BPR (Knights and Willmott 2000).

2.3.2.4 *Reengineering infrastructure: roles and change agents*
Leadership processes espoused above are proposed to work through an infrastructure of teams and committees consisting of personnel dedicated to reengineering. In addition to the leader of reengineering, Hammer and Champy (1993: 102–16) identify the following structure of roles and change agents as important to reengineering:

Process owners—senior line managers with prestige, credibility and influence, who assemble, motivate, and advise reengineering teams.

The reengineering team—a task group of between five and ten people including a mix of insiders and outsiders. Insiders are people who currently work inside the process undergoing reengineering but who are also capable of maverick thought. They are 'rising stars', with strong credibility with co-workers. Outsiders are required to provide a radically disruptive element. Management consultants are seen as such external change agents.

Steering committee—seen as an optional aspect of a reengineering infrastructure this committee could process overarching issues that transcend the scope of individual processes and projects.

Reengineering czar—acting as the leader's chief of staff for reengineering, enabling, and supporting each process owner, coordinating all reengineering activities.

2.3.2.5 *Process redesign*
The focus of change efforts is business processes. Hammer and Champy (1993) indicate that a company will have a relatively small number of processes, perhaps half a dozen. To identify processes companies are advised to 'process map' organizational activities and depict how work flows through the company. Having identified business processes, it is suggested that the next step is to decide which processes to reengineer and in what sequence. Criteria to apply to help choose the business processes to reengineer are business process dysfunction, importance, and feasibility. Having identified a business process to

reengineer, Hammer and Champy advise that a process owner be designated, a reengineering team convened, and the current process understood. Process redesign can only take place following process analysis ('diagnosis') leading to better understanding the performance of the process currently. Hammer and Champy describe the activity of process redesign to be about 'reenvisioning' the company and 'inventing' new ways of doing work. Process redesign requires, in their terms, imagination, inductive thinking, abandoning familiar ways of working, and suspending belief in time-honoured rules, values, and procedures. The reengineering team then has to take the redesigned process to the rest of the company. They suggest the keys to getting people to accept the idea of radical change to their working lives lie in processes of educating people about the need for change, communicating change, and selling change to employees. Senior managers must communicate the 'case for action'—detailing why the company must reengineer and offer a 'vision statement'—revealing the kind of organization the company needs to become.

In the light of BPR performance, 'classic' prescription has been challenged and revised by other advocates and proponents of BPR. Hall, Rosenthal, and Wade (1993) have recently isolated some of the signs and symptoms of faster BPR movement and impact, such as sustained top-level commitment, adequate diagnostic planning, a major communication drive, and the development of product champions throughout the organization. Dixon et al.'s (1994) analysis of fifteen reengineering projects found sustained top-level support and commitment to be essential to the success of BPR. Belmont and Murray (1993) purport to identify five factors that companies must satisfy to succeed at BPR. The first step toward success is recognizing the need to change. Organizations must then assess the readiness to undertake redesign. The involvement of senior managers is seen as vital to success. Organizations must then 'organize a campaign' of change management and implementation, in so doing, carefully examining how information technology can enable new decision-making capabilities. Belmont and Murray also suggest that organizations must understand the pitfalls other companies have encountered in their approaches to BPR. Peppard and Rowland (1995) describe five key phases of a BPR programme. First, create the environment, which includes recognizing the need for change, creating the vision of the future organization, and undertaking a cultural audit. Second, analyse, diagnose, and redesign processes. Third, redesign the organization infrastructure, including competencies, structure, form, and roles. Fourth, pilot and roll-out redesigned processes. Fifth, realize the vision set at the outset. Dale (1994) suggests three phases of reengineering toward transformation: awakening; radical evolution; and alignment. Awakening is a phase during which key activities are seeing and creating the need for change and creating the opportunity and vision for change, starting with a caucus of senior people. Radical evolution is a phase when work starts on process reengineering, building multi-disciplinary reengineering teams, and implementing change. The phase of alignment occurs when the physical implementation of change is complete and the organization moves to realizing ongoing business benefits of BPR.

For others, such revisionist thinking is insufficient and simplistic. The challenge of reengineering is much deeper than the deployment of effective change management techniques and leadership. Classical and revisionist BPR literatures are charged with adopting a unitarist view of organization and presuming consent whilst ignoring power relations inherent in organizations. A naively apolitical and acultural view stands opposite a view that sees organizational settings as political and contested arenas. Business processes are said to embody the cultural and political nature of organizations, both representing and constituting organizational politics and power relations. McCabe and Knights (2000) observe BPR's limited impact on hierarchies, functional organization, multi-skilling, and empowerment in the case of ProBank, a medium-sized UK clearing bank as going beyond matters of change implementation. Vested interests in hierarchy, including management interest in control and cost reductions represent conditions that exist in tension with BPR rhetoric and which cannot be removed by attending to the people issues and niceties of change implementation. Rather than being organization free, BPR is laden with politics (Taylor 1995).

The preceding commentary reveals the ideal of process organization and the resonance of BPR with this ideal. It provides a sense of structural and ideological change associated with the transformation ambitions of BPR. However, the mixed performance of BPR in practice suggests a gap between the promise and practice of BPR. The implications of the gap for the development of this study's conceptual framework are twofold. First, theorizing needs to be sensitive to BPR implementation failure as well as success, patchy as well as holistic impact. Second, the 'blank-page' rhetoric is best treated with scepticism. In theory and practice, BPR is more appropriately seen as a social process inseparable from the power and politics of organization settings. These points are discussed further as part of the conceptual framework of the study developed in the remainder of this chapter and Chapter 3.

2.4 Assessing BPR as transformation

A weakness of much of the literature about BPR and organizational transformation is that it is general or normative in tone and lacks a high-quality empirical base. Many of the cases are self-reports from sponsoring managers and other participants creating doubt as to whether information presented is partial and unduly positive. In addition, managerial interest in change programmes is often short lived, so that inadequate attention is accorded to assessing whether the benefits promised at the front end of the change process in the end materialized. Given such short attention spans, empirical research has a powerful role to play in holding managerial decision-makers to retrospective account and lengthening attention spans. However, this endeavour needs to be guided by a concept of organizational transformation and associated operational criteria.

To assess BPR against its own rhetoric of transformation it is necessary to search beyond a mostly unreliable literature to identify work that seeks to analyse, characterize, and theorize the scale and pace of change in organizations in a theoretical and empirically robust manner (Greenwood and Hinings 1996; Ferlie et al. 1996; Child and Smith 1987; Pettigrew 1985). These more reliable studies suggest organizational transformation to be a complex social process marked by change in organizational performance, and associated with challenge and change to established structure and action. Neither is it realistic to characterize transformation as either a single event or a linear process unfolding in the even-paced and sequential manner implied by rational, phased models promoting planned change.

Tushman and Romanelli's (1985) concept of 'transformation' involves sharp and simultaneous shifts in strategy, distribution of organizational power, structure, and control mechanisms. Transformation is presented as relatively short bursts of fundamental change (revolutionary periods). Pettigrew (1987, 1985) conceptualizes strategic change and transformation as change in dominant ideologies, cultural systems of meaning, and power relations within the organization (Pettigrew 1987, 1985). Corroborating Tushman and Romanelli (1985), Pettigrew's analysis of change in ICI reveals periods of incremental change punctuated by radical change. Over a thirty-year period, ICI is shown to have moved from a long period of inertia into a short period of radical change informed by shifts in the external environment, crisis, and leadership from internal agents.

Child and Smith's (1987) analysis of transformation in Cadbury Ltd is a little more circumspect about the punctuated equilibrium thesis suggesting an over-separation of continuities and discontinuities. Both the Cadbury and ICI studies reveal continuity and change to be key paradoxes of organizational life. In Cadbury Ltd, change is observed to take place in a 'dynamic tension' with continuity, meaning that the process of transformation did not represent a complete break with the past. Neither are the origins and sources of change located so easily as internal or external to the firm. Rather, sources for change may be a mixture of the 'endogenous' and 'exogenous'. Finally, in both ICI and Cadbury processes of strategic change and transformation were observed to have occurred over decades not years. This last point is noteworthy given the time-limited content of classical BPR prescription observed earlier (Hammer and Champy 1993).

Greenwood and Hinings (1996) use the concept of 'archetype' to operationalize organizational transformation. Archetype refers to a configuration of structures and systems of organizing with a common orientation or 'underlying interpretative scheme'. Organizational transformation is theorized to occur with a change in the dominant archetype. On the other hand, convergent change is fine-tuning within the parameters of an existing archetypal template. Revolutionary and evolutionary change is distinguished by the scale and pace of upheaval and adjustment. Whereas evolutionary change occurs slowly and gradually, revolutionary change happens swiftly and affects all parts of the organization simultaneously (Greenwood and Hinings 1996: 1024).

Cooper et al.'s (1996) examination of organizational change in two Canadian law firms is an empirical example of archetype analysis and shows organizational transformation as an ambiguous phenomenon. The explanation of change between archetypes—Partnership and Managed Professional Business—is not one of secure, unequivocal, and linear transformation involving the replacement of one archetype by another. Rather, the metaphor of sedimented structure and ideologies captures the process and effects of organizational change that sees a layering of one archetype on another. This layered sedimented outcome involves the simultaneous presence of more than one archetype, and the persistence of values, ideas, and practices, in spite of changes to formal structures and processes. The case exemplifies the idea of a 'competitive value commitment' whereby two or more archetypes exist in a competitive relationship within the same organizational system (Greenwood and Hinings 1996; Hinings and Greenwood 1988). Following the image of change moving along tracks, such archetype incoherence is associated with a track described as 'unresolved excursion'.

Also using an archetype conceptual framework, Denis, Langley, and Cazale (1996) draw a similar conclusion with respect to organizational change in a Canadian public hospital. This case study reveals an attempted shift to a more 'externally focused' hospital, involving change in managerial style and organization design. The conclusion is that strategic change in this case did not proceed in a linear incremental fashion but rather a cyclical non-linear pattern with periods of substantive change alternating with periods of political realignment. The 'final' phase of their analysis also uses the language of 'unresolved excursion' to report setbacks and stagnation in the movement between archetypes.

Archetypal analysis is a major contribution to understanding of organizational change and transformation in professional service contexts and is utilized later to explain the process and effects of reengineering in the case-study site. However, Ferlie et al.'s (1996) model of transformation in the policy and process of the UK public sector since the late 1970s is most central to our empirical assessment of the transformatory effects of BPR in the case-study site. Multiple indicators focused more on actions and related consequences than change in underlying meanings of professional work are developed within the model to assess organizational transformation. The indicators are: multiple and interrelated changes across the system as a whole; the creation of new organizational forms at a collective level; the development of multi-layered changes which impact below the whole system, at unit and individual level; the creation of changes in the services provided, and in the mode of delivery; the reconfiguration of power relations (especially the formation of new leadership groups); the development of a new culture, ideology, and organizational meaning. Only when all six criteria have been fulfilled it is possible to talk of a completed organizational transformation. Though the model has to date been applied at the level of sector more than single organization it is suitable for studying attempted BPR inspired organizational transformation at the organizational level. Core process redesign clearly implies system-wide change that privileges a lateral approach to organizing over a horizontal, functional approach to organizing. Organizing around the logic of core business processes as opposed to functions requires multiple interrelated and complementary changes to system procedures and processes. BPR also promotes and promises depth as well as breadth of change with system-wide change impacting upon the work and relations of units and individuals. The ideological and cultural accompaniment to the change in structures and processes is revealed by attention to value creation in a market context.

To summarize, organization transformation is viewed to involve change in organizational outputs such as services or products, associated with multiple and coherent changes in structure and action across the whole organizational system. Transformation is thus a complex social process operating simultaneously at several levels of organization with the sequencing and outcome of this process of challenge and change being highly uncertain. In the light of this definition, the preceding classic prescription of BPR appears highly ambitious in its rhetoric of organizational transformation. We are struck by confident assumptions about the ability of organizational leaders to choose and effect organizational transformation. Organizational leaders are urged to reshape organizations by reengineering organization form and process. However, the mixed evidence of results of BPR in practice serves only to support empirical studies of strategic change and transformation that encourage caution against supremely confident and simplistic linear connections between managerial action and change outcomes (Pettigrew 1987; Child and Smith 1987).

2.5 Explaining BPR as transformation: dynamics of action and context

Moving between assessment and explanation of the impact of BPR requires a more sophisticated theorization of action and context (Pettigrew 1987) than is displayed in much of the BPR and transformation literature. Complex dynamics stretching over time and space are implied in the above conceptualization of transformation. This section examines these dynamics further using recent developments in strategic choice theory and neo-institutional theory. Both theories understand managerial agency in relation to organization and environmental interaction. In so doing, they provide a more theorized sense of possibilities, problems, and processes involved in effecting organizational transformation than the BPR literature.

Agency is defined as the capability of human beings to deploy causal powers within the flow of daily life, to influence events, situations, processes, and the causal powers of others (Giddens 1984). Strategic choice theory argues for the role of agency in organizations pointing to the power of a 'dominant coalition' to decide upon courses of strategic action. Such action may be 'externally oriented' in the sense of moving in and out of markets or 'internally oriented' in ways implied by the ideal of the process organization and BPR. As observed earlier, process organization and BPR involves reconfiguring internal processes of work organization and practice. Strategic choice theory thus privileges acts as a central role in processes of organization change. However, in contrast to much of the BPR and transformation literature, choice- and change-related actions are not to be understood as voluntary, unbounded, or taking place in a contextual vacuum. Rather, processes of choice and change are bound up in the 'mutual pervasiveness' of organizations and the environment, and an interplay between struc- ture and action (Child 1997).

Strategic choice is presented as a process involving members of 'a dominant coalition' and relevant external parties, yielding action in the name of the organization conditioned by human purpose, pre- ference, and interpretation. As action in context, strategic choice is informed by relationships and interpretations in respect of organiza- tional environment, stakeholders, relevant events, organization per- formance, and internal working arrangements (Child 1997). At any point in time strategic choice is 'framed' by existing structures such as: information processes and channels; policies and priorities for action; configurations of competitors; regulators; suppliers; customers; and institutional obligations (Child 1997: 60). Child thus explains strategic choice as an example of structuration (Giddens 1984) in that,

action is bounded by the cognitive, material and relational structures existing within organizations and their networks but at the same time it impacts on those structures. Through their actions, agents endeavour to modify and rede- fine structures in ways that will admit of different possibilities for future action. The process is a continuing one. (Child 1997: 60)

Strategic choice specifically, and more generally human agency, is always 'socially contextualized'. Analysis of change therefore needs to attend to the interplay between processes, people, and events both internal and external to organizational settings (Lewin and Volberda 1999). Greenwood and Hinings's (1996) neo-institutional model of rad- ical change is valuable to this task. The model reveals neo-institutional theory more accommodating of agency than institutional theory. It is a necessary precursor to presenting the model to say a little more about institutional theory, both in terms of its contribution and critique.

Institutional theorists tend to view organizations and the individuals who populate them as suspended 'in a web of values, norms, beliefs, taken-for-granted assumptions, that are at least partially of their own making' (Barley and Tolbert 1997: 93). The wider environment is conceptualized as a constraint on managerial action, mediating processes of organizational inertia and resistance to change. Organizations are adjudged to operate in the ways they do because ideas, values, and beliefs initiated and legitimated in the wider environment or 'institutional field', become taken for granted as the acceptable way of doing things. Populations of organizations therefore exhibit similar characteristics as coercive, mimetic, and normative pressures in the wider environment or 'institutional field' tend organizations to convergence and isomorphism around norms and expectations of the institutional context. Organizational change is socially determined and organizational inertia and resistance to change is explained according to the 'normative embeddedness' of organizations in their institutional context or 'field'. Radical change is seen as problematic because of the 'embeddeness' of an organization within its institutional context. The prevailing nature of change is more likely to be convergent and reproducing of existing organization structures and ideas (Greenwood and Hinings 1996).

Criticisms of institutional theory are that whilst it recognizes a wide variety of social influences upon organizations and their members the power of agency is neglected (Beckert 1999; Barley and Tolbert 1997; Whittington 1992). Whittington (1992) and Child (1997) strongly argue the case for agency, suggesting that environment can be both enabling as well as constraining of organizational action. For Whittington (1992) the possibilities for agency lie in actors' exploitation of plural structural principles and their capacity to use their knowledge about system reproduction in a reflexive way to shape and influence system reproduction. Actors' participation in a plurality of organizations affords choice over the structural principles they enlist and exploit in organizational activities. Where systems cross-cut and structural properties are diverse, actors need only draw selectively on rules and resources, instantiating some and leaving others in reserve. Hence, structures do not crush agency by monolithic force, but enable it by complexity and contradiction. Whittington identifies two principal forms of managerial agency. First, agency that stems from managers exercising choice and discretion when faced with plural and ambiguous rules and resources within organizations, all with some legitimacy and plausibility. Second, agency that stems from managers using their connections with other social systems to import alien or contradictory structural rules and resources to 'inspire and empower their actions'. Such connections may occur through multiple organizational memberships or relationships acquired through necessary cross-cutting systems of activity. Whittington sees this second sense of agency as the greater because it carries the potential of 'defying immediate system logics altogether' (Whittington 1992: 704). It develops from managers' operation in a diversity of systems that exceed the bounds of the firm and the plural identities that such involvement may foster. Some of the limits observed by Whittington on these forms of managerial agency are inability to access alternative structural principles, lack of legitimacy of these principles amongst those they wish to influence, and 'economic constraints'. Hung and Whittington's (1997) study of strategies in nine Taiwanese computer firms illustrates agency and substantiates Whittington's (1992) earlier criticism that institutional theory inappropriately emphasizes the conformity of populations of organizations at the expense of seeing possibilities for organizations to experience an 'eclectic' and 'creative' relationship with the environment.

Greenwood and Hinings's (1996) neo-institutional model of radical change is more accommodating of agency than early institutional theory. The model sheds further light on the interrelations between agency and structure in radical change processes. Radical change is explained as an interaction between 'exogenous' dynamics (market context and institutional context) and 'endogenous' dynamics of interests, values, power dependencies, and capacity for action (Greenwood and Hinings 1996). Radical change is associated with following endogenous precipitating dynamics: group dissatisfaction with accommodation of interests within the existing dominant template for organizing coupled with a 'value-commitment' ('competitive' or 'reformative') to an alternative template. From these dynamics flow the internal pressure for change, the intensity of which is an outcome of links to market and institutional contexts. However, for radical change to occur, these precipitating dynamics have to be complemented by the 'enabling dynamics' of 'supportive power dependencies' and 'capacity for action'. The political nature of organizations and change requires power to be mobilized to promote preferences and interests. Individuals and groups differ in their ability to access and mobilize power resources in pursuit or defence of change. Radical change is specifically seen as requiring those in positions of power to favour proposed change. Institutional and market pressures may shift power dependencies in favour of an alternative template but radical change will only result if the 'dominant coalition' recognizes the weakness of the existing template and is aware of potential alternatives. A second enabler of radical change is 'capacity for action'. Capacity for action refers to 'the ability to manage the transition between templates of organizing' (Greenwood and Hinings 1996: 1039). It is a function of understanding the new conceptual destination, being able to manage how to get there, and having skills and competencies required to function in that new destination. In suggesting how capacity for action is related to market context, there is a resonance with Whittington's forms of agency. For instance, Greenwood and Hinings suggest that recruitment of new personnel whose previous employment experience involves experience of fundamentally different ways of operating to the host firm can increase the possibility for radical change. The institutional context may also serve to 'articulate the need for new competencies and promote the development of capacities for action' (Greenwood and Hinings 1996: 1041).

2.5.1　*Managing change and transformation*

The concept of capacity for action directs attention to managerial approaches, actions, and skill in accomplishing major organizational change. BPR's proposal of a Big Bang approach to change through high investment in a pre-packaged product and a prescribed technology stands in stark contrast to other studies that characterize major organizational change to result from longer-term processes of learning, conditioning, and influencing (Child and Smith 1987; Pettigrew 1985, 1987, 1998; Pettigrew and Whipp 1991).

　　Child and Smith (1987) argue that organizational transformation involves altering understanding of environmental pressures and recognizing new 'paths for survival'. This involves the reconstruction and reframing of conditions within the sector and their implications for the firm. Such a reconstruction ultimately has to be recognized, learned, and articulated to create awareness within the organization of a new linkage between firm and sector. In the case of Cadbury Ltd, Child and Smith identified the capacity for accomplishing this recognition and articulation to be limited to a number of managers, oriented to change by prior experience and external collaborative networks. Similarly, Pettigrew and Whipp (1991) identified 'environmental assessment' as a key feature of managing change for competitive success. Environmental assessment is regarded here not as a single act at a given point but a process subject to multiple influences over time. Individual and collective beliefs affect the way individuals conceive and enact the environment as well as exercise judgement and choice in respect of that environment (Pettigrew and Whipp 1991).

　　Processes of recognition and assessment are political. Pettigrew and Whipp (1991) reveal how assessments and their associated judgements and choices are controversial, conflicting with 'world-views' of others. Child and Smith (1987) characterize the process of transformation as a debate between 'mental constructs' whereby new ideas are put forward to challenge those which underpin existing organizational understandings and arrangements. They observe advocates for change pitting their visions against more established tangible recipes. The duality of action and structure may either serve to promote, protect, or preserve the interests and preferences of dominant groups and individuals within organizations (Pettigrew 1987). When strategic choice implies organizational transformation, agents pursuing change are faced with challenging and changing ideologies and structures that are dominant whilst interacting with them. In a similar way, Greenwood and Hinings (1996) identify a 'competitive value-commitment' as a precipitating condition of radical change. A competitive value commitment to change develops as individuals and groups associate disadvantage with the existing arrangements or 'organizing template' in use and seek to replace one template with another. In change processes, therefore, actions, reactions, and outcomes are not neutral but laden with competing ideas, rationalities, commitment, and interests of actors. For those with ambitions of change and transformation, establishing legitimacy for one's ideas and actions becomes critical to realizing intended effects.

As revealed earlier heroic leadership is typically associated with BPR. However, the emergence and expression of leadership in practice challenges the image of heroic visionary implied by much normative literature about leadership and change. Harvey-Jones's vision in ICI is described as neither simple-minded nor clear-cut but more additive and incremental in tying together change and continuity (Pettigrew 1985). Similarly, 'visioning' in the case of Cadbury Ltd was in advance of specific plans, and was more associated with proponents of change having a clear sense of direction and 'image of the future' (Child and Smith 1987; Pettigrew 1985). Pettigrew and Whipp (1991) conclude that whilst leadership can shape strategic change one should be cautious about assuming the efficacy and success of charismatic leaders and visionaries. For these writers the assumption of control implicit in such images is too great for a process that they understand to be unpredictable and highly sensitive to temporal and contextual dynamics. For these writers, the 'art of leadership' in management lies in 'the ability to shape in the long-term rather than direct it through a single episode' (Pettigrew and Whipp 1991: 143). 'Leading change' thus involves action by people at every level of the business and important preparatory actions of problem-sensing and climate-setting within the firm. The chairman of ICI, John Harvey-Jones, is reported to have spent much of his early years orchestrating an 'educational process' in an attempt to open up the organization to change. The educational process incorporated elements of formal and informal education. At the level of formal education, management development programmes focused attention on new management capabilities and skills. Other, more informal educational processes promoted new ideologies as challenges to traditional ways of thinking and acting. Child and Smith (1987) also describe how attitudes and behaviours within Cadbury Ltd were reshaped via simple 'slogans' and 'watchwords' that focused individuals' attention and effort and served as symbolic levers to secure complex change in working arrangements. Pettigrew (1985) labelled this process as the management of meaning, referring to a process of symbol construction and value use designed to create legitimacy for one's ideas, actions, and demands whilst simultaneously undermining demands of one's opponents.

Organizational change processes require influence to be exercised on a grand scale and mechanisms of influence can be wide and varied, ranging from symbol construction to direct and indirect interpersonal processes of confrontation, coercion, or subtle persuasion. In attempts to change large social systems will, skill, and persistence are critical ingredients of influencing behaviour. Skill is largely contextually determined, involving the matching of power resources and influence methods to the demands and sensitivities of the situations (Pettigrew and McNulty 1998, 1995). Denis, Langley, and Cazale (1996) illustrate the contextual sensitive nature of change leadership and influence processes through a study of radical change in a Canadian hospital. Focusing on the roles and influence tactics used by leaders within the hospital over a fourteen-year period, the study draws the following conclusions and propositions. In conditions of 'ambiguity' (unclear goals and lines of authority), substantive change requires collaborative leadership involving a tight-knit group of leaders performing specialized, differentiated and complementary roles. In functionally diverse arrangements with diffuse authority structures and plural lines of accountability, the leadership constellation has to involve the principal sources of authority, competence, and legitimacy within the organization (Denis, Langley, and Cazale 1996: 690). Momentum gain and momentum loss in this change process is associated with leaders' influence tactics, some of which were credibility enhancing, for instance, coalition-building, whilst others were credibility draining, for instance coercion and threat.

Permeating all the observations about managerial action is a recognition that change is not just about the actions of leaders, managers, and proponents of change. Change also involves other people, their actions, reactions, and interactions. Processes of recognizing, visioning, and leading change need to generate a force of critical mass. Greenwood and Hinings (1996) conceptualize radical change as requiring supportive 'power dependencies'. If transformation does involve multi-layered change processes (Ferlie et al. 1996) then ensuring that there is effective change capacity at each level of the organization and links between the different tiers seems crucial. Child's (1997, 1972) model of strategic choice starts with the assumption of individuals and groups having power to influence organization form and processes in line with their own preferences. In the case of Cadbury Ltd, transformation stemmed from champions of the vision moving into key positions. Movement of proponents and sympathizers of new interpretations into positions of power and creation of 'change agents' at different levels and locations of the organization are important parts of constructing the power base from which to mobilize change (Child and Smith 1987). Pettigrew and Whipp (1991) argue for linking change at strategic and operational levels. A gap between strategic and operational change occurs where the strategic change agenda is not effectively implemented at operational level. The gap raises questions about the change capacity within the organization (Pettigrew and Whipp 1991). Cascading down of the change agenda and building up of change capacity below the most senior levels of the organization down to middle management level appears to be a critical action for change proponents to accomplish. Linking strategic and operational change 'places a premium on the ability to link educational, analytical, and political dimensions of the change process—together' (Pettigrew and Whipp 1991: 199).

Is BPR then a way of accomplishing such effective change management in an accelerated fashion to enable rapid and radical change said to be necessary in contemporary organizations? High failure rates and a mixed picture emerging from the use of programmatic change strategies suggest BPR is a risky strategy. According to Pettigrew (1998), successful change programmes seemingly require the following supportive conditions and processes: persistent and consistent top-level support for the change programme with people in key posts long enough to see change initiatives through. Change programmes need also to be linked to the critical path of the business through ensuring that business objectives drive the change process. It is also critical to marry top-down pressure for change and bottom-up concerns so as to link strategic and operational change. Allowing individuals and groups within the organization to 'customize' change in the light of local needs and interests is also important as is inclusive rather than exclusive project team working and management. In so doing, it is possible to establish a coherence which links the change programme to multiple agendas and issues within the change setting (Pettigrew 1998).

In practice change programmes are often vulnerable to turnover at the top, issue succession, or sudden crises or panics which divert managerial attention elsewhere. They can suffer from uncertain legitimacy of those driving and leading change. They may be perceived as single issue 'off the shelf' interventions and become disadvantaged in the competition for resources and attention in complex multi-issue organizations. They can progress from being seen as solutions to being seen as problems in their own right. They may be unable to attract sustained support over a considerable period of time (rise to the top of a crowded agenda and even more problematical stay there) and rapid regression may set in as energy and momentum may rapidly drain away. They may be weakened when perceived as imposed, exclusive, unrealistic in ambition, and overzealous in approach. Cynical contexts, tainted by past attempts at change, can weaken the potency and impact of any change programme as can a failure to link change programmes to core business issues and political interests within the organization (Pettigrew 1998).

To conclude and summarize, the chapter has introduced and problematized the concept of business process reengineering using its own rhetoric of organizational transformation. Transformation is regarded as a relatively recent emphasis within the discourse of organization and management. The development of a process theory of organization engages clearly with the spirit and discourse of transformation by seeking to promote a new organizational form. As an example of a process-based theory of organization, business process reengineering promises to transform the practice and performance of organizations.

However, securing transformation through BPR is easier said than done in practice. Albeit from a weak empirical base BPR has not been found to deliver its promises in many instances. Both the promise and performance of BPR cause us to reflect more deeply on the nature of the transformation as both an organizational project and process. From a wider body of literature about strategic and organizational change the conclusion drawn is that transformation is a complex process of challenge and change to established structure and action in and around organizations. Empirical evidence suggests that such a process is unlikely to unfold at a uniform rate and pace over time, nor is it strictly amenable to manoeuvres and manipulation by organizational leaders and managers. Managerial action has a key part to play in processes of strategic choice and change but such influence must not be over-privileged or seen as divorced from other agency interests and institutional forces that influence the dynamic of organizational continuity and change. Rather to understand the process and effects of a BPR transformation initiative it is necessary to attend to the relation between agency and context. Having majored on managerial action and agency in the latter sections of this chapter, Chapter 3 is concerned with understanding the context of this empirical study of BPR with a view to better appreciating institutional and contextual influences that may shape the process and effect of BPR at an organizational level.

3

Process Redesign and Changing Contexts of Health Care

The previous chapter considered a novel process theory of organizing (Denison 1997) of which BPR could be seen as an important recent example. This literature also reflected a growing academic interest in processes of organizational transformation. Some authors have argued that process-based organizations represent a radically new organizational form different from the integrated hierarchies of the past. Proponents of BPR (Hammer and Champy 1993) state that generic principles of process redesign act as a powerful vehicle for organizational transformation. This aspiration is apparent within some health care organizations (as within other sectors) that adopted BPR as a corporate change programme in the 1990s.

We also outlined in Chapter 2 a theoretical framework for understanding organizational change that combined a concern for both agency and context within an interactive model. Structure and action are mutually constitutive through interaction (Child 1997), exemplifying Giddens's concept of structuration. Giddens's own account of structuration (Giddens 1993) suggests that social theory does not 'begin' either with the individual or society as a prime unit of analysis but rather there is a concern for the linkages between these two levels. In structuration theory, another core theme is with recurrent social practices and their transformations. Tracing the nature of the interactions between agency and structure within major social change processes is then a key research task. Nor do such arguments remain at the conceptual level but also have implications for empirical forms of research. Giddens (1993) argues that structuration theory can be used in social science field investigation and theoretical endeavour as an explanatory framework.

In the specific case of BPR, influential texts (Hammer and Champy 1993) adopt an excessively agency-centred approach, conceiving of change in a planned and top-down manner and according too much importance to senior managerial 'leadership' as the only factor within change. This lends excessive primacy to subjective factors and neglects other structural forces, which shape organizational change. Agency-led approaches should be complemented by a greater awareness that organizations are contextually embedded entities and display 'deep structures' which reproduce themselves and are highly resistant to change. The development and fate of a BPR 'intervention' designed to transform recurrent patterns of work practices thus needs to be studied within its organizational context.

How can this rather broad concept of organizational context be operationalized within analysis? At least three different levels of organizational context need to be analysed, and the interactions between them established. At the very broadest level, the macro or outer context (Pettigrew 1990, 1997) includes the broad social, economic, competitive, and technological framework within which organizations operate. We should also include the political economy that is of extreme significance to public sector organizations. Such parameters occasionally exhibit sustained and radical shifts that destabilize market recipes, niches, or established forms within organizations. Pettigrew's (1985) analysis of strategic change in ICI suggests that the dramatic economic recession of the early 1980s and rapid loss of traditional markets represented a clear externally generated crisis around which internal change agents could mobilize to force a shift of strategy. Without the external crisis, internal forces for change were disempowered. The more recent growth of stronger market pressures for private sector professional services such as accountancy has led to an erosion of traditional professional partnership-based forms of organization (Hinings, Greenwood, and Cooper 1999) and the growth of an alternative managed form.

An important macro-level shift in the UK context has been the development of a new political economy since the early 1980s with a shift from a social democratic regime to the New Right and then to New Labour. The New Right sought to curb the historic growth of the expanded public sector characteristic of the old social democratic order and 'reform' those public services that could not be privatized. This phenomenon has been characterized as the rise of the New Public Management and marks a radical break from the old models of Public Administration. The scale, significance, and impact of this macro-level shift in the political context facing UK public sector organizations will be explored within this chapter.

The concept of the meso-context (House, Rousseau, and Thomas-Hunt 1995) draws attention to dynamics at an intermediate level, here within a particular sector or specific population of organizations. We know that industrial sectors face specific conditions and 'recipes' are generated based on taken-for-granted assumptions (Child and Smith 1987; Pettigrew and Whipp 1991). Even within the public sector, different subsectors exhibit characteristic rates of movement towards New Public Management models. Such movement is faster in health care settings and within the Civil Service than in educational settings (Ferlie et al. 1996). So, the particular dynamics within the health sector need to be considered, such as the strengthening of management against traditionally dominant professional groupings (Freidson 1970, 1994) and introduction of quasi-markets within public services.

At the level of the micro-context, these broader forces play out within particular local sites. Local personalities and politics may skew the balance of forces within each site. The structure of the quasi-market is locally variable, with stronger forces in urban sites than in rural areas. Local actors may differentially seize opportunities presented by macro-level shifts to expand their roles, increase their power base, and to advance ideas that would previously have been heretical. There may be a historical pattern of path dependence, whereby a sequence builds up over time acting either to strengthen or weaken collective change capacity.

Such contextual analysis is easier to undertake where there is a readily recognizable past phenomenon, such as the economic recession of the early 1980s, which can be easily linked to pressures on organizations (such as in the case of strategic change in ICI, see Pettigrew 1985). The contextual effect was gross and direct. In other cases, macro-shifts are difficult to discern and may be partial in nature, contained in scope, or even reversed in a later period. Their effects may be more indirect, or their significance may be highly contested by various stakeholders within the organization.

3.1   Intersectoral analysis and process-based organizations

The first two questions that we ask are: which external forces encourage the adoption of process-based ways of working? Are they present in public service settings to the same degree as private sector settings? Denison (1997) remarks that from the era of Adam Smith (1770s) to the 1960s, the general principles of organizational design were concerned with the construction and control of ever-larger firms. If we are now seeing a mega-shift to process-based forms of organizing, then it is likely that some very substantial changes have taken place within the economy and society, which have prepared the ground. So, what might be the external drivers for the adoption of process-based forms of organization? Denison (1997) suggests that the following factors are important: (i) the growth of global scope or global competition (which is not present in a direct way within the public sector); (ii) the advent of distributed control systems linked by information technology (which is present in the public sector as in the private sector, but perhaps on a more gradual basis); (iii) the growth of internal market forces within firms (which is present in the current public sector as in the private); (iv) a shift from a sellers' market to a buyers' market, with the empowering of consumers (the decline of deference to public service producers is a noteworthy trend). Although such shifts would need to be radical and sustained in nature to destabilize highly institutionalized forms of organization, some of these forces are at work within public service settings as well as private firms.

Within similar work on the 'innovative organization', Pettigrew and Fenton (2000: 279) argue that new forms are arising as 'competitive pressures in many industries are demanding more rapid response times; greater flexibility and lower management costs; often alongside the sophisticated development and application of intellectual capital'. They highlight the growth of sophisticated IT systems capable of sustaining more complex horizontal links as a source of major organizational change. IT systems have developed in the public sector as in the private sector and specifically help underpin process redesign efforts as they can move quantities of data laterally around the organization. The corporate management of previously tacit and hidden forms of clinical knowledge has also emerged as an important development within the health care sector. While market-led competition has not been so prevalent in the public sector as in a globalizing private sector, analogous pressures for enhanced performance from an increasingly managerially conscious State have been apparent.

Another key issue that arises within a sectoral perspective is the potential applicability and hence the likely impact of private sector-based managerial ideas and methods as they move from the private sector into UK health care settings. Are American firms similar to UK public agencies and can methods readily be diffused from one sector to another? The sponsors of reengineering-based change advocate a 'blank sheet approach to change' (Hammer and Champy 1993) and radical organizational redesign, irrespective of local histories. Yet, contextualist forms of analysis (Pettigrew 1990, 1997) argue on the contrary that change processes are embedded within distinctive organizational contexts. General management models and tools may not be at all general in their impact, but vary sharply according to the setting. So UK public sector organizations such as the NHS may be less receptive to process redesign ideas than the American sites cited by Hammer and Champy (1993), which are often drawn from private sector manufacturing or routine service sector organizations (such as insurance companies).

Hammer and Champy (1993) consider whether BPR is relevant to public service agencies. They argue that BPR is applicable in principle, but that it poses special implementation challenges which explain why governmental agencies are often laggards in reengineering terms. First, the lack of a profits yardstick makes it more difficult to tell whether organizational performance is impaired or indeed improving. Agencies which provide measurable services (such as tax departments) or which are in competition with private sector providers (as the Veterans Administration is within the American health care system) are more likely to embrace reengineering. Secondly, competition for jurisdiction between different public services agencies means that complex inter-agency processes are difficult to reengineer. Thirdly, government agencies are policy rather than operations centred, so that techniques designed to improve operational management are not embraced. Clearly, the acute sector NHS hospitals do not demonstrate a profits yardstick, nor does the NHS provide easily measurable services, and it operates in a complex inter-organizational set (with strong links to community health services, social services, and the voluntary sector). Against these negative factors, there is within this organizational form a strong operational focus as well as a policy bias that might act to increase the ownership of process redesign ideas.

However, Hammer and Champy's (1993) analysis is cross-sectional in nature and does not consider how it is that public sector agencies may be changing their nature over time, possibly leading to the increased applicability of private sector-based management models, tools, and indeed personnel. Nor does it consider the distribution of organizational power and how this may promote or retard the adoption of process redesign ideas. Key questions are 'to what extent and how is the current public sector changing?' and 'do these changes increase the likelihood that generic or private sector based models of management will be adopted and sustained?'

Addressing these questions, this chapter reveals a number of processes operating at different levels of the context of health care with seemingly quite different implications for the introduction and fate of a process redesign intervention. At the most macro-level, the UK public sector is becoming less distinctive and to some extent converging with private sector templates. A number of nationalized industries have been privatized and those functions remaining in the public sector have been placed under sustained political pressure to become more 'businesslike'. This macro-level view reveals a public sector increasingly exposed to intersectoral transfer of generic models of organization and management. Differences between contemporary private sector firms and public sector health care organizations appear to be less pronounced through a process of intersectoral blurring, or rather the convergence of public sector organizations onto private sector templates. The greater the convergence the weaker the argument that models cannot be exported into the public sector because the work undertaken is intrinsically different.

On the other hand, are there still limits to this process of convergence specifically within the health care sector? The NHS has not been privatized and the growth of private health care has so far been of a highly contained nature. The NHS continues to be strongly located within the public sector and retains a high political profile. Within UK health care, government, legislatively based restructuring, political controversy, and defensive behaviour continue to play a greater role than in most private sector settings. Property rights remain public rather than private, and there are few functioning price mechanisms or market forces. Issues and decisions may quickly move into political or public arenas, and interventions that generate bad political news (even if they also produce efficiency or effectiveness improvements) may be dropped as too risky. There are still greater constraints on the behaviour and power base of public sector senior management than typically found within a private sector firm. There is an ingrained pattern of hyper-bureaucratization, risk aversion, and a political dislike of 'bad news' that tells against the use of radical organizational experiments to test alternative futures.

In addition, health care has traditionally been seen as highly professionalized so that professional workers such as doctors enjoy a high degree of organizational power and autonomy over work practices (Freidson 1970 has outlined the classic theory of professional dominance). Much professional work is based on tacit or craft-based forms of knowledge that resist easy formalization and rationalization. Management here plays a modest facilitative role rather than a directive function and has by itself little power to impose radical change. The real power has historically rested with a loose coalition of local clinical groups that are engaged in the incremental development of their own services, so that macro or strategic organizational change across such groups remains highly problematic. The strategic management capacity needed to implement complex change programmes across a large organization may well be undeveloped.

A further possible contextual difference relates to the highly complex and differentiated nature of the work undertaken within health care. The rationalization of work processes typically encountered within BPR (Knights and Willmott 2000) may be more applicable within simpler settings where there are a confined number of 'product lines' or where generic core processes can be more readily established. Re-engineering ideas may indeed fit best in engineering type settings. In sectors with high-volume, low-skill work processes, rapid developments in IT systems (often associated with the implementation of BPR programmes) may represent a truly profound driver of organizational change. Within health care, by contrast, more sophisticated IT systems have had an important impact in such contained areas as near patient testing, but the bulk of the diagnostic and intervention work is still undertaken by highly skilled humans and is resistant to change that is information technology led and involves actors operating outside clinical domains.

3.2 The macro-context: the rise of the new public management

At the most macro-level, some authors have argued that the UK public sector has moved 'down group' (Dunleavy and Hood 1994) since the 1980s, becoming less distinctive and converging with private sector models of management. Such a transition would increase the probability that business models and ideas such as process redesign will be imported and sustained. This macro-level transition is in large part a result of broad changes within the UK political economy that have had important knock-on effects at the organizational and managerial level (Pollitt 1990; Hood 1991; Hood 1995; Ferlie et al. 1996) across the public sector as a whole. The NPM movement represents a successor to the old Public Administration template that used to be dominant and which stressed the distinctive nature of government as opposed to private sector firms.

What were the major forces that were at work to create the new UK political economy of the 1980s? The growing problems of ungovernability and the large implementation deficits apparent within the extended social democratic state—and the high tax levels required to finance it—led eventually to a political outcome which took the form of a taxpayers' revolt, a desire to curb state growth, and restimulate the role of markets. The election of a radical right government in 1979 is the immediate expression of this change in political mood. There was increased political resentment against the supposed dominance of special interest groups such as trade unions and professional cartels that were seen as leading to poor performance, lack of value for money, and resistance to change within the public services. Politically and ideologically, the public sector was cast as part of the problem rather than being part of the solution to social need.

Ideas for the strategic restructuring of the public sector slowly emerged within the NPM umbrella. The NPM was sceptical about the claims to autonomy traditionally advanced by public sector professionals (Kirkpatrick 1999) and seeks ways of influencing patterns of professional practice (McNulty, Whittington, and Whipp 1996). Managerialization and marketization represent two high-level ideas. Such ideas were ideological as much as empirically grounded. Entrepreneurs and managers needed to be empowered ('the right to manage') and given greater incentives to revitalize the public services. Market forces should be restimulated and would lead to greater value, quality, and choice. The problems of the overextended social democratic state were seen at their most acute in the NHS of the late 1970s, with waves of strikes, over-mighty professional groupings, and a failure to implement proclaimed strategic plans. While the New Right first adopted these critical ideas in the 1980s, they were subsequently largely accepted by 'modernized' social democratic regimes such as New Labour.

Within this new political economy, reversing the growth of the social democratic state became a major priority. As a result, institutional reform within the public sector ceased to be a specialist domain controlled by technocrats and moved up the political agenda to a strategic level with Prime Ministers (such as Margaret Thatcher) providing top-level sponsorship for public sector restructuring over a sustained period during the 1980s. The UK emerged as one of a relatively small number of 'high-impact' settings for NPM ideas and models internationally, alongside Australia and New Zealand (Hood 1995). The UK NPM is a form of restructuring of real breadth and depth which is far more significant than the usual managerial 'fad or fashion' (Abrahamson 1991). While the earlier phases of the NPM were characterized by a number of submodels competing for attention (Ferlie et al. 1996), its later phases were dominated by an approach that was based on these twin guiding principles of 'markets and management'.

We now outline the guiding principles of the NPM paradigm (Ferlie 2000*a*) as apparent across the UK public sector and in particular the health care subsector. We suggest that the NHS can be seen as a 'high-impact' subsector of public services for NPM ideas, because it is under clearer national political direction than locally delivered services such as education and social work and because it was a clear political target for reform in the 1980s. Since the early 1980s, UK central government has increasingly acted to disturb inherited organizational forms within health care, imposing waves of top-down change. The introduction of general management was perhaps the first major example (Griffiths 1983) and came early on in the life of the Thatcher governments. Repeated interventions from the political and governmental environment represent potentially powerful disturbances to established roles and power balances (Brock, Powell, and Hinings 1999). The guiding principles of UK NPM as apparent by the early 1990s can be defined as follows.

3.2.1 *Greater focus on operational and strategic management rather than policy advice, constitutional, or judicial tasks*

Within the restructured public sector, the dominant focus of interest and attention moves from 'policy' to 'management'. The earlier public administration template stressed the distinctive role of the State as lawgiver, governor, and monopolist of legitimate force. While constitutional, judicial, and policy advisory functions represent the old core of the public sector, they have long been dwarfed by the mass service delivery tasks performed by large-scale welfare bureaux. Such tasks may have been larger scale, but they were also historically less prestigious or politically visible. With the rise of the NPM, political attention shifted to the more effective management of such bureaux that account for the bulk of public sector expenditure (such as social security programmes) where better value can be sought.

Moving down to the health care sector, policy-making in the 1970s was characterized by the development of ambitious long-range plans for service development that then encountered significant implementation difficulties, being blown off course by a deteriorating economic environment. In the 1980s there was a retreat from the overemphasis on policy-making and long-range planning with attempts to strengthen the implementation capacity of the system. 'Policy' gave way to 'strategy', where policy objectives were only seen as meaningful in so far as they were aligned with financial and human resources to enable implementation. Grand declarations of creative policy-making and service development (such as the novel care in the community policies of the 1970s) gave way to a more modest emphasis on effective resource management (such as the realizing of annual efficiency savings). The aim was to pursue fewer policies better, and if possible in a more cost-effective manner.

The introduction of general management (Griffiths 1983) within the NHS will be considered in more detail in a later section. In addition, a separate NHS Management Executive (NHSME) was created in the late 1980s and spun out of the Department of Health (DoH) to lead the operational management arm. Significantly, the NHSME was headed by its own chief executive rather than the Permanent Secretary. The Regional Health Authorities (RHAs) were brought into an integrated command structure for the first time, and developed a performance management function downwards. Individual target-setting and annual appraisals were brought in for both Health Authority (HA) chairs and chief executive officers (CEOs). All these developments represented a strengthening of the managerial focus and capacity of health care organizations which had until the 1980s been undeveloped.

3.2.2 *Disaggregation of public organizations and greater managerial autonomy*

The public administration model produced vertically integrated organizations with strong upwards lines of accountability. The NPM separates out responsibility for purchasing and providing public services, so that previously integrated organizations have been decoupled in order to increase pressure for performance and break up excessive collusion. On the providing side, greater managerial freedoms in the fields of budgeting and capital and human resources have been devolved to new operating units distinct from a policy-making core. These agencies still operate under a framework set by the centre and enforced through a contract, but have more internal freedoms (at least rhetorically). A good example would be the Benefits Agency that delivers a large-scale welfare programme as a 'hands-off' agency and as the operational arm of the Department of Social Security.

These organizations often display better-developed managerial capacity and possess (within the agreed framework) greater autonomy, choice, and flexibility. There is a debate about how much discretion has in reality been delegated, but it may be significant in some cases, opening up the possibility of some strategic choice and repositioning. An early view was that organizational diversity within the public sector might be increasing (Ferlie et al. 1996), rather than decreasing, as a wider range of organizational forms and management approaches are acceptable.

Within the health care sector, the two best examples of devolved management structures consist of General Practitioner (GP) Fund-holding and NHS Trust hospitals, both of which forms were created by the 1990 internal market reforms. The primary care sector within the NHS had been hyper-regulated since 1948, with the so-called 'red book' of rules and regulations used to govern payments to GPs in detail. This hyper-regulation coexisted with the small business orientation of many GPs (who were technically self-employed rather than salaried) that was if anything accentuated by GP Fundholding. The new group of GP Fundholders was given delegated budgets over certain elective services, which they could use to negotiate contracts with the NHS on indeed private sector hospitals. Smaller and more flexible than purchasing Health Authorities, they could 'spot purchase', relet contracts (or make credible threats so to do), and realize micro-gains and service improvements that could be spotted on a local basis. The first waves of GP Fundholders displayed a strong 'entrepreneurial' culture that made some of their purchasing decisions idiosyncratic. They also managed to shift power away from hospital consultants towards primary care. GP Fundholding grew at only a moderate rate, but in some areas (often affluent areas with well-organized practices) had become significant by the mid-1990s. Concerns centred on lack of equity across practices, a high administrative workload, and high transaction costs (Mays et al. 2000).

NHS Trust hospitals represented a potentially novel organizational form within hospital-based provision (Ferlie et al. 1996; Kitchener 1999; Mays et al. 2000). The new NHS Trust form rolled out rapidly, and most hospitals were in Trust status by 1994 (a much faster pace of diffusion than the analogous reforms within education services). While the operational level of the NHS consumes the vast bulk of resources, hospitals had enjoyed little managerial autonomy until 1990. The old Directly Managed Units (DMUs) reported to the HA, which acted as their formal governance structure. By contrast, each NHS Trust had its own board, chair, and CEO. Trusts' income was dependent on their ability to attract income from the macro- and micro-purchasers and so they needed to find effective strategies to compete. They were given more freedom to self-manage, including the ability to negotiate more local pay arrangements and more freedom over capital. They were permitted to develop new services without having to go to the HA.

3.2.3 *From plans to quasi-markets*

The public administration model used the hierarchy and the plan as key vehicles for resource allocation. The NPM facilitated the growth of quasi-markets, particularly where conventional public sector monopolies were seen to be failing. Public services could still be financed through public money but were increasingly delivered by a wider range of providers than the old public sector monopolists. Providers may include new entrants from the private sector, not for profit organizations or newly independent buyouts. Barriers to entry are high in some areas (such as clinical health services) but lower in others (such as cleaning services). A number of peripheral functions have been externalized, contracted out, or subjected to market testing, in order to stimulate performance and value for money. Such externalization was noticeable in such areas as nursing care and social care, although less so in acute hospitals. The letting and reletting of contracts represent key decision points, when the dynamics of the quasi-market become clear. The quasi-market stimulated the creation of 'quasi-firms' or 'social businesses' (including NHS Trusts), where the search for competitive advantage is no longer an entirely inappropriate concept.

Within the NHS quasi-market, there was potential for competition between NHS Trusts at least within urban areas where there were a number of competing providers within the same locality. Such providers were competing for an increasing number of GP Fundholder contracts over a range of elective services, and having to market their services in a much sharper fashion than before. Depending on the stance of the HA, there might also be periodic competition for major contracts in service areas which required rationalization (a reduction in the number of providing sites and concentration of provision). An important function of the HA was market development, where the market was as yet immature.

3.2.4 *Increased pressure for performance*

The transition to the NPM is associated with a demand for greater public sector performance and productivity. Within the managerial sphere, there is a greater use of efficiency targets, market-testing, performance indicators, and expanding audit systems (Power 1997). There is increased interest in assessing performance, developing performance management systems, and indeed in the creation of high-performance public sector organizations (Moore 1995). Far more sophisticated IT systems have led to the rapid development of performance indicator data systems and the comparative benchmarking of performance, in the public as in the private sector. Where market forces remain weak, public sector managers face individual performance targets set by their boards on which their careers may depend. There is a greater willingness to expose low-performing public sector providers and credible threats to replace them with new private providers (even in 'core' areas as education and prison services, although not yet within health care).

Within health care, the quasi-market was one mechanism for putting pressure on to reduce costs and increase quality. This was complemented by the growth of more managerially based performance management systems in the 1980s and 1990s. These would include the setting of efficiency and other targets and the development of comparative Performance Indicators which could be used to benchmark providers and of more sophisticated cost and information systems which facilitated scrutiny from the higher tiers. Audit systems began to develop (Power 1997), starting with the policy to sanction the expansion of the role of the Audit Commission from its traditional base in local government into health care.

Human Resource Management (HRM) practices shifted significantly in the NHS in the 1980s and 1990s, away from old public sector employer models and associated with a decline in the power of the public sector trade unions. There was a growth of annual target-setting and appraisal, reinforced by the use of short-term contracts and performance-related pay. There was an individualization of job contracts at the higher levels of NHS management and a move away from collective bargaining. There was also a growth in management education and development, designed to foster different and more managerial sets of skills. While senior managers were better paid, they also enjoyed much less job security: the days of a 'job for life' within NHS management were over.

3.2.5 *From producers to users*

Public sector organizations have historically been seen as inward facing, dominated by strong producer groups, and insulated from the expression of client preferences. The new quasi-markets within the public services led to the introduction of novel mechanisms (decentralized budgets; micro-purchasing; lessening of restrictions on client choice) designed to increase user voice. There has been a growth of 'customer care' initiatives designed to combat traditional producer dominance, associated with a new rhetoric of choice and quality.

This shift has perhaps been weaker in health care than in other public services, reflecting the dominant position of professional workers within health services. Purchasing power was delegated to consumer proxies (such as GPs), rather than consumers directly who still had little direct market power or ability to exit to alternative producers (public sector local area monopolies continued in many places such as rural areas). Patients had less real choice than parents in education services, who were more able to switch schools. Even in health care, however, there were by the 1990s some attempts to increase the power of users. Interestingly, there were calls as early as 1983 (Griffiths 1983) for more market research to assess the opinion of users. The new purchasing role of HAs was meant to recast them (somewhat optimistically) as 'tribunes of the people', accessing users' views through Health Needs Assessment (HNA) techniques and reflecting them in contracts. Quality initiatives such as TQM (Joss and Kogan 1995) operated with consumers' definition of a quality service as well as a clinical definition. The new NHS Trusts' marketing function often championed greater customer awareness. Nevertheless, health care producers remained largely dominant up to the end of the 1990s, when there were some signs that this pattern might shift radically with the breakdown of the concordat between the UK State and the medical profession.

3.2.6   *From administrators to managers*

These developments have had implications for individual careers as well as for corporate organizational forms, with a shift from the old public administrators to the new public managers. Within the public administration model, often the real power lay in the hands of senior professional staff (e.g. clinicians) with administrators taking on a modest, facilitative role. The New Public Managers often enact an expanded and directive role, with the hiring of CEOs (often brought in from outside) to act as change managers on higher salaries but also on short-term contracts. The newly created Non-Executive Director roles (NED) (rather than the old 'member' roles associated with the public administration model) on boards of public sector organizations provide another expanded focus for senior level leadership (Ferlie et al. 1996). More recently, senior professional managerial hybrid roles have been created (Montgomery 1990; FitzGerald 1994; Thorne 1997; FitzGerald and Ferlie 2000) in an attempt to tie together the historically different worlds of public sector managers and public sector professionals.

A managerialization process was evident within the health care organizations of the 1980s and 1990s. Managers were to enjoy the 'right to manage', and the public sector trade unions were marginalized through the introduction of new industrial relations legislation and changed HRM strategies. The introduction of general management roles (Griffiths 1983) to replace more facilitative public administrative roles was the most obvious change, but a less noticed development was Griffiths's second proposal to get more doctors into management. The clinical directorate (CD) model encouraged a clinician with a particular interest in management to move into a management role on a part-time basis, usually supported by a senior nurse and a business manager. A few early adopting hospitals experimented with CDs in the mid-1980s, and such structures later diffused rapidly in the early 1990s as a way of developing a subgroup of clinicians who were closer to the management agenda. Considerable education and training resources were made available to develop these clinico-managerial hybrids (Ferlie et al. 1996) that could potentially link the traditionally different worlds of medicine and management. Concerns centred on the skill and commitment levels of these CDs, as well as the dilemma of whether their improved relationship with management was bought at the expense of a deteriorating relationship with the clinical rank and file.

The empowerment of the board within health care organizations—and the emergence of assertive NEDs who relished the task of strategic management—was noticeable in the early 1990s, particularly in the large acute Trusts that were seen as more prestigious by many of those with substantial director-level experience in large private sector organizations (Ferlie et al. 1996). This represented an additional management force and greater capacity at the level of the governance structure.

3.2.7 *From maintenance management to the management of change*

The emphasis on due process and insulation from external forces characteristic of the old Public Administration model led to the reproduction of decision-making routines and standard operating procedures. Within the NPM model, steady state management has been replaced by an emphasis on the management of change as the old public sector is taken as a negative role model: as something to escape from, rather than to perpetuate. There was a noticeable growth of academic research interest in the empirical study of processes that accompany the management of change within health care (Stocking 1985; Pettigrew, Ferlie, and McKee 1992) and more speculative or normative talk of radical 'organizational transformation' to new styles of management (Osborne and Gaebler 1992). The earlier presumption of a dominant bureaucratic style with an emphasis on steady state management is being superseded by a post-bureaucratic or an entrepreneurial style of management (Barzelay 1992).

These basic principles of the NPM implied a massive change agenda for existing public service managers as they were enacted within local agencies. At the level of the individual career, the new general managers in the NHS were often tasked with accelerating the rate of service change, for example securing the closure of hospitals and the redevelopment of services. These plans had often drifted badly, and here was a much sharper managerial focus that was supposed to speed up implementation. However, apparently well-defined and hard-edged targets for change still became embroiled in a wider set of political and cultural forces that impeded planned change efforts. Given these obstacles, many general managerial staff took an increased interest in models and techniques that might help them implement major change effectively. This would include, for example, models for transition management (where Beckhard and Harris 1987, provided an influential framework) or culture change (Deal and Kennedy 1982).

Certainly, a novel discourse around the 'management of change' was noticeable in the NHS of the 1980s and 1990s, whereas it had been absent throughout the 1970s. Perhaps Peters and Waterman's (1982) *In Search of Excellence* can be seen as the first 'block-busting' text which crossed into the NHS and stimulated high levels of interest among management staff in accessible change models. Authors that are more scholarly also focused on background culture (Schein 1985) as an important shaper of organizational decisions and performance. This academic and consultancy interest was transmitted to the service by Organizational Development (OD) units within the NHS and a growing number of courses that taught the basic principles of the management of change. Staff were encouraged to act as 'internal change agents' and could make their managerial careers on that basis. Consultancy firms and management gurus acted as 'external change agents', and imported ideas into the NHS from outside, as the 'fads and fashions' model (Abrahamson 1991) suggests.

This interpretation of the dominant principles of the NPM movement as it consolidated itself within the UK public sector of the 1990s—in brief, 'markets plus managers'—suggests that underlying tendencies are apparent within the NHS, as across other public service settings.

Indeed, the NHS can be seen as an early moving subsector, reflecting its political visibility and high levels of central control. We see such shifts in the wider field of UK public services as radical, sustained, and significant. There are of course alternative interpretations of the guiding principles of the NPM movement, and of its level of significance. Some do not accept that it marks a major change in public service organization and argue that it is no more than a fad (Lynn 1998) and that the NPM bubble could burst. Others defend aspects of the old public administration paradigm against the NPM, stressing the positive role of the public administration ethos in supporting due process and ethical government (du Gay 2000). This critical perspective argues that the shift to the NPM increases low-trust games around contracts (at best) and levels of corruption (at worst) within the public services.

Our characterization applies to the 1979–97 period during which the NPM template emerged and developed (the case study is largely located within the same period). For the future, the question will arise as to whether the change of UK government in 1997 is of sufficient significance to lead to the de-institutionalization of this NPM paradigm. Our speculative view is that this remains unlikely (Ferlie and FitzGerald 2000) as the new government has retained many of these guiding principles of organization and because other of the social factors which have led to the growth of the NPM (such as the emergence of management as a new form of elite labour) remain undisturbed. We shall return to this theme in more detail in future work.

3.3 The meso-context: hospitals as organizations

The earlier sections of the chapter outlined very broad shifts in the UK political economy, and traced these changes through to the emergence of strategic ideas for the downsizing and restructuring of the UK public sector. In this next section on the 'meso-context', we introduce other literature that has analysed hospitals as organizations. This meso-level of analysis is an intermediate level that seeks to bridge macro- and micro-perspectives, and to trace the interactions between them (in this case, the attempted impact of the macro on the micro) (House, Rousseau, and Thomas-Hunt 1995; Klein, Tosi, and Cannella 1999). The macro-perspective draws attention to the changing political economy of the public sector and strategic ideas for public sector reform. The micro-perspective focuses on how these forces are enacted within one site. The intermediate level of meso-analysis focuses on the population of hospitals as an organizational field. The notion of an 'organizational field' refers to a community of organizations with a common meaning system, made up of organizations that produce similar services or products, and related to the same set of key suppliers, consumers, and regulatory agencies (Caronna and Scott 1999: 86). What kind of organizational field is apparent within health care? What are the implications for process redesign efforts of the dominant organizational forms that are apparent?

We start by asserting that organizations can be seen as more or less politicized. We share the view that hospitals should be seen as highly politicized and that health care management thus takes place within a politicized context (Harrison et al. 1992; Buchanan 1997). There is most obviously a party political element to such politicization in the UK, as different political parties proclaim 'solutions' for the reform of the NHS based on distinctive political ideologies. Thus, Conservative reform programmes emphasize consumer choice; while Labour reform programmes have recently emphasized service integration and consistency.

But the health care system can be seen as politicized in a second and wider sense. There are many different occupational and interest groups within the health care system with seemingly competing goals and agendas. Individuals often identify strongly with such collective bodies (for example, a doctor with the British Medical Association) and see them as protecting their preferences and interests. The various interest groups are cohesive internally and able to mobilize individuals within their own constituencies. There are also usually losers as well as winners associated with change processes and the potential losers may well be rational from their perspective in resisting imposed change. Political forms of behaviour may be expected from all parties involved in complex change processes, and not just from senior management who represent only one stakeholder in a multiple stakeholder system. Indeed, it would be odd if 'change victims', either real or potential, did not engage in political behaviour in order to minimize adverse outcomes as seen from their point of view.

Much organizational behaviour literature does not address such issues adequately, or considers the use of power as legitimate only when undertaken by senior management. We therefore need to consider the nature of organizational politics and power more directly and broadly (Hardy and Clegg 1996). We refer here to the micro-politics of the health care organization as well as the macro-politics of health care policy where the role of elected politicians is more apparent.

So how do we conceive the nature of organizational politics within hospitals? Morgan (1993) distinguishes between unitary, pluralist, and radical perspectives on organizational politics. The unitary perspective ignores the different perspectives, agendas, and interests held by individuals and groups within complex health care organizations. The radical perspective too readily assumes that such differences escalate into class conflict, whereas the pattern of activity and alliance-making within health care organizations may shift from one issue to another. Conflict may be of a contained and highly negotiated nature, rather than of a highly generalized form.

We argue therefore that health care organizations should be seen as 'boundedly pluralist' arenas with many interest groups. Pluralist forms of political analysis often focus on how institutions structure decision-making (here the micro-institutions of the hospital such as the different CDs); agenda formation processes; bargaining between different interest groups; and coalition formation processes. On the basis of early empirical work, some American political scientists (Dahl 1961; Polsby 1963) argued that the distribution of political power in American local politics was highly diffuse rather than concentrated in a small elite. Later work (Bachrach and Baratz 1970) qualified this view, suggesting that there were underlying processes at work excluding some issues from ever reaching the agenda. Some groups were more powerfully placed to shape the agenda creation process, and subordinated groups were excluded.

A 'boundedly pluralist' perspective argues that there are many interest groups within decision-making but that some have more influence and power than others. It qualifies the classically pluralist perspective by recognizing that there are imbalances in the underlying distribution of power (for example, doctors have traditionally been more powerful than nurses). Radical changes to a political or organizational system may be dependent on a prior shift in the distribution of political power. In his analysis of American health care politics, Alford (1975) distinguished between a dominant professional grouping, a challenging managerial grouping, and a repressed community grouping. One way of decoding the NPM movement is as an attempted mega-shift which empowers the managerial grouping as against the traditionally dominant professional grouping and which may result in more managerialized patterns of decision-making. The pluralists would argue that the outcomes of such bargaining processes are uncertain and may be shaped by local factors which 'tip the balance' one way or the other. Broad structural changes are by themselves unlikely to be the only factor that determines decision outcomes, as they are mediated by local contexts.

The possibility arises of bargaining between the different interest groups that may lead to the creation of a form of consensus, at least within the dominant coalition (so called 'win win' situations). This perspective is different from that of neo-Marxist or labour process organizational theory (Parkin 1979; Braverman 1974) which assumes a latent or indeed overt conflict between dominant and repressed classes within organizations, driven by different economic interests. Within hospitals, decisions are made within a large and complex organization rather than through markets and prices. There are thus specific institutional arenas in which such collective decisions are processed. There are formal and informal power centres within the organization that seek to shape such decision-making outcomes, such as the governance structure or collegial meetings of the senior clinicians.

3.3.1 *Organizational and occupational principles at work*

Within health care organizations, there are a range of stakeholders and occupational groups which seek to influence the decision-making process. However, we can focus on two alternative principles for the structuring of the clinical work, whose coexistence within hospital organizations forms one important basis of the micro-politics of health care.

These alternative occupational and administrative principles (Watson 1995) operate in conditions of both cooperation and tension and can be defined in the following ways. 'The occupational principle of work structuring emphasizes the way in which people with similar skills, traditions, and values cooperatively conceive, execute and regulate work tasks.' By contrast, he argues that, 'The organizational or administrative principle of structuring work emphasizes the ways in which some people conceive of and design tasks in the light of certain ends and then recruit, pay, coordinate and control the efforts of others who do not share those ends, to fulfill work tasks' (Watson 1995: 234). The former is a guild-based form; the latter a more conventionally managed form.

Concepts of profession and clinical specialty have conventionally been central to the organization of clinical work. Both exemplify the occupational principle of organization within practice. In the context of the medical profession, clinical specialties grow up around anatomical divisions or organs (such as nephrology or cardiology); medical technologies (such as radiology or anaesthetics) or age groups (such as paediatrics and geriatrics) (Montgomery 1990). The secular trend within the medical profession towards ever-greater specialization as the clinical knowledge base expands intensifies the organizational problem of how to integrate work processes across a growing number of clinical specialties, each of which displays occupational boundaries.

By contrast, CDs exemplify the organizational and administrative principle, diffusing rapidly as a new mode of organizing clinical work during the 1990s. Their emergence coincided with the development of the quasi-market and creation of NHS Trusts and they were seen as enhancing the managerial capacity of hospitals now operating in more demanding and businesslike conditions. CDs are managerially inspired and defined groupings of clinical specialities and service inputs, for example, surgical services, medical services, clinical support services. They have been created specifically for the purposes of resource management, control, and accountability. CDs seek to link previously unaligned processes of service provision and resource management through explicit business planning and the greater involvement of clinicians within management (Ferlie et al. 1996). Clinical directors may be beginning to exercise managerial influence over their clinical colleagues, but drawing on strategies of trading and reciprocity rather than the exercise of crude positional power (FitzGerald and Ferlie 2000).

The coexistence of the traditional occupational principle of organizing with an increasingly assertive organizational principle provides ample scope for political behaviour around attempts to alter or protect the historic division of labour. Such disputes are unlikely to remain at a purely technical level but have the potential to escalate as underlying ideologies (notably the claim to professional autonomy) are brought into the argument. A managerial skill may be not to take those actions that bring with them a high risk of escalation and polarization. Dispute may arise from the tension between the administrative principle's interest in control, as opposed to the occupational principle's orientation to autonomy. Without ignoring the potential for cooperative behaviour or consensus-building strategies that may contain conflict, the potential for intergroup dispute remains high.

These tensions are not novel but are well established and documented. Behaviour within health care organizations has often been conceptualized in terms of conflicting cultures, value systems, and ideas apparent between managerial and clinical groupings (Alford 1975; Pettigrew, Ferlie, and McKee 1992; Harrison et al. 1992). More recently, in his study of the introduction of reengineering into a hospital setting, Buchanan (1997) identifies the potential for conflict

emerging between managerial and clinical perspectives in relation to
the domains of 'costs', 'returns', and 'common purposes'. Kitchener
(1999) draws attention to a mixed picture of change within the UK's
experiment with the quasi-market in health care. Professionals have, in
his view, come to accept the diffusion of the clinical directorate model,
albeit under duress. However, there is little evidence that the primary
loyalty of UK hospital doctors has shifted from their peers or professional associations to their general managers or hospitals at a more
corporate level.

Denis et al.'s (1999) important investigation of why it was that
boundary redefinition exercises through hospital mergers often failed
to live up to their initial promise within Canadian hospitals started by
outlining a 'negotiated order' perspective on work definition within
hospitals. The 'real work' is done within clinical teams who negotiate
between themselves as to how the work can be best divided up (e.g.
surgeons and anaesthetists negotiate about how to make best use of
theatre time). Cross-boundary operating units emerge according to the
clinical logic of the workflow, albeit dominated by the most powerful
interest group (the clinicians). There are severe limits to the use of managerial power in forcing through change within these emergent operating units, especially as senior clinicians may be well represented in
the organization's governance structure. Nevertheless, 'reformers'
(managers, politicians, and experts) periodically propose transformation projects (such as mergers) that emerge within the political or policy domains and are incompatible with this core logic of professional
production. In these cases, clinicians may retain loyalty to the old negotiated order that is able to handle complex questions of clinical coordination at an operational level and resist the new imposed structures.
The construction of a new negotiated order across the newly merged
hospitals that went beyond relatively superficial structural change was
a task of enormous complexity and possibly beyond managerial capacity. Although this study was conducted in a different health care
system, many of the underlying themes have resonance for our UK
case-study site.

3.3.2   *Managers and professionals in health care*

Any managerially sponsored change programme within health care will
need to engage with the traditionally autonomous behaviour and power
base of professional workers, especially doctors (Clarke and Newman
1997; Exworthy and Halford 1999). Moreover, such professionals should

not be seen as passive victims of change, but possess high levels of knowledge and skill that they can use to adapt the change agenda to defend their core purposes.

Medicine can be seen historically as an ideal-typical case of professional dominance (Freidson 1970, 1994) where decisions are made by a college of senior professionals rather than line managers. Health care may be similar to other professionalized organizations such as law or accountancy firms which have been until recently resistant to managerially led forms of radical process design as senior professionals have retained their core organizational power (Brock, Powell, and Hinings 1999). Mintzberg's (1979) delineation of the professionalized bureaucracy—such as in a hospital—painted a picture of an organization dominated by senior professionals, which was changing constantly at a micro-level but in which strategic change was largely absent. It was difficult to envisage these systems as displaying any kind of strategic management capacity as the corporate core remained weak. Greenwood, Hinings, and Brown's professional partnership model (1990) (or the so-called P2 form) similarly described distinctive organizations in which professional workers were not only the operators of the organization, but also the senior managers and indeed the owners, as in partners within law firms (and also GPs in primary care settings).

There have been recurrent cycles of attempts to managerialize health care organizations (Flynn 1992; Harrison et al. 1992; Harrison and Pollitt 1994). Here we briefly summarize what we know about the outcome of such reform efforts and draw out the implications for the current study. Between the formation of the NHS and the early 1980s, health care organizations could be seen as professionalized bureaucracies, in which clinicians retained a high degree of autonomy over work practices through advancing an ideology of clinical autonomy which was at that stage largely accepted by the State. This organizational form was similar to the one described by Mintzberg (1979). From the early 1980s onwards, we have already argued that there was the rise of the NPM movement, with recurrent attempts to strengthen the management of the NHS. In addition, quasi-market forces were introduced to mimic the effects of real markets, even within a public sector context, and strengthen incentives for performance. So, the period can be seen as one of increased application of managerial control structures into a hitherto professionally dominated system.

Harrison and Pollitt (1994) argue that reform measures within health care can be grouped into three categories: challenging professionals;

incorporating professionals; and changing the environment in which professionals practice. We will briefly discuss each strategy and explore what they reveal about medical–managerial relations within hospitals.

Managerial work in the pre-1980s NHS was reactive rather than proactive (Harrison and Pollitt 1994). Organizational decisions emerged as an aggregate outcome of individual doctors' clinical decisions, rather than through the deliberate actions of politicians, policy-makers, or managers. Doctors controlled the 'real work', while managers took on a facilitative or diplomatic role, providing support for the key clinical workers. In the 1980s, the old facilitative model of management was discarded in favour of a more active general management model, which was better able to challenge inflated autonomy claims and promote value for money. Associated with the introduction of general management was the attempt to upgrade management cost and information systems and weaken the influence of trade unions and professional associations.

By contrast to this 'head-on' challenge, another strategy has been to incorporate subgroups of professionals into management activity. Harrison and Pollitt (1994: 74) define 'incorporation' as 'government/ managerial tactics to control health professionals by encouraging some of them to become involved on managers' terms, in management processes which include a degree of control over their professional colleagues'. Such mechanisms of incorporation include making doctors budget-holders through the introduction of resource management systems, GP Fundholding, and clinical directorates. While there was some retreat from a reliance on a pure general management model in the 1990s as public and political concern about the costs of management grew, there has been if anything an increasing stress on 'getting doctors into management'. For example, the recent changes within primary care organizations strengthen the role of clinico-managers within the new form of Primary Care Groups, providing for part-time managerial roles for senior GPs.

Professional autonomy has also been challenged by macro-changes in the environment. The separation of purchasers and providers within the quasi-market (a split which has been retained after 1997) offered the potential for purchasers to lever more influence over the work of clinicians as they placed contracts. Rising consumer expectations and education levels have also led to a decline of deference and a greater willingness to question the behaviour of clinicians.

So, what is the outcome of such change efforts? Harrison and Pollitt's (1994) assessment of the impact of two decades of reform efforts concludes that there has been some loss of traditional forms of autonomy for individual health care professionals and a significant enhancement in managerial control. Clinical decision-making is, and they suggest will continue to be, more subject to professional guidelines and diagnostic and treatment protocols. New processes of general management, financial audit, service contracting, and information systems are subjecting professionals to the rules, plans, and priorities of the organization. The loss of autonomy has been greater on the part of nurses and Professionals Allied to Medicine than doctors.

However, there remain some important limitations to pure forms of managerial control at hospital level. Ferlie et al. (1996) found substantial power shifts at the strategic apex of health care organizations away from a model of pure professional dominance, but it is unclear whether this shift is also apparent at the level of clinical practice. Attempts to incorporate doctors within managerial work have only been partly successful. Despite the introduction of clinical director roles, many doctors remain outside managerial processes. At the level of the individual physician, strategies vary and may include resistance or negotiation, as well as acceptance of the managerial agenda (Hoff and McCaffrey 1996). For some doctors, management is not seen as a valued activity and involvement in it may be construed as a betrayal of their primary profession. For those doctors who are involved in management, as clinical directors, their own level of commitment varies, as does the reaction of other doctors to them. One possibility is that there is a growing divide between the clinico-managerial hybrids and the professional rank and file (Kirkpatrick 1999), especially if the former are perceived as 'going over' to management, sometimes with the excessive zeal of the convert.

Managerial control remains confined because of the continuing 'micro-power' of clinicians (Harrison et al. 1992) over key processes of admission and discharge of patients, diagnosis, and treatment-planning. The hospital patient is a patient of a named consultant, not of a manager, nurse, or medical social worker. The consultants control the 'real work' in the hospital and it is difficult for management to influence care processes at the ward level. Early reform efforts—such as the introduction of general management—may have underestimated the power of local doctors to resist imposed change (Harrison et al. 1992) and evade attempts to standardize and monitor their activities. At the very least, constructive partnerships between managerial and clinical groupings may be necessary to progress strategic change (Pettigrew, Ferlie, and McKee 1992).

Lack of professional ownership continues to be a major predictor of low levels of impact within corporate change initiatives such as TQM programmes (Joss and Kogan 1995). Professionals may reject TQM ideas if they are seen as over-aligned with managerial agendas. Change programmes which succeed in reshaping non-clinical aspects of work (such as the condition of waiting areas) but which fail to reshape clinical processes cannot be seen as achieving a fundamental impact on the organization. In their evaluation of a BPR experiment in health care, Packwood, Pollitt, and Roberts (1998) found that many of these limitations were also present. Unless there has been very substantial recent change within professional roles and identities, these underlying tendencies that produce such limited impact can be expected to persist.

3.3.3 *Cooperation and conflict in health care*

The question of cooperation and conflict within health care organizations should not be conceived simply in terms of the interaction between clinicians and managers. Doctors and managers are not the only occupational groups within the health service, nor are these two groups always internally homogeneous either structurally or ideologically (McNulty, Whittington, and Whipp 1996; Harrison et al. 1992; Whittington, McNulty, and Whipp 1994; Pettigrew, Ferlie, and McKee 1992). It is not uncommon within the managerial cadre to find internal competition for status and scarce resources (Buchanan 1997), or for behaviour to embody a mixture of competitive and collaborative strategies. Similarly, processes of internal competition within the clinical grouping also arise from wider processes of professionalization that have operated at the societal level. There are many different professional groups within health care, which compete for turf and professional 'jurisdiction' (Abbott 1988).

Professionalization should be seen as the process by which an occupation seeks to increase the status, relative autonomy, rewards, and influence of its members. Anglo-American medicine has been seen as an ideal-typical example of a successful professionalization project (Freidson 1970, 1994), although such professional dominance has more recently come under challenge from sharper market forces or more assertive purchasers (Brock, Powell, and Hinings 1999). The core value underlying a strategy of professionalization is autonomy that enables professional workers to retain control over work tasks. Abbott (1988) uses the concept of 'jurisdiction' to define the relationship between a profession and a set of tasks. The jurisdictional ambitions of professions often contain three claims: (i) claims to classify a problem (diagnosis);

(ii) claims to reason about it (inference); and (iii) claims to take action on it (treatment). A successful strategy of professionalization has then consequences at a local as well as a societal level.

Within hospitals, clinicians not only control the flow of work, but also differentiate themselves into segments (clinical specialties) and resist managerial attempts to make their activity predictable, transparent, and standard. By comparison, the nursing and other caring professions have been less successful in translating their professionalization strategies into autonomy in the workplace. At local level, clinicians also seek to increase their status and extend the boundaries of their jurisdictions. Moreover, jurisdictional overlap between the professions may emerge in large and complex organizations (Abbott 1988: 64–7), and become apparent in the handling of interfaces between different segments. An example would be the process of role negotiation between senior nurses and junior doctors: one profession may expand; but the other may feel under pressure to contract. The extended range of professional groups further complicates attempts to introduce managerially sponsored innovations, as there are many different and competing professional lobbies to negotiate with. Specifically, process redesign's alleged interest in reduced task specialization and multi-skilling is likely to promote jurisdictional disputes at the local level.

In conclusion, this analysis of the meso-context of the health care field suggests that the challenges of process redesign within hospitals are considerable. Many reform cycles in the past have achieved only partial success. Hospitals are political systems within which managerial influence is bounded by the exercise of professional power and autonomy. There are also internal processes of competition over scarce resources and work jurisdictions. The impact of such organizational features on the fate of reform efforts is likely to be significant. This may be particularly the case in process redesign programmes as task differentiation and specialization—values challenged by process redesign— are core aspects of the dominant professional ideology.

3.4   Implications for the micro-context

Some important forces and shifts observable within the case-study hospital will be outlined in this section, linked to earlier analysis of the broader macro- and meso-contexts. The chapter has so far observed that over the period 1980–97 managerialization and marketization represent two key processes evident within the health care system.

These processes were indeed apparent in miniature within the case-study site. The remainder of the chapter will explore broader contextual processes as important antecedent and accompanying conditions of BPR within the case-study site. Some changes associated with these processes were mandated by legislation and imposed as top-down 'reforms' nationally. The hospital was however able to exert strategic choice in deciding to adopt the CD structure very early on (in the mid-1980s). It also developed a reputation for being a 'well-run hospital' in which managers and clinicians generally worked well together. It is true that the health care sector might be seen as an 'unreceptive' sector for BPR, given its differentiated workflows, high levels of professionaliza-tion, and jurisdictional disputes. Within the broader health care sector, however, it could be argued that this hospital displayed many of the con-ditions one might expect to be associated with successful change man-agement and was therefore a favourable site for a national experiment.

General management. General management roles were introduced in the hospital in the mid-1980s, as mandated nationally. Between 1985 and 1999 there were only two CEOs in the Trust. In 1990, the chief execu-tive who went on to lead the BPR programme was appointed, having previously been a general manager within the hospital. He remained in the hospital until 1999 and then departed (on promotion to a national-level post). The pattern is therefore one of stable, internal managerial leadership, which might be expected to strengthen organizational memory and the capacity to learn apparent in the site. The chief execu-tive who signed up to the BPR programme remained in post as a strong senior level supporter throughout its duration.

Clinical directorates. The hospital was a very early adopter nationally of the CD structure (in 1986) designed to draw at least some clinicians into the management arena through the creation of clinico-managerial roles. By the time the BPR programme started (1994), there had already been some eight years of local experience of the structure and process of clinical directorates. It terms of clinical-management structures there-fore the site was relatively well developed with a track record of clinical and managerial cooperation. For the BPR programme this entailed the potential advantage of accessing a cadre of established clinical directors whose interest in process redesign could be developed through experi-ence and also management development programmes (which were generously funded initially, as a potential incentive to adopters). BPR offered all clinical directors the opportunity to 'learn by doing', perhaps in a small-scale way initially. One of the key early change champions was the then clinical director within the medical directorate who had supported process redesign in his own clinical setting and was keen to expand the scope of the work. In the mid-1990s, the middle managerial capacity of the directorates was also expanding, with the responsibility to manage sizeable chunks of resource.

NHS Trust status. The case-study hospital was granted NHS Trust status in April 1993 and remained a Trust throughout the period of the BPR programme. As an NHS Trust the hospital developed its own governance structure, notably a board (a mix of executive and non-executive members), and a non-executive chair. The chair had previously been a member of the District HA. An engineer by profession, he had had very senior-level experience in industry. He too remained in post during the lifetime of the programme and acted as a senior-level supporter. The executive directors on the board included the medical director and director of nursing, both of which were key linking posts bringing together clinical and managerial communities. Both these post-holders played important roles in sponsoring the BPR programme. Trust status brought with it more managerial freedoms, including the freedom to launch the BPR change programme. Unusually, there was a period of strong and stable leadership in place that provided senior-level support for the programme.

Pressure from the quasi-market. The BPR experiment (1993–7) analysed here coincided with the strongest period of quasi-market pressures. By the mid-1990s, the site was facing increasing pressure from the developing local quasi-market. Before 1990, the city had three acute hospitals closely situated next to each other, integrated by a common Medical School (Ferlie et al. 1996: 78). In the era of planning, they were developed as a whole, leading to cross-site links and complementary strengths. This led to an original proposal that all three hospitals should go out into Trust status together. The Department of Health indicated that this was unacceptable, and in the end three Trusts were created. There has also been some rivalry between the three sites, with the two newer hospitals feeling that the third (the case-study site) was over-dominant. The District HA continued to conceive of the three Trusts as an entity, whose job was to serve the needs of the population. However, service rationalization decisions meant that Trusts faced the possibility of losing contracts to the other hospitals. In addition, the structure of the local quasi-market facilitated effective 'shopping around' behaviour from the growing number of GP Fundholders, whose business (mainly in relation to elective work and outpatients) was being courted actively by the three hospitals.

Over the period of the BPR programme therefore, the hospital was in competition with two other acute hospitals within the city and was under severe pressure to reduce its resource base and win contracts from GP Fundholders. This period was certainly characterized by the presence of growing competitive pressures within elective health care work (although not emergency services as the hospital provided a local monopoly in this area). There was the real possibility for competition with the other two acute hospitals in the city that were now separate Trusts. Such anticipated competition combined with the patients' charter initiative to create a managerial desire to strengthen the weak user orientation in some clinical settings such as outpatients' clinics (where there were often severe problems with waiting times and queues). This created an increased focus on strategic management, external communication, and a stronger user orientation as a way of reducing waiting times across the hospital. Trust management in particular saw BPR as a proactive way of coping with these looming pressures and avoiding a continuing situation of managing annual budgetary reductions.

A well-managed hospital. By the 1990s, the hospital was developing a reputation for being 'well managed'. It tended to perform well when benchmarked against other acute sector teaching hospitals within sets of Performance Indicators. More intangibly, it could attract and develop good-quality clinicians and managers whose relations were generally cooperative and constructive. Conflict had not escalated and there were signs of constructive partnerships between managerial and clinical groupings. Potentially important for the BPR programme, there were a number of well-placed clinical directors who were change leaders. The environment—while by no means simple—was less problematic than that faced by some of the London teaching hospitals. It had then some signs of being a 'receptive context for change' (Pettigrew, Ferlie, and McKee 1992), and of building up considerable internal change capability. From the point of view of the higher tiers of the NHS undertaking appraisals before deciding where to invest in local organizational experiments, it could be seen as a low-risk site. The underlying organizational conditions were seen as positive: if process redesign could work anywhere in the health care sector, it would be here.

3.5 Concluding discussion

Whereas the previous chapter characterized process redesign as a managerial change 'intervention', this chapter has analysed the implications of the changing context of the UK health care sector for the process redesign implementation process. Whilst proponents of BPR tend to privilege it with a generic transformational capability irrespective of organizational context, a key argument from the empirical study of the practice of organizational change is that the content and process of change cannot and should not be abstracted from the context that gives that change form meaning and dynamic (Pettigrew 1985).

Our analysis distinguished between three levels of context (the macro; the meso; and the micro), and traced the downward links between them. There were a number of important structural changes apparent in the case-study site that represented local manifestations of national-level policy and legislative changes. The role of legislative and policy mandates in determining the formal role and tasks of public sector agencies is as important as ever, although these changes are also of course enacted locally, and this represents an important aspect of the 'structuration' process.

Our analysis suggested that organizational change in the NHS must be seen within the context of a new political economy and a changing public sector and more narrowly within changes to health care organizations. The shift from a social democratic regime to a New Right regime was a major change that led to the rise of the NPM movement as a set of high-level ideas for restructuring the public sector. This in turn led to increased managerialization and marketization in health care as in other public services, along with increased suspicion of the high autonomy levels enjoyed by public sector professionals such as clinicians. While others would contest this interpretation of the long-run impact of the NPM movement, the possibility of radical internal change increases when linked to such major and sustained shifts in the environment (Brock, Powell, and Hinings 1999), including within the underlying political ideology.

Within the meso-context of the health care sector, hospitals should be seen as political systems where there is bargaining between many different interest groups. A boundedly pluralist perspective was advanced which recognized both the multiple stakeholders and the imbalance of power between them. Power relations were observed between clinical and managerial groupings. The difficult relationship between doctors and managers in health care was traced, together with the development of clinico-managerial hybrids as a potential bridge. Finally, some of the features of a highly professionalized organization, such as competition for work jurisdictions, were highlighted. An analysis of how major shifts in the organization of health care 'played out' within the micro-context of the local site was presented, with some suggestion that this might be a favourable site for managerial experiments such as BPR (albeit within a generally unreceptive sector).

We observed in Chapter 2 that organizational transformation was a complex challenge to dominant organizational ideologies and structures that entailed whole system change. BPR's concern with organizing around core business processes and enhancing value requires system-wide change, but one that emphasizes a lateral approach to organizing rather than the traditionally dominant vertical and functional approach to organizing. Organizing around the logic of core business processes as opposed to functions requires multiple interrelated and complementary changes to other system procedures and processes, for instance, payment and reward systems. The ideological and cultural accompaniment to these structural and system prescriptions is revealed by BPR's emphasis on value creation in a market context.

The overall conclusion is that we should be sceptical about the promises of 'blank sheet restructuring' and 'Big Bang change' associated with process redesign. A quasi-Leninist emphasis on charismatic leadership from health care managers as the vanguard of the salariat is too thin and fragile a base for organizational transformation. Organizational change processes are deeply shaped by their context, and a distinctive combination of high politicization and high professionalization within health care has blunted the impact of successive reform cycles. Public sector and NHS contexts have historically been highly distinctive and there are 'deep structures' in the organization of clinical work which act to dilute managerial power. So how much has changed this time? After twenty years of the New Public Management, the UK public services are now more businesslike, even if they are not yet a business. The specific question is whether these shifts are powerful enough to enable process redesign efforts to deliver sustainable change at the hospital level despite the strong and continuing professional power base or whether more nuanced outcomes are apparent (Cooper et al. 1996).

4

Organizational Process Research: Research Style and Methods

This chapter considers the methodological issues associated with the so-called process research approach used within the study, drawing on earlier reflections on method (Pettigrew 1990; Ferlie and McNulty 1997). Such craft-based and often implicit rules of method should be made explicit, so that they can be debated publicly and inform future studies. Indeed a self-conscious approach to research design and data analysis has been argued by Bryman and Burgess (1995) to be a hallmark of rigorous qualitative research.

4.1   Qualitative forms of analysis

The process research methods adopted by the team employ qualitative approaches to the study of organizations, often using the analysis of comparative and longitudinal case studies to produce evidence of patterns or tendencies across a contained grouping of organizations. There is a search for trends rather than 'laws'. Within this perspective, organizations are seen as complex and open systems where there are no causal laws but where on the other hand behaviour is not entirely random. There is in other words a patterning which is generally evident (e.g. a doctor is more powerful than a nurse), but which may break down perhaps under special circumstances (e.g. a nurse may become more powerful in moments of crisis).

In what sense can the knowledge generated by the qualitative methods often used within process research be said to be 'valid'? Validity is an important concept in many branches of social science research but there is a debate about how notions of validity can be operationalized within the interpretive rather than the positivist research paradigm. Often methodologists draw a distinction between external and internal forms of validity. In her discussion of survey methods, Bowling (1997: 162) defines external validity as the generalizability of the research results from the 'sample' to the population of interest. Where the sample is biased, then the level of external validity falls. Within quantitative research, internal validity can be described in relation to the properties of the measurement instrument (Bowling 1997: 132). An instrument is assigned validity after it has been satisfactorily tested repeatedly for the populations for which it has been designed, for example, in instruments that measure health status.

Within qualitative process research, such notions of validity are not so appropriate. Rather external validity may refer to the extent to which it is safe to generalize from the case-study site to other organizations. The analogous definition of internal validity is even more complex. How can we be sure that our conclusions about processes apparent within the case-study site are well founded? What determines whether a qualitative study should be seen as rigorous or well conducted? Bowling suggests (1997: 313) rather conservatively that internal validity within qualitative research may be enhanced by a number of research design strategies. These include the use of triangulated methods (a number of different data sources); the presence of more than one researcher in the site; and taking steps to minimize the bias of the researchers (so that they are not 'captured' by a particular group or 'go native'). There needs to be an explicit theoretical base and a structured and transparent approach to the collection and analysis of data. Consideration should also be given to sampling strategy, which is as much an issue in qualitative as quantitative research (see also the review of criteria for assessing the rigour of qualitative research by Mays and Pope 1995). Some of these criteria (such as the search for inter-rater 'reliability') would be contested by less conservative qualitative researchers as inappropriate and as belonging to the positivistic paradigm.

Altheide and Johnson's (1994: 485–99) review of validity criteria within ethnographic research argues that 'how a researcher accounts for his or her approach to certain aspects of research, including the routine sources of problems' is key for evaluating the work substantively and methodologically. This includes a clear and explicit description of the research process and the role of the researcher within the organization. Readers should wish to be informed of the role of the researcher vis-à-vis the phenomenon to be studied. There is a debate about the extent to which respondent validation is important or not as a test of quality. Some argue that the 'shock of recognition' is an important test; others that outsiders may generate insights that are denied to insiders, especially top management which may be insulated from the field level. Altheide and Johnson argue that the policy criterion of validity for ethnography is itself fraught with difficulty.

Murphy et al. (1998) consider a number of possible indicators of validity (here defined as 'the extent to which the likelihood of error has been reduced') within qualitative research as applied to health care organizations. This suggests that valid qualitative research is that which plausibly captures social reality; or rather, multiple social realities that may coexist within one setting. Certain stances and processes make qualitative research more likely to do this. They suggest that the following indicators of quality may be important, amongst others:

- an explicit account of the research process;
- the production and presentation of clear concepts, which have been produced within such research;
- the conclusions drawn should relate clearly to the data presented;
- the presentation of 'rich data' within the analysis as well as synoptic concepts;
- an extensive period of fieldwork spent in the site;
- the consideration of alternative plausible explanations;
- an empirical generalizability of their findings through negative or disconfirming cases and the use of systematic sampling;
- the use of a multiple stakeholder perspective;
- researchers should seek to enhance theory.

Given the possible trade-off between internal and external concepts of validity, our design choice has been first to assure high levels of internal validity through intensive and pluralistic forms of fieldwork within one major site. We will address questions of external validity later through reviewing related studies and also generating or confirming concepts that may apply to other organizations. Other process researchers operate in a more 'quantifying' manner, and these differences of approach will be explored in the chapter.

Our analysis is contextualist in nature, in that it studies organizational phenomena, including patterns of behaviour within their organizational and societal contexts, and is cautious about over-abstraction out of those contexts. Such trends and tendencies are much less 'law-like' than the causal relationships sought within natural science. Process methods are more inductive than deductive, where patterns emerge from data rather than through the testing of discrete hypotheses. While the aim of many quantitative researchers is to produce elegant models of the utmost parsimony, process researchers by contrast often seek to produce 'thick' or multi-layered analytic descriptions, in which analytic constructs emerge out of initial description (Eisenhardt 1989).

This represents a research style and tradition very different from the experimentalist paradigm common within HSR. In this research community, there is often a hierarchy of quantitative evidence models headed by the RCT (NHSCRD 1996). Methods are typically deductive, measurement based, and reductionist (i.e., attempting to isolate the effect of a particular intervention holding all other factors constant). The aim is to isolate 'laws' which operate at as high a level of generality as possible, following the model of the repeated scientific experiment. Whilst this should still be seen as the dominant research paradigm, the disappointing performance of experimental approaches to social evaluations over a long period of time has been recently highlighted and a more 'realistic' or naturalistic model of evaluative research advanced (Pawson and Tilley 1997).

There is increased interest in qualitative research even within the historically resistant field of health care research (Pope and Mays 1995; Murphy et al. 1998). This reflects an enhanced concern for exploring social processes that operate within health care systems. This perspective differs from the traditional focus on the natural scientific or technological base where the biomedical research paradigm has been most dominant. Many social scientists have criticized the over-dominance of experimentalist methods within HSR; and a few have defended them (Oakley 2000) in their quest for a new mode of 'evidence-based' policy.

For critics of experimentalism, there is a growing awareness that the study of input/output relations is not enough, and that the 'black box' of the organization exerts important mediating effects. The search for 'universal laws' within the organizational domain is seen as a chimera and the adoption of experimentalist methods in this field (e.g. by those who follow the Cochrane model of Evidence-Based Medicine (EBM) as applied to the organization of care) as unlikely to be fruitful.

There is a wider methodological debate within social science as a whole as well as within the smaller HSR community. Within many social sciences, there has been a meta-level shift over the last twenty years or so from quantitative to more qualitative approaches, and this trend has been echoed in organizational studies. Clegg, Hardy, and Nord's (1996) overview of the organizational field argues that the main shift has been from a functionalist paradigm (based on the assumptions of 'normal science') to an interpretive paradigm which accords particular importance to the question of meaning. Associated with this has been a drift from quantitative methods (such as surveys) to qualitative methods (such as case studies, action research or focus groups, or critical forms of research). This shift is partial and a diverse range of methods coexists within organizational research; for example, Donaldson (1996) continues to advocate the use of the 'normal science' model. This overall shift in the balance of the discipline to more qualitative methods is however an important one.

4.2   Issues within management research

There are methodological issues to be addressed specifically within management research that suffers from two weaknesses. The first is the frequent absence of a well-developed methodological base. While there has been a rapid growth of applied management literature over the last decade, much of this writing has not been undertaken by researchers but by others (perhaps self-reported 'success stories' from managers or consultancy-driven 'products'). The phenomenon of the management 'blockbuster' has been evident since the early 1980s. This raises the important question of the status of such knowledge, especially given its high impact on the field. This weakness is particularly evident within the BPR literature that is often written by those with a vested interest in producing an impression of success. So called case studies here become no more than 'success stories' that are narrated by top management, present top management in a heroic light, and act as selling vehicles for the reengineering product. As Fincham (2000: 184) remarks, acidly but accurately:

these simple, intense, narratives are thought to be extremely effective in creating receptive managerial audiences. In terms of any recognizable methodological standard, however, they are valueless. No hint of complexity or criticism is allowed, nor has critical analysis anything to do with these texts . . .

We hope that our contribution to the restricted corpus of BPR case study-based literature is methodologically sound in research terms.

Management research within health care faces a second typical weakness, that is a disconnection from a more general or theoretic base and a subsequent failure to build a cumulative body of knowledge (Stewart 1999). The evaluative and highly applied forms of research common within this field are typically captured by a short-term policy agenda and fail to add to long-term intellectual development. The time and cost constraints encountered in this style of work may lead to a research style that has been referred to as 'poverty in pragmatism' (Mark and Dopson 1999). In other words, we need to make problems, as well as take them from the field. In this study, we were fortunate enough to attain a level of funding from the Department of Health's Research and Development Directorate that enabled us to study the hospital over a sustained period. Given this relatively privileged position, we should be judged on our ability to link the results of our evaluation to wider bodies of organizational theory as well as contribute to site-specific or substantive learning.

4.3   Our choice of qualitative methods

So why were qualitative methods employed in this management research project and why would a quantitative design (such as an RCT) not have been appropriate or perhaps even possible? To recap, our task was to get inside the 'black box' of the hospital which was seeking to implement the BPR programme and explore *why* and *how* it was that the BPR programme unfolded as it did. The *what* questions (what organizational and indeed clinical outcomes were apparent) were explored in a complementary research project undertaken at the same time by quantitative evaluators based at ScHARR, the Health Services Research Unit located at the University of Sheffield. The two research teams enjoyed highly cooperative relations, used different methods, but it was hoped that the teams would 'triangulate' and examine the same clinical settings simultaneously from a qualitative and quantitative perspective.

It was decided by research commissioners at the Department of Health that the *why* and *how* questions were best explored through alternative qualitative methods. As the qualitative research team, we wanted to use a case study-based approach that moved beyond the investigation of causal chains typical of a quasi-experimental design (Pawson and Tilley 1997).

But did these two approaches turn out to represent incommensurable paradigms? A research paradigm can be seen as a set of assumptions upon which the formulation of research questions are based—deriving from a way of looking at the world and assumptions about the nature of knowledge (Bowling 1997: 103). Kuhn's (1962) famous work traced the evolution of scientific paradigms within a single discipline, arguing that each paradigm embodies such different assumptions that a *gestalt switch* is needed from one paradigm to another (e.g. to move from Newtonian to Einsteinian models in physics). Such competing paradigms are not only incompatible but also incommensurable (as Kuhn asserts, 1962: 103) so that proponents of different paradigms 'argue past each other', employing different assumptions and language. Within organizational studies, for example, Burrell and Morgan (1979) trace the emergence of different research paradigms within the discipline of organizational studies, which includes the functionalist and interpretive paradigms. The incommensurability of these paradigms led to language blocks that precluded effective communication between these groups of researchers.

Others (Clegg, Hardy, and Nord 1996) agree that there are important differences between practitioners of alternative research paradigms. Rather than engaging in isolationism or protectionism, however, a better strategy is to recognize these differences and bring in (rather than screen out) alternative viewpoints. Endorsing this perspective, we argue that we need to engage in conversation, dialogue, and open enquiry across traditional boundaries, without labouring under the illusion that this will produce the final answer or consensus. In this study, the process and quantitative strands of the evaluation suggested distinctive questions that were addressed in a way that respected the basic assumptions of the research paradigm being employed. Cross-paradigm working could also be fruitful, if it could be achieved. For instance, the qualitative work could in principle suggest 'interesting' clinical settings that could then be subjected to very different forms of quantitative analysis. Conversely, the quantitative analysis could throw up interesting effects—or indeed non-effects—which called out for further qualitative exploration in intensive case studies. Some settings analysed in Chapter 6 (for instance, menstrual disorders clinic, the Accident and Emergency department) were explored in depth by both a quantitative and a qualitative researcher, working in different ways. The two teams also produced a consolidated abbreviated final report (Bowns and McNulty 1999).

It should be noted that the quantitative analysis produced by ScHARR (Bowns and McNulty 1999) confirmed our view that the performance of the hospital (which was already a 'high performer' within its group of provincial teaching hospitals) had not been transformed to the extent and at the pace intended at the outset of the initiative. It had improved its efficiency marginally faster than a peer group of teaching hospitals during this period. While none of the initiatives examined in detail achieved the magnitude of benefit originally intended, it had generated some service improvements. ScHARR estimated that redesign resulted in cash releasing savings of about £500,000–600,000 per annum (less than 0.5 per cent of the hospital's annual revenue).

Despite this integrated short report, which suggests the same broad results from both quantitative and qualitative perspectives, it proved difficult to produce integrated writing on a wider scale, suggesting that sustained cross-paradigm working remains difficult. Many analyses (including this monograph) were in the end written up separately rather than in an integrated fashion, so different were the working styles of the two groups of researchers.

While the qualitative research tradition incorporates a wide variety of different approaches (with some internal tension and debate between them, as Denzin and Lincoln 1994 suggest), they tend to the interpretive rather than positivist paradigm. In many qualitative traditions, interpretation emerges during and after the systematic collection and analysis of empirical data in an interactive process of moving in and out of the research setting. Qualitative methods are united by their reluctance to embrace sophisticated forms of measurement such as econometric modelling (although they may produce simple classifications or counts of types of responses to questions). Qualitative research is generally concerned to explore social processes and questions of meaning to human actors rather than model input/output relationships. This involves the handling of subjective concepts of organizational culture, value systems, and ideologies that shape patterns of social action. Different occupational groups may display different meaning systems and definitions of reality, so that a multiple stakeholder approach to research will be needed to capture these various accounts. Action can only be understood in relation to the social and organizational contexts in which people operate, which cannot be abstracted away in an attempt to 'control' for extraneous variables.

Pope and Mays (2000) suggest that core features of design distinguish qualitative research. First of all, it seeks to *defamiliarize* social phenomena: the seemingly common sense is critically analysed and exposed as the product of certain socially constructed arrangements and assumptions. Local practices are then reinterpreted in the light of theory that is more general or of experience elsewhere. An implication of this may be that accounts of social and organizational life produced by insiders and by outside researchers may be very different in nature: external accounts may lack face validity to internal actors immersed in their local worlds.

Secondly, qualitative methods are often field based or *naturalistic* in nature, rather than based in artificial, manipulated, or experimental settings (as in the current study). People are studied within their own workplaces and using their own language rather than in a setting created and controlled by a researcher (such as a laboratory-based experiment). The focus is on social context and on a holistic form of analysis.

These methods enable researchers to locate patterns of meaningful behaviour (Murphy et al. 1998), especially where social reality contains various layers. For instance, the initial accounts surfaced by researchers as they go into an organization may consist of officially espoused or 'front-stage' versions of reality, and only when trust and rapport slowly build up over time will unofficially enacted or 'backstage' accounts be disclosed by participants or uncovered by researchers.

Thirdly, much qualitative research uses a strategy of *triangulation* or multiple methods, which may include a combination of documentary analysis, interviewing, observation, and informal talks and focus group work. While each of these methods displays its own balance of advantages and weaknesses, *internal validity* is enhanced if a similar picture emerges across the range of methods employed.

Many different qualitative methods are available to the researcher, which move from the near positivistic (such as the simple quantitative analysis of interview transcripts which have been coded up against a set of coding categories) to the highly inductive (such as the postmodernists' critical deconstruction of written texts). Case-study work is a staple method which has been widely employed within qualitative analysis, including at the organizational level (Goffman 1961; Pettigrew, Ferlie, and McKee 1992; Keen and Packwood 2000) and this method will be discussed in the next section.

Finally, qualitative work is often interested in the analysis of social process (Murphy et al. 1998), including the dynamic and interactive nature of social life. This is quite different from the focus on input/output relations characteristic of biomedical research and indicates a preference for longitudinal studies and prolonged immersion in the setting. Such research may become a 'lived experience', in which a researcher goes to live in the setting being observed (Goffman 1961 famously gathered his data on patterns of behaviour in a psychiatric hospital through working there as an administrator). This style also raises the question of how past time (as well as real or observed time) can be captured so as to add to the longitudinal nature of the study, possibly using the skills of a historian to conduct archival analysis or interviews with very long-standing personnel.

4.4   Process research within organizational studies

We now move down a level of analysis and consider process research as a subfield evident within certain branches of qualitative research. It has emerged particularly within the discipline of organizational studies as a key method over the last decade or so. Organizational studies is a social science discipline that has grown out of its original base within sociology (Ferlie 2000*b*). Compared with psychology or micro-sociology, however, it typically operates at a higher level of aggregation than these other disciplines' focus on the individual or the team, namely at the organization or system-wide level. An organization may be defined as a particular setting (such as an outpatients clinic), a large producing unit (such as a hospital, as in the current study), or an organizational field (the population of all hospitals within a health care system). The discipline thus operates at a relatively high level of analysis, between the meso- and the macro-level. However, it is less macro than other social science disciplines such as policy analysis, political science, or macro-sociology, which often concentrate on system-wide institutions or forces rather than local settings.

Organizational studies displays its own internal dynamics and debates, reflecting the mega-trends observable within social science as a whole. There are emerging feminist, neo-Marxist, and postmodernist interests alongside more orthodox groupings. A recent overview (Clegg, Hardy, and Nord 1996) suggests that there is not one organization theory, but many. But what kind of subject is it? Compared with some of the natural sciences, there is often less emphasis on discrete hypothesis-testing and more on more general theory-building. Organizational research is often grounded in an explicit body of theory, with a number of alternative theoretical positions on offer. Our own theoretical framework is rooted partly in contextualist approaches to organizational change theory and partly in a broader social action view of organizations as social, political, and cultural arenas (hence the interest in structuration). Others might have operated from a theoretical perspective rooted in contingency theory, or population ecology, or critical management.

Secondly, a position of explicit value commitment is sometimes evident within social sciences such as organizational analysis (see Willmott 1984, 1997). The application of the principles of critical analysis to the specific phenomenon of BPR has been elaborated within Knights and Willmott (2000). Cooke (1999) has traced the strong underlying values that lie behind the work of well-known organizational authors such as Kurt Lewin and Edgar Schein. These prominent organizational researchers are highly value committed rather than value neutral, proclaiming the emancipatory role of research for lower-level participants by exploring—and exposing—organizational power. Research here is seen as strongly connected to achieving organizational and social change: the point is not only to understand the world, but also to change it. Where do we stand on this debate? We would not of course claim a position of value neutrality as we are clearly committed to a multiple stakeholder perspective and hence are critical of models that see top management as the only legitimate actor within change processes. We did not wish to undertake an action research or change agent role, but instead wished to retain some critical distance from the site. High-quality data are dependent on access to a range of different stakeholder groups and might have been threatened if we were seen as over-aligned with top management. We wished to reflect the plurality of views expressed by different stakeholders so we wanted to avoid being 'captured' by any one group (such as management) to whom we might become too close.

Thirdly, much organizational analysis is contextual in orientation, arguing that organizational behaviour can only be understood within context. Forces apparent within individual organizations may reflect wider societal changes or shifts in the political economy (the so-called outer context). Certainly, this is true of the NHS, where (for example) the decline of traditionally strong trade unions and the rise of managers and then markets in the 1980s and 1990s reflected the rise of New Right ideas and governments. Such shifts may be played out in different organizations in various ways, so that attention also needs to be paid to the micro-politics and culture of single organizations (the so-called inner context).

Fourthly, there is a strong empirical tradition within organizational analysis. In particular, there has been a tradition of using field-based or case-study methods that communicate well to the user community of managers. Such case study-based work may spread into consultancy, where the reflective consultant tries to use the material generated to try to spot patterns across the cases (typically, a subset of apparent 'high performers'). Methodologists have considered the various ways in which patterning can be validly established across a contained set of cases (Eisenhardt 1989; Langley 1999). An important methodological concern is for internal validity within a contained set of cases rather than reliability or external validity. The concept of reliability is problematic within organizational research, since it could be argued that the researcher who has conducted fieldwork within a setting necessarily has a higher level of understanding of that local setting than other researchers. We will consider the consequent problem of low external validity later on in the chapter.

4.4.1   *The narrative approach to organizational process research*

There is a spread of methods used within organizational research, ranging from the experimental models to action research (Stablein 1996; Bryman 1989). So-called process-based research often builds on previous ethnographic studies of organizations (including health-care organizations, such as those conducted by Goffman (1961) and Becker et al. (1961)), but displays a more longitudinal and contextual approach than this early work. It is also more orientated to the study of decisions, especially higher-level or strategic decisions, reflecting its closer links with management. However, there are also quantitative approaches to the study of organizational process that need to be considered.

Process research can be defined as the dynamic study of behaviour within organizations, focusing on the core themes of organizational context, activities, and actions that unfold over time (Pettigrew 1990). It differs from other approaches within organizational studies such as structural contingency theory (Donaldson 1996) that measure dimensions of organizational structure and population ecology (Baum 1996) that employ techniques of organizational demography within whole populations of organizations. The handling of time distinguishes process research from other methods, which are more cross-sectional in nature.

There is an internal debate about narrative-based and quantitative approaches to organizational research. The former are more dominant in British and European studies; the latter in American studies (see Pettigrew's 1997 critique of the 'variables paradigm' proposed by Abbott 1992). Within narrative-based approaches, the aim is often to analyse a relatively contained set of organizations that can then be subjected to in-depth analysis. The techniques used are literary rather than numeric. While there is a search for patterning, this operates at a relatively contained level of empirical generality. It is similar in nature to the description of comparative causal research as outlined by Whitley (1989) in his typology of management research ideal types:

comparative causal research deals with phenomena and processes in more everyday terms as outcomes of causal structures and relations which are realized in particular ways in particular circumstances. The level of analysis is more concrete and more closely related to specific processes . . . but the goal is still to understand why events occurred through identification of the generative mechanisms at work.

This idea of 'generative' patterns of causation as opposed to so-called 'successionist' patterns (associated with experimentalism) has also been used to support the argument for so-called realistic evaluation strategies which seek to identify trends or patterns of association rather than predictive laws (Pawson and Tilley 1997). Process research is consistent with this approach within the analysis of organizations as it challenges formula-driven or rationalistic models of change management.

Process research is often seen as a qualitatively based form of research, but this distinction may not be absolute (Hinings 1997) or indeed valid. Process research also may include quantitative analysis of categories coded up from qualitative data, or may involve the use of computer-based approaches for data analysis. As process research 'scales up' beyond small-scale exploratory studies, so there is a greater concern for the adoption of more formalized approaches that can handle and reduce large volumes of data in a transparent manner and this may increase the probability that quantitative methods will be adopted. Langley (1999) usefully distinguishes between two radically different 'sense-making' strategies now apparent within process analysis. The 'narrative strategy' (which we adopt in this study) involves the construction of a detailed story from raw data. Time is a frequent structuring device and because of the focus informing the analysis of action by an awareness of contextual detail, this approach works best where there are a contained number of cases. Pentland (1999) suggests such narratives can provide the basis for many organizational theories and will often display the following key properties:

sequence in time; a chronology as a central organizing device;
focal actor or actors; narratives are about someone or something;
identifiable narrative voice; someone is telling the narrative;
canonical or evaluative frame of reference; there are implicit or explicit standards against which the actions of characters can be judged;
other indicators of content and context: rich detail that adds to the reader's understanding of the chronology presented.

These narratives are thus analytic descriptions that produce not only chronology but also (hopefully) concepts, understanding, and in the end theory.

At the other end of the pole to this narrative strategy (associated with the work of Pettigrew 1985 and Langley 1999, for example) lies the 'quantification strategy' apparent in the American work of Scott Poole, Van de Ven, and colleagues (2000). This builds on the tradition of quantitative sociology, as seen in the early work of Abbott (1992), and seeks to analyse sequences of organizational events (within a framework of so-called 'narrative positivism'). In this approach, an initial mass of qualitative data about 'events' is coded up by researchers according to a core set of agreed categories (Scott Poole et al. 2000). Inter-rater reliability checks are undertaken. This coding process creates a quantitative database that can be then be analysed using advanced statistical techniques, including advanced techniques such as regression and stochastic modelling.

We suggest that there are serious problems associated with this quantitative approach to process analysis. As Langley (1999) argues, this approach may lead to conceptual simplicity, but at the cost of a loss of contextual richness and failure to consider an organizational gestalt (Pettigrew 1997). Such quantitative methods may superficially appear accurate; but may also lack the internal validity which narrative approaches can provide. Narrative approaches can also build constructs and theories through stories and need not remain at the level of mere description (Pentland 1999). Within the quantitative approach, actors and interactions between actors disappear and they are replaced by passive 'occurrences'.

We were essentially interested in this study in exploring who sought to implement a reengineering programme within one hospital (i.e., an intensive study of one organization), how they did this (the strategies they employed), the resistance they encountered, and the extent to which change was achieved. We therefore made a decision to adopt a narrative approach to process methods as such an approach was much more likely to generate material which could shed light on these questions. Given this basic design decision, we then drew on previous studies undertaken by colleagues at the Centre for Corporate Strategy and Change, at the University of Warwick, to guide our methodology. Such texts include Pettigrew's work on strategic change processes. Pettigrew (1985) explored interdivisional variation in change capability within a large private sector organization, namely ICI. Pettigrew and Whipp (1991) applied the methods to their analysis of intrasector variations within the private sector. They were further applied to the study of local strategic change processes within the NHS (Pettigrew, Ferlie, and McKee 1992). Fuller expositions of CCSC methods have also been published (Pettigrew 1990; Ferlie and McNulty 1997). Johnson (1987) undertook an analogous analysis of one large private sector organization (Foster Brothers), although from a more cognitive perspective. In the last decade, such narrative-based process research has become a commonly used method within UK management studies. Such process research operates with five key assumptions (Pettigrew 1997):

Embeddedness: studying change within interconnected levels of analysis; including both the outer context and the inner context of the organization. Processes are embedded in these contexts and can only be studied as such.

Temporal interconnectedness: locating change in past, present, and anticipated future change in order to examine how antecedent conditions shape the present and emerging future. There can be no assumption of predetermined timetables or of ordered stages but rather of uncertain streams of events.

Exploring context and action: process research studies both context and human action; and the interaction between the two, for example, how actors mobilize features of context to support desired actions (Pettigrew, Ferlie, and McKee 1992). This follows Giddens's (1979) theoretical contribution of superseding the historic dualism of structure and agency by creating a bridge between the two.

Causation of change is neither linear nor singular: organizational change has multiple causes rather than a single cause. As such, the search is for multiple intersecting conditions which link context and process to outcomes. We will be searching for a holistic pattern of association rather than a simple input/output link. The analogy is that change patterns will be explained more through loops than lines. The task is to identify the variety of causes of change and explore through time how these forces interact and evolve to produce outcomes.

Complexity reduction: linking process to organizational outcomes. While some process research is interested in process in its own right, our view is that it is stronger if it can be linked to the study of differential organizational outcomes. Such a strategy reduces the complexity of the research design, and avoids the danger of drowning in qualitative data that are difficult to shape in any thematic fashion (Miles 1979). Such an outcome-based approach (in this case, the extent to which the transformational organizational change sought can be said to have occurred) also increases the possibility that key users of process research (especially the reflective managerial constituency) will engage with the work. By 'outcome', we refer to intermediate organizational outcomes rather than the final outcomes characteristic of biomedical research. For example, Pettigrew and Whipp's (1991) outcome indicator was differential performance of the eight firms in the study. Pettigrew, Ferlie, and McKee's (1992) outcome indicator within the health care sector was strategic change capability. This is of course a judgementally based outcome indicator which can be assessed on the basis of case-study data, but which is not obviously amenable to quantitative measurement. We would argue that many key underlying dimensions of organizational capability (the capacities to change, innovate, and learn) are of a similar nature and cannot be assessed through many quantitative approaches.

4.5 Evaluating reengineering as a social intervention: issues and challenges

Much early process research took the form of single case studies, usually undertaken by a single researcher. However, as the method has become established, there has been a move to much larger-scale empirical projects, with more ambitious data collection, larger teams, and hence a greater need to establish clear rules of method at the early stages of the project (Ferlie and McNulty 1997). Specialized research centres were constructed (e.g. Pettigrew founded the CCSC at Warwick University in 1985) to provide collective capacity and the benefits of critical mass. In America, Van de Ven et al.'s (1999) large-scale research programme is another example of this enhanced level of ambition. Moving to multiple research sites and many researchers implies that methods need to become more formalized and explicit strategies for data handling and reduction are crucial (Hinings 1997).

4.5.1 *Decision rules in design construction*

As Ovretveit (1997: 4) remarks: 'we are more familiar with methods of evaluating treatment interventions to patients, rather than social interventions (management technologies) to complex health care organizations operating in a volatile and changing political context'. Such complex interventions may consist of a diffuse mass of interlinked elements, which may be reinterpreted locally (as Joss and Kogan 1995 found in their analogous study of TQM experiments in the NHS), and interact with other forces for change evident within the same site or mutate through time.

Given these difficulties of standardization in the evaluation of complex organizational interventions, the first decision rule adopted within our evaluation design has been to treat reengineering as a dynamic rather than a static phenomenon, and to trace its evolution throughout a life cycle of birth, early development, maturity, and possibly decline. Social, administrative, and managerial innovations may evolve and mutate in unpredictable ways during their policy career (Van de Ven et al. 1999) rather than retain fixed characteristics over their lifetime. There may be important sources of variation that emerge either historically (different periods) or geographically (different settings). The evaluation design needs to be sensitive to such historical or geographical variation, for example, showing how the adopted corporate management strategies changed over the period of the programme, and how BPR ideas were renegotiated in local clinical settings.

This awareness of a time dimension suggests that the more we look at present-day events, the easier it is to identify change; the longer we stay with an emergent process and further back we go to disentangle its origins, the more likely we are to identify continuities in the deep structure of the organization. Thus, the chosen time frame of the research may be crucial in shaping empirical findings (Pettigrew 1985, 1990). In our study, we mixed real time and retrospective data collection, using interviews and documentary analysis to elongate the time frame under consideration. The empirical chapters explain the genesis of the re-engineering intervention with reference to the broader financial and political imperatives facing the site in the early 1990s, as well as the local history of previous quality initiatives. Our theoretical perspective on reengineering is also influenced by our knowledge of previous cycles of management reform in the NHS.

The second decision rule adopted was to recognize that managerial innovations such as BPR (but also other important interventions such as TQM or new Information Technologies) may be highly diffuse rather than specific in nature. BPR may entail a set of high-level and global objectives that are capable of many different interpretations. The extent of such diffuseness has to be captured within the evaluation and it cannot be assumed that there was necessarily consistent agreement across the hospital as to what BPR actually was. Ovretveit (1997) noted how quality improvement programmes might vary between being a carefully planned, coordinated, and implemented set of training and organizational changes to a series of loosely related activities that are retrospectively reconstructed as a quality strategy. These activities also span various organizational levels, from the strategic apex to the operating core. Similarly, Joss and Kogan (1995) found that approaches to TQM in the NHS varied considerably within the NHS, with many adopting highly localized approaches.

So our corporate overview contained within Chapter 5 reveals how, at the outset, the programme was highly specified in terms of ambition, focus on core processes, and central teams of reengineers. Over time, the originally high level of specificity was eroded as the reengineering programme became more disaggregated in terms of change activity; devolved in its management to the clinical directorates (who put their own 'spin' on the programme) and diffuse in its impact.

The third decision rule adopted was to ensure that the multiple perspectives on reengineering should be captured within the design.

Hospitals contain a large number of different occupational groupings (of which doctors, nurses, managers, and management consultants can be seen as distinct groupings), each of which may have different versions of reality. The more diffuse the intervention the more likely it is to involve a wide plurality of actors. The processes and fate of social interventions are closely tied to the conduct and perceptions of key individuals who are involved in sponsoring or blocking change. The study tried to get close to a wide range of individuals performing various roles within the site, in order to examine interpretations, motives, and conduct. We encountered widely differing opinions about reengineering, and have tried to incorporate this spread of views using a variety of methods.

Our focus has been on those actors involved in the decision-making process, rather than actors who were largely invisible at that level: we were interested in the process of decision-making as revealed empirically. However, service users or their representatives were not generally encountered within decision-making arenas. We did not therefore interview cohorts of service users, although this was done within the quantitative study by the parallel research team based at ScHARR, University of Sheffield.

A fourth decision rule has been to analyse reengineering in context. The dynamic and fluid character of managerial technologies and interventions owes much to the strong relationship between these technologies and their environments. Managerial technologies designed to change behaviour are not controlled experiments in which the many contextual influences can be separated out and controlled for. So how should such factors be identified and the impact explored? Within the case analyses, due attention needs to be paid to surfacing the additional factors operating within the site at the same time which reinforce or weaken the impact of the reengineering programme. In interview, the relative force of these alternative explanations can be discussed and an assessment made.

We can distinguish between the so-called *inner context* (the structural and cultural characteristics of the hospital under consideration, such as the movement to NHS Trust status, the top-down pressure for greater performance, the early investment in clinical director roles, the relatively benign inheritance, and high managerial capability) and the *outer context* of the health care system as a whole (the introduction of a quasi-market system nationally, the shift to NPM-based models of organization across the public sector, and broader background processes of managerialism and professionalism).

4.5.2 *The wider impact of reengineering: intangible effects, temporal lag, and multiple causation*

How are we to assess the impact of the reengineering programme? What might be considered as the 'outputs' of the programme? Here again there are different definitions of outputs, with broader indirect outputs being considered by some as important, alongside direct outputs. ScHARR's quantitative evaluation attempted to assess the direct impact of the reengineering programme, by using multiple measures of measurable performance (such as costs, service quality, and patient activity) rather than a single measure about which there might not have been consensus. But are there other indirect effects of the reengineering programme that need to be considered? If so, how can they be readily operationalized?

In their comparative study of high- and lower-performing forms in four sectors, Pettigrew and Whipp (1991) identified a range of organizational and managerial capabilities critical to the processes of change and competition. The most fundamental was the organizational capacity to learn and to change. We were keen to note any such indirect effects of the reengineering programme where this has proved possible. We have managed to make some progress towards this objective within empirical fieldwork, but critics could rightly say that we should have done more. We have tried to explore the extent to which there has been ongoing process redesign that has been 'kick started' by originally time-limited interventions. We wish that we had been able to do more in terms of assessing underlying learning and change capability processes.

A second issue in impact assessment refers to the question of *temporal lag*. Hackman and Wageman (1995) argue that the straightforward testing of the relationship between an intervention and organizational outcomes is prone to methodological and interpretive difficulties. Temporal lag can obscure this relationship, as there may be a discrepancy between short-term and long-term organizational outcomes. It is by no means straightforward to decide how long after an intervention one should wait before making an assessment. The more one waits, the more opportunity the intervention has to demonstrate impact, yet the more open these results are to confounding factors. Disentangling the effects of the intervention from other forces of change is also complex and has to be handled within case-study data collection. This problem of temporal lag was addressed in part by an extension of components of the evaluation and by assessment of intermediate change indicators. Hackman and Wageman (1995) argue that intermediate indicators of performance improvement (such as learning, change, and motivation) would lead to improvements in economic measures of effectiveness in the long run. We were able to assess processes and rates of service change in our study, but did not really explore changes to learning capacity or motivation levels. So, Hackman and Wageman (1995) have made important points about how to undertake a broad impact assessment. We agree with them that the indirect as well as the direct effects of reengineering need to be taken into account in any full evaluation. We have tried to do this where possible within the current study, but have found the assessment of indirect effects difficult to operationalize. Future studies should build on our experience and build in a much more sophisticated assessment of indirect effects.

In considering the relation between cause and effect, we have to beware of singular explanations of change. Here, causation is not seen as singular or linear in nature but rather observed changes have multiple causes so that the challenge is to identify the variety of these causes and to explore through time the conditions in which these forces occur and interact (Pettigrew 1990). The collection of data from multiple respondents, multiple levels of analysis, and in diverse settings has enabled us to identify many of the different causes of change and continuity within the site. In particular, an inductive analysis of the case-study settings outlined in Chapter 8 reveals generic factors critical to explaining the variable impact of reengineering interventions.

4.5.3 *Reengineering: variation in the rate and pace of change*

The more diffuse the intervention, the more likely that one may observe variation in the implementation and impact of change at the level of the clinical setting. A major contribution of process analysis has been to identify and explain such variation using comparative case-study methods (Pettigrew 1985; Pettigrew and Whipp 1991; Pettigrew, Ferlie, and McKee 1992), using the metaphor of receptive and non-receptive contexts for change. So, we have been conscious in this study not to assume that social interventions and later behaviour change occur at a uniform rate across the organization. Rather, we hope to spot and then explain inter-setting variability.

4.5.4 *Multiple levels of analysis and sampling strategy*

Complex change processes proceed through interconnected levels of analysis (Pettigrew 1990) and the interactions between these different levels may be highly significant. While the single hospital represents one case study, we further defined the case-study work to incorporate multiple micro-case studies within the one macro-case study (Yin 1989; Ovretveit 1997; Pettigrew 1985).

Sampling can be as much of an issue in qualitative as survey-based research. Given that there were many more clinical settings than researchers available to study them, how were selection decisions to be made? An initial selection framework was suggested by the site's declared reengineering strategy which envisaged radical change within two years to four so-called *core processes* (namely: emergency entry; patient stay; patient visit; and clinical support services). The ambition was both broad (across the hospital impact) and deep (intensive change within clinical settings).

Our first response was to distinguish between three different organizational tiers and to ensure that data were captured at each of them. At the *corporate level*, we wanted to establish whether the ambition to reengineer health care processes across the whole hospital was successful. At the *intermediate* or *clinical directorate level*, we wished to consider variation in impact between the clinical directorates within the hospital. We needed to consider these directorates as an important intermediate tier in their own right, linking the corporate centre and the clinical setting. The importance of the directorates increased during the course of the evaluation, especially after responsibility for operational implementation was devolved to them. The medical directorate was taken as the main case study at this level (our seventh intensive case).

The third level of analysis was at the level of the *clinical setting*. Comparing across different case studies, we considered both the technical changes made because of reengineering interventions and the social dynamics that were associated with such changes. These cases were chosen because they embodied planned change interventions designed to reengineer patient processes. Within the set, there was a spread across the four 'core processes' as represented in the site's high-level strategy. They also offered a spread across the main categories of service within the site (medical; surgical; Accident and Emergency; orthopaedics; obstetrics and gynaecology; also emergency in-patient; elective in-patient; and outpatient). These case studies where possible complemented work undertaken in the quantitative evaluation, so quantitative and qualitative methods were triangulated. A further pragmatic consideration was that the career of reengineering interventions within the cases should also advance enough to afford the opportunity of observing at least early outcomes of reengineering ideas.

Ideally, initiatives should be starting at the same point as we went into the field so that we could follow through their whole career in the site. We deliberately did not select those that were already well under way or even completed (such as work on the test centre or the Effective Clinic programme of work) as we felt that purely retrospective data would be weaker. A total of six clinical settings were chosen for intensive study.

Reengineering the care process for patients admitted with fractured neck of femur. This case study was selected to complement a detailed study being undertaken within the quantitative evaluation that focused on this patient group. The treatment pathway cuts across the three core processes of 'emergency entry', 'patient stay', and 'clinical support'.

Reengineering the care process for patients attending the Accident and Emergency department with minor injuries. This case study complements a detailed study being undertaken within the quantitative evaluation. The case study is revealing of emergency care processes.

Reengineering the care process for patients attending the menstrual disorders clinic. This case study complements another detailed study undertaken within the quantitative evaluation. This case study is revealing of the 'patient visit' process and the concept of a single-visit clinic.

Reengineering the care process for patients attending the gastroenterology clinic. This case study focuses on the redesign of an endoscopy clinic within gastroenterology (a specialty within the medical directorate). It provides an example of process redesign as applied to the 'patient visit' process.

Reengineering elective surgery within the specialties of ENT and gynaecology. These two case studies both focus on elective surgical procedures within different directorates. They are revealing about the reengineering of the core process of 'patient stay' as well as the provision of 'clinical support services'.

4.6 Operational design, data collection, and analysis

We now move from discussing our theory of method and high-level design to its operationalization within fieldwork. One of the authors entered the site briefly in March 1995 and collected very early data. Data collection started in earnest in July 1995 and was maintained at an even pace (rather than a 'peaks and troughs' strategy of intensive fieldwork interspersed with periods of low involvement) until March 1998.

This fieldwork over a three-year period brought the researchers into contact with many actors within the site. Such interaction was managed in order to minimize direct input from the researchers on the career of the change programme. This study was deliberately not designed as a piece of action research and from the outset its style was supposed to be summative rather than formative in nature. The intention was to provide substantial feedback to the site and the funder through the final evaluation report but not earlier. The funding came from the Department of Health rather than the site itself, and this external source of funding was an important influence on the summative style adopted. This design decision was taken in order to enhance the external validity, generalizability, and systemic learning provided by the evaluation, although critics argue that we could have done more to inform the site and ensure the optimal implementation of the programme as it unfolded. Neither did the researchers adopt a management consultancy role but remained separate from the consultancy inputs associated with the reengineering programme. There was, however, a great appetite from the site for formative feedback and one feedback session was provided from the research team to the Reengineering Steering Committee in May 1996 (the formal end of the programme).

In practice, therefore, the original desire to adopt a summative style had to be balanced somewhat against the need to retain a level of support for the project (and the motivation to continue to devote time to being interviewed) from participants in the site. It was impossible to undertake this type of work (in which close relationships were formed with key staff over a long period of time) by remaining totally aloof and independent of the issues and personalities within the research setting. Informal conversations with the researchers may also have triggered novel reflections by internal staff that would not otherwise have occurred. The issue is not then about achieving total independence but balancing involvement and distance (Pettigrew and McNulty 1995).

We collected retrospective or historical data as well as data in real time across the hospital as a whole. We also collected specific data relating to the particular clinical specialties sampled. Data collection was pluralistic, incorporating a range of stakeholders involved in the reengineering process. We collected data from four main sources: interview data; documentary and archival data; notes taken from informal conversations; and observational data gathered at meetings. This use of triangulation is an important check on the internal validity of the data collected (Pope and Mays 1995) which was further enhanced by the presence of two researchers working to the same core interview proforma and meeting to discuss the early interpretation of the data. They were also triangulated alongside quantitative data.

4.6.1 *Interviews: sampling strategy*

Some 144 semi-structured interviews were undertaken during fieldwork. On average, an interview lasted for an hour, with sessions audiotaped and transcribed. Here we comment on the selection of respondents and the conduct of the interview. Sampling can have a place in casestudy research as in survey and experimental research. Such interpretive studies may involve sampling in a universe of people, situations, behavioural events, and objects with which the researcher is confronted (Honigman 1982) and so a sampling strategy will need to be developed. However, statistical representativeness is not a prime requirement when the object is rather to understand social processes (Mays and Pope 1995).

The sampling strategy included a major component of judgement sampling (Honigman 1982). We attempted to identify individuals who were key actors in the reengineering process, because of their role, organizational status, or experience. Respondents were also sampled at the three levels identified earlier (corporate centre; directorate; and clinical setting), and across different occupational groups (clinicians; managers; nurses; and management consultants). This can be seen as an example of theoretical sampling as our change theory had sensitized us to the need to track change at multiple levels and to uncover the interactions between the different levels. Some role-holders were sampled across the different clinical settings studied (e.g. key clinical managers) so that comparisons could be drawn. Finally, there was an element of opportunistic or 'snowballing' sampling as names emerged in the course of early fieldwork. Appendices 4.1 and 4.2 provide further details on the sample interviewed.

4.6.2 *Conduct of interviews*

A conversational style of interviewing was employed in this study. Styles of interviewing range from the highly structured (where the researcher controls the interaction with the respondent using a prearranged order of questions, issues, and prompts); through the semi-structured (topic based); to the unstructured (where surfacing the personal agenda and experience of the respondent is a key task). The conversational style employed has varied between semi-structured and unstructured styles, as the researchers sought to gather a picture of organizational change as a whole rather than study causal relationships between an artificially constrained set of variables. This desire to construct a gestalt indicated the use of relatively unstructured techniques that would not preclude the disclosure of a wide range of material (Becker and Geer 1982).

The task within such interviews is to construct a natural conversation that will motivate the respondent to engage with the researcher whilst pursuing core research themes. Such conversations offer the chance to test themes generated by the literature review and earlier fieldwork, whilst also offering respondents a chance to raise issues and perspectives important to them. Schein (1985) spoke of the 'joint effort' required by interviewer and respondent to draw out and interpret culturally based material in a skilful fashion.

The two researchers agreed a 'core' pro forma, which was customized according to clinical settings. Interviews were conducted in natural settings, such as offices, reengineering laboratories, hospital restaurant and wards, as part of the respondent's normal working day. There are questions of interviewing skills to be considered. For example, it is important to conduct the interview in an empathetic but neutral manner and not to 'lead' the respondent towards particular responses. A researcher should be alert to what the respondent is saying, and probe to amplify short or unclear responses. Chance disclosure within an interview can open up another stream of activity within the hospital which has influenced the change programme but which has not so far been considered. Although the interview is conversational in nature, it is carefully planned so that the researcher should read background material prior to the interview in order to secure maximum value. With the consent of the respondent, interviews were taped to provide verbatim material, and playing back tapes and reviewing transcripts provided further cycles of reflection on the raw data as well as making such data reviewable by the other researcher.

4.6.3   *Observational data*

Observational methods used in social research involve the systematic, detailed, observation of behaviour and talk: watching and recording what people do and say . . . [a] crucial point about such qualitative observation is that it takes place in natural settings and not experimental ones. (Mays and Pope 1995: 182)

In the analysis of organizational change, it is important to balance what people say they do (*espoused behaviour*) against what they actually do (*observed behaviour*). So we observed many meetings of groups at the three levels of analysis identified earlier (corporate, clinical directorate, and clinical specialty), in order to complement the opinions expressed to us within individual interviews. This enabled us to observe actual behaviour rather than espoused beliefs. The observation was of a non-participant nature with the researchers on the periphery of decisions. However, when the researchers were on occasion asked directly to express an opinion by others in the meeting, then they would do so. Observation at these meetings enabled us to watch and record in a systematic way the behaviour of people within decision-making groups related to the reengineering programme. Approximately fifty meetings were attended across the three tiers already mentioned, at which notes were taken of talk and behaviour.

During the course of the evaluation, many more meetings were observed than envisaged at the outset as they proved to be an especially fruitful method of data collection. They provided an opportunity to observe group discussions about the progress of the reengineering programme as expressed by a wide range of individuals, both internal and external to the hospital. These contacts enabled the researchers to establish rapport and trust with individuals, which could lead on to fruitful individual interviews. The meetings enabled us to keep up to date with the reengineering programme as it evolved, simultaneously keeping a view of the 'big picture' whilst conducting intensive analysis in individual settings.

4.6.4 *Documentary and archival data*

Processual research should be sensitive to the passage of time, whether past, present, or anticipated future time. The case-study analysis should be longitudinal in nature rather than cross-sectional. History can play an important role as antecedent conditions in complex change may shape the eventual fate of the change programme. The more we stay with present-day events the easier it is to identify change; the longer we shadow an emergent process and seek to disentangle its origins, the more we identify continuity (Pettigrew 1990). For example, the local 'prehistory' can be dated back to the early creation of clinical directorates in the site in the mid-1980s that led to the development of a strong clinical director cadre locally. This development in turn can be seen as an important layer of basic system capability that indicated that it might be a receptive site for further change.

The collection and analysis of documentary materials was a way of incorporating an awareness of retrospective time. Archival data was gathered on the history of the hospital, the transition to Trust status, the introduction of clinical directorates, and earlier quality initiatives. More directly, as we entered the site after the formal commencement of the reengineering programme, archive data (especially minutes of meetings, background papers, internal memos, and letters to externals) were used to trace the genesis and early development of the programme. Such documents can be seen as a relatively non-reactive source of data, especially those internal documents which were not intended for external readers but which remain in internal files. They also enabled us to trace the career of groups over extended periods and help identify distinctive periods, as an important part of pattern development.

4.6.5   *Informal conversation*

Finally, data have been collected because of numerous informal conversations ('corridor chat') that we have conducted given our presence within the site over a long time. While these conversations have not been taped or transcribed, they yielded important data that served as a follow-up or as a precursor to an interview. For example, one chance encounter in the queue for sandwiches in Marks and Spencer led to some interesting 'off the record' remarks. Where these conversations were not signalled as 'off the record', the researchers captured the essence of these informal conversations through making field notes after the conversation.

Internal reliability and validity was promoted by the presence of two researchers on the team who on occasions jointly conducted interviews (about 10 per cent of all interviews); worked to a jointly agreed core pro forma; experienced meetings of the same groups; commented on each other's case reports; and in some cases worked jointly on the same cases (e.g. ENT).

4.6.6   *Data management and analysis*

A mass of raw data was collected, in the form of interview transcripts, notes of meetings, fieldwork notes, and minutes of meetings and reports. It was a major task to manage and analyse these data sources. Consistent with Miles's (1979) and Pettigrew's (1990) advice to develop 'structured understanding' out of complex qualitative data, the analytic strategy was conditioned by the original research protocol that provided initial direction and form. The protocol signalled early features of the design such as the adoption of a longitudinal approach; a multiple stakeholder perspective; a multi-tier approach to analysis which included both a broad overview and a 'drilling down' to the clinical level within intensive analysis.

Analysis of data was not left until the post-fieldwork period (i.e., March 1998) (Barley 1990*a*) but early analysis was undertaken during the course of data collection. The model of conducting research based on three distinct phases (preparation, data collection, and data analysis) was found to be artificial. In practice, the distinction between data collection and analysis was blurred, as indicated by the need to ensure the ecological validity of data and contextualism. As Turner (1988) suggests in his study of organizational culture, the processes of observation, analysis, and theory-building overlap in a cycle that continues in an iterative fashion until the researcher decides to end it.

In qualitative work, there is a tension between the need for focus and letting issues and themes evolve out of the data collection process in an emergent or a grounded way. Our approach was closer to that of Miles (1979)—who stresses the need for an early explicit if tentative organizing framework—than the purely grounded theoretic approach characteristic of Glaser and Strauss (1967). The provision of initial direction does not however mean that the research design cannot evolve over time. For example, more data were collected at the intermediate level of the clinical directorate than envisaged in the protocol as its potential shaping role became apparent. In addition, early empirical findings sensitized us to the need to collect and access further theoretical literature.

Fieldwork strategy also varied by time. During 1995, data collection was exploratory and only loosely structured as the researchers generated basic knowledge about the site, the genesis and ambition of the reengineering programme, and key players in the organization. The period was also one in which the evaluators gathered ideas about how to operationalize the original protocol in the site. After several months of fieldwork, an operational design was built up, along with a more detailed analytical framework. The analytical framework presented below organized the raw data collected and the following were the key themes identified.

4.6.6.1   *Corporate level*
A prime focus at this level was on the meta-level management of the reengineering programme across the hospital, and in particular the

following themes:

- change planning and preparation; the ambitions and objectives of the programme as a whole; resources provided to support the change programme;
- the change management methodology adopted, for instance the use of internal and external change agents, explicit and implicit change management theories; generic methods such as core process redesign; relations between specialist change agents and line managers;
- senior management input and support for reengineering;
- the development of a chronology and analytic phasing at a corporate level.

4.6.6.2 *Clinical directorate level*

During the course of the evaluation, more extensive data collection occurred at this level than had been envisaged. Some directorates (e.g. medicine; surgery) included very substantial chunks of service, staff, and finance and grouped together a number of clinical specialties. In early fieldwork, the role of the clinical directorate as a potentially powerful intermediate tier became clear, along with differences between the different directorates in the hospital in their management strategies adopted. A new question emerged, namely: how (if at all) does the clinical directorate shape the rate and pace of reengineering-led change at clinical specialty level? Indicators that helped us answer this question included:

- the nature and ambition of the overall directorate change agenda;
- perceptions of the reengineering programme within the context of the directorate change agenda;
- directorate culture, managerial competence, and organizational change capacity and approach;
- level of commitment to (and local ownership of) reengineering within the directorate; the spread of clinician opinion and clinical attitudes to management in general and reengineering in particular;
- the quality of interclinical and clinical managerial relationships within the directorate;
- relations with other directorates; the extent to which reengineering disturbed traditional directorate boundaries;

The medical directorate was chosen as an intensive case study of a large and significant block of services, but some data on the behaviour of other clinical directorates were also gathered through the six cases of particular clinical settings.

4.6.6.3   *Clinical settings*

Six clinical settings were selected to offer a range of intervention sites for reengineering ideas. These were made up of: ENT; Accident and Emergency; orthopaedics; gastroenterology; and two services within gynaecology (elective gynaecology and menstrual disorders clinic). Data collection and analysis at the level of the clinical setting were organized around the following themes:

- the context, background and ambition of attempts to reengineer patient processes;
- the chronology of the intervention, analysed by 'period' and theme;
- understanding the technical changes to the patient processes proposed through analysis of reengineering documentation and interviews;
- explaining these technical changes by examining the social and organizational context of the clinical setting. Organizing concepts included receptive or non-receptive contexts for change (Pettigrew, Ferlie, and McKee 1992). This encouraged us to examine the scale, scope, and complexity of the patient process; the extent of process interdependence between clinical settings and any competition for work jurisdiction between different professional segments (Abbott 1988); the resource implications of the planned change intervention and the change strategy adopted locally.

Within such a multi-tier change process, the relations and interlinkages across the three tiers involved may be crucial to determining the impact achieved by the change programme as a whole. In particular, the clinical directorate may have a key linking role, 'managing up' to the corporate centre, while 'managing down' to the clinical setting. If there is an absence of change ownership or capacity at any one of these three levels, the momentum behind the programme may quickly erode: the chain will break if there is one weak link.

4.6.7   *Approaches to data analysis*

Using Langley's (1999) typology of process research methods, how could one describe our approach to the analysis of the qualitative data we generated? Clearly, our dominant approach should be seen as a 'narrative strategy' in which the two researchers constructed detailed stories or narratives about the career of reengineering across the different settings studied. These included 'thick descriptions' of particular critical incidents or interactions that usefully revealed wider dynamics. These narratives indeed form the basis of the later empirical chapters in this monograph. These narratives were written up to a core pro forma that had been agreed by the two researchers as an initial structure so as to allow later cross-case comparison. All transcripts, documents, and notes of meetings were examined and any material that related to the categories contained within the pro forma extracted (verbatim, and not reduced to a binary code). The lead researcher who had worked within that setting wrote up the cases, but the other researcher would read and comment on them, again facilitating comparison. These case histories were designed not only to display high internal validity (possible through the highly intensive approaches that were adopted) but also to begin the process of construct derivation. Clearly, we did not follow the quantitative approach to data analysis, nor did we code up our data in the highly structured and 'shredded' fashion advocated by Scott Poole et al. (2000).

However, our analysis also includes elements of some of the other approaches to process-theorizing reviewed by Langley (1999). The narratives were organized around particular periods (a so-called strategy of 'temporal bracketing'), as in the narrative of the corporate centre contained in Chapter 5. This creation of adjacent periods is seen as appropriate within an approach which is theoretically informed by an awareness of structuration: the reader can see how change in one period informed change in later periods. A more grounded theoretical approach was also used to produce the inductive model contained in Chapter 8 that seeks to explain variation in change processes observed across the settings. The final form of this model is synthetic in nature: we would argue that it may well have some predictive power in relation to the outcomes of patient process redesign initiatives in other sites. Finally, some material (notably patient process redesign maps) was initially examined in a visual or chart-like form, allowing the presentation of much information in a condensed manner. They enabled us to identify the range of key actors and any jurisdictional issues.

It further appears that our approach shares some of the narrative features identified by Pentland (1999: 712):

- *event sequences*: event sequence can be seen as the core of a narrative structure. Thus, our case studies are organized chronologically over time. However, the chronology represents the start of an analytic task, through the construction of phases and then the inductive emergence of cross case concepts. Our approach has more in common with the discipline of history than the narrative positivism of quantitative sociology.

- *focal actors:* the focus is on the career of a reengineering programme within one hospital, and the individuals and groups that were involved in it. We are also concerned with tracing the interactions between the various characters apparent within this story.
- *narrative voice:* the narrating voice is that of an external organizational researcher who is immersed within the organization but at the same time critically distant from it;
- *the search for generative mechanisms* or 'deep structures' that drive the underlying process; here the nature of control over professionalized work practices.

4.7   Remaining methodological issues

4.7.1   *The issue of generalization*

It may be argued that research data from only one organization may provide high internal validity, but low levels of external validity. How might we respond to this criticism? While we were working within only one organization, we undertook eight different cases (at three different hierarchical levels) rather than just a single case, say of the corporate core. Another response is that such case-based approaches can generate theory or concepts that have wider applicability across wider populations of organizations. Thus, Goffman's (1961) ethnography of a single psychiatric hospital generated the concept of a 'total institution' that could be applied not only to other psychiatric hospitals but also to many other institutions such as prisons or medical schools. Susman and Evered's (1978) defence of the scientific merits of action research also argues that such research is valuable as far as it can generate knowledge of systemic relevance rather than purely local relevance. A theoretically informed approach enables us to achieve this wider systemic orientation.

Finally, Chapter 9 will compare the results of our study with other published studies on reengineering within health care and other public sector settings. Our findings can then be tested against other relevant literature to investigate whether they are 'out of line' or whether the cluster of studies reviewed is reporting similar findings.

4.7.2   *A summative evaluation—not action research*

The relationship with the site needs to be considered, as there are issues in conducting management research within a charged and high-profile policy context. The hospital was highly visible as it represented one of two national pioneers for BPR experiments within the NHS. Our research protocol explicitly proposed a *summative* rather than a *formative* evaluation as the key objective was to provide system-wide rather than local learning. It did not seek to engage in action research collabora- tively with the site. The research funder concurred with this position. Indeed, the researchers sought to minimize their involvement in the site so as to disentangle the researcher effect from the BPR effect, to reduce the danger of capture by the site, and to produce generalizable and the- orized knowledge rather than purely local knowledge. While we were unable to sustain this position in its entirety in the course of fieldwork as there was a great appetite from the site to learn early results, neverthe- less the amount of interim feedback provided was relatively slight.

We need therefore to distinguish our methods not only from the experimentalist paradigm (as previously discussed) but also from at least some action research models. Action research is increasing in pop- ularity as it is seen as effective in linking research to local development and change (while many other approaches are not), produces results in short time scales, and engages practitioners with the research agenda. Some action researchers stress the importance of providing systemic as well as local learning (Susman and Evered 1978) or substantive theory (Eden and Huxham 1996), but these positions—with which we would concur—are minority views within the action research community. Instead, many influential models of action research argue that a prime feature of action research should be utility to the practitioner at the moment of action (Reason 1988) or as a vehicle for empowerment of lower-level participants.

Adopting such an action research approach disproportionately geared to local learning and problem-solving would have in our view eroded the quality of the research design. Some action researchers have criticized this decision on the grounds that we could have done much more to inform the site from our early findings and enable them to take corrective action in those areas where performance was suboptimal. Effective local learning was in the critics' view sacrificed on the altar of research purity. However, we would argue that the site had access to many other local learning mechanisms—including a major input from a consulting firm—and the key task was to generate system-wide learning. Two sets of consultants operating in the site at the same time would also have produced severe role confusion. This dilemma raises the question of the relationship between the researchers and the researched, who were not 'co-investigators' in action research mode.

There was the need to keep good relationships with the various stake-holders in the site without being captured by them. In our view, the very close relationship between co-researchers (in action research terms) could lead to capture and an inability to keep critical distance.

4.7.3   *The problematic relationship between social science research and policy*

There are intriguing differences between alternative externally and internally produced accounts of this BPR experiment. There was an active commitment to a learning orientation in the site that could diffuse early lessons to the rest of the UK health care system. So, knowledge was produced and disseminated internally as well as externally by outside evaluators. There was a series of well-attended conferences that achieved this. Some senior managers used their experience on the programme for their own continuing professional development, including undertaking master and doctorate theses. The high-profile nature of the site also meant that it attracted a large number of visitors, keen to learn what had been going on from the experimenters there.

These internally produced accounts were often based on distinctive action-learning methods. Many of these early messages were positive, and helped raise interest and energy levels internally and elsewhere. Such site-led diffusion had substantial impact within the management and policy domain. These early dissemination events can be seen as a well-intentioned attempt to maximize the system-wide learning associated with the BPR experiment, as indeed was expected from a flagship site. The question is whether the early learning being diffused was unintentionally rather over-optimistic in the light of later findings from the external evaluation.

In part because of the understandable need to consider the full policy implications of the study, the final report from the outside evaluators did not reach the public domain until April 2000. Although the research team attempted to write in accessible terms, our judgement would be that the technical issues of research methods inevitably contained in the report do not communicate readily to many managers who prefer to hear strong and clear optimistic messages. Policy processes had meanwhile moved on: by 1997 or 1998 there was substantial policy interest in concepts of process redesign as a tool for 'modernizing' health care delivery and major 'roll-out' of these process redesign ideas (though not the original concept of BPR programmes) was decided upon nationally. A number of related programmes including ideas to promote better forms of patient access and the so-called 'Breakthrough Collaboratives' were set up on a national level in 1999 and 2000.

Our learning from this experience is that the relationship between social science research and the policy process is highly indirect. Health care managers may have a relatively weak level of interest in the findings of formal management research (Rosen 2000), placing more weight on experiential knowledge, group consensus, or high-profile role models. Klein (2000) argues that the whole concept of Evidence-Based Policy is suspect, as social science-based evidence will prove less timely or influential than other forms of evidence generated through political or administrative channels. Nevertheless, we believe that social science research may have an indirect and long-term role to play in influencing policy. We hope to have generated high-quality evidence that may be of use to the policy system at certain key points if not in the short term. Influence points for research may be greatest under certain circumstances: late on in the life cycle of policies, when anomalies accumulate within existing policies, when there is a strategic review set up, or when there are new policy-makers or ministers brought in to provide alternative leadership following a perception of 'failure'.

As this methodological chapter suggests, the empirical chapters that follow are a narrative constructed through the researchers' interpretation of a complex sequence of events that occurred in the site. Our interpretation of these events is grounded in a style of site-based fieldwork that is well adapted to generate intensive knowledge of a particular context, and also the multiple perspectives apparent within that context. The process style of research adopted is distinct both from experimentalism and from many action research models. Within the single macro-case, a number of micro-cases have been selected to facilitate comparative analysis. Our analysis has been sensitive to the importance of time and evolution rather than adopting a cross-sectional approach. Our interpretation of our data has also been developed in dialogue with an underlying conceptual framework which was itself refined as events took place and issues emerged. We believe that the use of this processual methodology is not confined to this single site or corporate change programme, but could be used as a framework to analyse complex change programmes in other health care settings or indeed other large organizations outside the health care sector. In a sense, BPR is merely a timely and high-profile example of the more general problem of change management within complex and professionalized health care settings.

Appendix 4.1 Interview Sample by Roles

Chairman
Chief executive
Executive director e.g. human resources, nursing, medical, operations
Reengineering programme leader
Reengineering team leader (NB: all four reengineering team leaders interviewed at least once)
Reengineering team member
Staff side union representative
Management consultant
Patient process director
Patient process manager
Business manager (NB: all business managers interviewed at least once)
Implementation leader
Head of service (specialty) (NB: 90% of heads of service interviewed at least once)
Clinical director (all clinical directors interviewed at least once)
Consultant (medical), including joint academic and NHS appointments
Clinic coordinator
Senior nurse
Sister
Ward sister
Nurse (various grades of nurse interviewed throughout the evaluation)
Clinical nurse manager
Physiotherapist
Occupational therapist
Pharmacist
Social worker
Director of purchasing
Training and development manager
Director of corporate management (purchaser organization)
Associate director, human resources
Specialty manager
Ward manager

Appendix 4.2   Interview Sample Statistics

	Frequency	%	Cumulative %
Senior management e.g. directors and members of the Trust Board (except clinical directors)	14	9.7	9.7
Clinical directors and heads of service	33	22.9	32.6
Middle management —business managers —process directors/managers —clinic coordinators	20	13.9	46.5
Reengineers and management consultants	30	20.8	67.3
Doctors, except clinical directors and heads of service	24	16.7	84.0
Nurses and other professionals allied to medicine	21	14.6	98.6
Representatives of trade unions and purchasing organizations	2	1.4	100.0
Total	144	100	

5

Reengineering as Strategic Choice and Change

5.1 Introduction

Mindful of the importance of qualitative description to the analysis of social and managerial interventions (Ovretveit 1997) this chapter provides a descriptive and analytical overview of the reengineering intervention at Leicester Royal Infirmary between 1992 and 1998. Implicit within the material presented in this chapter and subsequent chapters are answers to questions such as, why did LRI embark upon reengineering, how did the reengineering intervention start, how was the reengineering intervention organized and managed, and what methodologies have been used to reengineer the hospital?

Following Chapters 2 and 3, data reveal possibilities and problems of reengineering as a process of strategic choice and change within a hospital setting. Strategic choice was defined earlier as the ability of power-holders within organizations to decide upon courses of strategic action (Child 1997). The introduction of business process reengineering is here presented as a strategic choice aimed at transforming hospital processes and performance. More associated with private sector manufacturing practice than public service delivery, the adoption of reengineering in this case instances how managers are able to utilize ideas developed in one social system as a resource for change in another social system (Whittington 1992). In this case a small number of senior managers and clinicians within LRI articulated reengineering as a necessarily radical response to managerial and clinical challenges facing the hospital in the early to mid-1990s. Reengineering was simultaneously a reactive and proactive response by senior managers and clinicians on behalf of the hospital within the context of changing health care and public sector policy.

Notable factors and conditions associated with the adoption of reengineering include the hospital's prior participation in a region-wide service quality improvement initiative, difficult operating conditions characterized by cost and quality improvement pressures, and relations formed with the NHS Executive and reengineering guru Michael Hammer. In a financially hard-pressed environment, a loan by the NHS Executive offered some financial slack (Whittington 1992) to support LRI as a national pilot site for reengineering between 1994 and 1996. This policy-level support also helped establish the hospital's reputation as an innovative organization within the UK health care sector. Amidst somewhat isomorphic tendencies of the health care sector at that time, where national health policy strongly encouraged all hospitals to become NHS Trusts within a newly formed quasi-market context, LRI established and embraced its national innovator status through very early adoption of reengineering within the health care sector. The adoption of reengineering by LRI confirms that organizations subject to the similar institutional pressures can indeed respond very differently (Whittington 1992; Greenwood and Hinings 1996).

Against this backdrop, reengineering developed as a programmatic approach to organizational transformation (Pettigrew 1998). The programme was characterized initially by the rhetoric of transformation, a language and method of core process redesign, and a distinct infrastructure of reengineering roles and relationships. In these respects LRI adhered very closely to the classic reengineering prescription of Hammer and Champy (1993). The change programme served to develop a 'capacity for action' to transform LRI from a functional to a process-based organization (Greenwood and Hinings 1996). Reengineers drawn from inside and outside the hospital were responsible for advocating and implementing process-oriented solutions that would transform performance and practice of the hospital. That they were unable to do so in many parts of the hospital brings to mind Giddens's (1984: 27) remark that 'human history is created by intentional activities but is not an intended project; it persistently eludes efforts to bring it under conscious direction'.

The end of the chapter observes a distinction between the intended and realized strategy of reengineering (Mintzberg and Waters 1985). The intended strategy of reengineering was radical and transformatory in ambition, method, and organization. By contrast the emergent or realized strategy of reengineering proved to be more evolutionary than revolutionary, more convergent than transformational in its impact on organization process and performance (Greenwood and Hinings 1996). In keeping with evidence from other studies of strategic choice and change reengineering was a politicized process within a politicized setting (Child and Smith 1987; Pettigrew 1985). As a change initiative the process and fate of reengineering is revealed to have been shaped and framed by the context it sought to reshape and reframe (Child 1997; Giddens 1984). The chapter reports how as the reengineering programme unfolded the initial radical ambition for organizational process redesign was tempered and reshaped in line with functional organization principles that underpinned the existing pattern of specialties and clinical directorates. Reengineers learned quickly that they were dependent on the support of managers and clinicians, especially doctors, to effect change at specialty and clinical directorate levels. In spite of the rhetoric of core process redesign, reengineering change methodology and ambition were adapted to accommodate existing organizational arrangements and relations. These observations are at the heart of the study's conclusion of more continuity than change in organizational processes and performance.

The remainder of the chapter is organized as follows. Following this introduction, the chapter reflects on the origins of reengineering within LRI. In so doing the reader is further informed about the hospital as a case-study site and the antecedent conditions inside and outside the hospital prior to reengineering. The chapter then proceeds to provide a chronological overview of reengineering within LRI organized into five phases, spanning a period between 1992 and 1997. Thereafter the chapter develops a number of themes and issues identified in relation to each of the phases. This fuller discussion of the reengineering intervention is organized under the following headings: preparation for reengineering; ambition and formal objectives of the reengineering intervention; the scale, scope, and methodology of the reengineering intervention; and the governance and organization of the reengineering intervention.

5.2   Introducing reengineering into the Leicester Royal Infirmary NHS Trust

The Leicester Royal Infirmary dates back to 1771. Progressive development of the hospital on a city centre site, including the establishment of the Medical School in 1971, has resulted in the Leicester Royal Infirmary becoming one of the largest teaching hospitals in England and Wales. At the start of reengineering in 1994 the hospital was resourced with an annual revenue budget of approximately £130 million, 1,100 beds, and 4,200 staff. Over 400 medical staff worked at the hospital ranging from consultants to part-time medical officers. Approximately

40 per cent of staff were employed part-time and nearly half the staff had worked at the hospital for five or more years. The hospital's clinical activity approximated to 103,000 in-patient episodes, 120,000 accidence and emergency episodes, and 400,000 outpatient attendances each year. An unusual feature of the hospital was the relatively high proportion of emergency work undertaken, compared with elective or planned activity, with up to 80 per cent of in-patient cases admitted as emergencies.

It is reasonable to characterize the hospital prior to reengineering as a mature and relatively efficient organization. Researchers at the Sheffield Centre for Health and Related Research (ScHARR) have confirmed that LRI was indeed near or at the top of the NHS 'efficiency league' tables for provincial teaching hospitals (Bowns and McNulty 1999). LRI enjoyed low turnover in the most senior management positions. Between 1985 and 1999 the hospital had just two chief executives (previously called hospital general manager), with the changeover occurring in 1990. The period of 1990 to 1999 during which the hospital attained NHS Trust status and embarked on reengineering is one characterized by consistency of hospital leadership. The hospital was an early adopter of the clinical directorate structure for organizing clinical and managerial relations in 1986 and by the mid-1990s was able to point to an established approach for organizing and managing clinical and managerial relations.

Figure 5.1 indicates clinical directorates and clinical specialties as key features of the organization and management of the hospital immediately prior to reengineering. There were nine clinical directorates in total, all, with the exception of support services, headed by a triumvirate of a clinical director, a business manager, and a senior nurse or midwife. There was also a head of service for many of the specialties located within directorates. Typically, a head of service is a medical consultant in that specialty. Data about staffing, beds, and specialties show quite different patterns of resources for each directorate. As indicators of directorate size, these data reveal the medical directorate to be by far the largest of eight directorates within the hospital. The medical directorate contained 319 beds on 14 wards, employed 670 staff, and accounted for an annual budget of about £14 m. Subsequent modifications to these organization and managing arrangements are commented on throughout the monograph.

The development of reengineering at Leicester Royal Infirmary in 1994 has been traced back to a service quality improvement initiative developed by Trent Regional Health Authority called Project Sigma in

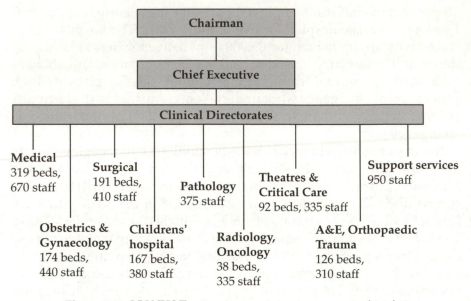

Figure 5.1 *LRI NHS Trust management structure: pre-reengineering*

Note: Each directorate headed by a clinical director, supported by a senior nurse and business manager.

September 1992. Two of the five Sigma projects, in the specialties of neurology and hearing services resulted in faster treatment and reduced costs. A single-visit neurology clinic reportedly reduced time from visit to diagnosis of neurological problems from twelve weeks to one day, whilst a hearing services clinic reduced time to fit hearing aids from fourteen months to six weeks after referral. Senior managers attributed improvements in these two services to the redesign of services from a process perspective.

Identification of a link between the Sigma quality improvement initiative and the subsequent reengineering programme supports the argument that managers can import 'resources' from one social system to another social system to inspire their actions (Whittington 1992). In this instance, the resource was business process reengineering. The manager responsible for quality recalled that the diverse results of the first generation of Sigma projects started to 'make sense' after encountering the concept of BPR during a 'Quality Masterclass' run by a University Business School in the summer of 1993. Thereafter a small but powerful coalition started to form behind reengineering, comprising a manager responsible for quality improvement, the hospital chief executive, the hospital medical director, and the clinical director of the medical directorate.

To further conceptualize the development of reengineering within LRI, it is important to locate reengineering within wider organization and institutional conditions in and around LRI in the early to mid-1990s. Most notable here are the conditions of the 'NHS Internal Market' and the emergence of a new organizing template called the NHS Trust. The introduction of the NHS Internal Market in April 1991 required purchasers and providers to enter into contracts or service agreements. The internal market in theory sharpened the role of economic incentives. Hospitals were to compete for business with an extended range of purchasers (notably GP Fundholders). Soft budgetary constraints were to be hardened. New capital charging regimes were introduced which increased the pressure to make more effective use of capital stock and downsize the large and dilapidated estate. Hospitals were given delegated freedoms over their human resource management strategies, to encourage them to move away from conventional public sector modes of industrial relations.

Elsewhere the emergence of strong internal market forces has been observed as an external pressure to adopt more radical change strategies than would conventionally have been the case. For example, the move away from the Partnership (P2) form in accountancy has been encouraged by the growth of market pressures within the accountancy market and a shift to a more deregulatory policy stance by government (Hinings, Greenwood, and Cooper 1999). Stronger market forces have also acted to de-institutionalize conventional forms of provision in the American health care sector (Shortell et al. 1995; Caronna and Scott 1999) and may provoke the emergence of alternative organizational forms. It was possible therefore that the internal market period would result in the effective mimicry of market forces within the public sector itself and that these internal market pressures would force hospitals to up the pace of organizational change. Performance pressures and economic incentives to change would become sharper, perhaps proving stronger than the pattern of social relations (Granovetter 1985) between a narrow range of institutionalized interest groups which has often acted to prevent radical change within UK health care.

We know now that the internal market experiment did not lead to a full transition to a market-based health care system. UK health care remains overwhelmingly located within the public sector, with few market forces evident and resources typically allocated through planning-based mechanisms. After the first couple of years, internal market pressures were reined back, as the policy system attempted to reassert effective control. There were increasingly mergers between small and potentially unviable providers, leading to a reduction in competition on the supply side. There was, in any case, a lack of competition in many services (such as emergency work) and no market entry or exit. Over time, market forces became weaker and management stronger.

The emergence of business process reengineering in 1994 coincided with the period when 'market pressures' were at their strongest in the NHS and in this locality. Within the case-study locality, the early to mid-1990s were characterized by the presence of growing competitive pressures upon elective services (although not emergency services as the hospital provided a local monopoly in this area). The old integrated configuration of local hospitals had been broken up as a deliberate act of policy and there was the real possibility for competition with the other two acute hospitals in the locality, which were now separate NHS Hospital Trusts. The hospital became the Leicester Royal Infirmary NHS Trust in April 1993. In private, senior managers used the terms 'desperate' and 'hard-pressed' to describe circumstances of the hospital at that time. In 1992/3 the hospital had a large overspend on budget. There was a major shortage of medical equipment and the hospital site was in need of both maintenance and development. These 'internal' pressures coincided with 'external' demands for improvements in both the volume and quality of health services emanating from national government and local purchasers (health authorities). The first year of contracting in the new NHS internal market between the hospital and the Local Health Authority revealed referrals to the hospital were in excess of contract targets by 6 per cent for in-patient and day-cases. GP Fundholders, covering about 10 per cent of a population of one million were beginning to exercise purchasing muscle, demanding shorter waiting times. Over and above the government's Patients' Charter, the hospital had agreements with the local purchaser for 'special initiatives' in the specialties of plastic surgery, oral surgery, and ENT, whereby no patient on any of the hospital's waiting lists would wait longer than two years for surgery. Purchasers were also pushing that the hospital achieve a waiting time standard of no longer than one year for in-patient or day-case surgery. There was reported a sense of 'increasing frustration' of staff, both managerial and clinical, with service provision at LRI. There was also what a senior manager described as a 'punishing cycle of annual cost-improvement programmes'.

The internal NHS market was beginning to assert itself . . . purchasers had become more demanding of quality standards . . . when we looked at our level of productivity compared to other sites we were a reasonably high unit in terms of efficiency . . . we knew our ability to take one or two per cent off year after year and continue to have to improve our volume of services, as well as quality was just not a realistic prospect. (Senior manager, August 1995)

The adoption of NHS Trust status crystallized these pressures upon the hospital, while at the same time offering senior management greater freedom and discretion in how to manage such pressures. In keeping with organizational environments being enabling as well as constraining of managerial agency (Child 1997; Whittington 1992) these conditions allied to Trust status lent managers resources to construct and mobilize a case for change. Words and phrases such as 'innovation' and 'greater freedom to organize [our] own affairs' accompanied the hospital's application to become an NHS Trust. Traditionally, management responsibility in the health care sector was decentralized to individual clinical settings rather than being corporate or strategic in nature (Mintzberg 1979). Notwithstanding central planning initiatives emanating from a national policy level, service development at the hospital level is reasonably characterized as having been bottom-up and emergent in nature, rather than top-down or planned. The extended range of stakeholders, competing objectives, and the presence of many professional groups have historically made the development of any strategic management capacity difficult at hospital level. In the early 1990s newly formed boards within NHS Trusts were emerging as more powerful centres of decision-making than had been predicted, attempting to develop novel strategic management approaches across the organization (Ferlie et al. 1996). Approval of Trust status in April 1993 demanded some explicit statement of strategic direction for the hospital. Production of a concept paper about reengineering coincided with a process by which senior managers and clinicians met to identify and discuss the strategic direction for the hospital. At least some senior managers and clinicians began to recognize and articulate a gap between practice at LRI and those aspirations informing the strategic direction of the hospital and the following mission statement of the hospital.

We at the Leicester Royal Infirmary NHS Trust will work together to become the best hospital in the country, with outstanding local and national reputation for our treatment, research and teaching. We will give to each patient the same care and consideration we would to our own family. (LRI NHS Trust 1994*a*: 2)

A senior manager and a board member recalled the circumstances of the Trust prior to the reengineering programme.

We had a broad sense that in many areas we were relatively reasonably efficient and that when we looked at the strategic environment the demand to
achieve more for less would be greater. The level of uncertainty of income
coming into the hospital was getting greater and yet we were required to produce more and more . . . Though not saying that we could not become more
efficient easy options for improvement in efficiency were not that abundant . . .
there was a sense of anxiety and unease given all this strategic stuff that we
knew was ahead of us, some of it very close, about responding in a way that
would allow us to achieve more for less, but at the same time provide staff and
patients with a very much better quality environment in which to be cared for
and provide services within. And to teach and research . . . I think one of the
things we did was we made a connection between the quality Sigma initiative
and the strategic direction of the organization and we locked in some very
powerful players. We enrolled them in the exercise. All that happened at a
time when I think it was particularly fertile in terms of organizational change
and becoming a Trust. (Senior manager, August 1995)

I believe there is no way that we could improve the effectiveness and efficiency
of this hospital simply by trying to do better that which we already do. Unless
you take a fundamental look at the way a place is run, organized, and what its
priorities are, you cannot, I believe, make a significant change in the way
things are done. When I looked at the range of quality initiatives so called that
we had running when I came here in 1992 we were simply getting nowhere
with them—a little bit done here, a little bit there, terribly worthy but not really
making a difference. We looked at the ways in which we were trying to save
money in accordance with the need each year to produce X per cent reduction
in cost or Y per cent more work done but the attention was always going to
those areas which were the softest. A few less cleaners here, squeezing a bit on
the restaurant staff, looking at the telephone exchange, at how we could
reduce the numbers of porters we were using. This was not getting to the root
of the problem. That demanded a fundamental approach and process reengineering is for us that way of doing things differently. (Member of the Trust
board, December 1995)

Concluding this part of the discussion, business process reengineering
is identified as a strategic choice that developed as part of an embry-
onic process of strategic management amidst a pressurized but energized corporate core of senior managers within a newly created NHS
Trust. These managers were simultaneously acting to exploit and
mobilize the new found freedoms of Trust status, to cope with the
developing pressures and constraints on the hospital, not least the
thresholds of patient care quality and activity demanded by local purchasers and the government. Institutional imperatives associated with

the NHS internal market, the Patients' Charter and the onset of NHS Trust status, were perceived by members of senior management within LRI to require of the hospital more health care services, of better quality, whilst meeting cost improvement targets set by national government. Some senior managers and clinicians within LRI developed a belief that a 'radical' solution was necessary to be able to meet this challenge. Reengineering was perceived as the 'radical solution'. Reengineering was a strategic choice by senior managers of hospital intended to reconfigure the pattern and performance of work throughout the hospital. It displayed simultaneously a reactive and proactive response by senior managers on behalf of LRI to institutional forces and pressures that were perceived by senior managers as enabling and constraining. The remainder of the chapter reports how the reengineering intervention developed over the period between 1994 and 1998.

5.3   Reengineering LRI: a chronological overview

Table 5.1 offers a tabulated overview of a change programme using a set of milestones of the reengineering intervention between 1992 and 1997. A more discursive overview of the reengineering intervention over the period is provided below organized around a chronology of five phases. The five phases are:

phase one: the genesis of the reengineering intervention at Leicester Royal Infirmary (September 1992–July 1994);
phase two: reengineering diagnostic services & outpatient clinics (August 1994–February 1995);
phase three: reengineering the 'clinical heartlands' of the hospital (March 1995–August 1995);
phase four: reengineering implementation lags the reengineering transformation vision (October 1995–May 1996);
phase five: the end of the beginning and 'incremental revolution' (June 1996–1997).

5.3.1   *Phase one: the origins of the reengineering intervention at Leicester Royal Infirmary (September 1992–July 1994)*

Though the reengineering programme formally commenced in August 1994, the preceding discussion associated reengineering, at least in

Table 5.1   *The LRI reengineering programme: milestones of a planned change intervention*

September 1992	LRI initiates five projects as part of Trent Health's Project Sigma initiative designed to improve the quality of outpatient services.
July 1993	Senior Managers and Clinicians use the concept of reengineering to make sense of variable results of five Project Sigma initiatives.
October 1993	A concept paper about reengineering is prepared by LRI and King's Healthcare. The paper is part of formal submission to the NHS for the Trusts to pilot the application of reengineering to health care.
November 1993	Clinical, managerial and trade union leaders are introduced to the concept of reengineering at a strategic direction 'time-out'.
January 1994	A programme initiation document titled *Reengineering the Healthcare Process* is prepared by LRI. The document invites NHS Management Executive to sponsor the reengineering intervention at LRI.
July 1994	The report of a scoping study identifies core organizational processes to be reengineered, programme objectives, and time scales.
July 1994	NHS Executive recognizes, with financial support, LRI as the national pilot site for reengineering.
August 1994	The reengineering intervention formally commences. Work starts on the redesign of the core processes of patient visit and diagnostic test processes.
January 1995	LRI seeks and receives continuing support of the NHS Executive to move onto the next phase of reengineering.
March 1995	Four new reengineering laboratories are created for the purposes of redesigning the four core processes of 'emergency entry', 'patient stay', 'patient visit', and 'clinical support services'.
October 1995	The process of dissolving reengineering laboratories starts as part of a process that sees formal responsibility for reengineering shift from a centralized programme to clinical directorates.
May 1996	The Reengineering Steering Group recognizes that reengineering will have to continue beyond May 1996. Senior management of the hospital is committed to continuing to reengineer the hospital. 31 May, the date for formal completion of the programme, is spoken of as 'the end of the beginning'.
August 1997	The language of radical performance transformation has been replaced by talk amongst leaders of the reengineering intervention of 'incremental revolution'.

part, to the successful establishment of a 'one-stop' or single-visit clinic in the specialty of neurology. The concept of reengineering was used by some senior managers and clinicians within LRI to 'make sense' of the relative success of this project compared to other projects undertaken as part of the same quality improvement initiative (Project Sigma) within the hospital. In this newly created NHS Trust, reengineering was championed by some senior managers, including the chief executive and medical director as a radical change methodology by which the hospital could meet the intensifying demands upon the hospital related to the volume, quality, efficiency, and effectiveness of patient care. Senior management at the LRI developed plans for an organization-wide reengineering initiative to produce dramatic improvements in patient care processes and performance. The energy and enthusiasm of champions of reengineering within LRI were also fuelled by the endorsement of a reengineering intervention within LRI by reengineering 'guru' Michael Hammer and initial financial support provided by the NHS Executive.

5.3.2 *Phase two: reengineering diagnostic services and outpatient clinics (August 1994–February 1995)*

With financial support of the NHS Executive, the reengineering intervention formally commenced in August 1994. The intervention was akin to the classical reengineering prescription in terms of ambition and organization (Hammer and Champy 1993). The stated ambition was dramatic improvement in organizational performance within two years. Management consultants were appointed as external change agents. Internal change agents were also appointed using individuals seconded from their existing roles within LRI. Both internal change agents and external change agents were located in three specially created reengineering laboratories, to work together in teams to identify and reengineer health care processes. Six core processes within the hospital were identified and plans to reengineer these processes in a sequential order were developed.

Starting with two of the six core care processes, namely 'patient visit' and 'patient test', the sequence of reengineering commenced with redesign of some diagnostic testing services and services provided in some outpatient clinics. LRI reported that these early attempts to reengineer processes culminated in some radical process improvements. On the back of this reported success, a further successful bid for more substantial funding from the NHS Executive was prepared.

5.3.3　*Phase three: reengineering the 'clinical heartlands' of the hospital (March 1995–August 1995)*

In the initial months of 1995, ambitions for the programme peaked as illustrated by the aspirations of those leading the intervention to move from a 'sequential' to 'concurrent' core process redesign. The change was justified on the grounds that the hospital core processes were interconnected and maximum benefit could only be gained if all core processes were reengineered rapidly and concurrently.

Buoyed by progress made reengineering both diagnostic services and outpatient services, the reengineering intervention within LRI continued with additional financial support from the NHS Executive. Over a two-year period until July 1996, financial support would allegedly total approximately £4 million. In this phase, four new reengineering laboratories were created, comprising approximately 30 LRI staff plus management consultants, to extend reengineering into what some members of senior management described at the time 'as the clinical heartlands' of the hospital. Newly defined core processes covering all patient services within LRI were identified. In addition to diagnostic and visit processes, the concept of reengineering was extended to the core processes of 'emergency entry' and 'patient stay' (see later in the chapter). Administrative processes were also to be reengineered by mid-1996.

In this phase the scale and scope of the reengineering activity increased enormously. There were 50–70 reengineering projects spanning a wide breadth of clinical directorates, departments, and specialties in LRI. This increased amount of change activity made the change intervention more complex to manage. Those responsible for managing the reengineering intervention became increasingly concerned about the integration and coherence of the plurality of reengineering change projects within the organization. In spite of plans to reengineer core processes across the hospital, it was not always apparent how reengineering interventions at specialty and directorate levels related to the four 'core organizational processes' previously identified. Major differences were observable in the rate and pace of change across specialties and clinical directorates within the hospital. Some directorates and specialties were being given greater attention by reengineers, notably, A&E services, orthopaedic services, and some surgical specialties. Across surgical specialties, progress in piloting redesigned patient processes was slow and uneven. Reengineering of in-patient services within the medical directorate had not started at this point.

Managers and clinicians at clinical specialty and clinical directorate levels were emerging as important regulators of the rate and pace of the reengineering intervention at clinical directorate and specialty levels. At directorate and specialty levels, it was common to hear managers and clinicians questioning the idea that patient services could be interpreted as generic core processes to be redesigned and 'rolled out' across specialties. Senior members of the reengineering intervention started to articulate that process reengineering needed to be tailored to the needs of particular patient groups and wants of clinicians. Management consultants expressed concern that senior managers within the hospital could not force medical consultants to accept change.

By the end of August 1995, the progress of reengineering emergency care and in-patient elective care appeared slower than anticipated in the original plans for the reengineering intervention. Senior reengineers and managers started to openly acknowledge for the first time that time scales for realizing some of the benefits of reengineering would need to be extended beyond May 1996. However, faced with limited and reducing (as planned) financial and staffing resources for the purposes of reengineering an extended time scale presented difficulties. By the end of this phase of the intervention, responsibility for reengineering was shifting from a centralized team of reengineers located within laboratories, focusing on a limited number of core processes, to managers and clinicians within clinical directorates and specialties.

5.3.4 *Phase four: reengineering implementation lags the reengineering vision (October 1995–May 1996)*

The process of formally shifting responsibility and accountability for reengineering change interventions from reengineers located in centralized laboratories to managers within clinical directorates continued throughout this phase. To this point, the reengineering intervention had focused more on changing processes of patient care than the formal pattern of roles and responsibilities within and between clinical directorates. However, as reengineering laboratories were being dissolved changes to the organizational structure started to emerge. Some senior 'reengineers', for instance, 'reengineering team leaders' who headed the reengineering laboratories were appointed to senior 'process management roles' within clinical directorates. Most notable was the appointment of a reengineering team leader to the post of patient process director alongside the clinical director within the clinical directorate of A&E and orthopaedic trauma services. The change was intended to help develop 'process management' at the expense of 'functional management' at directorate and specialty levels. At the head of this directorate, there was now a clinical director and patient process director, with three process managers, rather than the trium-virate of clinical director, senior nurse, and business management. Indeed, this was a precursor to the further introduction of process management throughout the hospital during 1996 and 1997.

The remaining, though reducing, number of reengineers and manage-ment consultants perceived a changed role for themselves in motivating, supporting, and coaching those within clinical directorates and clinical specialties to engage in patient process redesign. With varying degrees of enthusiasm managers and clinicians within clinical directorates and specialties received responsibility for reengineering interventions. By November 1995, the number of reengineering change projects swelled to over 100, spanning many different areas across the hospital. However, the increased number of change projects served to cause further concern about both the coherence of change projects across the LRI and account-ability for results. The reengineering programme manager and a small team of people spent much of their time in late 1995 and early 1996 attempting to establish a performance management process through which directorates would be accountable for the performance of reengi-neering projects in their directorate against predetermined objectives.

It was apparent that whilst the breadth of the change activity appeared to span the majority of clinical directorates and specialties within LRI, the depth of impact was variable across the hospital. To this point reengineering appeared to have made greatest impact in areas of patient testing such as pathology and in some outpatient clinics. Progress made reengineering the corpus of emergency and elective services provided to patients admitted into hospital was relatively slow. It was widely acknowledged that LRI would not be a 'reengi-neered organization' by May 1996. Whilst radical transformation remained the ambition, May 1996 was no longer seen as the end of a major, time-limited change programme, and senior managers started to talk of LRI being committed to the 'continuous reengineering' of the hospital's processes.

5.3.5 *Phase five: the end of the beginning and 'incremental revolution' (June 1996–March 1998)*

The period post-May 1996, the formal end point for the reengineering intervention, saw those at the forefront, including the chief executive, reengineering programme leader, and medical director, continuing to espouse the need for radical change albeit through a more incremental and evolutionary change philosophy. The philosophy at March 1995, of quick 'Big Bang' organizational transformation had been tempered by the experiences of implementation over the previous 12–18 months.

Senior managers continued to communicate to the organization their belief in targeting organizational processes in pursuit of radical performance improvements. Process thinking and process management remained particularly enduring features of the reengineering intervention, though some other features of earlier phases of the reengineering programme had disappeared. The shift of responsibility for patient process redesign interventions from 'reengineers' working in 'reengineering laboratories' to managers in clinical directorates was completed. With reengineering laboratories dissolved, all that remained of the centralized reengineering infrastructure set up to promote and support process redesign was a 'Centre for Best Practice', consisting of a small number of former reengineers, including the reengineering programme leader. These individuals were now working without the support of the firm of external management consultants who had left the organization as planned in the later months of summer and early autumn 1996.

Specially created committees for managing the reengineering intervention were also dissolved. The Reengineering Steering Group, discussed later in this chapter, met for the last time in May 1996. The Reengineering Management Group met for the last time in January 1997. In 1997 the reengineering change agenda was subsumed as part of the remit of a reconstituted Hospital Executive Group. At specialty and clinical directorate levels, the reengineering change agenda was subsumed into new 'process management' arrangements. Plans issued by the chief executive to reconfigure and reduce the existing pattern of clinical directorates did not materialize. The language of reengineering largely disappeared from the parlance of LRI. Indeed, in instances when it was used it was often referred to with negative connotation, as the 'r-word'. Whilst the word 'reengineering' disappeared from everyday parlance within LRI, the language of 'process change', 'process-driven organization', 'process thinking' persisted amongst some managers and clinicians within the hospital.

Though variable, there remained in this period some momentum for process redesign at senior management, clinical, and directorate specialty levels of the hospital. Many change interventions dating back to earlier phases of the reengineering intervention continued. New

change interventions started post-May 1996 explicitly using methodologies and expertise developed during earlier phases of the reengineering programme. Some of the new projects developed in this period
were a deliberate attempt by some senior managers and clinicians
within the hospital to both increase coherence of change initiatives
across specialties and clinical directorates and address chronic ongoing
problems facing the hospital, for instance, redesign of elective and
emergency admissions at a hospital-wide level. Some senior managers
heralded these efforts as a return to thinking about change in terms of
generic core processes at the corporate level. These projects were ongoing as fieldwork for the study was completed in mid-1998.

The preceding discussion is an introductory overview of the reengineering intervention. The remainder of this chapter will elaborate
on events and issues raised in the preceding commentary under the following headings: preparing to reengineer; reengineering ambition and
objectives; scale, scope, and methodology of the reengineering intervention; and governance and organization of the reengineering
programme.

5.4　Reengineering LRI: a thematic overview

5.4.1　*Preparing to reengineer*

Between June 1993 and August 1994 a small cadre of the Trust's most
senior managers, including clinicians with senior managerial responsibilities, engaged in a number of change-related activities. These activities are reported here to provide a sense of formal preparation by senior
management for the reengineering intervention. Activities identified
include: researching the concept of reengineering; assessing the potential risks to the reengineering intervention presented by stakeholders
both inside and outside LRI; gauging and mobilizing support for the
reengineering intervention; organizing and managing the reengineering intervention; and procuring the input of management consultants.

During 1993, time was invested researching the concept of reengineering. This research included reflecting upon the experience of
Project Sigma within LRI and other organizations' experiences of
reengineering. It is alleged that the Trust investigated reengineering
initiatives undertaken by more than fifty organizations worldwide
resulting in an audit of reengineering success factors produced by the
reengineering programme leader and Trust chief executive. In the

autumn of 1993, this research was referenced in a concept paper about reengineering produced jointly by LRI and a London teaching hospital for the NHS Executive. The submission represented a formal approach to the NHS Executive by the hospitals to pilot reengineering within the respective hospitals. Speculatively the concept paper was sent to Michael Hammer, reengineering guru and co-author of *Reengineering the Corporation: A Manifesto for Business Revolution* (Hammer and Champy 1993). At the invitation of Michael Hammer, representatives from LRI and King's attended a seminar by Hammer in America. Senior managers and clinicians described Hammer as 'interested, encouraging, and reinforcing' of proposals to reengineer the hospitals. One senior manager recalled that

He was very interested in what we were doing and that was a very influential piece of encouragement. Material picked up from his seminar and through private discussion with him was interesting. Our meeting him encouraged us that what we had written and what we were thinking was not completely bizarre . . . the discussion we had with Hammer was very useful and basically he gave us advice of what not to do and reinforced our ideas about doing a whole hospital piece of work. He was recommending that there was no point in trying to do it half-baked as that would fail. (Senior manager, August 1995)

Closer to home, a reengineering programme leader was appointed in November 1993, and some senior managers and clinicians endeavoured to mobilize support for a reengineering programme both inside and outside LRI. There were a number of stands of activity related to gauging and mobilizing support for reengineering. As part of a process of formulating a strategic direction for this new NHS Trust a number of 'think-tanks' and 'events' occurred.

We decided to create a number of different think-tanks and events to bring peoples' ideas together. We were also trying to put into place ideas about best practice from an analysis we had conducted about strategic analysis and planning in other organizations. We tried to identify the critical mass of leaders within the hospital that in a sense would add some weight and momentum to try to move the organization. We knew that simply the management team or the clinical directors could not do it on their own given the size of the organization and its culture. (Senior manager, August 1995)

One event in November 1993 involved over 100 clinical, managerial, and trade union 'leaders' meeting at a local stately home to work on 'facets of our strategic direction including a mission statement' (Senior manager, August 1995). Two of the notable recollections of senior executives of this event are that this 'time-out' was the first opportunity for a very diverse multi-disciplinary group of people to work together in small teams. Second, the concept paper produced for the NHS Executive was used within small team workshops to introduce a wider set of individuals to the notion of reengineering.

. . . the event was a powerful gathering in terms of a whole load of aspirations and ambitions to improve what we do. What was clear to those of us who had been involved in the process analysis stuff [following Project Sigma] was that there was no way that you could get close to some of the aspirations we had got. The [patient] process is just too complex and byzantine . . . processes were intrinsically inefficient, they created delays, duplication, and errors. They had simply been put in through convention over the year . . . Through events at that time-out it became clearer why we had those weaknesses. We had a roll of wallpaper or something with a series of sticky labels looking at the different activities in outpatients . . . the exercise simply demonstrated inadequacies of our present working arrangements and explained for example why we fail to get 100 per cent of medical records to outpatients clinics and why staff in clinics often have a difficult time. (Senior manager, August 1995)

Simultaneously and somewhat 'behind the scenes' there were iterative, informal processes whereby a small collection of reengineering champions at senior management level talked to colleagues within the Trust and members of the Trust board about a reengineering intervention. A senior manager recalled that

I spent a lot of time talking to the movers and shakers of the hospital about the idea of reengineering. This involved a lot of time refining ideas, working out what it was that we needed to do in order to have a proposition to enthuse them. So, a lot of my time was spent nurturing that leadership. (Senior manager, September 1995)

The process of mobilizing support for the programme was also informed by a risk analysis of the reengineering intervention carried out by the Trust with the help of a management consultant. Risks to the programme were identified both inside and outside LRI. Inside LRI, there was a concern amongst those leading the intervention to minimize cynicism and opposition to the reengineering intervention from trade unions and staff. Outside LRI there was concern that the NHS Executive should not intervene in the intervention through loss of confidence, and that the major purchaser, Leicestershire Health, should not endeavour to block the intervention. It was also acknowledged that reengineering could be undermined by factors such as: poor information for measuring performance of the hospital and the reengineering intervention; loss of key people during implementation; distraction of the chief executive and senior management from the intervention due to, for example, pressures of contracting; underestimation of the complexity of the reengineering task and the financial resources required for the intervention; an inability to release senior clinicians to work on the intervention; and the failure of management consultants to deliver. Particularly important 'stakeholders' in the programme were identified as the NHS Management Executive, the Trust's medical profession, and nursing staff.

The concept paper prepared for the NHS Executive in November 1993 was superseded by a 'programme initiation document' in January 1994 inviting the NHS Executive to support the reengineering intervention at LRI (LRI NHS Trust 1994b). In seeking to secure the support of the NHS Executive, the Trust demonstrated its confidence in the ability to achieve the dramatic improvements promised by reengineering by allegedly pledging to pay back 50 per cent of net savings to the major local purchaser resulting from the reengineering intervention. Since the visit to America contact with Michael Hammer enabled LRI to present the application to the NHS Management Executive with a personal endorsement of the programme by the reengineering guru.

Following this submission to the NHS Executive, the LRI received a visitation from the then chief executive of the NHS who met with senior clinicians and managers of the Trust, prior to granting the hospital a loan to support reengineering at LRI. With the support of the NHS Executive, the LRI became one of two national pilot sites for re-engineering. The remainder of the chapter provides a sense of how re-engineering subsequently unfolded and impacted within the hospital.

5.4.2 *Reengineering ambition and objectives: from rapid organizational transformation to incremental revolution*

This part of the chapter discusses the formal ambition and objectives of the reengineering intervention over the period of 1994 and 1997. It is shown that the ambition and objectives of the intervention changed over time. The formal ambition behind the reengineering intervention, at least initially, adhered to the reengineering orthodoxy as preached by Hammer and Champy (1993). From the outset, the reengineering intervention was conceived of and publicly projected by leaders of the intervention as one intended to create dramatic performance improvement. In January 1994, a formal 'invitation' was made to the NHS Management Executive to sponsor the Trust to achieve major cost savings and service excellence improvements in two years. The Trust assumed that savings from the programme would outweigh the costs. Specific 'hospital performance' objectives related to service quality, service cost, service activity levels, and perceived contributors to hospital performance such as staff satisfaction, processes of research and teaching, and the managerial process. A scoping study in July 1994 (LRI NHS Trust 1994c) proposed that reduction of administrative errors, patient process delays, and duplication could achieve significant reductions in hospital costs, patient process times for outpatient clinics, and reduced length of stay in hospital.

Ambitions for the reengineering intervention further increased following the period of reengineering between July 1994 and January 1995. Following on from claimed successes in reengineering processes of diagnostic testing and outpatient clinics, this point in the history of the reengineering change intervention reveals a heightened level of ambition for reengineering. The anticipated deadline for radical performance improvement was brought forward three months to May 1996 and reengineering ambition also spread beyond outpatient services and diagnostic testing toward emergency and elective in-patient care. In emergency services the thrust of reengineering would be to dramatically improve times by which patients attending the A&E department would be assessed, seen by an A&E doctor, and if necessary, admitted into hospital. It was also hoped that by mid-1996, the hospital would achieve zero rate of cancelled operations (LRI NHS Trust 1995).

May 1996 marked the intended point of completion of the reengineering intervention. By this time, senior managers within the hospital and leaders of reengineering had amended their ambitions for reengineering within LRI. In March 1996, LRI published a document entitled *Reengineering the Healthcare Process: Achieving Results* for the NHS Management Executive (LRI NHS Trust 1996). The document pointed to a large number of reengineering projects within the hospital. Some benefits of the programme were reported in terms of cost reduction and service quality improvements. However, with some exceptions, results of reengineering in the 'clinical heartlands' of medical and surgical services for in-patients over the period of March 1995 to March 1996 were less apparent. In summary, much of the report talked about the potential rather than the actual impact of the reengineering intervention to date. New ways of justifying the intervention were presented as the report noted that reengineering had increased the organizational capability to change and provided learning for the NHS community. Certainly, eighteen months into the programme, it was apparent that the aim of transforming the performance and capability of the entire hospital had not been realized.

Subsequently the date for completing the reengineering programme passed with a commitment by senior management to continue the reengineering programme in LRI. At the final meeting of the Reengineering Steering Group in May 1996, a senior member of the group and Trust board remarked that 'May 1996 does not mark the end of the reengineering programme but merely the end of the beginning'.

Following the formal end date of the reengineering programme members of senior management, including the chief executive, remained committed to process redesign as a methodology for bringing about organizational change. However, whilst holding onto the desire to create dramatic improvements in hospital performance the language of radical performance transformation was replaced by talk amongst hospital leaders and some former reengineers of 'incremental revolution' (Senior manager, August 1997). An internal evaluation of the Reengineering Programme in late 1997 (LRI NHS Trust 1997) indicated that reengineering had impacted on every directorate and department of the hospital though at a pace and level of impact more uneven than anticipated at the outset of the programme.

5.4.3 Scale, scope, and methodology of the reengineering intervention

From the outset, the reengineering programme at LRI was intended to be total rather than partial in its coverage of clinical and non-clinical services within LRI. In keeping with classic reengineering prescription (Hammer and Champy 1993) the intervention was based upon the identification and redesign of core organizational processes. The programme of reengineering was planned into a number of phases over a two-year period. Over the period, there have been three generations of core processes identified. The first generation of core processes emerged in 1994. Akin to the industrial models of reengineering (Hammer and Champy 1993) six core organizational processes were to be reengineered. The six processes to be reengineered covered care for patients admitted as emergencies, in-patients, and outpatients. Diagnostic services provided to clinicians and patients were also to be reengineered. Complementing the redesign of patient care disciplines was the intent to redesign processes of teaching and research at LRI and relations with purchasers via the NHS internal market.

A 'phased' approach was taken to reengineering in order to produce early results and manage risk. The 'phased' (sequential) approach started with the reengineering of patient visit and patient test processes.

The decision to start with the processes of patient visit and patient test was justified at the time as offering opportunities to make improvements in the high-profile area of outpatient services and benefit hospital performance against the government's Patients' Charter standards.

The reengineering intervention started in August 1994 in accordance with plans. Initially reengineering work focused upon improving waiting times and organization within outpatient clinics as well as the provision of diagnostic tests and X-rays required by outpatients. It was soon realized that the change management methodology imported from industry needed to be adapted to the needs of a health care context. By January 1995, those leading the reengineering work were speaking of a need to modify reengineering to suit the health care context. The standard reengineering methodology of defining the project scope, baselining/benchmarking existing performance, visioning change, planning change, and implementing change had proved difficult to use during the period between August 1994 and January 1995. Reengineering teams found the method of baselining to be 'time consuming' and 'frustrating'. It was felt that the method of 'visioning' did not adequately engage clinicians who were more engaged with the practicalities of providing patient services. For the future development of the programme the 'classic reengineering methodology' would be adapted by a methodology more attuned to speeding up the process of piloting newly designed processes through directorate-based teams of people acting within a methodological framework facilitated and validated by reengineering laboratories.

The programme was structured around core processes. However, the first generation of six core processes identified in July 1994 was replaced by a set of four core processes. The core processes to be reengineered in the next phase of the programme covered were articulated as: 'emergency entry'; 'patient visit'; 'patient stay'; and 'clinical support services'. It was identified that a patient's entry to the hospital is either planned or emergency. A patient's treatment takes place as a visit, if there is no overnight stay, or a stay if there is an overnight stay. A patient's process of aftercare involves discharge to primary care and ongoing monitoring. Clinical support processes include services such as diagnostic tests, pharmacy, and theatres. The identification of the four core processes indicated that the scope of reengineering was in practice being extended to cover elective and emergency activities and in-patient and outpatient services. At this point in the programme administrative and management processes were included in reengineering plans for the first time. To integrate reengineering within the management of the hospital attention would be given to reengineering the hospital infrastructure (non-clinical services), organizational structures, roles, and accountabilities and patient information systems.

Also, by January 1995, the sequential and phased approach to reengineering had been replaced by plans to redesign concurrently the four core processes. From March 1995, a strategy of concurrent change was adopted in place of the phased (sequential) strategy of change. The decision to adopt a concurrent process of change was justified by senior managers on the grounds of: reducing the chances of creating a partially reengineered organization; managing 'interaction' between hospital processes; and challenging 'existing departmental and functional boundaries'.

After March 1995, reengineering went beyond outpatient services and diagnostic testing into in-patient elective and emergency activities. As the application of reengineering to the majority of specialties and directorates within LRI unfolded two issues emerged related to the scale, scope, and methodology of the reengineering intervention. The application of reengineering across specialties and directorates was uneven and patchy. It was also evident that the practice and rationale of change interventions at specialty and directorate level did not necessarily relate to the second generation of core processes identified.

Generating momentum for reengineering interventions within the range of clinical directorates and specialties within LRI created its own problems for those leading reengineering programmes. Most notably, the anticipated coherence of reengineering interventions based upon a set of interrelated core organization processes was being undermined by the practice of process redesign tailored to the needs and circumstances of directorates and specialties. Following some work in the specialty of ENT by members of the patient visit reengineering laboratory in June 1995, the idea of care group-specific patient processes was articulated by reengineers (see Chapter 6). Reengineers talked of the need to be able to redesign care process for particular patient groups from 'end to end' of the care process. This thinking was not consistent with the rationale and activities of four separate reengineering laboratories created to focus on a limited number of generic core processes.

By September 1995 the mass of reengineering change activity and projects appeared to be organized more around imperatives and idiosyncrasies of individual specialties, directorates, patient groups, and medical consultants rather than guided by some overarching set of core processes. The four core processes of patient stay, patient visit, emergency entry, and clinical support were not proving to be a robust organizing logic guiding the practice of reengineering. The process of reengineering became more local than corporate in the way it was shaped and managed at directorate and specialty levels. The planned methodology for change based around core processes was weak in the face of organizing forces at the clinical specialty and clinical directorate levels. Temporally, these observations of the reengineering intervention coincided with the dismantling of reengineering laboratories and a shifting of responsibility and accountability for reengineering projects from reengineers in laboratories to clinical directorates. Within a mass of change activity, the anticipated focus on previously identified core processes appeared blurred, generating debate about whether the 'right core processes had been identified in the first place' (reengineer). Some individuals went as far as to articulate that there were really only two core processes in LRI and these were related to 'emergency' and 'elective' care. Core processes had proved to be indeterminate (Buchanan 1997).

It was nearly twelve months later before corporate core process thinking re-emerged within the reengineering intervention. In June 1996, three new reengineering projects were revealed at the Reengineering Steering Group. The projects were described as a 'planned admissions project'; a 'prioritizing emergency demand project'; and a 'trust-wide discharge project'. Some senior managers and reengineers heralded the emergence of these projects as a return to thinking about change at a 'corporate level'. For some people these projects represented a refocusing of change activity around core processes of 'emergency care', 'elective care', 'discharge planning', and 'clinical support services'. These new projects were pursued at the same time as other change interventions more focused at clinical specialty and clinical directorate level proceeded. In practice, the coexistence of multiple change interventions at multiple levels of organizational functioning represented a dynamic tension within the reengineering change process between change activity focused on the particular needs and imperatives of patient groups, specialties, and directorates and change activity focused on what some people perceive as wider, more generic issues and problems within the Trust.

5.4.4 *Governance and organization of the reengineering programme*

5.4.4.1 *Formal reengineering committees: a corporate core*
In contrast to the incremental and decentralized approach to strategy within professionalized service organizations such as hospitals painted

by Mintzberg (1979) the reengineering programme was conceived as an exercise in top-down strategic management. The whole of the hospital was to change quickly and dramatically. The gradual construction since the 1980s of a managerial and clinical managerial cadre that operated outside conventional clinical areas represented an additional power resource that could be used to help realize this ambition. There was a corporate core—reporting to the highest levels of the organization—which was actively monitoring the overall progress of the programme across the hospital.

Like the ambition and methodology of the programme, the formal approach to organizing the reengineering intervention closely resembled the structure of committees and roles suggested by Hammer and Champy (1993). Figure 5.2 shows three groups were created, all dedicated to the reengineering intervention: the Reengineering Steering Group; the Reengineering Management Group; and the Reengineering Team Leaders' Review. Established in May 1994 the Reengineering Steering Group met monthly to monitor and review progress of the reengineering intervention. The group was chaired by the chairman of the Trust and reported to the Trust board. The chief executive of the Trust attended meetings of the group. In addition, the Steering Group comprised major internal and external stakeholders. Internal stakeholders were, for

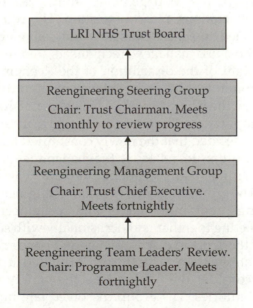

Figure 5.2   *Reengineering programme management structure*

instance, clinical directors and executive directors of the Trust. Major external stakeholders included representatives of the NHS Executive, the local Health Authority, the Audit Commission, and members of the evaluation team (Bowns and McNulty 1999). Also in attendance at meetings of the Steering Group were the reengineering programme leader and leaders of the reengineering laboratories and management consultants. Other individuals with reengineering responsibilities attended meetings of the Steering Group on an ad hoc basis to report progress with particular interventions. The group met for the last time in May 1996. The group was dissolved in line with the formal date for completing the reengineering programme.

Change in both the ambition and scope of the reengineering programme at February 1995 also marked changes in the organization and governance of the programme. Responsibility for direction and management of the programme remained with the Trust chief executive and reengineering programme leader respectively. In addition to the Reengineering Steering Group, a Reengineering Management Group was formed. The Reengineering Management Group met fortnightly to track progress of the reengineering intervention and resolve issues to do with the interface between the reengineering initiative and broader operational and management issues within the Trust. Established in February 1995 the group was chaired by the chief executive. By comparison with the Steering Group, the Management Group was more internally focused in its deliberations and composition. The composition of the group was restricted to senior clinicians and senior managers of the Trust, including business managers, reengineers, and management consultants. In the light of the dissolution of the Reengineering Steering Group and a commitment by senior management to continue reengineering the hospital, the Reengineering Management Group appeared to take on greater importance. The group continued to meet until the end of 1996 when it was decided that the newly constituted hospital executive would address future issues related to the change agenda of the hospital.

The Reengineering Team Leaders' Review was established in February 1995. The group consisted of senior reengineers, for instance, the reengineering programme leader and reengineering laboratory team leaders, meeting together and occasionally with senior managers and directors of the Trust to discuss issues and concerns related to the reengineering intervention. This forum provided a more informal opportunity to consider the work across the variety of different reengineering laboratories. The group dissolved late in 1995 as the reengineering laboratories were dissolved.

5.4.4.2   *Reengineering laboratories*

In addition to the formal structure of Reengineering Committees, the concept of the reengineering laboratory was also developed as a key feature of the formal process for organizing and managing the reengineering intervention. Reengineering laboratories were 'physical facilities' accommodating teams of reengineers working on the development and implementation of concepts for redesigning patient processes. The laboratories were designed to remove team members from their existing working environment and encourage them to 'take a fresh look at work processes in those areas' (Senior manager, March 1995). The creation of the laboratories indicated that the change programme was being organized using specially created reengineering change management teams whose members were without responsibilities for the day-to-day operational management of the hospital.

In practice, over the period of the reengineering programme there were two generations of reengineering laboratories formed to redesign the core processes discussed above. Between July 1994 and January 1995, three reengineering laboratories were formed to focus upon the core processes of patient visit and patient test. The laboratories were called the 'patient test reengineering laboratory', the '20-minute wait reengineering laboratory', and the 'patient visit reengineering laboratory'. In addition to the programme leader and a management consultant, approximately six people were seconded from existing roles within the Trust to work full-time in each laboratory. The individuals came from a range of administrative and clinical backgrounds.

Reengineers in the patient test laboratory reengineering team sought to dramatically improve the delivery of accurate, timely, and relevant information for patient diagnosis and therapy. The objective of the 20-minute wait laboratory reengineering team was to reduce waiting time in outpatient clinics so that no patient would wait longer than 20 minutes. The patient visit reengineering laboratory team sought to streamline outpatient processes toward improved clinical outcomes and service quality.

At March 1995, four new reengineering laboratories replaced the three reengineering laboratories. Numerically, the composition of each laboratory was greater than previously, involving twenty-eight individuals seconded from their posts. Each laboratory had a team leader and the leaders of the laboratories met as a group once a fortnight in a 'team leaders' review meeting'. The four new reengineering laboratories were created to support the redesign of four newly identified core processes of emergency entry, patient stay, patient visit, and clinical support services. The laboratories were located on former wards on one level of a wing of the hospital.

The patient visit team continued to redesign the patient visit process throughout the hospital. The clinical support services laboratory absorbed the activities of the former 'patient test reengineering laboratory'. The emergency entry laboratory was set up to reengineer the process by which patients enter the hospital via the Accident and Emergency department (A&E) and are admitted to wards. It was suggested that redesigned processes could lead to a reorganization of the flow of patients through the A&E department as well as some nursing roles in the department. The patient stay laboratory was created to reengineer the process of patient stay in the hospital with a remit covering processes of patient admission into hospital and discharge from the hospital.

The overall composition of reengineers comprised a mix of disciplines and seniority. Reengineering teams consisted of some clinical professionals with backgrounds in nursing and therapeutic occupations, professional administrators and managers, and some clerical staff. Few doctors were seconded to work as reengineers full-time. Seniority levels varied, for example senior nurses acted as reengineers alongside more junior nursing peers. Secretaries and clerical officers were reengineers alongside managers seconded from middle-to-senior business manager roles. In March 1995, all members of the four reengineering laboratories attended a three-day training programme. The training event was designed to develop teamwork amongst the newly appointed reengineers spanning the four laboratories. The objectives of the training event were to: inform new reengineers of the objectives of the programme; increase their understanding of their roles as reengineers; and develop their understanding of the tools, techniques, and concepts they would use to reengineer the organization. Management consultants and the reengineering programme manager led the training programme. Those at the training event were observed to be told by a senior hospital manager that they had been selected as reengineers because they were the 'brightest and the best' in the organization and that they 'will [over the period of reengineering] open the door of the hospital to the future' (Senior manager, March 1995).

Following the training event, members of the four laboratories proceeded with the task of reengineering Leicester Royal Infirmary. The laboratories continued in existence until September 1995, when the decision was taken to shift formal responsibility and accountability for reengineering to the clinical directorates. Following the decision occupants of the laboratories began to disperse. Some left LRI for other posts, others returned to their former roles, whilst some were appointed to senior process management roles within clinical directorates. By February 1996, the number of full-time reengineers had reduced to single figures. Located within a newly formed unit within LRI called the 'Centre for Best Practice' these individuals continued to promote organization development through process redesign.

Following the shift of reengineering responsibility to the clinical directorates the mechanisms for governing the programme rested on the creation of a performance management system, reporting by directorates at both the Reengineering Management Group and Reengineering Steering Group, and the creation of a Centre for Best Practice.

5.4.5 *Management consultants*

Two firms of management consultants contributed to the reengineering programme at LRI. In the 'programme initiation document' published in January 1994 (LRI 1994*a*) management consultant advice and expertise was reported to be a prerequisite for the programme. LRI was looking for consultant partners to: provide a methodological framework for the programme; assist the laboratories in improving core business processes; provide executive-level coaching and strategic guidance; and assess IT infrastructure and needs. The tender document issued by LRI criteria for selecting consultants included: demonstrable experience of supporting successful reengineering projects in organizations with £100 million turnover; willingness to share risk; ability to support reengineering laboratories; an approach which incorporates a time scale for the total project of two years or less; and an ability to develop performance measurement models which link service quality with cost, case-mix adjusted activity, and clinical effectiveness factors. Despite this last criterion there was allegedly little emphasis on previous experience of consultancy support in the health care sector amongst the criteria.

Figure 5.3 provides a broad overview of the consultancy input over the course of the reengineering programme between May 1994 and May 1996. The first group of consultants within LRI acted for three months between May and July 1994 and worked on a scoping study of reengineering within LRI. Three individuals, providing a level of support of two whole-time equivalents, worked as members of the scoping team alongside eight senior doctors, nurses, and administrators from within LRI. In the context of the whole programme the work of the

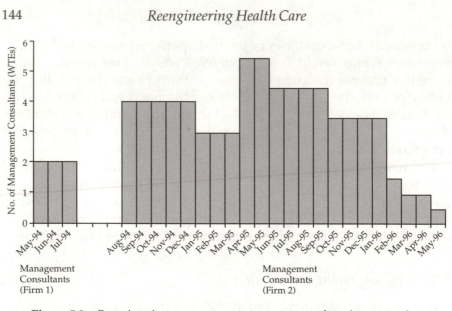

Figure 5.3   *Reengineering programme: management consultant input over time*

scoping team was important and shaped much of the ambition and methodology used throughout the reengineering programme. However, the consultants were not involved in the programme thereafter. A second consultancy firm joined the programme in August 1994. The firm had allegedly acquired its experience of reengineering in US health care and the automotive sector. Figure 5.3 provides a view of the level and length of involvement of the management consultants between August 1994 and May 1996. It is alleged that the cost of the consultancy support accounted for approximately 50 per cent of the loan from the NHS Executive (Bowns and McNulty 1999). The consultants joined LRI at the inception of the reengineering laboratories and reengineering of visit and stay processes. With consultants attached to each laboratory, key elements of the consultancy input were facilitating the redesign of patient processes through the transfer of knowledge, analytical models, and techniques for redesigning patient processes.

To summarize and conclude the chapter it is possible to draw a distinction between the intended and emergent strategies of reengineering in this case (Mintzberg and Waters 1985). The intended strategy of reengineering within LRI was radical and transformational in its ambition and organization. The stated ambition for the reengineering initiative in its preparatory and early phases (pre-March 1995) revealed LRI's adoption of the classical BPR ambition and method as expressed by Hammer and Champy (1993). The ambition and objectives of the programme reflected a rejection of incremental change and improvement strategies in favour of radically changing processes of organizing and managing health care in order to create dramatic and rapid organization-wide improvement. Supported by top management and significant financial investment, a reengineering capability was created within LRI using an infrastructure of reengineering committees, reengineering laboratories, and internal and external change agents. Reengineers and management consultants also articulated a belief in the orthodox reengineering methodology of identifying core processes, redesigning core processes, piloting redesigned processes, and rolling out new processes across the organization (Hammer and Champy 1993).

Relatively early in the reengineering programme the philosophy began to shift from one of rapid organizational transformation toward continuous incremental change and improvement. Plans to reengineer a set of core processes floundered by mid-1995 and the methodology of core process redesign, pilot, and roll-out dissipated to be replaced by a process redesign methodology more focused on distinct patient services at clinical specialty and directorate levels. Responsibility for reengineering shifted from a dedicated team of reengineers to managers within clinical directorates who were expected to incorporate reengineering into their existing responsibilities.

From the middle of 1996, further attempts to raise once again the level of redesign activity above specialties and directorates were observed. Articulation of emergency and elective care as the core processes of the LRI indicated a renewed attempt by some senior managers and process directors to again think about patient process redesign at a 'corporate' level. Within LRI, there continued a dynamic tension between centralized and decentralized approaches to managing change; also, between change methodologies that focus on what are perceived to be corporate core processes as distinct from methodologies focused on discrete patient services at specialty level.

Ultimately the emergent strategy deviated from the intended 'classical' reengineering strategy, in a number of important respects. Responsibility for reengineering initially rested with a distinct group of individuals working within a specially created set of change management facilities. Responsibility was later devolved to managers and clinicians within clinical directorates and specialties, supported by a small, dedicated, change management infrastructure. The focus on core process redesign processes shifted to patient process redesign attuned, in inception, purpose, and methodology to imperatives at specialty and directorate levels. The ambition to transform organizational processes and performance within two years shifted to an incremental philosophy of continuous change over a 5–10-year time scale.

The intended strategy of reengineering was radical and transformatory in ambition, method, and organization. By contrast, the emergent or realized strategy of reengineering proved to be more evolutionary than revolutionary. The pace of change was more convergent than transformational in its impact on the processes of organizing and managing LRI. In keeping with a structurationist view of social practice, the process and fate of reengineering as a transformatory change initiative is shown to have been reshaped and transformed by features and dynamics of the very organizational setting it sought to change (Child 1997; Giddens 1984). The following chapters of the monograph will proceed to analyse and explain the process and fate of reengineering in more detail, moving between corporate, specialty, and directorate levels of analysis.

6

Patient Process Reengineering: Six Case Studies

6.1 Introduction to case studies

The preceding chapter identified reengineering as a programmatic change strategy introduced by senior management to transform the hospital. This chapter examines the transformational claims and rhetoric of BPR further by focusing on empirically observable change to patient services as key indicators of hospital process and performance. The central question addressed within this chapter is, has reengineering transformed patient services within LRI?

The question is addressed using the comparative case-study method outlined in Chapter 4. A total of six in-depth case studies are presented ranging across emergency services, elective surgery, and outpatient services. The cases represent studies in real time of planned attempts to reengineer patient services. In each case, patient process redesign is viewed as action designed to challenge and change behaviour and role relations amongst actors involved in the provision of patient care. Case studies report activities, procedures, roles, and relations that are established features of patient care processes and how individuals and groups have sought to modify or defend these established features. The extent to which service provision now accords with reengineers' visions and aspirations suggests the scale and scope of change in patient processes. The path and effects of change interventions are thereafter explained with reference to behavioural and relational dynamics in and around clinical settings of the hospital (Child 1997; Barley and Tolbert 1997; Giddens 1984).

Collectively, the cases provide a comparative overview of the progress and fate of a number of planned change interventions informed by reengineering ideas and resources within the same organizational setting. The cases offer an opportunity to further examine the marked variation in the pace and impact of reengineering alluded to in the preceding chapter at the 'operational' levels of clinical specialties and directorates. To facilitate comparison a standard format is adopted for reporting each case. Initially, the patient process studied is placed in a context of relevant service and organizational arrangements. Thereafter, each case study reports aims and objectives of a patient process redesign intervention. Attention is drawn to changes both sought and attained by those championing redesign of patient processes. A chronology of the change intervention is included to provide a sense of the timing and unfolding of patient process redesign indicating associated actions, reactions, and interpretations. A concluding discussion in each case provides a first-level analysis of the impact of the intervention and factors that help to explain implementation and impact of the intervention. Chapter 8 subsequently returns to the case data to undertake a second level of analysis of the possibilities and problems of reengineering by identifying patterns and tendencies of patient process reengineering across widely dispersed services of emergency and orthopaedic trauma, medicine, gynaecology, ENT, and gastroenterology.

The six case studies are introduced below in the order they are presented within the chapter. Complementing discussion of the selection of case studies in Chapter 4, further details are here provided about the period of study and empirical data collected for each case.

Reengineering the process of care for patients attending the A&E department with minor injuries. The case study covers a period of data collection between March 1995 and September 1997. The case has been developed using data collected from twenty-three in-depth interviews with: members of the reengineering programme; directorate and specialty management; and clinicians within the A&E and trauma directorate. Data gathered from meetings of the Reengineering Steering Group and Reengineering Management Group are also used.

Reengineering the process of care for patients admitted with a fractured neck of femur. This case study covers a period of data collection from March 1995 to March 1998. The case has been developed using material from eighteen in-depth interviews with members of: the reengineering programme; directorate and specialty management; doctors in the specialty of orthopaedics and the A&E department; nurses and other professionals allied to medicine. Data gathered from meetings of the Reengineering Steering Group, Reengineering Management Group, and the Orthopaedics Process Link Group are also used.

Reengineering elective surgery within the specialty of gynaecology. The case study is based on data collected from twenty in-depth interviews with: senior managers within the hospital; members of the reengineering programme; managers and clinicians in the obstetrics and gynaecology directorate. Data gathered from meetings of the Reengineering Management Group, Reengineering Steering Group, and the Obstetrics and Gynaecology Directorate Reengineering Steering Group are also used.

Reengineering outpatient services in the specialty of gynaecology. The case study is based on notes from twenty in-depth interviews with: senior managers within the hospital; members of the reengineering programme; managers in the obstetrics and gynaecology directorate; and gynaecology clinicians. Data have also been used from meetings of the Reengineering Management Group, Reengineering Steering Group, and the Obstetrics and Gynaecology Directorate Reengineering Steering Group.

Reengineering elective surgery within the specialty of ENT. The case is based on data collected between March 1995 and October 1997 from twenty-five in-depth interviews with: members of the reengineering programme; managers in ENT and operating theatres; ENT consultants; anaesthetists; and nursing staff. Data collected as a result of attendance and observation at meetings of the Reengineering Steering Group, Reengineering Management Group, and ENT Working Party are also used.

Reengineering outpatient services in the specialty of gastroenterology. The case is based on data collected between late 1995 and October 1997. Data for this case are drawn from notes of seventeen in-depth interviews with managers and clinicians in the specialty. Data collected as a result of attendance and observation at meetings of the Reengineering Steering Group, Reengineering Management Group, and medical directorate are also used.

6.2 Reengineering the care process for patients attending the A&E department with minor injuries

6.2.1 *Introduction*

This case study reports a change intervention designed to reengineer the process of care for patients attending the Accident and Emergency (A&E) department of LRI with minor injuries. These patients are a large majority of the total number of attendances to the A&E department each year. A&E represented a visible and politically high-profile department within the hospital where it is important that reengineering should demonstrate an impact. The department acted as the filter for all emergency work coming into the hospital. As the provider of

A&E services for the whole county it was an extremely busy department and at the time of study there was much political and public concern nationally about the time patients have to wait in A&E departments.

The intervention occurred at a time when A&E attendances were increasing and the government's Patients' Charter initiative demanded demonstrable improvements in service waiting times. Reengineers sought to improve overall waiting times in A&E by quickening the treatment of people with minor injuries. This entailed important changes to the interprofessional division of labour. Key proposals by reengineers were that nurses in A&E take on some existing responsibility of A&E doctors for X-ray and treatment of patients with minor injuries. The case reports that from 1995 a significant proportion of nurses in A&E were trained to order a limited range of X-rays and administer minor treatments subject to clinical protocol. However, at the end of the study period there was considerable shortfall between waiting time performance of the A&E department and waiting time targets set by reengineers in 1995. The expected impact of reengineering on overall waiting times within the A&E department did not materialize and this must be seen as a disappointing outcome in such a strategic department.

The A&E department is shown to be a difficult environment in which to reengineer patient services. Growing workload in A&E allied to staffing problems are factors that shaped the possibilities and progress of change over the period of the intervention. Also, reengineers and management consultants failed to generate sufficient clinical support for the changes amongst senior doctors and nurses. In A&E, the approach to reengineering proved controversial in its objectives and method. Both this case and the case of fractured neck of femur patients are notable for the underlying conflict between process and functional views of organizing. Reengineers' 'process' view of the purpose and activities of the A&E department manifested itself in the language and objectives of 'queue management'. It was a concept resented and successfully resisted by A&E doctors who sought to defend A&E specialty status and the department's role in treating patients attending the hospital.

6.2.2 *Context and recent history of A&E services at LRI*

Leicester Royal Infirmary has one of the largest Accident and Emergency departments in the UK. In the year ending 31 April 1996, 109,000 patients attended the A&E department. In the period of study, the department was the only 24-hour major A&E department within the county of Leicestershire. There were three consultants in the A&E department whose appointments dated back to 1977, 1986, and 1994. The department also employed sixteen senior house officers (SHO). Recruitment and retention of nurses is a major theme within the case study. At November 1995 there were fourteen staff nurses vacancies. However, all vacancies were filled by end of 1996 following a departmental restructuring and recruitment drive. There was also considerable improvement in turnover and sickness rates amongst qualified nurses between December 1995 and March 1997.

Over the last twenty years, A&E medicine has emerged as a medical specialty in its own right. A&E consultants regarded A&E as a 'different specialty' to other specialties because of the number of staff needed to care for patients and the unpredictability of workload. The 1990s saw A&E services subject to increased demand. In line with national averages, attendance at the A&E department increased by 6 per cent. Simultaneously, the national NHS Patients' Charter initiative increased pressure for demonstrable service quality improvements. A Patients' Charter standard was that people in A&E should receive their initial triage assessment in five minutes. Staff in the department saw the 'big issues' facing the department to be: an inadequate number of staff to meet increasing demands upon the service; an outdated physical structure and departmental design inadequate for the volume of patients; and a department facing political pressure to improve waiting time at the same time as an increased number of emergency referrals exposed bed shortages throughout the locality.

A&E services were organized through the A&E and orthopaedic trauma directorate. In 1995, an orthopaedic consultant replaced an A&E consultant as clinical director. In early 1996, a senior management proposal to dismantle the directorate and merge the accident and emergency department with the medical directorate and orthopaedics within the surgical directorate did not proceed. Late in 1995, the administrative structure of the directorate was changed to introduce the philosophy of 'process management'.

Figures 6.1 and 6.2 show the structure of roles within the directorate pre- and post-reengineering respectively. Following the dismantling of the reengineering laboratories in late 1995, several members of the emergency entry reengineering laboratory moved into newly created process management roles within the directorate. An emergency entry patient process director was appointed in October 1995, alongside a newly appointed clinical director. All four occupants of the process management positions were from a nursing background, including

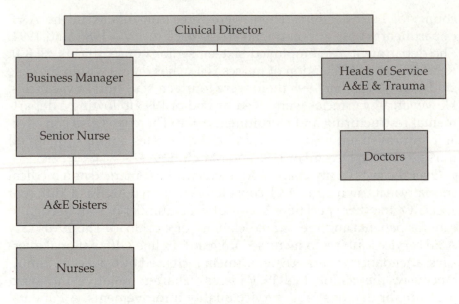

Figure 6.1 *A&E and trauma orthopaedics directorate: organization structure (pre-reengineering)*

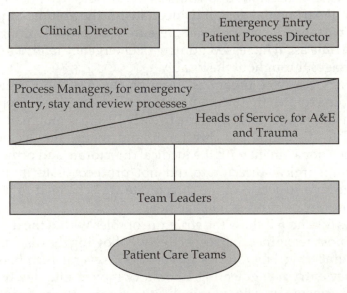

Figure 6.2 *A&E and trauma orthopaedics directorate: organization structure (post-reengineering)*

two who had worked in the A&E department albeit in a relatively junior nursing capacity. These were senior roles that replaced established 'functional management' roles such as business manager and senior nurse. The then vacant role of 'business manager' was not filled. The role of senior nurse disappeared as part of a Trust-wide restructuring of nursing management.

In 1996 the organization and management of nursing staff was restructured from top to bottom across the directorate. Figure 6.2 reveals the staffing structure within the A&E department post-reengineering. Six clinical manager posts were created with the occupants reporting to the emergency entry process manager. The role of clinical manager replaced the role of sister within the Accident and Emergency department. Only four of the previous sisters were appointed to clinical manager roles. On a day-to-day level, staff within the Accident and Emergency department were reorganized into shifts of six teams under the leadership of a clinical manager and lead clinician.

A number of reengineering initiatives related to A&E services were launched during 1995 and 1996. This case study concentrates on initiatives introduced as part of a planned change intervention designed to reengineer the care process for patients attending the A&E department with minor injuries.

6.2.3   Reengineering the care process for the 'walking wounded'

Objectives. At 1995, approximately 70 per cent of patients admitted to LRI were emergencies. Estimates of patients referred to the A&E department with 'minor injuries' ranged from '60,000–70,000' (a consultant in A&E) to '90,000' (reengineer). Patients with minor injuries are sometimes described as 'walking wounded'. 'Walking wounded' refers to patients that do not need to be admitted to LRI as in-patients. An A&E doctor defined the walking wounded as

patients who are injured but do not require to be laid on a trolley. In other words, patients who can walk up to a doctor or nurse and be seen. For example, someone with a wrist fracture. Less than 1% of these patients will require admission. They require admission because their treatment requires them to have a general anaesthetic or cannot be instituted as an outpatient. (A&E consultant, December 1996)

A formal set of deliverables registered by reengineers from the emergency entry laboratory with the Reengineering Programme Steering Group in August 1995 were contentious as doctors within the A&E

department thought them in conflict with triage guidelines published by the British Association of Emergency Medicine. Waiting times targets for patients attending to be achieved by January 1997 included: 100 per cent initial patient assessment in 5 minutes; 85 per cent of patients to be first seen by an A&E doctor in less than 20 minutes; and 85 per cent of patients to spend a total time of less than 75 minutes in A&E. Data for October 1994 reported 13 per cent of patients first see a doctor in less than 20 minutes, whilst 27 per cent of patients spend less than 75 minutes in A&E.

The above targets covered waiting times for all patients in A&E, not just those with minor injuries. The logic employed by reengineers was that by reducing the waiting times within the Accident and Emergency department of the largest group of patients, those with minor injuries, there would be a positive knock-on effect on the waiting times for all other patients attending the Accident and Emergency department. To achieve the targets reengineering worked on improving what they termed 'queue management in A&E'. A former reengineer in the A&E and orthopaedic trauma directorate remarked, 'the only important thing in A&E is getting people seen quickly. To get them to the right place. So you could call the whole of A&E queue management' (reengineer, November 1995).

Three initiatives were piloted in summer 1995 to reduce the queue of 'walking wounded' patients waiting to see a doctor in the Accident and Emergency department. These were: A&E nurses at triage ordering X-rays; A&E nurses at triage providing minor treatments and advice; and single queue management within the A&E department. Each initiative is described in more detail below. The brief chronology presented below further provides a sense of the unfolding of the change intervention.

Nurse ordered X-rays. In the summer of 1995, members of the emergency entry reengineering laboratory reported that 'baselining' of patient activity in A&E showed that the biggest delay for patients attending A&E with minor injuries was waiting for a doctor in A&E to order an X-ray. They further said that 40 per cent of all walking wounded patients needed an X-ray and 80 per cent of the X-rays for walking wounded patients were for minor injuries below either the knee or elbow. Consequently, they argued that nurses ordering X-rays for some patients with minor injuries would reduce the workload of the doctors and reduce waiting times in the department.

Established practice within the A&E department at that time was that medical staff ordered patient X-rays after the patient had been triaged. Having had an X-ray, the patient returned to the A&E department for diagnosis by a member of the medical staff. In effect, those patients requiring X-ray would have two separate consultations with medical staff in the A&E department. 'Baselining' revealed that the time to see a doctor for the initial consultation averaged 59 minutes though it could be as high as 2–3 hours depending on the overall workload within the A&E department. The initiative of nurses ordering X-rays was designed to reduce both the wait of the patient and the number of consultations with A&E doctors. The ordering of X-rays by nurses in the A&E department was piloted in July 1995. Protocols were developed to satisfy concerns of the doctors and to guide nurses on the appropriate ordering of X-rays. Protocols enabled A&E nurses of an appropriate grade and training to order X-rays of patients admitted with minor injuries below the elbow and below the knee.

Nurses carrying out simple treatments. It was accepted practice that all patients attending the A&E department are seen by a doctor. Along with nurse-ordered X-rays, the idea of simple treatments being administered by a nurse was perceived by reengineers to have the potential to make a big impact on the work of the doctor because patients treated at this stage would 'never get into the queue' (reengineer, August 1995). Using 'baselining' analysis reengineers argued that up to 20 per cent of walking wounded patients could be treated without having to see an A&E doctor. The idea of nurses administering simple treatments and ordering X-rays was piloted in July 1995. Between July 1995 and July 1997 75 per cent of qualified nurses in the department were trained to order X-rays and carryout simple treatments at triage. However, the case study will later reveal that the introduction of nurse-ordered X-rays and simple treatments was problematic and the impact of these initiatives were a disappointment to former reengineers and some managers within the department.

Single queue. In addition to the walking wounded category of patients, a second category of patient admitted to the A&E department is those patients who are not seriously ill or injured to the extent of requiring resuscitation but they do have to lie on a trolley. The seriousness of injuries to patients lying on trolleys can vary quite considerably. The physical layout of the department and availability of staff was felt by doctors to justify the management of the A&E workload via two queues of patients. First, patients on trolleys and second, patients who represent the walking wounded. Reengineers challenged the practice of two types of queue within the department,

if one is busy and the other one is quiet they rarely interchange—there is not a lot of flexibility. So we thought you would get better utilization out of the doctors if you were to put everybody [all patients] in one queue. (Former reengineer and department manager, March 1996)

Nurses and doctors raised doubts about the practicality of the idea of a single queue citing the structural layout of the department and concerns over the prioritization of patients. However, in November 1995 a pilot of the 'single queue' was set up under conditions, which a reengineer at the time described as 'sufferance' of nursing and medical staff. A system of prioritizing patients was used as part of the pilot. The pilot was stopped within hours of it starting. One doctor recalled in December 1996 that 'all hell broke loose and waiting times quadrupled'. The idea has never been tried again within the department. Within the department, members of medical and nursing staff perceived it as a 'disaster'. Former members of reengineering later regarded the pilot as a 'mistake'.

6.3   Chronology of reengineering the care process within A&E

March 1995. Emergency entry reengineering laboratory formed.

May 1995. Members of the emergency entry laboratory 'process-map' and 'baseline' patient activity in the A&E department.

June 1995. Reengineers report to the reengineering steering group that 'the major delay for the largest group of patients [walking wounded] is waiting for the doctor'. The A&E head of service announces to the Steering Group that a pilot will start in August to test two 'reengineering hypotheses' about nurses ordering X-rays and treating minor injuries. A&E doctors suggest to the Steering Group that waiting time in A&E is a 'multi-factoral' problem.

August 1995. Reengineers argue that the 'pilot' shows that nurses can order 70 per cent of X-rays for patients with minor injuries. Currently, seventeen out of an establishment of seventy-seven nurses are skilled to order X-rays and treat minor injuries at triage. At the Reengineering Steering Group, reengineers and A&E consultants disagree about reengineering targets for reducing waiting time in A&E.

October 1995. 'Process management' is created within the A&E/ orthopaedic and trauma directorate. The role of senior nurse in the directorate is replaced. The role of sister in A&E is to be replaced by the role of clinical manager within A&E.

November 1995. Single queue pilot in A&E is stopped within hours.

January 1996. The department has major problems recruiting and retaining nursing staff with 30 per cent of nursing posts vacant.

March 1996. A newly appointed patient process manager instigates a nurse recruitment drive.

June 1996. To facilitate nurses ordering X-rays and administering minor treatments nursing resource at triage has been increased since January.

September 1996. Six clinical managers have now been appointed. Four of the positions went to former A&E sisters. Some former sisters in A&E have been demoted.

December 1996. All nursing posts are filled. Three-quarters of nurses in the department are now trained to order X-rays and provide minor treatments at triage. Waiting times in the A&E department are not decreasing as reengineers anticipated and only a small number of minor injuries are treated by nurses. Managers in the department say that there needs to be an increase in the numbers of X-rays ordered by A&E nurses in triage. They want to: recruit more nurses; use nursing establishment in a more efficient way; improve sickness and turnover rates; alter nursing shift patterns in keeping with peak-times for demand; train more nurses to order X-rays; recruit extra D-grade nurses to enable more senior nurses to be located in triage. They are also hoping that a relaxation of the Patient Charter triage standard from five to fifteen minutes in 1997 will ease the pressure on nurses at triage and give more time to order X-rays and administer simple treatments.

January 1997. The number of nurses in triage has fallen in this month to help with the management of emergency admissions. The nursing resource at triage in this month is less than half the level of resource in June 1996.

April 1997. An extra 5.5 D-grade nurses are to be appointed.

May 1997. Alteration of nursing shift patterns within the department. Expected change in patient charter standards does not happen because of election and the change of government.

May 1997. Following a district audit report on A&E services a working group is established to develop minor treatment by nurses.

June 1997. The nursing resource at triage is higher than it has ever been since reengineering started. Three-quarters of working shifts had two triage nurses.

6.4 The impact of reengineering queue management in A&E

In terms of A&E we have not impacted on waiting times whatsoever. I think we have impacted on staff morale, training, development and education.

I think they are better informed, a better workforce, but in terms of what you would call key measures we have not impacted at all . . . we have nurses ordering X-rays and that has got to relieve the workload to the doctors and it does, but it has not impacted on wait-time for patients in A&E . . . (Former reengineer and directorate manager, November 1996)

6.4.1 *Waiting times*

Using data collected from managers within the A&E department in 1997, Table 6.1 reports waiting times in A&E using four measures. The column headed 'baseline (October 1994)' reports pre-reengineering performance. The third column notes 'reengineering target' (at August 1995). Performance figures up to and including the period of April–June 1997 are presented in a number of columns. 'Waiting times all patients, April–June 1997' includes patients with minor injuries. For the purposes of this case, waiting times for patients with minor injuries are also separated out. 'Best practice' over the period between 1995 and June 1997 is also recorded for both 'all patients' and 'minor injuries'.

Waiting times show that reengineering targets on all four measures were not met. There is a considerable shortfall between targets and performance on three out of the four indicators: time from entry to see the doctor; time from entry to start of treatment; and total time spent in A&E. A reengineering target was 85 per cent of patients to be seen by a doctor within 20 minutes of entering the A&E department. Data collected between April and June 1997 reported that only 13 per cent of patients attending the A&E department see a doctor in less than 30 minutes. The best performance on this measure occurred in the period January to March 1996 when 21.2 per cent of patients waited less than 30 minutes to see a doctor.

A second reengineering target was that 85 per cent of patients would start their treatment within one hour of entering the A&E department. Data measuring time from entry to start of treatment is not available from A&E PAS data. Managers believed that this measure is however 'patient-focused and important' and started to collect such data for walking wounded by occasional 'spot checks within the department'. The limited data available reported that 50 per cent of patients with minor injuries started treatment within an hour of entering the A&E department.

A third reengineering target was 85 per cent of patients attending the A&E department would have definitive treatment within 75 minutes

Table 6.1 Waiting times in A&E: reengineering targets and performance 1995–7

Measure	Baseline (Oct. 94)	Reengineering target (Aug. 95)	Waiting times all patients (Apr.–Jun. 97)	Waiting times all patients best practice	Waiting times minor injuries (Apr.–Jun. 97)	Waiting times minor injuries best practice
Initial assessment	94% in 5 mins	100% in 5 mins	96% in 5 mins	96% in 5 mins	See note 1	See note 1
Time from entry to see doctor	13% in < 20 mins	85% in < 20 mins	13% < 30 mins 20% < 45 mins 28% < 60 mins 54% < 120 mins 78% < 240 mins (See note 2)	21.2% < 30 mins 30.7% < 45 mins 39.7% < 60 mins 64.9% < 120 mins 79% < 240 mins (See note 2)	6% < 30 mins 25% < 45 mins 45% < 60 mins 81% < 120 mins 100% < 240 mins (See note 3)	16% < 30 mins 30% < 45 mins 69% < 60 mins 88% < 120 mins 100% < 240 mins (See note 3)
Time from entry to start of treatment	27% in < 60 mins	85% in < 60 mins	See note 3	See note 3	50% < 60 mins (See note 4)	72% < 60 mins (See note 4)
Total time in A+E	27% in < 75 mins	85% in < 75 mins	12.5% < 75 mins	12.5% < 75 mins	51% < 75 mins (See note 3)	73% < 75 mins (See note 3)

[1] Time to initial assessment is 'normally about 5% lower than times for all patients' (A&E manager, 1997).

[2] Data are taken from A&E PAS.

[3] Data are taken from A&E PAS. Data for walking wounded patients are not available on PAS system and have been collected from 'manual' spot checks by managers within the department.

[4] Data relating to measure of 'time from entry to start of treatment' is not available from A&E PAS data. Also 'staff rarely clearly document time to treatment'. Managers believe that this measure is however 'patient-focused and important'. Data for walking wounded is collected by 'spot checks within the department'.

of entering the department. Data show that only 12.5 per cent of patients spent a total time of less than 75 minutes in the A&E department.

Contributing to these performance figures for all patients are a set of performance figures for patients with minor injuries. Indeed reengineering targets set in 1995 assumed that speeding up the care for the large proportion of patients with minor injuries would have a positive knock-on effect on the waiting times for all patients attending A&E. The effect of reengineering the care process for patients with minor injuries did not materialize. Waiting times for minor injuries show that only a small proportion (6 per cent) saw a doctor in less than 30 minutes in the period April–June 1997; 50 per cent of walking wounded patients started their treatment within one hour. A similar proportion waited less than 75 minutes in the A&E department.

At June 1997, managers within the department conceded that in spite of nurses ordering X-rays and administering minor treatments there is 'no direct evidence that we have reduced overall waiting times' within the department. This is a major disappointment to managers, especially those former reengineers who went on to process management roles within the department and directorate. In December 1996, medical staff within A&E also expressed disappointment with reengineering, describing its impact as 'disappointing' and 'slight'.

Independent of this study, a survey of satisfaction amongst patients attending the A&E department at LRI with minor injuries between November 1995 and May 1997 concluded that reengineering did not result in measurable changes in patient satisfaction or reduce total time in A&E for patients attending with minor injuries. For patients attending LRI with minor injuries, mean time in A&E was 220 minutes in November/December 1995, 219 minutes in May 1997, and 215 minutes in May 1997. The proportion of patients attending LRI with a total visit time of less than 75 minutes remained at around 5 per cent for all three periods studied (Thomas et al. 1998).

6.4.2 *Explaining impact on waiting times and patient process*

After piloting in summer 1995, the practices of nurses ordering X-rays and administering simple treatments were slow to develop. Nurse shortages and nurse training requirements were major contributors to the slow pace of change since 1995. It took two years to develop the skills of a reasonable number of nurses in A&E to order X-rays and administer minor treatments. Between July 1995 and July 1997, 75 per cent of qualified nurses in the department were trained to order X-rays and perform simple treatments at triage. At June 1997, 56 per cent of walking wounded patients had X-rays and nurses at triage ordered 78 per cent of them. The idea of nurses administering minor treatments was relatively less developed in practice. At May 1997, 7.8 per cent of walking wounded patients received simple treatments at triage. The figure falls short of the speculation by reengineers that up to 20 per cent of patients could be treated without seeing the doctor. The single queue initiative never progressed beyond its pilot phase. What is the explanation of the slow progress of these initiatives?

The A&E department proved to be a difficult context in which to redesign patient processes. The rate and pace of change in this case is inextricably linked to reengineers' struggle to engender sufficient support for these changes amongst key clinical staff within the department. The process-based philosophy behind the change initiatives was seen to threaten both the established function of the A&E department in the broader context of the hospital and the established roles of doctors within the department. Reengineering initiatives were further undermined by resource shortages and the physical limitations of the A&E department.

A variety of conditions in and around the A&E department shaped the possibilities and progress of reengineering interventions in the A&E department over the period. Since the 1970s, the department grew into one of the largest A&E departments in the UK. With growth, it is perceived to have acquired status, power, and a strategic position in the hospital. Over the same period pressure on the performance of the department increased. This pressure became more public in the 1990s context of contracting and patient charter standards. Reengineering represented further pressure upon A&E, from outside the department, to perform better.

Against a background of severe nurse recruitment and retention problems, limited physical space, problems of patient prioritization, and an established sense of purpose amongst consultants, 'external' pressures on performance were received with some scepticism by A&E doctors and staff within the department. Reengineering was also subject to scepticism amongst A&E staff who regarded it as further 'interference' in the operation department from 'outside' the department. Increasing service demand throughout the period of reengineering allied to ongoing nurse staffing problems and nursing reorganization further reduced the receptivity of senior staff to reengineering-inspired change. The structural design of the department also proved incapable of supporting reengineering visions for change.

In these conditions, it was imperative that reengineers approached change in ways that generated support amongst clinical staff. However, reengineering proved to be controversial in the department. Both former reengineers and managers within the department recognize a failure to establish 'ownership' of patient process redesign within A&E. A&E doctors charged reengineers with being limited by a desire to achieve cost savings over radical service improvement and not being focused on core problems of the department.

I went to many, many meetings. It quickly unfolded that those things that could improve the service but would cost money were rapidly ditched, but the possibility of cutting down on nursing sisters was picked up very quickly . . . I am disappointed after initially being excited by the idea of looking at the whole concept of an emergency process . . . it is a wasted opportunity. We wasted time looking at an ideal service. 6–9 months down the road, it became obvious that the better objectives that were identified were not going to be taken on. (A&E doctor, December 1996)

I went along [to reengineering meetings] looking for sustainable change, not short-term paper exercises . . . I thought the concept of reengineering was to look at the process, identify that part of the process that was driving the problem . . . We had two problems with our waiting times, patients on trolleys and patients in E-bay [walking wounded]. 20 per cent of our work is on trolleys but they are the ones that tie up resources and make life a misery. In E-bay the doctors can fly through. The whole of reengineering focused on E-bay to start with. In E-bay you can have nurses ordering X-rays, it is a very quick turnover of patients, it is measurable. It was a paper exercise. It was always an easy target . . . but trolleys is different. The only way to improve it is to get more trolleys, more doctors, quicker investigations, more blood-gas analysers, and more beds. There is no other way. Yet, they did not start with that. I wanted them to go and hit the trolley bays and go and use treatment time and trolley time as markers of success. They said 'it was too difficult to start with'. They said 'it is better to start with something tangible which will give you a quick result'. They lost credibility with me straight away. I thought this is a paper exercise . . . . It was not radical enough . . . . Initially we thought it was a great thing, that we were going to change things and make things better. Any consultant does not want a six-hour wait in his department but it proved to be neither well thought out or radical enough. (A&E doctor, December 1996)

Reengineering was also undermined by claims that it was led not by A&E specialists but by reengineers without adequate experience and understanding of A&E services.

Though we got involved in it and made suggestions the overriding thing was that it was a group of people making decisions who were apart from A&E . . .

Our suggestions were not taken seriously because I always thought that they were not what they wanted. For example, we said at the beginning that we needed six more SHOs, more nurses and more space. They said we did not need that, we needed to do different things, like, single queue. (A&E doctor, December 1996)

I felt when we started reengineering, and I still believe that there is a potential to improve the system. The potential is there, because it allows us to think where the problems are and it allows us to look at the problem with a fresh look. What is essential is that it should be looked at by the people who work in that particular part of the hospital on that specialty . . . the ideal thing would be to let the medical staff lead the process of change and give them full authority, full commitment and responsibility. The day when non-specialist people who have no knowledge of that particular area or specialty come and tell you what to do the whole thing will collapse. (A&E doctor, December 1996)

. . . Someone who has never done a job has a different concept of what happens. A lot of those reengineering were people who had never worked in A&E. It seems daft. You would have thought that if you want someone to change things in a department you would at least get, perhaps leading it, someone from that department. (A&E clinician, September 1997)

Several staff within the departments were highly critical of a reengineering 'rush to pilot'. There was also talk of reengineering creating 'pilot fatigue' within the department.

the reason single queue pathway failed was that it was done too soon and not resourced. It was not planned or resourced . . . There was so many pilots going on that we had pilot fatigue. (A&E doctor, December 1996)

They [reengineering] failed hopelessly because it was not paced well. Quick hits and all this were thrown at us. I found that very insulting to come in here and talk about 'quick hits'. (A&E doctor, December 1996)

. . . there was some hyper motivation. People who came from outside A&E to implement changes were rather over-enthusiastic occasionally. (A&E nurse, August 1997)

Reengineering was also criticized for promoting an image of A&E doctors as resistant to change.

[about the single queue pilot] The impression came through to us that we were being resistant. That made me mad. We were not being resistant. We were proved right in the end . . . I think that was very unfair in that this was used as a stick to beat us, to make the change, bad change. They gave the impression that a lot of time had been put in and here we were being bad people. For it to be interpreted as going wrong because of us makes me mad because it is quite the opposite. We had gone along and tried to influence it, to make the change successful and it was not allowed . . . . Single queue was not 'supervised neglect'. (A&E doctor, December 1996)

Reengineering was not well received by nurses either.

reengineering has not been the most popular thing in A&E. The nurses want the change but are not happy with the word reengineering . . . I am sure if the programme had been called the patient care improvement programme, there would not have been the same response. (Department manager, March 1996)

Nursing staff were reportedly distracted and threatened by changes to the nursing structure introduced at the same time as reengineering.

we are short of people and people are distracted by the fact that they have to reapply for their jobs and that some people may not even have jobs at the end of the day. (Reengineer, November 1995)

Former reengineers acknowledged that 'mistakes' were made in piloting some initiatives.

It [single queue] was not piloted at a good time. They were low on staff, low on morale. Non-qualified nurses were being introduced which was contentious, and it did not have the backing of people. It was very stressful on the nurse. The nurse was not experienced enough to be doing that job even though they were quite an experienced A&E person. As far as the times went, the E-bay patients went down from the average, so they were actually being seen faster, but the waiting times of the trolley patients went up. Staff had a problem with that. Staff said 'we should not be delaying people on trolleys as they are likely to be more poorly'. And to a certain extent, they are right. The nurses were getting uptight because the trolley patients were waiting . . . we could still have better utilization of the doctors but I am not now convinced single queue is the way forward. (Reengineer, March 1996)

However, criticisms of the approach to this change intervention in A&E are countered by reengineers' and managers' claims of a lack of will to change amongst doctors in the A&E department. It is also said that they were resistant to influence from people outside the department and unwilling to change working practices. Specifically, A&E doctors are criticized as being unwilling to recognize the importance of walking wounded patients relative to other patients attending A&E such as those more seriously injured.

A&E said you are not looking at the critical patients. We said, 'we are looking at the largest volume of patients'. By critical they meant the most poorly. As far as A&E are concerned, the patients in resuscitation never wait. The patients on trolleys should not wait and E-bay patients [walking wounded] can wait as long as they like. These are very much the second-class citizens because they will not deteriorate if they do wait. So, it is probably most sensible that if anyone has to wait it should be them. But what we are trying to say is 'they should not have to wait that long anyway'. It is a culture that A&E should be resuscitation . . . we are trying to say, 'these are also very important people that are here legitimately and we are not offering them a very good service'. (Department manager, November 1995)

The waiting times are still an issue because we have not got over the culture that waiting times matter with some people. (Directorate manager, May 1997)

the attitude [of the A&E consultants] is 'we have built this department up since the year dot and we do not see how anybody who has never worked in this department can come in from outside and tell us how it should work. You do not understand' . . . this is directed at us all [members of reengineering]. (Directorate manager, November 1996)

It has been suggested outside and inside the department that A&E consultants have resisted changes to established patterns of work within the department:

They perceive that reengineering is taking everything out of A&E. (Reengineer, November 1995)

they [A&E doctors] did restrict them [nurse-ordered X-rays] sufficiently to know that it was not going to have huge impacts. The nurses would like to X-ray above the elbow, and above the knee . . . You would only ever be looking at minor injuries but you would then be getting into the realms of the nurse making a diagnosis. That is where the threat comes in. We have had nurse practitioner schemes in the past where a handful of nurses go off and do very superior training and they were quashed when they came back. They were not getting the supervision they needed, in the skills to get them to perform properly. (A&E nurse, September 1997)

All of these things affect nurses [nurses ordering X-rays, providing simple treatments, and single queue management]. We are asking doctors to do something different and every time we have approached anything that has been the doctors' domain it has been much harder . . . (Directorate manager, October 1996)

The reengineering philosophy and associated initiatives did indeed challenge the established role of the A&E department within the hospital. Statements by a reengineer and a doctor in the A&E department illustrate contrasting 'process' and 'functional' views of A&E services held by key actors within the change process.

We are not trying to achieve anything for the area of A&E. We are trying to achieve something for emergency entry. A&E is a department along the emergency entry process ... the main aim [for patients admitted to A&E] has been about getting them [patients] from A to B in the quickest possible time for them to reach a [clinical] outcome ... the patients' charter has driven that as well [as reengineering] because it has made us look at how patients flow through the department and why there are delays ... (Senior reengineer, September 1995)

... there was some lack of understanding [by reengineering]. A&E is a specialty in its own right ... A&E is very important and has a vital role to play in the hospital structure and it should be regarded as a separate specialty. (A&E doctor, December 1996)

Ultimately process ambitions were further undermined by shortage of resources and the structural design of the department. Former reengineers and managers in the department later accepted that nurses in the department were both insufficient in number and underskilled to take on responsibilities envisaged by reengineers in the summer of 1995. There was insufficient staffing resource to fully operate processes whereby nurses ordered X-rays and administered minor treatments. Latterly they conceded earlier arguments put forward by A&E doctors that nursing resources in A&E were inadequate to fully operate systems of nurses ordering X-rays and administering minor treatments.

[nurses ordering effects and providing minor treatments] is having some effect on the workload of doctors. It will not realize its fullest effect until we have the required number of staff at the front door in triage and the structure of the department has changed ... it requires staffing, it requires space and it requires restructuring of the department. (A&E consultant, December 1996)

The waiting time has gone down but not to the extent we had hoped for. That is about resources. If you want to introduce this system of nurses ordering X-rays and carrying out treatments at its fullest, it will require more staff ... it will not have its fullest effect until we have the required number of nursing staff available and the structure of the department is changed. (A&E clinician, December 1996)

Former reengineers and managers in the department increasingly accepted A&E doctors' concern about the resources, physical design, and size of the A&E department. During 1997 managers in the department took action in respect of investing in nursing staff and staff training to increase both the number of X-rays ordered by A&E nurses in triage and the administering of minor treatments by nurses. They also accepted the physical design of the A&E department to be a major impediment to any radical change to 'patient flows' around the department. The design of the department dates back to the late 1970s. Management within the directorate and A&E doctors prepared a major capital development plan to senior management within the Trust for the redesign of the A&E department.

To conclude the case, reengineering in respect of the care of patients with minor injuries can be seen as having had limited impact. Given the size, power base, and visibility of the A&E department this failure to achieve high impact is highly significant for the overall effect of the reengineering programme. This case study and the case study of fractured neck of femur reported later on in this chapter are both characterized by conflict between process and functional views of organizing. The functional principle remained largely dominant, supported as it was by most clinical and nursing staff. The reengineers were not able to win over a critical mass of clinical and nursing staff, nor to impose their process-based way of thinking on them.

In this case study reengineers sought to reduce waiting times by quickening treatment processes for patients with minor injuries. The language of emergency entry process as well as objectives and changes introduced to improve 'queue management' reveal reengineers' concept of the purpose and work of the A&E department to be fundamentally different to that held by clinical staff within A&E, especially the doctors and consultants. The lack of ownership from many nursing staff is an additional feature of the case. In spite of the promise of role expansion reengineering coincided with a review of traditional nursing structures and was seen as a further unsettling force in its own right.

In practice, A&E doctors effectively defended their concept of A&E as a specialty in its own right and their control over patient processes within the confines of the A&E department. Unlike the case of orthopaedics, reengineers never gained the trust and confidence of staff within A&E, and their projects and plans were subsequently undermined by a mix of inadequate change management and clinical resources. They were seen as outsiders who had little understanding of the 'real' world and work of the A&E department. It quickly became apparent that major change depended on wider and longer-term factors, such as changing the physical plant and dealing with major nursing shortages. In addition, some of the core change management tools adopted by reengineers, such as 'quick hits' and 'pilots', encountered considerable resistance from within the department.

6.5   Reengineering the process of care for patients admitted to LRI with a fractured neck of femur

6.5.1   *Introduction*

This case study reports a change intervention designed to reengineer the process of care for patients admitted to LRI with a fractured neck of femur. The injury is commonly described as a hip fracture. At the time of study patients admitted with a fractured neck of femur comprised approximately 20 per cent of emergency orthopaedic admissions. The formal objectives of the intervention were to improve the quality of care for patients by quickening referral from the A&E department to an orthopaedic specialist and reducing length of stay in line with national 'best practice' guidelines. Reengineering the process of care for patients admitted with a fractured neck of femur commenced during the summer of 1995. It took place in the context of a development of a new strategy for trauma services developed jointly by local purchasers and providers.

Orthopaedics faced long-standing problems in relation to coping with increased demands upon the service. Effective solutions to these problems were welcomed by clinicians. However, a mixed picture of the impact of the intervention is presented in this case. On the one hand, the formal objectives set by reengineers did not materialize and significant improvement in the quality of care in respect of admission times and length of stay cannot be demonstrated. On the other hand, changes made to the patient process support an argument that reengineering contributed to a 'culture of improvement' in orthopaedic services inspired by a coalition of reengineers and orthopaedic consultants (Haworth 1997).

Explanation of a failure to deliver demonstrable improvement to the care process in the time of this study takes account of unrealistic reengineering targets and the scope and complexity of the patient process being reengineered. Even a strong coalition between reengineers and orthopaedic doctors is shown to be limited in its ability to direct change beyond the specialty of orthopaedics and its associated ward areas. A feature of the case is how resource shortages and jurisdictional conflicts inside and outside the hospital regulated the rate and pace of change. Contests for control of work processes and resources between the A&E department, operating theatres, and the specialty of orthopaedics reveal an unresolved tension between process and functional models of organizing.

6.5.2   *Context and recent history of orthopaedic services at LRI*

At the outset of reengineering orthopaedic services were organized within the A&E and orthopaedic trauma directorate. In 1995, an orthopaedic consultant with a special interest in trauma management replaced an A&E consultant as clinical director. The administrative structure of the directorate also changed in late 1995 to introduce the philosophy of 'process management' at the expense of 'functional management'. An 'emergency entry patient process director' was appointed alongside the clinical director with three 'patient process managers', each with management responsibility for aspects of the care process within A&E and orthopaedics. All four occupants of the process management positions were from a nursing background. All four were former members of the emergency entry reengineering laboratory. These were senior roles and they replaced established 'functional management' roles such as business manager and senior nurse. At the time, the business manager post was vacant and the role of senior nurse as one of a triumvirate managing the directorate disappeared as part of a reorganization of nursing services across the Trust.

All trauma orthopaedic care was provided at Leicester Royal Infirmary with elective orthopaedic care provided at two neighbouring acute NHS Trusts. Demand for orthopaedic services at LRI was increasing. There was a 13 per cent increase in orthopaedic admissions between 1993/4 and 1996/7. Over the same period, emergency admissions increased by 11 per cent. The number of patients admitted with a fractured neck of femur was approximately 800 patients per year. As an aspect of trauma orthopaedics, care for patients with a fractured neck of femur must be seen in the context of overall demand and development of trauma orthopaedic services within Leicestershire since 1995. The period of reengineering within LRI ran in parallel with the development of a Leicestershire orthopaedic trauma service strategy.

A review of services in 1994 suggested that waiting list initiatives and governmental pressure over waiting times during the 1990s had contributed to a concentration of resources on elective orthopaedic care and routine surgery at the expense of trauma orthopaedics. The trauma strategy was an attempt to address serious deficiencies in trauma orthopaedics over a three-year period. It was recognized in 1995 that more orthopaedic trauma sessions were needed and senior orthopaedic appointments would need to be made to support the additional sessions. During 1997 and 1998, the numbers of consultant posts increased from eight to twelve and a professor of orthopaedic trauma was appointed. At the time of final data collection one consultant post was vacant.

At the outset of the study, practical effects of the relatively poorer resourcing of trauma orthopaedic care within the locality were apparent to medical and nursing staff. In the face of increasing demand for the service, consultant and nursing staff morale were perceived as low. Ward organization was considered inappropriate to meet increased demand for care. During the period of study this changed with both the clinical director and the head of orthopaedic services sharing a 'special interest' in improving the practice of trauma orthopaedics with the locality.

Not that reengineering was perceived as a panacea to these ills. In 1994, reengineering work aimed at 'scheduling' the fracture clinic had not whetted the appetite of staff for further reengineering-style change. At the outset of the change initiative, the vast majority of medical and nursing staff was sceptical about reengineering. However, some orthopaedic consultants, including the then new clinical director and head of orthopaedic services at LRI were looking to change a 'desperate situation'. Their particular interest in improving trauma service and their desire that further reengineering work in the specialty of orthopaedics should not recreate the 'ill-feeling amongst staff' generated by work in the fracture clinic contributed to the development of a dialogue between orthopaedic consultants, nursing staff, and members of the emergency entry reengineering laboratory.

6.5.3 *Redesigning the process for patients with a fractured neck of femur*

Objectives. The majority of patients admitted to LRI with a fractured neck of femur are admitted via the Accident and Emergency department. Two objectives for this intervention formally recorded with the Reengineering Programme Steering Group in November 1995 were to reduce length of stay in hospital to less than 20 days for 95 per cent of patients by March 1998. Also, to improve the quality of care by reducing the time between referral from A&E to an orthopaedic ward from an average of nearly three hours to 40 minutes of admission.

Patient process redesign. Redesign of the care process for patients with a fractured neck of femur was informed by both reengineers' aspiration to reengineer emergency entry processes and orthopaedic consultants' wish to improve the care process for the population of musculo-skeletal patients treated at LRI. Collaboration was evident between members of the emergency entry reengineering laboratory, some orthopaedic consultants, and ward staff. Changes to the care process, both proposed and effected involved changing the way patients are: assessed in the Accident and Emergency department; admitted to the ward and assessed on the ward; rehabilitated and discharged from the hospital. A brief chronological overview of the change intervention is included below indicating an unfolding array of initiatives and ideas associated with the intervention. In keeping with an intervention that has proved to be more incremental and iterative than radical and transformatory, the ideas are shown neither to have all emerged at the same time nor been implemented at the same time or with the same degree of impact.

Arrival in A&E to admission on to the ward, nurses ordering X-rays, assessment of X-rays on the ward. In the summer of 1995, reengineers produced data suggesting that the average time spent in the Accident & Emergency department by patients admitted with a fractured neck of femur was 2 hours and 50 minutes. Greatest 'delays' were attributed to patients having to wait to see an A&E doctor for X-rays to be requested and subsequently assessed. In September 1995, a member of the emergency entry reengineering laboratory described the 'vision' of change in the following way:

The vision is to get the patient through the A&E department to the orthopaedic ward area quickly—ideally 35–40 minutes. This would be achieved by removing the A&E doctor from the process. We think we could get them to an orthopaedic doctor on the ward quicker than the time it would take them to see an A&E doctor . . . We think we could do this by crossing out certain steps in the process. (Reengineer, September 1995)

In the vision of a reengineered process for patients admitted with isolated fractured neck of femur, A&E doctors would be replaced by: A&E nurses trained to order X-rays; radiographers assessing X-rays (guided by medical protocol); and orthopaedic doctors admitting patients to the ward. The vision has been partly implemented. The idea of nurses ordering X-rays for patients admitted with a fractured neck of femur was first piloted in November 1995. By July 1997, over 60 per cent of all patients admitted with a fractured neck of femur had their X-ray requested by A&E nursing staff. However, the idea that radiographers assess X-rays and then refer the patient to an orthopaedic specialist on the ward was not implemented. In August 1997, nearly two years after the idea was first identified, it was reported that in principle doctors in Accident and Emergency had finally agreed that subject to the development of medical protocols, patients admitted with an isolated fractured neck of femur could be transferred directly to an orthopaedic ward after X-ray. However, at March 1998, the process was still not happening. In December 1996, a doctor in the Accident and Emergency department had explained concerns about the idea:

If the patient has an isolated fractured neck of femur and that is the only injury they have, you are maybe on fairly safe ground . . . You do not know what is going on with that patient until you have had a look at them from top to bottom . . . What I would not want the patient to do is, without being assessed, sit in an X-ray queue for an hour gradually dying from a head injury. The patient must be assessed first, however brief that may be . . .

An alternative view of an orthopaedic consultant in December 1996 was that:

. . . we have resistance to this within the A&E department from a variety of staff. I think that is because of a fear of work being taken away . . . A&E is genuinely frightened and has not a clear view of what the role of an A&E department is in a changed world. They say, 'this is not true' of course. They perhaps need to be brought on with the ideas, and need to think more of where A&E should be going. Rather than just going back to how it was they should be looking at where it is going . . . The argument is that, 'someone is going to be seen by a nurse, seen by a radiographer, sent to the ward and have a cardiac arrest in the lift'. It is about risk management. The initial triage nurse is perfectly capable of assessing whether a patient is sick, or like most of our fractured neck of femurs not desperately sick and much better off being whisked to a bed on the ward straight away.

Admission and assessment on the ward: ward reconfiguration, theatre scheduling, auto-screening, collaborative notes, discharge planning. Following a pilot in October 1995, four orthopaedic wards were reconfigured into an acute dependent area and a rehabilitation area. Nurse staffing on orthopaedic wards was reorganized during 1995 and 1996 as the concept of team-based nursing on orthopaedic wards was introduced at the expense of 'functional' ward management. The traditional structure of four orthopaedic wards headed by a ward sister was perceived by process managers to prevent coordination of the patient care process both in terms of acute care and rehabilitation care. Subsequently, four wards were divided into an acute area and a rehabilitation area. At ward level, four acute nursing teams and four rehabilitation nursing teams were formed with each team able to access to multi-professional inputs by for example, occupational therapists and physiotherapists. Each team was linked to three orthopaedic consultants and headed by a nurse acting as 'team leader'. Collectively, the team leaders shared operational management responsibilities, for example, coordinating the flow of patients between the acute and rehabilitation areas, staffing, recruitment, and bed allocation.

National guidelines suggested that patients admitted with a fractured neck of femur need to be operated on within 48 hours, depending on their physical condition. In 1997, an internal report identified that significant numbers of patients admitted to LRI with fractured neck of femur waited over 48 hours for their operation. A number of issues impeded reengineers' and managers' desire to change the process of scheduling patient operations. Until the appointment of additional consultants and the allocation of extra operating sessions during 1997 and 1998, operating within 48 hours was seen as hampered by a lack of available theatre time. In addition, managers and nursing staff within the orthopaedic and trauma directorate commented on surgeons' lack of faith in a newly introduced computerized way of scheduling operations and preference to keep their own private schedule of operating lists in a 'blue book' that is passed around the doctors in the department. In February 1998, a manager within the directorate commented:

With the increase in the number of consultants and theatre sessions a greater number of patients get to theatre within their clinical need time. But theatre scheduling is not happening by computerization. Computerization has fallen by the wayside. The difficulty has been that we have not been able to prove that our system is better than the blue book. We still have the blue book but what is a huge step forward made in the last few months is that the team leaders are now liaising with doctors in terms of what is in the blue book and how admissions are prioritized. It is still a manual system but it is a more open manual system now with collaboration between medical and nursing staff that was not there before.

Changes were made to hasten assessment of patients' rehabilitation needs. A process of auto-screening was designed and piloted to automatically start the process of preparing for patient rehabilitation at the point of patient admission to the ward. Pre-reengineering, rehabilitation referrals were made after patients had had their operation. Though auto-screening proved to be a temporary innovation developed at the outset of reengineering it is perceived to have been a catalyst to assessing the level of therapeutic resources within the ward area and changing working patterns of therapists. Patients are now automatically referred to a physiotherapist on admission. Also, after June 1997,

patients were automatically being screened by an occupational therapist on their admission to the ward.

Collaborative notes and care plans intended to aid communication,
discharge planning, and multi-disciplinary team working were also
introduced. Post-reengineering, a system of integrated collaborative
notes was established at the point of patient admission on to the ward.
The notes contain a patient's social needs assessment, occupational
therapy needs assessment, nursing needs assessment, and physiotherapy needs assessment. The aim was to produce an integrated care plan
for the patient.

Pre-reengineering, each of the professionals involved in the care
process collected their own notes. It is widely viewed that collaborative
notes have enabled a group approach to be taken to planning the care
for each patient. Informed by the experience in orthopaedics the
practice of collaborative notes was being considered Trust-wide.

High lengths of stay were in part attributed to weaknesses in the
process of discharge planning. Mindful of national best practice length
of stay of fifteen days a rehabilitation coordinator was appointed in
May 1996 to improve patient rehabilitation and discharge. This
appointment helped to establish the concept of identifying patients'
discharge dates early in the care process. Discharge dates were increasingly monitored in order to identify if and why patients do not meet the
planned discharge date. Discharge dates were reviewed weekly at
multi-disciplinary team meetings with team leaders in the acute area
responsible for ensuring teams set discharge dates at the point when
patients are admitted. Data collected by orthopaedic staff revealed that
in October 1997 planned discharge dates were set for 60 per cent of
patients.

A number of factors were viewed to impede the process of discharging patients from hospital. One impediment was a weakness in the
process of discharge planning in the hospital. A second impediment
was perceived to be needs assessment by social services. A third
impediment was said to be an inadequate interface with social services
and alleged slowness of response by social services in providing social
care packages for patients once they have left hospital.

6.5.4   *Chronological overview of a reengineering intervention*

1994. A partnership of purchasers and providers develop an orthopaedic
trauma strategy for the county.

April 1995. Reengineers identify five steps within a 'high-level emergency entry process': referral; assessment; diagnosis; treatment; and disposal.

May 1995. Reengineers identify 'opportunities' to improve the flow of patients admitted through A&E into the hospital.

June 1995. Orthopaedic surgeons and reengineers 'process-map' the care process for patients admitted with musculo-skeletal injuries.

October 1995. The team leader of the emergency entry laboratory is appointed 'patient process director' within the A&E/orthopaedic and trauma directorate.

November 1995. The concept of nurses in A&E ordering X-rays for patients admitted with a fractured neck of femur is piloted.

December 1995. Within the orthopaedic and trauma directorate it is believed senior management in the hospital must decide who manages the resource called operating theatres.

May 1996. A rehabilitation coordinator is appointed. Team leader roles are created in nursing. A 'process link group' is created bringing together on a weekly basis team leaders on the wards, therapy professions involved in the care process, and staff from operating theatres.

October 1996. Radiologists and doctors have agreed to pilot and audit nurse-ordered post-operative X-rays, using protocols, in the hope that it will speed up the X-ray process and mobilization of the patient after operation.

November 1996. There is a 'winter beds crisis looming' and a conflict emerging between managing the hospital's emergency work and its elective work. Managers in the orthopaedic directorate acknowledge that it could take another two to three years to reduce length of stay in line with original targets.

April 1997. An audit service report about services for older people with fractured neck of femur at LRI concludes that: 'reengineering work has created a culture of improvement'. Its recommendations include better communication between the A&E department and orthopaedic wards about admissions.

May 1997. Nurses ordering post-op X-rays are judged successful. All the consultants have agreed that all patients who are admitted will have a planned discharge date. From June monitoring of discharge practice for each patient will begin.

October 1997. The first of three additional orthopaedic consultants appointed as a consequence of the trauma strategy takes up post. Additional operating theatre time accompanies the appointment.

6.5.5 *The impact of reengineering the care process for patients admitted with a fractured neck of femur*

Assessment of the impact of this intervention must take account of objectives stated as reengineering deliverables in November 1995. At March 1998, objectives set by reengineers in 1995 had not materialized. The changes described previously have apparently not impacted significantly upon the time of admission onto a ward and length of patient stay in hospital. A study of the impact of reengineering on the care of patients admitted to LRI with a fractured neck of femur, aged 65 and over, found that between 1995 and 1997 there was a reduction in the time taken to X-ray patients after arrival at the A&E department. However, there was no overall improvement in the time taken to transfer a patient to an orthopaedic ward (Bowns et al. 1998). Similarly, a district audit report in 1997 concluded that admission times at LRI on average far exceeded the guidelines of the Royal College of Physicians and the Trust's own target of forty minutes (Haworth 1997).

Length of patient stay was not reduced as anticipated. Initially, reengineers hoped to reduce length of stay for 95 per cent of patients to 20 days. In 1997, the target was further revised, in line with national best practice, to discharge 80 per cent of patients from hospital in 15 days or less. Evidence suggests these objectives were not met. Data suggest that patients aged under 70, without complications, comprised only 9 per cent of cases. The average length of stay for this group of patients for the four years between 1993 and 1997 was below 15 days. For the remaining majority of patients, average length of stay fluctuated slightly from 24.4 days in 1995 to 24 days in 1996 and 1997 (Bowns et al. 1998). In 1997 and 1998 managers and orthopaedic consultants expressed a view that the objectives set by reengineers were unrealistic and that it may be only realistic to expect such short lengths of stay for the small proportion of patients without complications.

To restrict assessment of impact to these measures would ignore the view of the District Audit Service that reengineering has contributed to the development of a culture of improvement in orthopaedic care (Haworth 1997). In addition to the trauma strategy, ongoing redesign of the care process and improved communication between staff involved in the care process created conditions conducive to further performance improvement in the future. This study observed a number of changes having been made to the process of care for patients with a fractured neck of femur. Out of the array of ideas first piloted in the summer of 1995 a number became routine practice by a multi-disciplinary team of individuals, for example, nurse-ordered X-rays, collaborative patient notes, dedicated rehabilitation care. Some changes to the care process were still bedding in, for example, discharge planning. Other changes were in their infancy, for example, theatre scheduling and patient admission direct to the ward. However, it is an indicator of the culture of improvement that a change vision first developed in 1995 was still being refined and implemented some three years later.

Much of the dynamic for ongoing improvement lies in sustained collaboration between managers and orthopaedic consultants and improved working amongst a range of clinical staff involved in orthopaedic care. A whole range of new attitudes, practices, and lines of communication developed between 1995 and 1997. Reflecting upon relations amongst orthopaedic consultants, an orthopaedic consultant commented in December 1996:

We have changed to become a closer-knit group, working together in the interests of the patient . . . Now do not for a minute think we all speak with one voice, but all of us feel we are part of a group who can bring change forward.

Some of the work practices and routines of doctors have been subject to change and influence of other staff. Responsibility for patient X-rays showed some sign of shifting, albeit slowly from Accident and Emergency doctors to nurses and orthopaedic specialists. Orthopaedic doctors and therapy professionals started to operate a system of integrated notes. Theatre scheduling promises to extend processes of prioritization beyond the decision-making of individual consultants.

Team-based nursing was a new development on the wards. Learning about the team-based working on orthopaedic wards was being transferred across the Trust. Therapy professions were brought into the change process and operated changed working practices. Improved communication between the Accident and Emergency department and the acute orthopaedic ward areas developed. As part of the attempt to improve the speed of patient admission through the Accident and Emergency department, clinical managers in A&E notify the ward that a patient with a suspected fractured neck of femur has been admitted and will require a bed on the ward.

A multi-disciplinary group of individuals involved in orthopaedic care processes called the 'process-link group' was formed to meet once a week. Managers, nurses, and therapists working on orthopaedic wards attend the group with representatives from the Accident and Emergency department and operating theatres. The group is a forum that discusses and seeks to resolve problems identified in the care process across professional and functional boundaries. The group developed a performance measurement and management function as it became accepted practice that members of the group report the performance of the process for which they are responsible. For example, physiotherapists and occupational therapists report on a monthly basis the time it takes them to respond to the patients' needs for assessment.

A number of factors are relevant to explaining how a change intervention has simultaneously contributed to a culture of improvement yet failed to realize reengineering objectives set in 1995. On the one hand, change was facilitated by a coalition of reengineers and orthopaedic consultants. This coalition subsequently grew to embrace other professionals in the care process. On the other hand, reengineers underestimated the scope and complexity of the patient process being redesigned.

6.5.5.1   *A coalition for change*

Changes to patient processes and working practices observed above are rooted in a partnership between reengineers and orthopaedic doctors. Orthopaedic specialists participated in the change process from the outset. A senior member of the reengineering team commented on the participation of orthopaedic specialists in the change programme:

. . . I think they were so desperate with the situation which they found themselves in, they were just keen for someone to listen to them and then say 'OK let us try this or that' . . . they are one group of medical staff in this hospital who have subjected themselves to change, i.e. total change from everything they do from the patient entering hospital, to the patient staying to the patient going . . . if you asked them 'why they allowed themselves to be subjected to this'? I think they will say that 'things were so bad it could not get any worse, and I would say that somebody gave time to them and they dedicated time back. So it was reciprocal, giving and taking, and the fact that people came up with ideas that we tried and implemented. (Reengineer, November 1996)

A senior consultant confirmed that

the process of consultation evolved partly because of our dissatisfaction with the initial fracture clinic project and our willingness to become involved.

We were all involved to varying degrees with the consultative process because we were desperate for change. We were so unhappy with the pre-existing situation that we were desperate for change and we were prepared to experiment with new ideas. (Orthopaedic consultant, December 1996)

Analysis of the situation facing the specialty before reengineering suggests that there existed a momentum for change within the specialty. The development of a trauma strategy for the district during 1995 symbolized a new willingness amongst purchasers and providers across the district to address historical underinvestment in trauma management. Furthermore, within the body of orthopaedic consultants there were willing leaders of change in trauma services. In 1995, one of the champions of trauma services was appointed clinical director of the orthopaedic and trauma directorate with LRI. This individual took on the post with a clear change agenda: 'there was a job that needed to be done. The Trauma service needed to be sorted out and I felt that I could do it' (clinical director, December 1996).

Reengineers were effective in tapping and mobilizing receptivity to change amongst orthopaedic doctors in ways that did not alienate the doctors. For instance, orthopaedic consultants do not appear to have had the same fears about 'ownership' of the change process as the A&E consultants had in the case study of minor injuries. An orthopaedic doctor commented that 'there was wide consultation within our directorate. It was very much a consultative process rather than reengineering being done to us' (orthopaedic consultant, December 1996).

Thereafter the process of change represented a fusion of a clinical agenda with a reengineering agenda. For clinicians, reengineering presented an opportunity to accelerate the changes envisaged in the trauma strategy.

I was not charged to deliver the reengineering programme and did not see myself as doing that. But when I became clinical director I had my own agenda of change, which actually fitted in with the concept of reengineering. I was involved in reengineering before I became clinical director . . . reengineering was a big opportunity. If reengineering had not happened I think things would have developed with the change in directorate management anyway but I do not think it would have developed quite so quickly . . . reengineering provided an opportunity at the right time with the right group of people who wanted it. (Clinical director, December 1996)

Reengineers provided the consultants with resources to accelerate the pace of service change such as change project management, ideas, information, and a change methodology. In turn, clinicians provided vital legitimacy to reengineers' use of methodologies and ideas to change patient processes. Three aspects of the reengineering methodology stand out as important to the change process in this case. First, 'baselining' activity by reengineers produced 'facts' about patient activity on which the case for change has been built. Second, 'process-mapping' enabled reengineers and doctors to analyse and understand current care practice and develop a vision of change. It also provided an opportunity to identify the people and roles critical to the process being reengineered. Having identified people and resources critical to the care process, those responsible for organizing and leading change were able to identify individuals who needed to be drawn into the change process. Third, 'piloting' allowed changes to patient processes to be introduced.

we find piloting a very useful way of bringing in the change programme. Often people do not realize that the pilot has occurred. There is no real change in their perception of the way patients are managed. Therefore you can go back to people and say 'well we have done this for a month and there has not been a problem, so should this continue' . . . piloting is critical. If you move forward with a pilot that works, people do accept it. (Orthopaedic doctor, March 1997)

A feature of the change process in this case is the coalition of people acting for change. The intervention was not dependent on a single partnership of a reengineer and clinical champion, as displayed initially in the case of ENT reported in this chapter. The presence of a corpus of people working for change is critical to explaining the sustained effort for change over the period of the case. The coalition initially emerged in mid-1995, and involved members of the reengineering emergency entry laboratory and some orthopaedic consultants. Later, the strength of the partnership was further reinforced by the appointment of a reengineer from the emergency entry laboratory to the senior post of patient process director for the orthopaedic and trauma directorate. Coinciding with the appointment of the clinical director, this appointment served to embed within the hospital structure of organizational and managerial roles a change management partnership that had emerged over the previous months.

we are partners, of equal weight and equal responsibility. I am not her clinical director; she is not my business manager. We are two people working together within the directorate. (Clinical director, December 1996)

From the middle of 1995, the team functioned to bring together various parties involved in the process of care for fractured neck of femur patients. It strengthened as it became more inclusive of the range of professionals involved in the care process being changed. In the last few months of 1996, the concept of a 'process link group' emerged to bring together the multitude of therapy professionals involved in the care process. Through the process link group all parties to the care process have an opportunity to communicate, problem solve, and fashion changes to the process of care for orthopaedic patients. At the point of concluding fieldwork, the provision of operating theatres and discharge planning were two major issues being explicitly addressed by this multi-disciplinary group.

6.5.5.2 *Problems of change: resources and jurisdictions*

Having observed several features of the approach to change that contributed to changing the process of care for patients with a fractured neck of femur, it does appear that those responsible for producing the original reengineering targets created unrealistic performance improvement targets. In this case, ambitions of radical process redesign have been tempered by the reality of an incremental change process. The following comments of managers involved in the reengineering of the care process for patients with a fractured neck of femur are revealing about the pace and progress of implementing change:

. . . radical discussions have taken place but implementation is a whole different ball-game. (Directorate manager, May 1997)

Change management is such a long process. When I first started to look at these things, I was under the impression that you had to get all these things in quickly for them to be effective. The reality of having to do that shows you cannot do it like that. It is changing cultures and people's ideas that they have built over years. To put challenges to people is quite difficult to do and for them to accept new working practices is also difficult and it does not happen overnight. That is what I have found difficult. You can almost see yourself that the ideas are not the difficult part, in fact, that is the easy bit. It is the implementation that is the battle. (Directorate manager, May 1997)

A key finding in this case is that whilst some changes have been made to the process of care, changes aspired to across the whole care process have not materialized. Much of the explanation for this patchy picture of change across the patient process lies with recognizing clinical, directorate, and agency interdependence within the care process for patients with a fractured neck of femur. The care process involves doctors from the specialties of A&E and orthopaedics as well as nurses, occupational therapists, physiotherapists, and social workers. Agency interdependence is revealed as the process of discharging patients from LRI requires resources from social services. Securing change across the process of care for patients with a fractured neck of femur has proven difficult because of problems of resource availability. Also, at junctures of interdependence, jurisdictional disputes have developed, not all of which have been resolved (Abbott 1988). Over the period of study, a lack of beds, theatre time, and staff has adversely impacted upon implementation of change and improvement of the care process for patients with a fractured neck of femur.

At the moment we get 90% of patients into bed within two hours. Our target was 40 minutes . . . the problem in getting patients to bed is not always A&E getting them out, it is us having a bed available. It is about us releasing beds and discharging patients more quickly in order to release beds for new admissions. (Orthopaedic consultant, December 1996)

I think where we went wrong at first with fractured neck of femur is that there are many issues about discharging patients. Whatever you do at the front-end [nurses ordering X-rays] there are no beds to put them into. So, at first we almost went about it the wrong way around. What we found when we first implemented A&E X-ray was that it did not make any difference to A&E length of stay because we would still be waiting for a bed to become available on the ward. (Directorate manager, October 1996)

Adequate theatre operating time is critical to patients receiving their operation in the clinical need time. A former nurse and manager within the orthopaedic directorate commented:

for trauma patients there is an ongoing historical issue of the increasing workload and how much theatre and surgeon time there is available . . . in reality, people's operations are still cancelled because of the amount of theatre time . . . its full implementation is still working through because the reengineering of theatres throughout the hospital is still working through. (Directorate manager, October 1997)

It was alleged that an effective process of discharge was undermined in past by the availability of social services. Physiotherapy staff have traditionally not been available on the wards at weekends. The new processes of rehabilitation require physiotherapists to be available at weekends. A specialty manager commented:

It has taken a long time but they are starting to be more flexible, for example, the physios are now talking about piloting physio at weekends. Three months ago that was a big battle. So, the thinking has started to change. (Specialty manager, October 1997)

The case shows that clinical and agency interdependence do not simply create resource problems. Jurisdictional disputes are also triggered when planned change challenges established roles and routines at the junctures of interdependence (Abbott 1988). In this case, jurisdictional disputes slowed down the rate and pace of change considerably. This change intervention occurred in the context of professional competition between orthopaedic specialists and A&E specialists.

All the consultants [A&E and orthopaedic] were involved in the consultation at the start of reengineering. Being frank, the A&E consultants were perhaps less willing to change than we [orthopaedic consultants] were. There were conflicts, for example, we interface closely with the A&E department, 99% of our patients come through A&E and we have always felt we would like, what some of my colleagues crudely call control over it . . . what we are looking for is a more integrated service. I think A&E consultants see that as a threat. It is perceived as 'we would be taking over control of their patients' but I see it as more of a partnership, though many of my colleagues would like to take over the care of their patients. (Orthopaedic doctor, December 1996)

The quicker ordering of X-rays in A&E is a result of A&E nurses ordering X-rays. However, a reengineer recalled that achieving this change was not a straightforward process:

The A&E consultants finally agreed to nurses X-raying patients. Initially they came out with a number of clinical issues to suggest that we would not be giving optimum care to the patient. After a lot of discussion, we decided as a group they were not issues and just delaying tactics. (Directorate manager, October 1996)

However, the idea that patients should be referred to a ward after X-ray (hence not returning to A&E) has been difficult to introduce in practice.

We have still not been able to get over radiographers reviewing X-rays. The A&E medical staff are against this one because it threatens their professional standing. They start saying 'well, why do you need doctors at all in that case if radiographers and nurses can do the job'. It is difficult to persuade them on that one. They also feel there is a risk to patient care if that happens. Personally, I feel we could get patients reviewed by a doctor on the acute ward in a shorter time than they see an A&E doctor. (Directorate manager, May 1997)

The reengineered process is requiring greater interdisciplinary teamwork. New procedures for assessing patients' rehabilitation needs and discharge procedures have had to be worked through carefully with the therapy professions. A specialty manager commented:

The key people in rehabilitation are occupational therapists, physios, social workers and nurses. There are lots of issues with them and I am working closely with them looking at issues of professional boundaries and the way they work together. (Directorate manager, October 1997)

The reconfiguration of the four orthopaedic wards into one area of acute/dependent patients and another area for patients in need of rehabilitation initially received a mixed reception amongst professional groups and took time to be accepted as a way of working. Procedures like auto-screening challenged occupational therapists' control over assessment and referral practices. Early in the process of introducing this change, a reengineer commented:

we have a problem with occupational therapy due to professional boundaries . . . they have a lot of control in the assessment and discharge processes that we have to look at. (Directorate manager, May 1997)

Jurisdictional disputes in this case were not simply based on inter- and intra-professional competition. The process of implementing changes to the patient process triggered a number of disputes rooted in competition for resources and control of resources between clinical directorates. A major jurisdictional dispute within the hospital concerned the availability and control of operating theatres as a centralized organizational resource. An orthopaedic consultant remarked:

things like increased theatre lists, increased theatre time, availability of surgeons are only just beginning to come into place . . . there is a debate about who manages theatres and that is part of the problem. It is being resolved by the process link group because the theatre team leader is part of the process link group. (September 1997)

The performance of those in new 'process management' roles in the orthopaedic and trauma directorate to complement a reengineered care process is perceived to have been impeded by traditional 'functional management' roles within other directorates. A manager in the orthopaedic directorate remarked in December 1996:

The patient process director is a concept that is not yet in place. It is that you have a director who oversees the patient process. But we are still a mix of business managers and process directors and that is a quite a big step because it means having the process managers becoming much more a self-contained team and self-running team. There are big issues here. One is people's reluctance and fear of losing their directorate. (Orthopaedic consultant, December 1996)

The walls of directorates are perceived by those managing change as barriers to people's involvement with changing the process of care. An orthopaedic consultant suggested the organization of radiographers impeded the introduction of the idea of radiographers assessing X-rays:

some radiographers want to assess X-rays, others do not. There is no cohesive view. That is partly because they are not yet part of the process because they have their own directorate. (Orthopaedic consultant, December 1996)

A former reengineer commented in October 1996:

it is very difficult to get over barriers between directorates and departments. They know that is how the process is managed now, I think they understand but they refuse to accept it. The managers in the orthopaedic directorate are a team, they see it as a patient process . . . the nurses in A&E, for example, only saw fractured neck of femur as a patient who comes in, needs pain relief, requires an X-ray and then they are handed over to the ward and that is their responsibility finished. But they can now see that with effective communication between areas and with the ambulance service, they can get the patient through the process quicker. But those barriers are still there and will not come down overnight. They have been reinforced over time.

To conclude the case, reengineering the process of care for patients with a fractured neck of femur has produced a mixed picture of impact. The intervention largely failed to realize formal objectives developed by reengineers. This might be thought to be disappointing given that orthopaedics was potentially a receptive context for this intervention, given its problems with handling increased levels of patient demand that had not been resolved internally. In this respect it can be compared to the gastroenterology case where reengineering was embraced as a way of helping the team manage increasing referrals. However, some important changes have been made to the patient process.

It is a notable feature of the case that changes to the patient process tended to be those related to the routines and practices in and around the specialty of orthopaedics and its associated wards. The possibility of jurisdictional dispute between clinical groups within a complex care pathway remains strong and was evident within this case. Moreover, all the cases in this chapter show that for reengineering to effect change in clinical areas, clinicians (especially medical consultants) need to be supportive. In this case, a coalition for change developed between reengineers and orthopaedic consultants. Interestingly, the same group of reengineers who were able to develop collaborative change-oriented relations with orthopaedic consultants failed to do so in the

A&E case described in this chapter. Over time, the coalition strengthened as reengineers moved into management positions within the
directorate and the therapy professions became more involved in
change processes. As such, the case reveals one of the strongest examples of collaboration between reengineers and clinicians in the LRI
reengineering programme.

At the same time, the case reveals how difficult it is for individuals and
groups to effect change in patient processes that draw upon a diverse
range of clinical skills and organizational resources. Notwithstanding
the changes made to the care process, there remain a number of issues
related to inter-professional, interdirectorate, and inter-agency working
to be overcome before the vision of the reengineered care process is
implemented in full. The issues ongoing as we left the site reveal the limited ability, in this case, of both reengineers and orthopaedic consultants
to direct change beyond the boundaries of the specialty of orthopaedics.
The scope of the patient process for patients with a fractured neck of
femur involves A&E, operating theatres, and social services. The vision
of the patient process for A&E and operating theatres reveals the political nature of process redesign in the sense that it implies, for both the
areas of A&E and operating theatres, a loosening of control over the
patient process and resources respectively. As such, change in respect of
both areas remains contested and is a sign of a tension between process
and functional models of organizing unleashed by reengineering.

6.6   Reengineering elective surgery in the specialty of gynaecology

6.6.1   *Introduction*

This case study reports a change intervention designed to reengineer
processes preceding and following elective surgery in the specialty of
gynaecology. Elective surgery represented a significant portion of the
clinical workload within the specialty of gynaecology. The intervention
took place against a background of a specialty preparing to open a new
women's hospital on the main hospital site. The reduced bed base
planned for the new hospital was in line with long-term trends away
from in-patient care models within gynaecology. A notable feature of
the case is the fusion of reengineering ideas and resources with a clinical
agenda for the specialty. The intervention was designed to reengineer
the process by which patients are admitted for surgery, discharged

from hospital, and cared for at home by nurses in gynaecology. The key formal objective was to reduce length of patient stay to effect higher quality care and more efficient utilization of resources.

The intervention was successful in a number of important respects. The redesigned care process was adopted by nurses and doctors and became an established work process in the specialty. Six months after an initial pilot of the new care process by two consultants, the wider group of nine gynaecology consultants and their nursing teams were practising the new process. This process of 'roll-out' is impressive when compared with that of the menstrual clinic among exactly the same set of consultants. The objective of reducing length of stay for patients in hospital was achieved which in turn contributed to a more efficient utilization of hospital resources and increased patient satisfaction.

The pace of change contrasts with a similar intervention in the specialty of ENT. Unlike the case of ENT, this change intervention proved not to be highly contentious either clinically or organizationally. Actions taken in preparing, planning, and implementing change avoided the sort of conflict and competition evident within the early phases of the ENT experience and contributed to the change observed in this case. Those leading the change were skilful in learning from the experience of ENT and mobilizing a more receptive set of conditions for reengineering than those presented in ENT. Unlike ENT, it was possible to confine patient process redesign and its implications largely to the resources and staff dedicated to the specialty of gynaecology.

6.6.2 *Reengineering the gynaecology elective process: issues of context, background, and ambition*

Gynaecology services in LRI were organized via the obstetrics and gynaecology directorate. Obstetrics and gynaecology was a smaller and relatively self-contained directorate with a track record of effective management and relative financial stability. Recent organization and management of the directorate revealed a sense of internal direction. As part of the early discussion of reengineering, a senior manager in the directorate articulated a sense of strategy for gynaecological services in LRI. On the back of the national trend away from in-patient gynaecology services the strategy reflected an intent to move to more complex and high-skill forms of work as a way of ensuring clinical excellence in a competitive environment.

The specialty contained the medical director of the hospital and an important champion of reengineering. Processes of preparation and planning for reengineering were managed through the directorate; for instance, reengineering interventions were carefully targeted at gynaecology. Maternity services were seen as clinically far more complex and unpredictable, and carrying a high risk of medico-legal intervention. In 1995/6, three reengineering projects were identified within gynaecology. One initiative was designed to reengineer the process by which emergency gynaecological care was provided within LRI. The other two initiatives were designed to reengineer in-patient and outpatient processes of care. An outpatient clinic for patients referred to LRI with menstrual problems was created. This initiative is reported as a separate case study in this chapter. This case study focuses on another change intervention launched in 1995/6, designed to reengineer the process by which gynaecology patients were admitted for elective surgery, discharged from hospital, and cared for at home after elective surgery.

Within gynaecology, elective services accounted for 60 per cent of all admissions, so the elective project can be seen as referring to a major stream of patient activity and clinical work. However, it is important to see the genesis and ambition of the project not simply in reengineering terms. Within reengineering texts (Hammer and Champy 1993) change interventions are seen as transformatory in nature, breaking with the legacy of the past in a 'frame-breaking' way. However, this case study suggests another view of a reengineering intervention as a catalyst for change, accelerating the pace of already established clinical, nursing, and administrative changes and ambitions. 'The logic is just to take forward in a quantum step, changes which have been occurring by accident if you like over the last ten years' (consultant gynaecologist, July 1996).

Long-term national trends in the pattern of clinical services in gynaecology suggested a movement away from a traditional in-patient care model to more stress on outpatient and community-based care. There was increased use of minimally invasive surgery (MIS) techniques and a trend to greater clinical sub-specialization within the clinical group. Within gynaecology the trend was toward a reduced use of in-patient beds. In ten years since 1987, the number of gynaecological beds within LRI had reduced from 82 to 36. At the outset of the initiative in 1995, it was known that the bed base of the specialty would be reduced from 42 to 36 as part of a move of the service into a new women's hospital on the LRI site during 1997. There was also a large private sector, where consultant practice already favoured early discharge in relation to elective gynaecology. Indeed one of the themes of the case is that for the consultants this change intervention was not clinically controversial, relative to, for example, the creation of the menstrual clinic in the same specialty.

Many senior and experienced gynaecology nurses were keen to broaden their pattern of work and undertake—under protocol—a more extensive range of tasks. This project owed much to the initiative of gynaecology nurses and their desire to take on an extended role using protocols. From the outset, clinicians and managers recognized the potential for more efficient bed management as a result of reengineering the gynaecology elective process. Furthermore, more efficient bed management was considered fundamental to the move to the new women's hospital. Uniquely in the hospital, it was agreed that savings achieved by reengineering gynaecological services would be 'ring-fenced' for reinvestment in the new Women's Hospital rather than be released back in their entirety to the corporate centre. This ring-fencing of the savings of course acted as an extremely powerful incentive for change as some of the key clinicians had long been campaigning for this new hospital whilst recognizing that in exchange they might have a reduced bed base.

6.6.3 *Patient process redesign of elective surgery in gynaecology*

Late in 1995 directorate management expressed objectives for the project in the following terms to the Hospital Reengineering Management Group:

we are looking to reduce overnight stays prior to theatre [and] discharge delays by allowing nurses to discharge against protocols. If we reduce the length of stay down from 2.5 days to 2 days, we can fit into the new women's hospital which has a reduced bed base . . . the project plan is to pilot the new systems with two consultants by the end of January 1996. (Manager, obstetrics and gynaecology directorate, December 1995)

For those leading the reengineering programme the appeal of the project also lay in the opportunity to 'roll out' reengineering to another surgical specialty. To this point in the reengineering programme only surgical processes in ENT had been subjected to reengineering.

Subsequently, the following changes were made to the process of care for patients requiring major surgical procedures including abdominal hysterectomies and vaginal hysterectomies. Changes spanned the breadth of the care process covering admission into hospital on the day of operation, quicker discharge home from hospital after the operation, and follow-up nursing care for the patient in their own home. Patient process redesign is a dynamic process and the chronology below is intended to provide a sense of how the initiative unfolded over time.

Pre-clerking. Patients were admitted to hospital on the morning of their operation, rather than the night before. To make this change possible women visited the hospital for pre-clerking prior to their operation. Pre-clerking is organized by the clinic coordinator and serves to plan a 'package of care' for the patient. Pre-clerking involves clinicians such as a junior doctor, a nurse, a pharmacist, and a physiotherapist identifying women suitable for early discharge and the hospital at home scheme following operation (see below). Blood and other tests are also done. All the gynaecology consultants practised pre-clerking patients, though the time of pre-clerking prior to admission varied for each consultant. Also, pre-clerking varied for cases of oncology due to the complexity of care required.

Direct to theatre. Having been pre-clerked, women arrive at the hospital on the day of their operation. On the ward, patients are prepared for their operation and walk to the operating theatre where they are assessed by an anaesthetist. After operation, patients are recovered by theatre nursing staff not ward nursing staff.

Early discharge. Patients that satisfy predetermined criteria for early discharge are discharged from hospital two to three days after operation. After early discharge, patients receive follow-up care at home. Discharging protocols were developed to enable the primary nurse of each consultant to make decisions about early discharge. These protocols still varied subtly from one consultant to another, as they resisted complete standardization.

Hospital at home. Patients discharged early are visited by consultants' primary nurses at home in the days immediately after discharge. There is continuing liaison with the hospital, and a mechanism for emergency readmission is available, should there be complications (this proviso has been used only very occasionally but has shown itself to be effective). The patient is then discharged to the GP.

6.6.4 *Chronology of reengineering elective gynaecological services*

Spring 1995. First (negative) experience of reengineering in gynaecology with the introduction of clinic coordinator roles. The initiative is viewed by nursing staff as imposed and threatening to job security.

September 1995. Coinciding with the decentralization of responsibility for reengineering laboratories, clinical and managerial staff in the directorate prepare plans to reengineer gynaecological services.

October 1995. An obstetrics and gynaecology Reengineering Steering Group meets, chaired by the clinical director and identifies elective surgery as an early candidate for reengineering. 'Visioning' and baselining activity starts. Two staff, one with reengineering experience, the other with nursing experience in gynaecology, are seconded as full-time internal change agents on reengineering projects within the directorate.

January 1996. Baselining suggests 38 per cent of elective stay patients spend 'non-value adding time' in hospital prior to their operation. It is recommended that 'faults of the care process' be eradicated through a new 'reengineered process' (manager). A pilot will start in late January with two consultants who had volunteered participation.

January–March 1996. A two-month long pilot occurs of a reengineered process with the participation of two well-functioning clinical teams. Active selling of the project to GP and local community managers and nurses occurs.

March 1996. Positive early results from the pilot are presented to the hospital's Reengineering Steering and Management groups. The project is reported to have the backing of gynaecological consultants.

April 1996. A third consultant 'buys in' as the new elective patient process begins to 'roll out' amongst gynaecology consultants.

June 1996. It is reported to the Reengineering Steering and Management groups that eight of the nine consultants have 'bought in' to the new patient process.

November 1996. The suite of gynaecology projects win a *Health Services Journal* award. Elective project is seen as stable and as embedded in practice. Nurses are strongly positive.

March 1998. The processes of pre-clerking, early discharge, and the hospital at home scheme are widely regarded as embedded into the processes of clinical care within gynaecology.

6.6.5 *Impact of reengineering elective gynaecology*

This intervention in elective gynaecology was relatively successful in both its implementation and impact. The redesigned care process enjoyed nursing and consultant support and yielded sustained change in care processes, improved length of patient stay, an extended role for nurses, and evidence of user, purchaser, and nurse satisfaction.

Planning of the elective project began in autumn 1995 and by summer 1996, the vast majority of consultant gynaecologists had adopted the new process. Following a two-month pilot in December 1995 there was rapid diffusion of the redesigned care process from two to nine consultants. Though each consultant customized the new care process to his or her preference practices of pre-clerking, admission on the day of operation, early discharge, and the hospital at home scheme were employed by all the consultants and their nursing teams. After initial trepidation amongst some nurses, there is evidence of considerable nurse support for the reengineered process. Like the consultants, nurses quickly adopted the innovation once it had been shown to be viable at a pilot stage. Primary nurses expressed a high level of support for the project viewing it to have led to both better quality care for women and a broadening of the nurse role. The nurse is now expected—under protocol—to make more decisions about discharge. The nurse is also expected to work more in the patient's home, with a far higher level of autonomy than in the hospital.

Practices such as pre-clerking, early discharge, and the hospital at home scheme were extended to further gynaecological procedures. Reduction in the length of stay in hospital for patients following surgery reduced pressure on the provision and availability of gynaecological beds enabling a 'straightforward' transfer of the service into the new women's hospital despite the lesser number of beds in the women's hospital.

From the outset of the intervention a representative of General Practice was involved in preparing documentation relevant to the new care process. As a result of continued contact with GPs and the Health Authority staff within gynaecology believed there to be external satisfaction with the new care process. It is also reported that questionnaires issued by gynaecology staff measuring patient satisfaction and GP satisfaction with the hospital at home scheme yielded good results.

It is noteworthy that clinical and nursing opinion within gynaecology about reengineering interventions within the directorate underwent a radical shift over time. Initially, the view within gynaecology was negative, reinforced by the early delayering at ward manager level and the imposed appointment of a clinical coordinator. The beginning of the recovery coincided with the hospital-wide shift of responsibility for reengineering from the central reengineering laboratories to the clinical directorates.

The view has shifted in terms of reengineering. It was first introduced into the Trust very much as a top-down thing. Shrouded in mystery, with very little understanding of what it was about. There was a paradigm shift once it was devolved down to the directorates, people took ownership of the projects, they wanted to initiate what was important to them. (Consultant gynaecologist, October 1996)

6.6.6 *Explaining the impact of reengineering elective gynaecology*

There are a number of contributory factors to the 'successful' outcomes indicated. The context in gynaecology can be seen as having provided a set of antecedent conditions that were mobilized and enabled this intervention. The directorate is smaller, relatively self-contained, and had a good history of doctor, nurse, and managerial relations. It was seen as well managed with balanced budgets, contracts, and activity. By contrast to the surgical directorate, obstetrics and gynaecology had not been plunged into crisis management. Change processes and energies had not been impeded or diverted by pressing operational problems as was the case in some other surgical specialties within LRI during the course of the reengineering programme.

The development of a new Women's Hospital also represented a powerful inducement for change and reengineering was seen as a tool for making the bed reductions promised in order to secure the investment. Ring-fencing savings for the Women's Hospital was unique in the context of the reengineering programme and acted as a strong incentive for change. Clinically, elective gynaecology services were seen as relatively routine and non-complex. It is noteworthy that it was most difficult to apply the reengineered elective process to more complex gynaecological cases involving oncology.

Yet a comparison with the slower 'roll-out' pattern displayed in the new menstrual clinic is instructive (see the discussion of the menstrual clinic initiative in this chapter). Here were two reengineering style ideas proceeding through the same group of clinical and nursing staff at the same time, yet with different outcomes. The context in gynaecology was not then uniformly benign and additional explanations must be sought for the effectiveness of the elective project as a change initiative.

This reengineering intervention in elective surgery did not generate conflicts about clinical efficacy, the extension of nurses' roles, or conflicts of jurisdiction. The initiative was non-controversial for gynaecologists as it was not perceived as adversely affecting levels of professional autonomy over core clinical practice or clinical efficacy. Core clinical practice in elective gynaecology for some time had been moving toward a reduction of the in-patient beds, less invasive techniques, and early nurse-supported discharge. This reengineering project merely accelerated this long-term trend at a local level. Gynaecology consultants were supportive of nurses in gynaecology extending their roles. The established nature of the teams of consultant and primary nurse appears to have provided the conditions within which delegation (subject to protocol) and trust between doctors and nurses has been fostered enabling practice of the reengineered care process. Unlike the case of ENT, the new care process did not draw the directorate of gynaecology into conflicts with clinicians and managers in other directorates. The absence of conflict, which could have derailed or slowed down the rate and pace of change, owes much to effective processes of change management. While the relatively receptive nature of the setting and the non-threatening nature of the intervention are important explanatory factors, some actions undertaken as part of the planned change contributed to the impact of the intervention.

It is noteworthy that this change intervention was prepared and managed by clinical and managerial staff from within the clinical specialty rather than by individuals outside the specialty or directorate such as reengineers. The launching of the reengineering work in gynaecology coincided with devolution of responsibility for the change programme from specialist reengineering laboratories to the clinical directorates. The reengineering of the elective gynaecological process was thus fundamentally directorate driven, but with support from reengineering. The level of direct input by management consultants to the reengineering programme was small, although the internal change agents had themselves earlier been trained by the management consultants and acted as 'coaches' to other people within the directorate. Some elements of the approach to change within gynaecology can be seen as orthodox reengineering, such as the decision in November 1995 to go for 'quick wins':

we need to get some small projects going which give nurses some quick wins. They will then be less fearful about reengineering when something major happens. (Manager, obstetrics and gynaecology directorate, January 1996)

Techniques of baselining, visioning, piloting, and roll-out can be seen as reengineering orthodoxy. On the other hand, the directorate clearly wanted to put a 'spin' on the programme, in order to customize re-engineering ideas to better suit the setting and the intervention:

one of my criticisms of reengineering is that it has a model and everything fits in, instead of changing the model to fit the specialty. They have words and everything fits the words . . . (Manager, obstetrics and gynaecology directorate, January 1996)

A stress on 'bottom-up ownership of the change', internal (rather than external) change agents, intense communication, and the translation of reengineering ideas into professional worlds distinguished the approach to change evident in gynaecology from some other settings within LRI. Indeed, several nurses interviewed reported that they saw the innovation as essentially a nursing innovation rather than a re-engineering innovation. Core ideas had here been successfully translated from one world (reengineering) to another (nursing practice). This highly unusual translation process explains why it was that nursing opinion about reengineering had been turned round in gynaecology to a much greater extent than in other specialties. In essence, this innovation appears to have been nurse led and consultant supported, with the primary nurses helping persuade the consultants to take part:

I personally think that if you went onto the gynae ward and talked to the primary nurses who are willing to do this, they feel that they own this because they have made many of the decisions about how it is to work. Now to me the people who will make it work—because it is a nurse-orientated project—are the primary nurses. So, it has been important to get them involved. (Manager, obstetrics and gynaecology directorate, January 1996)

In this elective gynaecology case, there was a period of preparation for change in advance of moving into action such as consultation with key stakeholders in the care process and risk analysis. Attention was paid to ensuring that key stakeholders were scripted in rather than scripted out of the change process. The previous clinical director was enrolled as a key supporter at the pilot phase, ensuring that an important clinician developed into an ally. There was communication with external purchasing agencies and GPs about the movement of LRI nurses into the community.

we very much thought about how we were going to implement things, 'who did we need to get on board, and for how long, how we were going to roll it out, what was our strategy for rolling it out?' We took the view very early on that we were not going to develop a generic project. (Manager, obstetrics and gynaecology directorate, January 1996)

Another important feature of the case is the construction of a championing team rather than reliance on a single individual to drive forward change. The championing team included not only two complementary internal change agents (themselves combining reengineering laboratory experience and clinical practice experience and credibility), but also a subgroup of supportive nurses and consultants. The clinical director also quietly acted as a higher-level 'umbrella' and 'unblocker' for the project, persuading clinical colleagues to buy into the new process. Increased stress on intensive—and time-consuming—communication efforts arose as part of the learning drawn from the earlier ENT project. This was

indicated by the decision of the internal change agents to base themselves next to the ward, rather than in a central reengineering laboratory.

Building a credible communications strategy required intensive
effort by advocates of the intervention over a long period. Communication with consultants was frequently through informal conversations
on a one-on-one basis early in the evening after the close of ordinary
business. The two internal change agents in particular would attempt to
'sell' the project to individual consultants by going to them when they
were available. There was less reliance on impersonal methods of
communication (e.g. newsletters):

you cannot make them [medical consultants] toe the line. You have to make it
good for them to toe the line. It is about getting solutions to their problems that
are also solutions to yours, but it is a one-to-one thing, it is not a meetings
thing. (Manager, obstetrics and gynaecology directorate, September 1996)

Indeed the rapid 'roll-out' of the process amongst consultants is partly
explained by the use of effective but essentially informal persuasion
mechanisms within the setting. First, the then business manager and
two internal change agents worked hard at building up communication levels with consultants on a one-to-one basis, going to see the key
clinicians individually and at times and places that suited consultants.
Secondly, primary nurses—who relished the prospect of role expansion—were instrumental in persuading 'their' consultants to pilot and
adopt the new process, as the level of trust between the two groups of
workers was very high:

we used the primary nurses to persuade the consultants on a number of
issues . . . we used the primary nurses to sell messages, which was useful.
They have quite a lot of influence with the consultants. (Manager, obstetrics
and gynaecology directorate, August 1996)

one of the nurses actually persuaded the consultant because she wanted to
go out into the community, she wanted continuity of care. So, it was peer persuasion. If the nurses were happy, he would be happy. (Internal change agent,
August 1996)

Persuasive information also spread from one consultant to another:

we were having a difficult meeting one day and we were being shot down in
all directions. Then a piloting consultant walked in and said, 'how wonderful
it is, it works and I am happy, let's get on with it.' The response was 'well,
alright, we will do it then'. (Internal change agent, August 1996)

The pilot scheme was seen as a practical success, if only as another
new technique which had been tried and which had been found to

work. There was felt to be a spirit of emulation and strong concern about peer reputation amongst the body of consultants, which could be used to spread the innovation.

they saw, they came, they looked and said: 'I want it too please.' They saw it work. They saw the whole system was very much more efficient. (Consultant gynaecologist, July 1996)

some of the nurses thought it was a silly idea but the two teams that led it were enthusiastic and motivated. They worked at the protocols and were really committed to making it work. The consultants were also. Having made it work within the pilot with nurses who have credibility the others then knew it worked. Similarly, the pilot was with the right doctors. When it was such a success with the two teams it was harder for other consultants to say 'we will not do it'. (Primary nurse, March 1998)

An important task for directorate personnel was managing up to the corporate centre as monthly reports on progress were presented to the Reengineering Steering and Management Groups. The relationship between these groups and the directorate was one of potential tension as the centre was frequently pushing for harder-edged 'deliverables' to be achieved within a shorter time scale. There was already evidence elsewhere in the hospital that this central reengineering programme pressure, if pushed too far, could jeopardize the strategy of gaining bottom-up ownership of the intervention within the directorate. Targets might be set which in the view of the directorate were over-ambitious and could not be delivered.

A view from the centre was that macro-level interventions would be far more likely to be targeted on directorates where there was less evidence of forward movement, and that directorates such as obstetrics and gynaecology would be allowed far more delegated responsibility. Indeed, evidence of sophisticated change preparation within the directorate was favourably remarked upon at a meeting of the hospital-wide Reengineering Management Group. A good example of the central/local tension would be the shaping of the strategy for roll-out of the elective gynaecology project amongst the consultants:

the next step after the pilot—if it is successful—is to ask other consultants whether they want to participate and get it introduced through them opting into it. Rather than us saying: 'right, we will roll this out among everybody'. That may not be what reengineering wants to do. (Manager, obstetrics and gynaecology directorate, September 1996)

In the end, the directorate's own strategy for roll-out went successfully ahead without central intervention. There is clear evidence in the case study of learning from the early experience of reengineering elective surgery in ENT. This is seen at the most basic level in the use of internal change agents and their deliberate location in an office on the ward rather than some distant reengineering laboratory. In addition, there was reflection on why certain aspects of the ENT experience were disappointing and lessons drawn. Much greater stress was placed on a sustained one-to-one communication effort in order to win 'hearts and minds' of doctors and nurses. There was a reluctance to set overambitious targets.

I think the learning is not to be up front about what you are going to achieve until you know you are going to achieve it. Let's not start talking about the 20 per cent increase in throughput through theatre until we achieve 20 per cent increases in throughput. (Manager, obstetrics and gynaecology directorate, September 1996)

At a more generic level, learning from ENT suggested that interventions would have to be tailored to clinical contexts and that 'roll-out' was not as mechanistic as originally perceived. Finally, a conscious decision was made to avoid the level of conflict evident in the ENT initiative between professional groups located within other parts of the hospital. Implementation proceeded without triggering major 'jurisdictional disputes'. Much effort was spent on communicating with anaesthetists to ensure that they did not challenge the reengineered process. After due consideration there was also a deliberate decision not to attempt to undertake internally the tasks traditionally undertaken by nursing staff in the operating theatre recovery area. This represented an important piece of learning from a major hiatus in ENT. This change to nurses' roles was to be left until the opening of the new women's hospital that would control its own theatres in any case.

To conclude, this case represents an example of a very effective patient process redesign intervention from a change management perspective. A feature of the case is how change was piloted and diffused throughout a surgical specialty within a relatively short time period. An interesting comparison can be drawn between this case and that of ENT also reported in this chapter. The two interventions show similar elements of process redesign, for instance, pre-clerking, whilst displaying marked differences in the rate and pace of change. Between 1995 and 1997 the ENT intervention ebbed and flowed within a context of conflict and competition, taking a long time to generate consultant support. By contrast, the intervention in gynaecology proceeded relatively smoothly from inception to impact within a matter of months.

A combination of reengineers, managers, and clinicians were skilful in spotting and mobilizing a set of conditions receptive to this intervention. Most notably, reengineering ideas and resources were introduced to complement and support a strategic and clinical agenda within the specialty. Patient process redesign was not highly contentious in clinical terms and attracted the support of nurses and doctors. Operating facilities dedicated to gynaecological surgery meant that conflict was not generated with other departments and specialties about the provision and scheduling of operating time. The case is a good example of the relatively successful and accepted development of a process perspective to patient care implemented albeit within the confines and resources of a single specialty.

6.7 Reengineering outpatient services in the specialty of gynaecology

6.7.1 *Introduction*

The creation of a menstrual clinic within the specialty of gynaecology is a rare example within the LRI reengineering programme of an intervention designed to change clinical processes of diagnosis, inference, and treatment (Abbott 1988). As such, it can be seen as a particularly challenging intervention. The development of the menstrual clinic reveals a fusion of different streams of ideas drawn both from reengineering and evidence-based medicine. It indicates possibilities for a juxtaposition of clinical and organizational change agendas within patient process redesign.

In autumn 1995, clinical audit data in LRI suggested that a third of gynaecological outpatients presented with menstrual problems. These women were being treated in general gynaecology clinics in LRI and around the county with different treatment regimes according to the consultant. Existing simultaneously was a large private sector, where practice had traditionally been seen to favour surgery (hysterectomy) rather than medical modes of intervention. The menstrual clinic in part arose out of a view that here was an important patient grouping that merited a response in terms of a specialist clinic based on evidence.

A menstrual clinic was developed but initial aspirations to diffuse the concept into the practice of the corpus of gynaecological consultants were not realized. At the final point of data collection in March 1998 only the two original sponsoring consultants were actually operating a menstrual clinic, though it was being reported at this time that a further two consultants were to operate a menstrual clinic from October 1998. Problems of 'rolling out' the menstrual clinic amongst consultants indicate some limitations of a reengineering methodology for developing evidence-based medicine. One of the features of this case is that the degree of clinical controversy was much higher than in the case of elective gynaecological services in which roll-out among exactly the same group of consultants proved much less problematic. In particular, alternative medical and surgical models of clinical practice are evident and the treatment of menstrual problems can be seen as clinically controversial. Managers and reengineering and even clinical leaders may endeavour to shape and influence clinical behaviour but they cannot readily enforce such radical and disputed changes in clinical practice.

6.7.2 *Organization and service context of the menstrual clinic*

Gynaecology services in LRI were organized through the obstetrics and gynaecology directorate. By contrast, with the medical or surgical directorates, it was one of the smaller directorates in the hospital with a group of nine consultant gynaecologists who work with nurses and support staff. One of the gynaecologists at the time was also medical director of the LRI NHS Trust.

Obstetrics and gynaecology was regarded as a small, cohesive, and relatively self-contained directorate with a track record of effective management and relative financial stability. The planning and preparation of change described in this case study was largely managed formally through the directorate organization and management process. In 1995/6, three reengineering projects were identified within gynaecology. One initiative was designed to reengineer the process by which emergency gynaecological care is provided within LRI. The other two initiatives were designed to reengineer in-patient and outpatient processes. Elsewhere in this chapter there is described an initiative designed to reengineer the process by which gynaecology patients were admitted for elective surgery, discharged from hospital, and cared for at home after elective surgery. This case study reports the development of a menstrual clinic for women presenting with menstrual problems.

During the period of the study, the gynaecology service reduced its bed usage from 42 beds to 36 following the move to a purpose-designed Women's Hospital which opened in December 1996. There were long-term trends evident in the pattern of clinical services in gynae-cology—not only in Leicester but much more widely—which indicated a move away from a traditional in-patient model to more stress on out-patient and community-based care. There was increased use of min-imally invasive surgery (MIS) techniques and a trend to greater clinical sub-specialization. The formation of a menstrual clinic represents a good example of the trend towards clinical sub-specialization within the gynaecological outpatient setting.

6.7.3 *Objectives and operation of the menstrual clinic*

Over the period of study a range of objectives were articulated or intim-ated, both formally and informally in respect of the menstrual clinic. Informally there were suggestions by managers and clinicians within the obstetrics and gynaecology directorate that the clinic would free up capacity in outpatients that could then respond to presently unmet demand for service (with some £90,000 extra income). Conversations with some parties directly involved in the setting up of the clinic revealed that the menstrual clinic was more informally seen as strengthening the competitive position of the LRI in what was seen as a functioning quasi-market for gynaecology services. At the inception of the menstrual clinic no such specialist clinic was available at the neigh-bouring General Hospital—the key competitor within the local NHS internal market. It was perceived that many GPs have only limited experience in the management of menstrual problems and would wel-come a specialist centre that they could refer on to. Thus, the scheme was seen as capable of attracting strong support from purchasers, both the Health Authority and GP Fundholders. It was seen as capable of being a higher-quality service that would be welcomed by an articulate and demanding patient group. However, there is no evidence to sug-gest that the hospital ever marketed the service to GPs in these terms.

   More formally, a report produced and presented to the Reengineering Steering Committee in January 1996 stated broadly that the purpose of the menstrual clinic was to improve the use of resources and increase customer satisfaction. By February 1996 some of these objectives had evolved into the following formally agreed 'deliverables' with the lead-ers of the hospital reengineering programme: 50 per cent reduction in visits by patient with menstrual disorders from 4 to 2; 15 per cent reduc-tion in patient tests; and 90 per cent treatment by protocol. No objectives in relation to patient throughput were recorded at that stage. Neither was it specified that the clinic would result in changes to levels of contracts.

Some of the most notable developments in the creation of the menstrual clinic over the period between summer 1995 and October 1998 are now identified with the help of a chronological overview below. In the autumn of 1995, clinical audit data about treatment of patients with menstrual disorders was fed into discussion and plans for reengineering within the specialty of gynaecology. Data revealed 30 per cent of gynaecological outpatients presented with menstrual disorders and treatment regimes differed according to the consultant. In November 1995 two reengineers seconded to the directorate undertook analysis described by reengineers as 'baselining', 'scoping', and 'visioning' in relation to a menstrual clinic project. This analysis involved service users and GPs and linked into the wider 'effective clinic' concept and creation of clinic coordinators across the hospital. This work preceded the creation of a menstrual clinic working party involving consultant representation, a senior registrar in public health from the Health Authority seconded to work on protocol formation, and a manager from the 'effective clinic' programme. By January 1996, the development of agreed protocols for investigation and treatment in the menstrual clinic was being championed by two consultants in LRI and facilitated by the senior registrar. An 'Interim Report' from within the directorate projected a vision of a one-stop and evidence-based menstrual clinic. Initial ambition reported to the hospital Reengineering Management Committee was to have 'a full Menstrual clinic at pilot stage' by March 1996 involving three consultants.

After piloting in March 1996, the clinic was operated by two consultants. In keeping with the philosophy of reengineering the creation of a menstrual clinic involved changes to the process of care for patients with menstrual problems. The new patient process was one whereby clinic coordinators screen referral letters from GPs according to protocols and appointments are made for attendance at clinic. Pre-assessment documentation is sent out to the patient. In line with the aim of the clinic being to significantly reduce waiting time to diagnosis and agree a plan of treatment, all tests are generally taken during the clinic visit to reach diagnosis. Test results—including histology—are made available and are assessed by the two consultants at the end of the day of visit. Diagnosis and treatment options are discussed under agreed protocols. Pre-developed medical and surgical guidelines are used to agree the choice of treatment. Internal documentation suggests that surgical procedures are to be offered only if necessary criteria are fulfilled. The two consultants who operate the clinic debrief and audit each other's practice at the end of the clinic.

6.7.4 *Chronology of the development of a menstrual clinic*

Summer 1995. Retrospective case note audit undertaken—30 per cent of the sample of gynaecology outpatients presented with menstrual disorders. Data feed into reengineering visioning.

September 1995. Directorate begins to prepare plans for the reengineering of gynaecology, coinciding with the decentralization of reengineering activity from reengineering laboratories to the directorates.

October 1995. Obstetrics and gynaecology Reengineering Steering Group begins to meet and identifies the development of a menstrual clinic as a possible project. Reengineering resources will support the development. Work baselining and visioning the patient process starts. A menstrual clinic project Working Party is set up, including a senior registrar in public health seconded from the Health Authority, working on protocol formation.

Late 1995. More advanced plans for change are reported but the first overt signs of possible clinical resistance emerge.

January 1996. Development of protocols, accessing of evidence-based guidelines from the University of York. An 'Interim Report' presents the results of the baselining, suggesting a flawed patient process is in operation at present.

March 1996. A two-month-long pilot starts with two consultants participating. Initial scheduling problems are quickly resolved.

June 1996. Internal evaluation of the pilot suggests a successful clinic. However, the scheme remains a pilot as there is not enough evidence of consultant 'buy-in' for it to be rolled out.

August 1996. One of the process reengineers leaves for a post in marketing, diluting the reengineering resource.

November 1996. The suite of gynaecology projects wins a *Health Services Journal* award.

December 1996. Menstrual clinics continue to operate but only the two original consultants are participating. Efforts are being made to persuade two further consultants to adopt the practice of the menstrual clinic, but this may require customization of the clinic to their working practices.

February 1997. The menstrual clinic is relocated in the recently opened Women's Hospital. Testing facilities such as historoscopy are now directly available in the clinic making it more convenient for patients to undergo tests.

January 1998. It is reported that long-standing efforts designed to spread the operation of the menstrual clinic amongst other gynaecology consultants have been renewed after being 'put on hold for a while' (specialty manager).

March 1998. A manager within the specialty of gynaecology expresses the view that other gynaecology consultants will adopt a menstrual clinic but there are 'issues' still to be resolved.

July 1998. Reported that a further two consultants will operate a menstrual clinic from October.

6.7.5 *Understanding the impact of patient process redesign*

The menstrual clinic was the product of fusion between two sets of powerful ideas and the efforts of a number of doctors, nurses, and managers. Three doctors were instrumental in the development of the menstrual clinic—two gynaecology consultants (one an academic, the other is medical director of the Trust) and a senior registrar in public health. For the academic consultant and senior registrar, the evidence-based medicine movement, which seeks to ensure that clinical practice is based on scientific evidence, proved influential. Meta-analytical guidelines produced by the University of York were critical to the development of guidelines used to operate the menstrual clinic. Further, the process of clinical audit reinforced the impression of wide variation in clinical practice in this field, with alternative surgical and medical models of care evident in practice. There was also evidence of duplication of tests and patients becoming stuck in long-drawn-out pathways into treatment.

Ideas about evidence-based medicine fused with change methodologies and concepts associated with the reengineering, for instance the spirit of change associated with the reengineering programme, the concept of patient process redesign, and practice of single visit clinics. Particular advocates of these ideas were a gynaecology consultant who was also medical director of the Trust and two internal change agents. Reengineering played an important catalytic role in enabling other actors, for instance, the two gynaecology consultants and senior registrar, to operationalize their ideas for a menstrual clinic.

... the project would not have been possible without reengineering. (Consultant gynaecologist, July 1996)

However, it proved difficult to roll out (diffuse) the operation of a menstrual clinic from two consultants to the wider body of gynaecology consultants. In January 1998, long-standing efforts designed to spread the operation of the menstrual clinic amongst other gynaecology consultants were renewed after being 'put on hold for a while' (specialty manager). In July 1998, it was reported that two more consultants would operate a menstrual clinic from October 1998. The issue of roll-out is particularly significant given that standardization of the care process for patients with a menstrual disorder, according to clinical protocol, was fundamental to the spirit and purpose of the menstrual clinic. The process of standardizing care for this group of patients according to clinical protocols was undermined by the difficulties of roll-out. The progress of roll-out of the menstrual clinic amongst consultants within the specialty of gynaecology was in stark contrast to the progress made rolling out changes to elective gynaecological services amongst the same group of consultants. The two gynaecology case studies represent a naturally occurring experiment, whereby two reengineering-style change interventions proceeded through the same group of staff at the same time albeit with very different implementation processes and 'roll-out' success amongst consultants. The reengineered elective gynaecology process 'rolled out' amongst all consultants within eight months of the idea being piloted by two consultants. By comparison, rolling out the menstrual clinic to a wider group of gynaecological consultants took much longer. The case of the menstrual clinic is characterized by consultant gynaecologists emphasizing retention of clinical autonomy and control over practice in the face of arguments about standardization and protocol-driven medicine.

By comparison with the case of reengineering elective surgery in gynaecology the menstrual clinic did not enjoy the same level of support amongst nurses within the specialty. The menstrual clinic did not offer nurses in the specialty the same degree of incentive and benefit in respect of role extension and development. A major feature of the case study of reengineering elective surgery in gynaecology relates to the expanded role of the nurse. The menstrual clinic opened with two consultants and their two primary nurses, together with two clinic coordinators, representing the basic pattern of staffing. While nursing role change was also a feature of the menstrual clinic, it was more incremental nurse development than in the elective surgery setting. The primary nurse certainly undertook more of a counselling role than hitherto, given that the collapsing of the care process has resulted in more personal contact with the women. However, the new discharge role of the nurse was obviously not evident in this scheme (unlike the elective surgery process) as there was no automatic overnight stay as part of the care process. Furthermore, amongst the wider group of nurses in gynaecology there was uncertainty about the purpose or benefits of the clinic to patients.

the hospital at home [elective surgery project] is a more dynamic thing than menstrual disorders. A lot more people benefit from the hospital at home than menstrual clinic . . . . I cannot see the reason for the menstrual clinic . . . overall there is less enthusiasm for the menstrual clinic amongst the nurses—they are not as involved as in the hospital at home. (Nurse, March 1998)

It is noteworthy that in the case describing the elective surgery project in gynaecology the nurses were instrumental in persuading consultants to pilot and ultimately adopt the reengineered patient process. Nurse ambivalence about the menstrual clinic meant that an important internal pressure for change on consultants was not applied in this case.

The menstrual clinic also generated and exposed strains within a group of gynaecological consultants. The consultant-based form of leadership of the menstrual clinic somewhat paradoxically created its own strains and impeded wider consultant support for the menstrual clinic. It is observed here that the fusion of ideas of evidence-based medicine and reengineering proved powerful in creating and piloting the menstrual clinic in the first instance. However, somewhat paradoxically deeper analysis of the development of the clinic over time suggests that this combination of ideas led to some counter-reactions amongst clinicians within the specialty which help to explain the lack of progress made in the rolling-out of the menstrual clinic.

The menstrual clinic was one of the few 'reengineering'-related change interventions to directly address doctors' practice in diagnosing and treating patients. In so doing, it challenged established care practices, roles, and routines of gynaecologists within the specialty. There were several lines of counter-reaction to the development of the menstrual clinic that had a powerful effect of regulating the rate and pace of change considerably. A part of the explanation for the failure of the menstrual clinic to roll out is that the clinic was perceived as not appropriate or adoptable across the whole body of clinicians. It was suggested that some consultants did not do much menstrual disorder work and concentrated on more complex cases involving oncology. For others, the menstrual clinic did not fit in with their working patterns and routines. For those consultants working in peripheral clinics outside the city it was said that a highly specialized approach would be unlikely to generate the numbers to be successful. It was also argued that the original numbers of patients had been severely overestimated so that it was difficult to generate the workload needed for additional clinics. One such consultant described his approach to adopting the menstrual clinic innovation as follows:

I think it is probably a good thing if you can set it up and do it. It won't be for me, I have to do something different . . . I think the idea is great, it is the same as the one-stop hypertension clinic, it is great. I think the one-stop menstrual disorder clinic is a good one. Not quite right for me in my rounds, but I am stealing bits of it. (Consultant gynaecologist, August 1996)

Nevertheless, the menstrual clinic innovation was potentially adoptable by a rather wider group of gynaecologists than the two original innovators, yet by March 1998 this had not yet happened—why? Further counter-arguments to the development of the menstrual clinic are revealing.

This [the menstrual clinic] scheme affects them [the consultants] whereas the hospital at home scheme [the elective surgery project] is a change but it is very much underpinned by the nursing teams. It was the nurses who really had to change. The medical staff are not doing anything greatly different. (Specialty nurse, March 1998)

I suppose it is much more threatening in a way. And things that threaten us, we don't automatically adopt. (Consultant gynaecologist, August 1996)

The menstrual clinic was far more clinically controversial than the elective surgery project, and reached into the heartland of clinical practice. The menstrual clinic protocol essentially contraindicated surgical intervention—except where other methods had been tried and failed—and yet some consultant gynaecologists within the group espoused the use of surgical techniques. Moreover, the approach taken to the treatment of menstrual disorder was seen as a core part of the professional identity of many of the gynaecologists:

Menorrhagia is something between conservatively 30 per cent and bullishly 50 per cent of all referrals that are made to our gynaecological outpatients. We have 6,500 referrals made on an annual basis to this hospital. The bread and butter of private practice is menorrhagia dysfunction and so people like to have a reputation for their management in that particular field. . . . (Consultant gynaecologist, September 1996)

It was sometimes argued that the flourishing private sector in menstrual work—where hysterectomies were often the intervention of choice—helped explain clinical resistance to the adoption of a protocol that tipped practice away from surgical models and towards medical models. Menstrual problems represented a large proportion of the work done privately. So, while such private practice chimed with the objectives of the elective surgery project, it essentially contradicted the objectives of the menstrual clinic. There was no evidence of this consideration appearing formally in the documentation accessed, but

a number of respondents argued that it was an important consideration hidden away in the background.

Some of the core ideas lying behind the menstrual clinic were highly
controversial and were resisted by some clinical colleagues in the
group. A fundamental component of the menstrual clinic related to the
development of evidence-based protocols, which can be seen as a significant new development within the period of reengineering. This
raised the question of the extent to which such protocols were accepted
as 'scientific' and a legitimate guide to practice by the consultant body.
Some consultants argued that the definition of best practice was not
easy, and could depend as much on clinical judgement, experience, and
tacit knowledge as formal academic research:

I think that there is caution. It has not been properly thought out and I think
that there is a lot of uncertainty about so-called evidence-based medicine. It
depends on what you read what best practice is and we have all got our own
ideas about what best practice is and it does not necessarily mean evidence
backed up by 26 publications in particular journals. (Consultant gynaecologist, August 1996)

I think that protocols have to be flexible. And I think that sometimes you can
interpret them too rigidly. (Consultant gynaecologist, September 1996)

Some respondents further stated that menstrual disorder was if
anything a poor choice for an evidence-based medicine project because
there was an absence of incontrovertible scientific evidence. The meta-
analytic guidelines produced by the University of York were not
always accepted as genuinely authoritative. It was remarked by some
doctors that infertility would have been a better place in which to start
if an evidence-based medicine project were wanted.

Another view expressed was that the subgroup championing the
clinic was more preoccupied with getting the project up and running
than persuading other gynaecologists to join in. Intensive—and successful—external diplomatic efforts were being made to ensure that
the pathologists and other diagnostic departments cooperated. However, there was a feeling that the two original innovators essentially
'owned' this project within gynaecology. Some of the intensive internal
persuasive effort evident in the elective surgery case was not replicated
in the development of the menstrual clinic case.

To conclude, the case of the menstrual clinic is characterized by a
prominent emphasis displayed by consultant gynaecologists on the
retention of clinical autonomy and control over practice. Protocol-
based medicine was seen by its supporters as a way of standardizing

clinical practice and of aligning it more closely with the evidence. Critics, however, argued that the basis in evidence for the menstrual clinic was still equivocal and that senior practitioners such as consultants should rightly continue to retain autonomy over practice through the exercise of their clinical judgement. Consequently, there was in fact resistance to the core ideas of standardization and of protocol-driven medicine.

There was evidence of subgroups forming within the group of nine consultants with different—perhaps even opposing—views of the clinical care process. Change interventions which are seen as encroaching on core clinical territory (which the menstrual clinic did to a far greater extent than the elective surgery project) are likely to meet with higher levels of clinical resistance at the 'roll-out' stage (moving from a pilot to generic practice). The menstrual clinic was seen as very much led by two consultants. They were in turn supported by the two reengineers that undertook much of the detailed planning. This consultant-based form of change leadership was shown to act in a contrasuggestible manner to much prescription about the need for clinicians to lead change. Why might this be the case? It should be remembered that a group of consultants has traditionally operated as a college of equals. Although this has changed somewhat in recent years with the emergence of clinical managerial roles in hospitals, individual clinicians have retained much control over their day-to-day working practices. Sapiential authority is at least as important as the power of a formal role. In this case, the presence of the medical director within the gynaecology group acting as an advocate for the menstrual clinic innovation was seen by some as provoking resistance amongst colleagues keen to demonstrate their continuing autonomy over practice. Managers, reengineers, and clinical leaders of change may be able to shape or to influence clinical behaviour if they act with some subtlety and skill, but they still cannot readily enforce change at the level of the core clinical practice.

6.8   Reengineering elective surgery in the specialty of ENT

6.8.1   *Introduction*

This case study reports a change intervention designed to reengineer care processes that precede and follow ear, nose, and throat (ENT) surgery. ENT is an important surgical specialty within a hospital facing pressures to increase the number of patients treated (activity) and reduce waiting times. In this case, purchasers were keen to reduce long waiting lists, whilst the hospital sought to preserve its contracts for elective surgery and monopoly provider status for ENT surgery. In addition to reducing the length of patient stay in hospital, reengineers and management consultants hoped that a reengineered patient process would enable a 20 per cent per annum increase in routine elective ENT surgery. Following a pilot in summer 1995, the intervention quickly attained 'flagship project' status on account of its being the first attempt within the reengineering programme to redesign 'patient stay' processes. Reengineers saw this attempt to reengineer ENT as an opportunity to create a prototype patient stay process that could be 'rolled out' to other specialties in the hospital. It was an important early intervention designed to create momentum in what was at that stage perceived as a receptive setting with strong clinical leadership for reengineering.

In practice, reengineering elective ENT surgery proved controversial and took far longer and involved more managerial effort than reengineers first anticipated. The flagship change project on occasion sailed into dangerous waters and for a period was grounded. The case captures the process ambitions of reengineering coming into conflict with established functional models of organizing with LRI. The intervention did eventually succeed in defining and implementing substantial changes to the patient process experienced by substantial groups of elective ENT patients. Some of the targets of reengineers for improving the quality of patient care were achieved. Redesign of the patient process contributed to a significantly shorter length of stay in hospital as patients requiring routine elective surgery were admitted into hospital on the day of surgery rather that the day before surgery. The specialty of ENT increased patient throughput and waiting times for surgery have improved by comparison to the period prior to reengineering.

However, the ambitious activity targets set by reengineers at the outset of the intervention did not materialize. Reengineering did not contribute to faster working by ENT consultants. The pace of work, as measured by patients per operating list, remained largely unchanged compared with the period before reengineering. Increased patient throughput is attributed to the appointment of an additional consultant and improved operational management as much as to changes made to the patient process, though reengineering must be given some credit for improving operational management. The creation of a process template that could be 'rolled out' to other surgical specialties did not materialize though some of the concepts introduced as part of the

ENT project are evident in other surgical specialties, such as gynaecology. Learning derived from the ENT case by internal change agents was based on the limitations of the early ENT case as much as its successes.

6.8.2 *The specialty of ENT: recent history and basic mode of organization*

ENT is a major surgical specialty within the hospital that in 1994/5 accounted for approximately 28 per cent of the elective surgical workload of the hospital. It was part of a group of services managed via the surgical directorate within the hospital. Over the period of this case study, the surgical directorate faced considerable operational management problems of staffing, finance, and contracts. The directorate was concerned to save its contract base, both with the Health Authority and with GP Fundholders. The LRI was the only major hospital in the county providing an ENT service. In 1994/5 fears existed that purchasers might take steps to end this monopoly. There were long waiting lists for ENT surgery and purchasers were trying to increase the level of contracted activity. Clinical services contained within the surgical directorate were located across the vast site of the LRI, reportedly making communication within the directorate difficult. The work of the ENT specialty required the use of the hospital's operating theatres and anaesthetic staff. There were long-standing problems between surgical specialties, including ENT over the provision of these resources. Over the period of the case, a particular problem facing the directorate was the cancellation of operating theatre sessions.

At the start of the study, there were six ENT consultants who met as an ENT division chaired by the ENT head of service. The ENT head of service played a major part in piloting a reengineered patient process in 1995. A new head of service was appointed in summer 1996. The division is the forum for forming collective consultant opinion within the group and plays an important role in the case. Amongst the group of six ENT consultants, there was a pattern of sub-specialization. For example, one consultant specialized in major head and neck surgery. There was also cross-referral between consultants. No strong clinical controversies were evident amongst consultants. Many of the nursing staff were long established and the case study shows that reengineering entailed changes to their mode of working.

Within ENT, there were identified by reengineering four relatively well-defined groups of patients for surgical procedures such as

tonsillectomies, septoplasties, and ears (all relatively minor procedures) and head and neck surgery (major procedures, including oncology). Across the four groups 90 per cent of the procedures performed
are elective rather than emergency. The bulk of the workload was seen
as relatively routine and involving young and fit patients. The subgroup of head and neck cases was seen as the more complex work. The
reengineering intervention described in this case study was confined to
the large elective component of the ENT work. The case study reports
how a reengineering intervention started with those patients being
admitted for tonsillectomies and septoplasties. The timing of the
reengineering intervention coincided with an emerging trend of
shorter length of stay for patients and earlier discharge. Reengineering
at LRI also coincided with the growing demand for clinical audit and a
teaching and research agenda driven by the 1996 implementation of
the Calman Report. The Calman Report on medical training intensified
teaching demands made on the ENT surgeons at the same time as
reengineering and purchasers tried to intensify service workloads.

6.8.3   *Objectives of reengineering elective surgery in ENT*

Several objectives surfaced in this case, some more tangible than others.
Of particular interest is the formal hard-edged objective of substantially
increasing patient care activity. In November 1995, senior management
formally recorded the following quality improvement objectives for
this reengineering intervention in ENT: to increase direct patient care
time by 20–30 per cent; to reduce length of stay in hospital by 40–50 per
cent for 90 per cent of in-patients; and enhance nursing skills for 50 per
cent of registered nurses. These quality improvements were seen to
facilitate increases in 'patient throughput'. Management consultants
and senior reengineers argued that through reduced length of stay there
was an opportunity to increase the volume of patient care by up to
20 per cent within existing resources. Also, in November 1995, the objective of increasing patient activity by 20 per cent by March 1997 was
lodged with senior management as an official 'deliverable' of the
reengineering programme. To achieve these improvements reengineers
identified that £42,000 of capital investment was required immediately.

   More symbolic, the intervention in ENT was the first attempt within
LRI at reengineering patient stay processes. Prior to the ENT initiative,
reengineering efforts had been concentrated on changing clinical support services such as patient testing and outpatient clinics. The work in
ENT symbolized a movement of the reengineering programme into the

'clinical heartlands' of the hospital. The ambition for the project in ENT thus went far beyond the specialty of ENT. At the outset of the case study, members of reengineering believed that ENT offered a starting point to develop a template of a reengineered elective stay process. In June 1995, a senior reengineer commented:

we have chosen ENT because it is an area that has got a lot of patients going through . . . if you can get it right for lots of people going through, it should be transferable to an area with a slower pace. (Reengineer, June 1995)

Reengineers believed that learning from the reengineering intervention in ENT would provide a template of a reengineered elective stay process that would be transferable and 'rolled out' across other surgical specialties such as gynaecology.

To achieve performance objectives changes in work practices of consultants were seen by some as necessary. In August 1995, a reengineer commented:

we do need the consultants to do more routine work, which again is breaking tradition, because they do like to do the big interesting work. But this is the waiting list; this is the bread and butter stuff. We are trying to get them to increase throughput, particularly on the routine list . . . what is happening is that all the routine stuff, what we call the urgent stuff, is on the back burner all the time. (Reengineer on the ENT consultant surgeons, October 1995)

Reengineering the elective stay process in ENT had implications for doctors' practice in relation to: bed management; routine and urgent work; the pace of work; contract management; and discharge practices. Attaining reengineering objectives seemingly required some standardization and intensification of clinical practice.

6.8.4 *Patient process redesign in ENT*

Reengineering ENT started in mid-1995 when members of the patient stay reengineering laboratory and the ENT head of service began to redesign a process whereby patients requiring minor ENT surgery were admitted into hospital, had their operation, and were discharged from the hospital. The ENT head of service was seen as providing strong clinical leadership for reengineering ideas, but the clinical leadership remained individualistic in tone and some key clinical colleagues were not persuaded. Reengineers leading the change were looking at the ENT process to identify work practices that were judged to be unnecessary, wasteful, or duplicating and which could be rejected from the vision of a reengineered care process. The essence of the reengineered care process lay in a number of concepts such a pre-clerking, scheduling, direct access to theatre, and early discharge from hospital. The commentary below reports the extent of change in the patient process over the period of study, including a chronology of how the process of redesigning ENT surgery unfolded over time. The chronology provides both a sense of the changes to the process in a wider temporal and organizational context and reveals how momentum for reengineering the ENT process was developed, lost, and rediscovered.

Pre-clerking. Patients were pre-clerked in an outpatient clinic approximately one to two weeks before operation rather than on the ward the day before their operation. Pre-clerking replaced the practice of admitting patients into hospital twenty-four hours before their operation. It is a process of assessment of the patient prior to surgery. Of the six consultants one consultant does the pre-clerking personally, other consultants use their junior medical staff or nursing staff. Pre-clerking relies on new forms of multi-disciplinary documentation and protocols agreed amongst clinical staff. Piloted by one consultant in August 1995, pre-clerking became accepted practice amongst ENT consultants, for routine surgery, on otherwise fit and healthy patients by May 1996. At October 1997, an ENT consultant remarked that pre-clerking is perceived by medical and nursing staff as 'working well' and it is 'rare for it not to happen now.'

Integrated Notes. An idea associated with pre-clerking is integrated medical and nursing notes to reduce duplication of effort resulting from doctors and nurses asking patients the same questions. At October 1997, an ENT consultant commented that 'it is a good idea but we still have some duplication. On the medical side, the junior staff welcomed the fact that they do not have to go through the same thing with the patients as the nurses.'

Direct to theatre. A pilot took place in August 1995, involving one ENT consultant admitting patients to hospital on the day of operation. By June 1996 it had become accepted practice amongst all ENT consultants and anaesthetists that patients requiring routine ENT surgery are admitted into hospital on the same day of their operation and go straight to a newly built 'arrivals lounge' and then into theatre for their operation. At October 1997 an ENT consultant commented:

the arrivals lounge idea is not working too badly. It took quite a bit of bedding in. At peaks of activity, it can be a bit congested. There have been one or two detail problems in the way it was set up; for example, patients felt cubicles for changing did not offer enough privacy. We have got over teething problems of patients coming in at the right time. Nobody is clamouring that the patient should go back to the ward and come from there. Nobody is complaining now because we have got used to it.

Theatre recovery by ENT ward nursing staff. Senior members of the patient stay reengineering laboratory proposed that nurses from the ENT ward should recover patients in theatre after their operation. They argued that this practice would extend the skills of ENT nurses, and provide better continuity of care for the patient. The idea was proposed in mid-1995, and opposed by nursing staff in operating theatres already responsible for recovering the patient. Nurses who recovered patients in theatre expressed concern about the skills and competence of ENT ward nurses to recover patients. Though some training of ENT ward nurses in recovery skills occurred the idea was not implemented given resistance of nursing staff in theatres who perceived it as a threat to their jobs. Nurses on ENT wards also felt that they did not have time to recover patients. In August 1997, a senior manager for ENT commented that 'Recovery does not really fit the ENT group of patients who are here today and gone tomorrow.'

Nurse discharge process. To improve the process of discharging patients from hospital, reengineers proposed that a nurse should discharge patients guided by protocols developed with medical staff. Piloted in August 1995, the idea was tried but did not become practice. The idea lacked support amongst doctors and nurses. Reflecting upon the idea in October 1997 a consultant in ENT remarked:

the idea of early discharge planning is a load of old cod. We have always had a good record of discharging people reasonably early. It was always done around 8.30–9.00 a.m. For a period, it was decided the day before when people could go home. But it was always going to be subject to their condition the following morning. It was a lot of hot air. I do not think it delivered anything. It may have achieved an extra hour but in principal all the decisions had been made anyway by 9.00 a.m. If you made a decision today, and you were supposed to fill in on the operation sheet that the patient could go home at 7.00 a.m. tomorrow morning, they were still dependent on someone seeing them. I certainly was not happy that the decision would be made purely by nurses and neither were they happy that they would take responsibility for that. I think it was a load of hot air.

Scheduling of operating lists. Scheduling is about planning the case mix of operating lists to enable maximum use of scarce theatre time. One ENT consultant piloted the idea in February 1996. After some initial problems, the idea was 'rolled out' amongst all consultants by summer 1996.

Team-based nursing. Team-based nursing involves each consultant working with a dedicated group of nurses and other staff. In February 1996, team-based nursing was identified as a way of replacing the shift-based system of nursing in ENT. Team-based working was promoted by reengineers as enabling nurses to become more expert. Nurses would gain expertise congruent with the expertise of the consultant in the team. Team-based nursing would also provide continuity of care for patients because the same nurses would be involved in pre-clerking, the post-operative care of the patient on the ward, and in the outpatient clinic. Nurses would not be purely ward-based staff. The idea was not implemented in the period of study. Reasons given include there being insufficient nurses for individual teams. However, the idea was controversial amongst the ENT consultants. Whilst nurses appeared to accept the idea in principle some doctors differed in their views. Doctors whose work was predominantly short-term 'stay' work accepted the idea, whilst doctors who did the small amount of ENT work requiring patients to have a longer stay in hospital were concerned that team-based nursing may impede their work with other specialties such as plastic surgery. Concerns were expressed that their ward team would not correspond with their own joint working arrangements.

6.8.5   *Chronology of patient process redesign in ENT*

March 1995. Reengineers in the patient stay laboratory identify ENT as a good specialty to start reengineering.

June 1995. Patient process redesign is increasingly seen as creating care pathways for groups of patients with common characteristics, rather than effecting generic core process redesign. ENT is the first attempt at creating such a care pathway focusing on the procedures of tonsillectomy and septoplasty. An ENT Working Party is established led by the leader of the patient stay reengineering laboratory. Plans are developed for one ENT consultant to pilot ideas of pre-clerking, direct access to theatres, ENT nurses recovering patients.

July 1995. The head of the ENT service pilots a redesigned ENT process.

August 1995. Nurses on the ENT wards are unhappy about the poor communication prior to the pilot and fearful of the additional responsibilities incorporated into the new process. A senior anaesthetist expresses concern about the time to assess patients pre-operatively within a new process of admitting patients direct to theatre.

September 1995. The results of the ENT pilot ($n = 49$) are presented to the ENT division. The pilot is reported to have achieved a higher throughput of patients per operating list (4.5 to 7), reduced length of patient stay in hospital (39 to 22 hours), and evidence of high patient satisfaction. ENT consultants suggest that the good results are largely due to the selective case-mix used in the pilot. In the Reengineering Steering Group ENT is presented as a flagship project revealing what is possible through reengineering and applicable beyond ENT. Management consultants and reengineers suggest ENT patient activity can be increased by 20 per cent. Elsewhere, discontent about the new process is festering among recovery staff in operating theatre and anaesthetists. ENT consultants are unhappy that reengineers have circulated a job description for a new post of 'ENT process manager' without consulting the ENT division. Reengineering programme leaders are told 'if you want to change the structure of the department you must talk to us first' (ENT consultant). The head of the service suggests that piloting of new processes should continue but that processes do need refining. In particular, a new reception area for patients needs to be built in theatres. This requires capital investment by the hospital of £42 million. The hospital is performing badly against its contracts for elective surgery with ENT a particularly poor performer. The surgical directorate is said to be in 'crisis' with urgent short-term work needed to stabilize budgets and contracts. The surgical directorate is attempting to manage resource shortages in ENT and contractual underperformance at the same time as ENT nurses are being encouraged to undertake training in the recovery of patients. Furthermore, responsibility for reengineering is being shifted from centrally led reengineering laboratories to the clinical directorates.

October 1995. Increasing political difficulties emerge around the ENT intervention. Within operating theatres, nursing staff that recover patients after operation feel their jobs are under threat. Senior managers within the theatres and critical care directorate are keen to resist perceived fragmentation of the service. The unions are also increasingly concerned about possible job implications of changes in the process of patient recovery. Anaesthetists are seen as sympathizing with the concerns of the recovery staff in theatres. The head of service announces at the ENT division that the 'roll-out' of the ENT pilot is being stopped until the hospital agrees to build an arrival lounge for patients in theatres. He is also reported to be getting 'aggro' from theatre staff and anaesthetists. Reengineers hear that the pilot is being stopped from a third party and say 'it came out of the blue'.

November 1995. It is reported that senior management of the hospital supports the construction of a patient arrival lounge in ENT though senior members of the anaesthesia and theatres directorate are reported to be unhappy about the facility. Within the surgical directorate a set of 'implementation leaders' are to be appointed, one for each clinical specialty in the directorate.

December 1995. The ENT pilot has stalled. The only process redesign idea now being practised is pre-clerking. Only 80 patients have been through the new process. This figure is way short of an estimate of 1,000 by January 1996 made by a management consultant to the reengineering steering group after the pilot. Senior management approve plans for construction of the arrival lounge in operating theatres. It is announced at Reengineering Steering Group that from January 1996 'four of the six ENT surgeons are going to run the previously piloted process'. Training of ENT ward staff in recovery is to start in January.

January 1996. Recommencement of the pilot project is delayed by a 'winter beds crisis' which forces the cancellation of operating lists. The ENT pilot finally recommences at the end of this month.

February 1996. Five of the six ENT consultants are reported to be working with the new elective process.

March 1996. The surgical business manager reports to the Steering Group that 'roll-out' of the newly reengineered ENT process is happening amongst the ENT surgeons. Senior management within LRI are unhappy with the progress of the ENT project against original targets. A senior manager in the surgical directorate retorts that a 20 per cent increase in ENT activity is 'ambitious'.

April 1996. ENT is subject to further pressure to perform. The maximum waiting time for non-urgent ENT surgery is 16 months. The hospital reportedly agrees with the Health Authority that this will be reduced to 12 months maximum by April 1997.

May 1996. Team-based nursing in ENT is delayed and theatre scheduling is delayed. The patient arrival lounge is built. All ENT consultants are pre-clerking (but in slightly different ways). All ENT consultants are reported to be using the new arrival lounge. It is reported that patient length of stay in hospital is being reduced by between 20 and 50 per cent, but scheduling is seen as the key to hitting throughput targets. The very big increases in throughput predicted by reengineers and management consultants are not yet coming through. Deliverables identified by theatres management conflict with throughput objectives developed for ENT.

June 1996. The former leader of the Patient Stay Reengineering laboratory is appointed as associate process director of the surgical directorate. An ENT implementation leader is appointed. The implementation leader is a former senior nurse and ENT sister who reportedly has a good relationship with the ENT consultants. She attempts to build a broader base of support for the new patient process amongst the ENT surgeons through intensive one-to-one communication with ENT consultants. Matters for decision are taken to ENT division meetings (e.g. team-based working), to be decided by majority voting.

July 1996. Work is under way in an attempt to reach shared targets with managers of operating theatres.

August 1996. All ENT consultants are using the new theatre scheduling system.

September 1996. Roll-out of theatre scheduling across all six consultants is seen as a way of increasing throughput to meet contract targets. A change of head of ENT services follows a summer 'palace coup'. The coup is perceived not to be the result of reengineering issues but poor communication within the group.

October 1996. All the ENT consultants are working the new reengineered process. The new head of ENT services publicly declares himself as a convert to reengineering citing evidence of quality improvements, increased patient satisfaction, and reduced length of patient stay.

November 1996. The ENT implementation leader is appointed as process manager for ENT.

April 1997. ENT achieve a near 12 per cent increase in activity over the previous year. ENT has treated all patients waiting over twelve months for their operations.

October 1997. Confirmation that some changes to the patient process in ENT have been sustained whilst others have been rejected.

6.8.6   *The impact of reengineering in ENT*

The process by which patients are admitted for elective ENT surgery was redesigned. Out of the array of ideas first piloted in the summer of 1995, a number became routine practice amongst ENT consultants and nursing staff, such as pre-clerking, direct access to theatre, and scheduling of operating lists. Some other concepts piloted during 1995 did not become part of the patient process, for example, recovery of the patient by ENT nurses, discharge by nurses, and team-based nursing. Patients reported their satisfaction with the new process. ENT consultants reported satisfaction with the 'reengineered' process. Some improvements in the quality of care and the activity were made. The plan to extend ENT ward nurses' skills to recovering patients in theatres did not materialize. Doctors, not nurses, discharge patients. ENT did not prove to be the first of many new care pathways for elective patients throughout the hospital. A subsequent intervention designed to reengineer elective surgery in gynaecology (reported elsewhere in this chapter) if anything regarded ENT as much as a negative role model about how to manage change. There were major setbacks—indeed a 'crisis' late 1995—in the process of implementation in ENT, which took far longer and involved much more management effort than originally envisaged. There were difficult boundary disputes with theatres, anaesthetists, and nursing staff that undertake recovery of patients after operation. It proved very difficult to meet the very ambitious throughput targets agreed at the front end of the process. At the very least, it can be reasonably concluded that the ENT project encountered greater implementation difficulties than originally envisaged.

Some of the quality improvements stated in November 1995 were achieved. The major achievement was a reduction in patient length of stay in hospital. Figures from the hospital suggest that 98 per cent of ENT patients were admitted to hospital on the day of their operation. Consequently, the average pre-operative stay time for patients was reduced from 17 hours to 90 minutes. This shortened length of stay is attributed to a combination of the process of pre-clerking and effective functioning of the concept of patients going direct to theatre. ENT did not achieve the 20 per cent activity increases first envisaged by reengineers in March 1995. ENT increased its activity in the financial year 1996/7 by 11.3 per cent. In so doing, it reversed an activity fall of 4 per cent in the previous year. Prior to reengineering activity, increases were 8 per cent in years 1993/4 and 1994/5. Furthermore, by April 1997, ENT had no patients waiting longer than twelve months for their operation (the authors are grateful to colleagues from ScHARR for these performance data).

Interestingly, improvement in activity appeared not to be a consequence of faster working by ENT consultants as the pace of work remained largely unchanged compared with the period before reengineering (on average 4.5 patients were treated per operating list). Rather the improvement in activity was attributed to an additional consultant funded specifically to reduce waiting lists and better operational management within the ENT specialty. Improved management of waiting lists, improved utilization of theatre time, better communication between consultants and other ENT staff, improved communication between ENT and operating theatres are all signs of improved operational management. It was acknowledged by clinical staff that reengineering encouraged some of these improvements. Amongst members of the specialty of ENT it was said that the process of reengineering raised awareness about the need for change and focused energies on change. There is particular reference to the important role of reengineering in 'opening a few eyes and ears to change', 'helping to highlight problems we did not know or did not believe we had', 'focusing energies for change', 'providing the will to change and the commitment to change'. In October 1997 an ENT consultant commented:

one of the things that reengineering did of course, was look at our utilization of allocated theatre time. We were absolutely flabbergasted to hear how many operating lists were being cancelled every month. We had no true idea of it. The first time that somebody said, 'oh you cancelled twenty operating lists last month' and we all said 'no it can't be true, that's wrong'. The following month it would be twenty-five and it really brought home to us that we did not have the ability to cover things when people were away.

Having identified the scope for improvements in performance, improvements in activity have been achieved by new processes and extra resources to address problems.

Patients' going direct to theatre is also enabling better use of operating time. There is a lot less hanging around waiting for the next patient. The transfer of the patient from ward to theatre was a huge failing. The transfer of patients was previously one of the great limiting steps. We have removed that and there is much more even activity. With less hanging around you have a little less pressure per case. There are fewer complaints about waiting and that is because of the arrivals lounge and the team associates. (ENT consultant, October 1997)

Theatre scheduling has helped maximize the use of theatres. In 1995/96, many ENT lists were lost due to annual leave, sickness . . . scheduling has made all the difference along with greater management of waiting lists, plus extra lists. (Process manager, September 1997)

To meet the purchaser requirement to treat all twelve-month waiters an extra consultant was appointed in November 1996. The extra consultant has enabled the specialty to maintain a huge amount of operating lists through the year. We have literally been cancelling one or two in a month instead of twenty. That helped us enormously. (ENT consultant, October 1997).

6.8.7   *Explaining the impact of reengineering within ENT*

As the first attempt to reengineer in-patient services in LRI the project displayed a level of ambition typically associated with classic reengineering prescription (Hammer and Champy 1993). ENT was adjudged by reengineers as conducive to radical and rapid performance improvement and process redesign that could be quickly transferred to other parts of the hospital. The pattern of work within ENT was such that patient groupings and flows were reasonably simply identified and could be segmented. ENT was predominantly an elective specialty with many generally well patients with minor ailments. There was major external pressure for change coming from purchasers and there were long waiting lists. The consultant body was seen as relatively open-minded with a consultant willing to champion and pilot the intervention. The core ideas of the intervention were not regarded as new or threatening to ENT consultants given that many of the consultants utilized them already in their private sector work.

Yet, in practice the intervention was laced with controversy. Three particular controversies informed the intra-professional conflict and interdirectorate competition that materialized as the reengineering intervention unfolded. First, there was an initial failure to generate the anticipated support for the new process amongst the body of ENT consultants. Consultant support was critical given that reengineers recognized that achievement of ambitious performance targets required change to routines and work patterns of ENT doctors. Unlike, say, the elective gynaecology project, part of the agenda in the ENT case involved an attempt to reshape the practice of ENT consultants in the face of contract and waiting list pressure. The project in ENT involved an attempt to secure work intensification and an element of patient process standardization in order to achieve patient throughput targets. However, throughout the intervention the process of change was not helped by periods when the intervention lacked support amongst ENT consultants and later managers within the surgical directorate. For instance, ENT consultants did not automatically follow up the initial pilot with wholesale adoption of a new process. Neither did they sign up to hard-edged objectives of substantial increases in patient throughput. Even managers within the surgical directorate who later became responsible for delivering the project during 1996 also felt a lack of ownership of the throughput targets developed by the reengineers in the patient stay laboratory and the management consultants at the outset of the intervention.

Reengineers' vision of the process by which patients should receive elective ENT surgery implied change at some important junctures of clinical and directorate interdependence. Clinical inputs into the elective ENT patient process involved doctors and nurses within the specialty of

ENT and doctors and nurses within operating theatres. Organization-ally, the care process spanned the two major clinical directorates of sur-gery and theatres and critical care. Another major controversy in this case was the reengineering ambition that ENT nurses should take responsibility for the total process of care including recovery of patients after operation. This change to the process was perceived as a direct challenge to the work jurisdiction and job security of those nurses who recovered patients within operating theatres. This percep-tion was held by the trade unions, anaesthetists as well as the theatre recovery nurses themselves. Neither were ENT nurses committed to the idea of recovering patients after operation. They identified that the potential for extending their role was counterbalanced by unwel-come additional responsibilities of the task and the unpleasant intra-professional competition engendered by the idea. Ultimately this idea proceeded only as far as some initial training for ENT in the skills of recovery.

Consistent with a process perspective of organizing, reengineers were seeking a smoother, integrated ENT patient process. To achieve this they perceived that ENT staff needed to exercise greater control over the whole process of care. From the outset of the intervention reengineers argued that the only way to remove 'non-value adding tasks' from the care process and eliminate 'unnecessary hand-offs' was for ENT doctors and nurses to be responsible for the total process of patient care. In addition to moving ENT nurses into the physical area of theatres to recover patients greater responsibility implied greater control over the scheduling and management of theatre resources. Whereas the ideas of moving ENT nurses into theatre for recovery pur-poses created intra-professional conflict, this latter idea created ten-sions between the reengineers, the specialty of ENT, and the clinical directorate of Theatres and Critical Care. The reengineering vision tapped the deeper underlying conflict that already existed about the level of control that surgical specialties have over the resource of oper-ating theatres within the hospital.

On reflection there was contained within the ambition of the inter-vention and the vision of a reengineered process a high potential for the intervention to be controversial. However, to appreciate why the potential for conflict manifested itself in practice in the ways described one has to look more closely at the approach to planning and imple-menting this reengineering initiative. There are a number of factors relating to the approach to change in this case that adversely affected the implementation and impact of the intervention.

It was not until 1996 that a broader base of clinical leadership and support for the elective ENT project emerged. This change itself came after the reengineering laboratories had been dissolved and a new head of ENT service and process manager were appointed. The process manager was a nurse within ENT who first became an implementation leader and subsequently process manager. Momentum for change was re-established and consultant trust was developed through intensive, persuasive, one-to-one communication between the process manager and consultants. Reengineers had previously failed to do this. A failure to bring the wider grouping of ENT consultants into the change process early was a major impediment to change. The ENT project was characterized in its early stages by restricted and individualized leadership. Despite the formation of an ENT working party the change intervention was taken forward and progressed to pilot on the basis of a relatively narrow alliance between a senior reengineer and a championing ENT consultant. There was no sense of change being led by a wider team or coalition of people involved across the overall patient process. The consultant champion in this case was seen as committed, hard working, and able to present persuasively in meetings. Yet, the leadership base was to prove narrow, subject to volatility, and ultimately brittle.

[when he stopped the pilot] he pulled up the drawbridge behind him . . . 'I am not doing any more, I am fed up, it is not working, it is not doing what I want'. (Reengineer, December, 1995)

Soon after piloting a new patient process, the consultant began to doubt the motives of the reengineering programme. The preservation of good relations with other clinical colleagues—and particularly anaesthetists who are key partners for ENT surgeons—was apparently more important than the timetable of the project.

I think reengineering has got a different objective to ours . . . they wanted us to be able to do more work and they wanted us to prove that you can actually get through more patients in theatre on a regular basis by a substantial margin. So, what they wanted was the maximum number rolled through week in week out on every list. (ENT consultant, September 1996)

I did present at a meeting of the Reengineering Steering Group and one of the most interesting things about that was that [a senior manager] of the Trust said 'this will mean that you can do more patients', and I said 'no, it does not mean that we can do more patients'. I said 'it will mean that we will use the resources that we have more effectively'. He was looking for a change from an average of 4.2 patients on a list to 7. And I said 'no that is not what is going to happen. You will not get that.' (ENT consultant, September 1996)

The body of ENT consultants perceived that there was inadequate consultation with them in contract and target setting. As a consultant body, they never accepted the target of 20 per cent increased patient throughput. ENT consultants also resisted an automatic 'roll-out' of a redesigned patient process following the 'pilot' pointing out that the lists on the pilot had been restricted to tonsils and septoplasties, both relatively minor operations. Nursing support was also conspicuous by its absence throughout most of the implementation phase.

My gut feeling was that there was not a lot of ownership from the working side of the project, from the nursing side. They felt that we had devolved this project to them, and roll-out is the time we pulled back. I do not think they understood it enough. . . . (Former reengineer on the project, November 1995)

. . . clearly reengineering was still in the lab phase, and people thought it was going to stay in the lab phase and pass by and not really impact on them. So, when it did go out to the wards, they felt very threatened. I do not think they got people on board—we really did not develop ownership as well as we ought. They did not see it as their project; they did not see the value in terms of quality of care and what they could actually achieve as a team. They did not have a particularly well-developed team structure. (Former reengineer on the project, November 1995)

In the critical early stages, the ENT project was seen as essentially led by reengineers with little work going on building a broader climate and base of support for change within ENT. Reengineering had committed itself publicly to achieving ambitious targets within tight time scales, with frequent reporting to the corporate centre, and a strong action orientation. It was not with the benefit of hindsight always clear how robust these initial targets were and how they had been derived. There was evidence of indifference or even covert resistance from certain staff groups, particularly those whose job security was under threat, such as nursing staff who recovered patients in operating theatre. Amongst managers in the surgical directorate and ENT there was some uncertainty as to how the ambitious early throughput targets had been set. The uncertainty became public towards the formal end-date of the reengineering programme in May 1996 as it became apparent that managers in the directorate and specialty were being made accountable to senior management on the hospital Reengineering Steering Group for progress against the objectives:

They are being treated as a commitment that they made and if they vary from that commitment, we want to know why. This is what they are committed to . . . . (Senior reengineer, July 1996)

There was some uncertainty within the surgical directorate where the extra 20 per cent would come from. It appeared from a directorate point of view that some of the baselining analysis carried by members of the patient stay reengineering laboratory and subsequently recorded as official deliverables was inaccurate and over-optimistic.

we were not involved from day one. We are inheriting these tablets of stone. Had we been [involved] I am sure that some of the predictions and potential would perhaps have had a tinge more realism at times, along with some of the numbers. . . . (Manager, surgical directorate, May 1996)

There was also a significant gap between the disbanding of the reengineering laboratory in autumn 1995 and the formal appointment of an ENT implementation leader in summer 1996. There was a period during which it proved difficult to resource the project managerially and sustain momentum for change. The change management resources available to the directorate had a much broader span of specialties to cover than ENT. This period also coincided with a financial crisis in the surgical directorate and a withdrawal of clinical support within ENT: 'when the reengineering laboratories had gone it was harder to keep the project afloat' (former reengineer on the project, July 1996). The reengineering vision of end-to-end patient process redesign in ENT raised important interface issues with theatres and anaesthetics that proved difficult to resolve. Traditionally, a process of mutual negative stereotyping had been evident between the groupings of clinicians:

it is very much a them and us situation and it has never been a healthy relationship, surgeons blame anaesthetists and vice versa and we did have problems in recovery with staff thinking we were taking their jobs. (Reengineer, December 1995)

The concerns of theatre recovery staff about job insecurity were relayed to the anaesthetists, who then lobbied the ENT surgeons with whom they had very close working relationships. Concerns and conflicts manifested themselves in complaints about a lack of consultation with theatres. For example, the patient arrival lounge was seen as taking a third of available reception space away from the theatres department to give to relatively small groups of ENT patients:

it was presented as a fait accompli and 'you in theatres will do this anyway' and before you know it contractors are in—people were in there putting up curtains and cubicles and doing that kind of thing. (Manager, operating theatres, September 1997)

Perhaps this situation could have been ameliorated by intensive early diplomatic effort, but this was not always seen as evident in the ENT case. Perhaps however the conflict was deeper and not so amenable to resolution through diplomatic change management. A reasonable interpretation is that this controversy was symptomatic of a more fundamental and ongoing conflict within LRI between process and functional models of organizing patient services. Reengineers in this case were seeking to develop a lateral 'end-to-end' model of organizing ENT services in a context where specialties, directorates, and operating theatres are organized on a functional basis. As such, the process perspective challenged existing patterns of control over clinical work and resources. A functional perspective sees central operating theatres as a hospital-wide resource offering expertise, flexibility across clinical settings, and economies of scale. However, both this case and that of fractured neck of femur described elsewhere in this chapter see a process perspective asking the question of 'who really runs theatres anyway?' This particular conflict between process and functional thinking could potentially have been solved by a macro-level shift across the hospital away from the directorate structure. As will be revealed in Chapter 7, such macro-organizational change was to prove far more modest in scope than originally envisaged.

To summarize the case study, the ENT intervention can be seen as important in the history of the reengineering programme as it represented the first major attempt at reengineering processes of admission, stay, and discharge related to surgery. Even though ENT was initially held up as the 'flagship' by the corporate centre, change was slow and contested. The case captures the process ambitions of reengineering coming into conflict with established functional models of organizing with LRI. In practice, change to the patient process was realized but not with the speed or demonstrable impact reengineers hoped to achieve. The process that unfolded was characterized by, at times, highly charged conflict and competition involving groups of clinicians and managers. The momentum of the change ebbed and flowed in accordance with the conflict. Conflict became apparent as reengineers challenged established functional relations and patterns of control with a process model of organizing. Initial momentum for change that propelled the intervention rapidly to pilot was quickly lost to be regained only when change management responsibilities were shifted to another set of actors operating at directorate level and linked to a broader hospital initiative to reduce waiting lists in ENT. These lessons about the need for widespread internal ownership were effectively drawn and used to inform later interventions, as in the elective gynaecology case.

6.9   Reengineering out- and in-patient services in the specialty of gastroenterology

6.9.1   *Introduction*

This case study reports the process and outcome of a planned change intervention designed to reengineer services within the specialty of gastroenterology, including the design of a new endoscopy outpatient clinic. This redesign entailed role expansion for the newly appointed nurse endoscopists and a different way of working with the consultant. Redesign work was later applied to linked in-patient settings. Gastroenterology is a relatively small-scale specialty located within the medical directorate. It was widely seen as an early and fast mover within medicine, being held up as a role model by the directorate and the corporate centre. It displayed a history of internally led recent development (albeit from a low base) and a relatively simple and self-contained character. However, it also exhibited some important interdependencies with other services which were effectively managed. There was only one consultant at the start of the process, who supported the reengineering intervention throughout, so that there was a high level of clinical ownership.

Reengineering ideas were used to redesign an outpatients' clinic in this setting which increased throughput substantially, reduced waiting times for patients (although importantly this improvement was not sustained due to Health Authority contractual changes outside the power of the team in the setting), and led to high levels of expressed patient satisfaction. The case study demonstrates some important successes. Reengineering ideas were seen as helpful as they provided solutions to problems that had already been diagnosed internally. The clinical team recognized the problem of escalating patient flows and welcomed suggestions for their more effective management. Process redesign within gastroenterology started within outpatient settings, but later moved into more complex ward settings and sustained itself over time. Even so, the interface with the wider system could threaten internal achievements. For example, substantial delays in implementation were experienced due to the need to get higher-level approval for minor capital works.

The rapid and sustained pace of process redesign is in marked contrast to other settings within the medical directorate: gastroenterology was seen very much as a positive outlier. Why this might be so will be explored in Chapter 7.

6.9.2 *Organization and service context of gastroenterology*

The gastroenterology specialty is located within the medical directorate. The specialty contains the integrated endoscopy unit (offering a diagnostic facility both for outpatients and also some in-patients) and had access to a cluster of beds on two wards. It had recently gained some additional beds. Under active clinical leadership, it had expanded considerably over the preceding decade, as historically the service had been provided from six beds 'donated' by surgeons and no junior medical staff were in post. It was regarded as a successful and self-confident setting, with a track record of effective management as well as clinical excellence.

Gastroenterology services were also provided from the two other acute hospitals locally, so there was effective local competition for General Practitioner Fundholder referrals. Before reengineering, there was a twenty-week wait for an outpatient appointment, with increasing Fundholder pressure to get the waiting times down. The patient group is seen as less assertive than in other case studies (such as gynaecology) so patient-led pressure was less evident than fundholder-led pressure. Until 1996, there was only one consultant physician who specialized in gastroenterology in the hospital. Although this increased to two, the size of the clinical group is much smaller than in other case studies.

Although the bulk of the work (approximately 3,500 gastrointestinal endoscopies are currently undertaken per annum) is of an elective and outpatient-based nature, there is also a block of 'hot' diagnostic work, undertaken for the Accident and Emergency directorate and the surgeons. This case study relates initially to the outpatients' clinic established to handle the bulk of the elective work rather than the emergency work.

Gastroenterology was seen within the medical directorate as a relatively contained and routine setting in which standard reengineering tools such as patient segmentation and the plotting of patient flows were helpful structuring devices. As such, it was chosen as a site for early intervention. Until 1996, gastroenterology clinics had been located on two different sites in the hospital. The possibility of centralizing them on one location—and producing upgraded space for patients—provided a strong incentive for the setting. The adoption of process redesign was also a way of substantially increasing throughput and coping with a rising tide of referrals. Patient attendances had built up substantially (approximately doubling over the preceding three years) placing the service under considerable pressure.

The gastroenterology case is notable not only for strong consultant leadership, but also for a wider and mixed leadership group that included the specialty process manager (previously the nurse manager of the unit) and the clinic coordinator. There was an effective and sustained partnership between all three role-holders, which together drove forward change in this setting.

6.9.3 *Redesigning the process for gastroenterology patients*

Objectives. The formal objectives agreed for the gastroenterology Visit Process Project within the reengineering programme represented a mix of quality improvement objectives, increased activity and purchaser value, and some generalized hospital benefits. It should be noted that some objectives (e.g. reduced process time, decreased waiting times, increased activity) were of a stepwise rather than an incremental nature. They were seen as largely having been implemented as of late 1996, although sustaining all these gains over a longer period proved difficult.

Another formulation of informal objectives was contained in another internal policy document designed to support a presentation by team members. While this presentation certainly made reference to the purchaser perspective, there was perhaps less emphasis on activity increases and even more concern with quality. This document again highlighted the gains achieved for a range of stakeholders, including nursing: there seemed in this setting to be a range of winners with few losers. This document also emphasized the opportunity to move to a greater reliance on teamwork, better training opportunities, and more time for research as important indirect objectives.

Patient process redesign—screening by clinic coordinators. An expanded clinic coordinator role was created to manage the referral process more effectively. Clinic coordinators now dealt with referrals from General Practitioners and more actively managed appointments and waiting lists, trying to minimize the previously high number of 'Did Not Attends'. A direct telephone line was installed, making it easier for patients to ring in and cancel appointments they could not keep.

Single-visit clinic. The introduction of a new single-visit clinic reduced the number of visits for 66 per cent of patients from three to one, and greatly reduced the typical time for the diagnostic process. Waiting times to get a consultation reduced initially (although these improvements were not sustained due to changes in the volume of contracted activity), as did the time taken by the diagnostic process once the patient had arrived in clinic. Elective patients were now being admitted to a redesigned and centralized outpatients' area, received an initial consultation, underwent endoscopy, were recovered, and received their diagnosis in one day. The old outpatients' service on a different site was effectively moved across to a centralized site within the endoscopy unit within the main hospital site as a key part of the faster redesigned process. The quality of the space was also upgraded.

Nurse endoscopy and support worker roles. New roles were developed to support the new process and so achieve key project objectives such as an increase in patient throughput. Previously, doctors were performing all endoscopy procedures regardless of their complexity. Trained nurses were also spending little time on direct patient care and the bulk of their time on indirect support.

Baselining analysis by reengineers working within the medical directorate identified that certain procedures (such as upper gastrointestinal endoscopy and flexible sigmoidoscopy) could be seen as relatively routine and low risk. Experienced nurses were therefore encouraged to develop into nurse endoscopists with responsibility—under consultant supervision and clinical guidelines—for their own lists, assessment, overseeing recovery, and giving health education and advice to patients. Individual nurses varied in the extent to which they quickly adapted to these new roles. New support worker roles were in turn devised to support these nurse endoscopists with responsibility for all indirect care activities.

Redesigning in-patient settings. In 1996, there had been little process design work undertaken on the two wards linked to the gastroenterology service. They were seen as more difficult areas in which to work at that stage. By the end of 1997, process redesign work on the two wards was much more evident. Nurses were being rotated around the different settings in order to broaden their skills base. Care coordinators were appointed on the wards to manage the whole care pathway in a more proactive fashion. New clinical team leader roles were created to strengthen overall leadership. They were seen as less ward based and more likely to take a broader view of the whole care process, including linkages with other clinical directorates and wards.

6.9.4   *Chronological overview of a reengineering intervention*

April 1995. Gastroenterology moves into the medical directorate and a new nurse manager is appointed. This is seen as facilitating further development and change in the setting.

Summer 1995. Appointment of clinic coordinators within endoscopy. Endoscopy emerges as the first process redesign intervention. A reengineering training package on ensuring no more than a twenty-minute wait is seen as helpful and reinforces the internal appetite for change. Baselining and 'process-mapping' begins, involving consultant, manager, and clinic coordinator and identifies distinct patient segments—66 per cent of referrals have an endoscopy. Of these, there are distinct care pathways for 70 per cent of patients. Baselining identifies a 33-week process for diagnosis with many 'hands offs'.

September 1995. Internally led pilot with eleven patients presenting with dyspepsia tests a new patient process and produces evidence of high patient satisfaction.

October 1995. Reengineers move into the medical directorate. Gastroenterology is identified as a promising setting at directorate level. The two seconded reengineers within the medicine directorate work with the gastroenterology team on further process redesign.

October 1995–April 1996. Period of inertia while the capital needed to centralize gastroenterology outpatients on the new site could not be identified by Trust directors. Clinicians report this as 'six months of excruciating frustration'.

November 1995. Nurse manager in gastroenterology is reappointed as one of the first specialty process managers in medicine. Seen as helpful continuity in key staffing and triggers off further role expansion.

Spring 1996. Search for capital monies. Expenditure levels pared down. Upgrading work undertaken and facilities centralized onto one site. First new clinic in early May. Number of gastroenterology clinics increases from 2 to 5 per week.

July 1996. Waiting list down from 20 to 5 weeks, attracting GP Fundholder interest. Big increases (133 per cent) achieved in capacity. Seen as embedded and sustainable in the long run. Big reductions in the time taken by the diagnostic process. New nurse endoscopy and support worker posts introduced, with competency-based skills training. New process eliminates eleven 'hands offs'.

Late 1996. Early wave of changes stabilize within gastroenterology, new administration block opens.

1997. A second ward comes in to the service following a directorate-wide reconfiguration of firms. General picture of consolidation within the outpatients' service but process redesign accelerates on the wards (e.g. appointment of care coordinators and clinical team leaders to the wards; nurse rotation across the settings). Increased emphasis on close inter-directorate and setting working, for example, with the gastrointestinal surgeons, radiology, and the admissions ward within the medical directorate. Restrictive Health Authority contract chokes back elective activity to protect emergency work and waiting lists once more rise as the specialty has to remain within contract.

September 1997. Average outpatients' wait now 30 weeks (as opposed to 16 weeks in September 1996).

6.9.5 *The impact of reengineering in gastroenterology*

The endoscopy case can be seen as one of the very first clinical settings within the medical directorate to engage in process redesign—in a directorate which at least initially was slow to embrace reengineering ideas. It displays many signs of considerable success. Within a year, the entire outpatients' service was redesigned, centralized, and housed in upgraded space. A number of 'hands offs' were eliminated within the process and waiting times dropped. This centralization permitted a major expansion in the number of clinics run each week. Nursing, support worker, and administrative roles were all enhanced, and skills training opportunities made available. The creation of the nurse endo-scopist role—under consultant supervision—was an important role shift. Process redesign was seen as unleashing latent energy and enthusiasm for service development that could be detected in post-holders not normally engaged in the management of change, for exam-ple, by the clinic coordinator, who had many ideas for improving services.

Process redesign ideas had an initial impact in outpatients but then diffused into more complex in-patients settings. New and broader roles were introduced in the two linked wards. There was finally an emphasis on building effective interdirectorate and inter-setting relationships within a care pathways approach. There was strong and collective internal leadership and an effective partnership with reengin-eering personnel, especially after they had been devolved to the med-ical directorate. There was evidence of patient satisfaction with the redesigned process.

Where there was regression (as in the case of the waiting list), it was due to factors outside the control of the setting, although this indicates that such macro-level factors can have important effects, which in the end 'swamp' change effected at a more micro-level. For example, wait-ing lists did go up again, in order for the specialty to remain within the contract agreed with its Health Authority purchaser. It was suggested that the endoscopy centre was having only 25 per cent of the activity purchased which it theoretically was able to produce. As of October 1997, it was reported that 280 patients were waiting for an outpatients appointment, with an average wait of 30 weeks (as opposed to 16 weeks in September 1996). So the initial reductions in patient waiting times achieved were not sustained because of contractual changes as the Health Authority moved to protect emergency admissions, if need be at the expense of elective admissions in such service areas as endoscopy.

Why did reengineering in gastroenterology achieve a higher level of impact? There are various explanatory factors that in essence came together. The first relates to the organization, management, and timing of the reengineering programme itself. There was little direct intervention from the reengineering programme in the initial central laboratories phase apparent in this setting where process redesign came on stream rather later than, say, ENT. As a result, reengineering of the gastroenterology setting was largely internally led, with the process manager, consultant, and new clinic coordinator all playing important roles. The early process-mapping and pilot activity, for example, was largely internally driven. However, the internal appetite for change had been increased by the very early and centrally sponsored Effective Clinic work (20-minute wait; appointment of clinic coordinator) which was well received in this setting. Their limited experience of centrally led reengineering in 1995 had then been positive and fed an appetite for more locally driven work in 1996.

In late 1995, the medical directorate took increasing responsibility for the reengineering programme, reflected in the appointment of a new business manager and the secondment of two reengineers to the directorate. In the search for possible 'quick wins', gastroenterology was identified as a promising site for intervention because of its track record. The directorate also provided development opportunities for cooperating settings—the reengineers within medicine assisted the team in gastroenterology further with process redesign.

A second explanation lies in the history, local context, and configuration of key personnel that had emerged within gastroenterology. The endoscopy service had previously been small scale and underdeveloped, lying (until spring 1995) within the critical care directorate. The consultant had for some time been trying to build up the service from its low base, displaying innovative and entrepreneurial behaviours. The move to the medical directorate, the appointment of the consultant to a head of service role and then the appointment of a new nurse manager (then process manager) all opened up opportunities for a period of significant change, activity increases, and development of roles. The small-scale nature of the clinical grouping meant that internal splits were less likely to occur, although there may be a different pattern if more consultants are appointed. Reengineering was consistent with a pre-existing clinical development agenda which involved the centralization of activity within an expanded and upgraded endoscopy centre. Internal change capacity was high, but initially seen as stronger in the simpler outpatients setting:

you have got a strong team. A team that can change. A team that is flexible. So, you have all the right ingredients. But it just demonstrates, on the endoscopy side of gastro, they control everything that they are doing, and they can influence, change, and move it. On the ward, yes, they can control the ward aspect but there are so many interdependencies as soon as you open one lid three more open behind it. . . . (Management respondent, July 1996)

In fact, this early view rather underestimated the subsequent impact that was to occur in the ward-based settings. There was certainly strong evidence of internal ownership and leadership within endoscopy across a core multi-disciplinary team, including the clinic coordinator as well as the consultant and process manager. This division of roles and responsibilities offered a powerful combination:

it is absolutely critical that the clinical team is headed up by a competent, focused manager and that competent, focused manager shares a good relationship with a clinical head of service who shares the same vision as they do and can therefore give them the weight of authority to get on and do things that they would not otherwise have. (Senior clinician, December 1996)

This core team was kept together over a long period of time, when compared to other settings within the medical directorate, so that there was the benefit of continuity in key personnel over the whole of the process redesign period. The appointment of clinical team leaders and care coordinators in late 1997 also created a wider group that could support the process manager who had been a single managerial focus until that point.

There was little reported direct top-down intervention from the directorate management within gastroenterology so that the change process was led by the clinical setting. First, the physical layout of the hospital means that the key medical directorate personnel were physically distant from endoscopy. Secondly, gastroenterology was seen as a strong performer in any case so they were left 'to get on with it'. The directorate level was influential in selecting gastroenterology as a setting where an early appointment would be made to a specialty process manager post and influencing that appointment. Endoscopy was soon held up as a role model both by the directorate and indeed the corporate centre.

A third explanation lies in the local perception that reengineering could be a solution to the problems of operational management that had already been diagnosed internally. Given the operational problems of split site working, long waiting lists, and historic underperformance, reengineering was seen as a useful tool that made it easier to achieve what they had wanted to do anyway:

reengineering has created a culture, perhaps an environment, in which you can say, 'I want to change things' and do it. We have actually used some of the techniques that have become familiar to us. (Management respondent, July 1996)

reengineering obviously irritates people like crazy but it is quite good at breaking things down to what is actually happening and viewing them that way, and I think it has a lot to be said for it. . . . (Clinician, March 1996)

The reengineering agenda was here consistent with and enabled the service to achieve internally owned operational objectives: centralization and upgrading of activity; changing skill mix; retaining the confidence of GP Fundholders. The service was not distracted from the change agenda by successive operational crises or firefighting and managed to retain a focus on longer-term and more strategic issues.

Nor was reengineering seen as threatening to the underlying division of professional labour. There were few changes to consultant clinical roles through reengineering the endoscopy process, beyond a greater degree of delegation (under personal supervision and within clinical guidelines) of the more routine work to nurse endoscopists. This was a helpful coping device that enabled the consultant to concentrate on more intensive cases. Major changes to nursing roles were reported as part of the reengineering process. A small number of experienced nurses were encouraged to develop into nurse endoscopists with far greater devolved responsibility than before. Individual nurses varied in the extent to which they adapted rapidly to these new and broader roles. Secondly, new support worker roles were introduced to support these nurse endoscopists with responsibility for all indirect care activities. Thirdly, clinical team leaders were appointed on the wards to bring in more proactive case management. The new process manager role was considerably broader than the old nurse manager role (although the same person occupied both positions) and led to more personal development opportunities. The role was also seen as more 'empowered'. A new clinic coordinator role was created which was broader and more proactive than the old ward clerk role.

The leadership team in the setting remained enthusiastic and supportive of the utility of patient process ideas throughout the period of fieldwork. However, there was also some criticism from those—such as some nursing staff—who saw themselves as victims of change. A number of respondents felt that the pace of work was being progressively intensified as case numbers continued to increase. There might well be limits beyond which it would not be possible to go:

there is constant pressure on the people working here, there does not seem to be any let up at all. At the moment, people are enthusiastic and keen, and we have to keep that enthusiasm going by levelling out a bit. I think that you can only keep going with the promise that it will get better. (Management respondent, July 1996)

The view was reported in late 1997 that a number of nursing staff remained disengaged from the new process-based mode of thinking. It was argued that some of the highest calibre staff were being taken out of clinical roles and being put into more managerial roles, with a consequent threat to the quality of clinical nursing care.

Fourthly, some argued that gastroenterology was seen as a relatively simple setting within which (certainly for elective outpatient work) a high degree of patient segmentation was possible. The 'objective' conditions of clinical work favoured process redesign, as well as the subjective factors of history and leadership. Many patients are symptom specific and it was relatively easy to predict from referral letters whether they would require an upper or lower gastrointestinal endoscopy. It was also relatively easy to design specific care pathways. For example, work was also going on to devise a care pathway for gastrointestinal bleeds right up from initial presentation in Accident and Emergency to the gastrointestinal ward.

This argument that gastroenterology was a simple and contained setting needs to be qualified. It exhibited some important interdependencies and handled them well, for example, with the gastrointestinal surgeons with whom joint clinical working and joint contracts had developed strongly during 1997. Better relations were also reported in 1997 with surgery, with radiology, and with the admissions ward within the medical directorate itself, with which relations had not always been good. The building up of such links was an important feature of the work reported during 1997. Nevertheless, the initial work in endoscopy did take place in a relatively simple setting where the team was in control of most of the process, when compared to other settings such as orthopaedics.

In summary, gastroenterology should be seen as a generally high-impact setting for reengineering ideas within the medical directorate. The redesign of the endoscopy clinic was rapid and radical. There was high internal ownership of reengineering ideas (unlike the situation in Accident and Emergency) and a strong team-based approach to leadership. Local history was one important explanation as to why the setting welcomed reengineering ideas. There were effective working relations with the reengineers working within the medical directorate. Within process redesign, changes to interprofessional roles and relationships were generally well handled with good relationships reported between the clinicians and the newly created nurse endoscopists. Gastroenterology managed to use the reengineering intervention to progress its pre-existing internal agenda, winning upgraded physical space through embracing process redesign. The consultant was looking for solutions to the problem of managing escalating referral flows. The space upgrade also acted as a major incentive. Gastroenterology was a relatively contained and simple setting, although by no means free from potential jurisdictional issues. There was only one consultant in post in the setting in the early phases of process redesign, so the problem of diffusion across a large group of consultants (as in the gynaecology group) did not arise.

The approach to change within gastroenterology can be best described as internally led but externally supported. The internal leadership came from a small team and included a process manager, a management friendly clinician, and the newly appointed clinic coordinator. This team provided the impetus for change and developed their ideas further over time, moving from an initial focus on outpatient clinics onto more complex ward settings. Continuity in team membership also contributed to a higher level of change management capacity.

The case study also suggests that micro-change at the level of the clinical setting can be swamped by powerful macro-factors, such as shifts in the purchasing behaviour of the Health Authority, which could cause rapid regression, despite the best efforts of the team on the ground.

6.10 Concluding remarks

Having observed the transformational rhetoric and ambition associated with reengineering, this chapter has focused upon patient care processes as important indicators of organizational practice and performance. Six case studies of patient process redesign have been presented to assess whether reengineering transformed patient processes within LRI. The comparative case-study approach covering several different types of service provided within the hospital has enabled further examination and analysis of the finding reported in Chapter 5 that there was marked variation in the process and impact of reengineering across the array of services and settings within the hospital. The overall conclusion with respect to patient processes is that reengineering led to some redesign of patient processes but did not effect transformation in either the organization or delivery of patient services. Some patient process redesign interventions studied have proved to be more clinically controversial than others. The case of the menstrual clinic is exceptional in seeking to change core clinical practices relating to inference, treatment, and diagnosis (Abbott 1988). In practice, however, progress standardizing clinical practice amongst the corpus of gynaecology consultants via the menstrual clinic is reported as slow and contested, as consultants displayed retention of individual clinical autonomy and defence of control over practice. The menstrual case is thus reasonably characterized as having had a mixed impact when judged against original aspirations and objectives.

The other cases reported engaged less with redesign of core clinical practice and more with reorganizing the provision of patient care processes. Of the cases reported greatest impact was observed in redesign of outpatient services in gastroenterology and elective surgery in gynaecology. Both initiatives involved extended roles for nursing staff within redesigned patient care processes. Other cases revealed a lesser impact of reengineering interventions against original ambitions. Like the menstrual clinic, cases of process redesign in the specialties of ENT and orthopaedics revealed the process of change to be slow and contested, and notwithstanding some change to patient process, to have fallen short of initial reengineering aspirations and objectives. The case of least impact is that of redesign of care processes for patients admitted to the A&E department with minor injuries. Given the hospital's high emergency workload and the role of the A&E department within processes of patient admission to hospital this inability to effect radical process redesign in the area of A&E is significant to any judgement about the overall impact of the reengineering programme.

Chapter 8 is dedicated to further explaining the pattern of marked variation found in the process and impact of the reengineering programme within the hospital. However, in beginning to understand variation in the process and impact of patient process redesign one can observe in the cases that comprise this chapter a tension between a process model of organizing and existing functional arrangements as manifested in clinical specialties and directorates. In the high-impact cases, change was largely confined to either a single specialty or settings and process redesign did not contradict administrative or organizational practices in other settings and services. By contrast, case studies in the specialties of ENT, orthopaedics, and A&E medicine reveal redesign ambitions were in tension with existing specialty and directorate arrangements. Using patient processes as indicators of everyday action in clinical domains of the hospital the overall impression created by the impact of the interventions is that patient process redesign more reinforced than transformed practices that existed prior to reengineering. Distributions of authority and discretion between clinicians within patient processes remained largely unchanged. Patterns of professional action and jurisdiction within and between clinical directorates and specialties were largely maintained. In this way we can see the constraining nature of structure manifest through the ability of some individuals and groups to preserve established processes and arrangements in the face of reengineering action designed to transform those arrangements. The implications of the conflict between functional and process models of organizing are significant for a transformation agenda that desires change across the system. The point is now developed further as Chapter 7 analyses the relationship between functional and process models of organizing in respect of wider processes of organization and management within LRI. Continuing the discussion from Chapter 5, Chapter 7 reveals how organizational arrangements in place prior to reengineering remained intact and served to shape and structure the process and impact of reengineering (Child 1997; Giddens 1984).

7

Reengineering Organizational Form and Process: The Old Shapes the New

7.1 Introduction

Following on the preceding discussion of patient process redesign, this chapter moves on to examine the relationship between reengineering and organizing arrangements within the hospital. In Chapter 2, reengineering was presented as a contemporary prescription for organizational transformation that involves reconfiguring internal processes of work organization and practice. Reengineering was also identified to be part of a novel process perspective of organizing. The process organization is idealized as one wherein value creation is secured through lateral coordination of a chain of events taking place inside and outside the formal boundaries of organization. The process-based organization is seen by some to represent a radically new organizational form different from integrated hierarchies of the past (Denison 1997). In keeping with the process perspective reengineering emphasizes system-wide change that privileges a lateral approach to organizing over a functional approach through (re)organizing around core processes.

Building upon the preceding corporate and case-study analyses presented in Chapters 5 and 6 respectively, this chapter considers the nature of changes to organization form and managerial arrangements within LRI associated with reengineering ideas, interventions, and resources. These include, role change at service delivery levels of the hospital, the introduction of process management with clinical directorates and specialties, a new cadre of hospital leaders, and ongoing process redesign. However, it is argued that these changes do not constitute compelling evidence of organizational transformation. The changes outlined above are located within a pattern of clinical directorates and specialties that existed prior to reengineering, organized on a functional basis.

Exemplifying Giddens's (1984) theory of structuration in an organizational setting, clinical directorates and specialties represent important continuities that shaped the process and effects of this attempted programme of organizational transformation to such an extent that change is considered more convergent with, than transformational of the organizational form and process that existed before the reengineering programme started. The attempt to develop a process philosophy of organizing within the hospital occurred within an established structure of directorates and specialties, each with distinctive and enduring managerial and professional jurisdictions (Abbott 1988). In respect of both organizational and patient processes there was neither the breadth nor the depth of change across LRI as an organizational system to justify a conclusion of organizational transformation (Ferlie et al. 1996). We are thus reminded that within processes of strategic change and transformation, choices and actions of managerial and other agents are mediated by the very same cognitive and relational structures that such choices and actions are designed to modify (Child 1997; Giddens 1984). The first half of the chapter develops the argument further, whilst the second half illustrates the argument with reference to reengineering within the medical directorate, the largest clinical directorate within the hospital.

7.2   Organizational form and process within LRI

In Chapter 3, we suggested that clinical directorates and specialties were important features of organizational form and process within hospitals. These arrangements represent the coexistence in practice of organizational and occupational principles of work organization. Clinical specialties are mechanisms that serve to promote and preserve occupational specialization and jurisdiction within the hospital. The trend within medicine toward greater specialization seemingly intensifies the organizational problem of how to integrate work processes across a growing number of clinical specialties each representing work boundaries and jurisdictions. Clinical directorates are a mode of organization developed in the late 1980s and 1990s in an attempt to increase managerial capacity and capability within UK hospitals. Clinical directorates are managerially inspired and defined groupings of clinical specialties and service inputs, created for specific purpose of resource management, control, and accountability. This study has been particularly curious about the relationship between reengineering and arrangements that appear to embody functional organizational principles and not the process perspective of organizing described in Chapter 2. A key finding is that reengineering did not effect major challenge or change to the pattern of clinical directorates and specialties within the hospital. Clinical directorates and specialties remained as central features of organizational form and process within LRI.

7.2.1 *Important but not transformational changes associated with reengineering*

Within this fundamental continuity of organizational form, there is evidence of some important change to organizational processes and roles. At service delivery level, there were changes to organization and staffing; for instance, Chapter 6 reported how ward management was replaced by team-based nursing in the specialty of orthopaedics. Whilst team-based nursing is not a reengineering idea *per se*, its adoption within the specialty of orthopaedics followed a reengineering process that reconfigured orthopaedic wards and redesigned the care for patients with patients admitted within musculo-skeletal injuries, including a fractured neck of femur. Within a framework of process management (discussed in more detail below), the A&E department has been reorganized into six clinical teams, each under the leadership of a clinical manager and a lead clinician. Later in this chapter, it is observed how within the medical directorate specialty process teams were created.

New roles were developed within LRI as part of the redesign of patient processes. Gastroenterology introduced nurse-led endoscopy. Nurses in gynaecology discharged patients and provided follow-up care of the patient at the patient's home after operation, whilst nurses in A&E were trained to order a limited number of X-rays and apply minor treatments at triage. There were also changes in clerical support roles. The concept of the effective clinic involved the introduction of the role of clinic coordinator within outpatient departments across LRI. The role of 'clinic coordinator' was created across the Trust to improve the efficiency of clerical support within clinics and represented an exercise in multi-skilling, combining a number of clinic-related clerical roles within a single role. Clinic coordinators became a key role within the organization and management of outpatient services within the vast majority of specialties within LRI. Evidence that is more detailed was collected about the role in practice in the specialties of gastroenterology and gynaecology reported in Chapter 6. In these cases, the role of clinic coordinator is confirmed as broader in both concept and practice than the previous clinic clerk role and has led to more proactive management of waiting lists and a better operational management capability within clinics. Clinic coordinators were seen as important players in the redesigned patient processes offered within these outpatient clinics. In ENT and gastroenterology, the new role of 'team associate' within the patient process was developed as one of a multi-skilled porter who books patients in on arrival at hospital, helps the ward clerk, and transports the patient between the operating theatre and ward after operation.

'Process management' was introduced at the clinical directorate and clinical specialty levels of management. First introduced in late 1995 in the directorate of A&E and orthopaedic trauma, process management was extended across all directorates and specialties within the Trust during 1996 and 1997. Reengineering revealed the patient process to be a key level of organizational activity. Process management was an attempt to strengthen managerial accountability and responsibility for patient processes at specialty and directorate levels. It was also an attempt to improve managerial communication and decision-making across specialties and directorates. Process management was promoted through new roles and relationships at directorate and specialty levels including a clinical director working with a patient process director within each directorate. Other key roles were those of process manager, responsible to a process director, and head of service. These process management roles were designed to replace the following triumvirate of 'functional management' roles at directorate level: clinical director, business manager, and senior nurse. Our detailed studies in orthopaedics, gastroenterology, ENT, gynaecology, and the medical directorate reveal process directors and managers making a major contribution to patient process redesign.

There is also some important evidence to suggest that process directors and managers from different directorates and specialties were beginning to work together to improve joint-directorate working and the flow of patient processes that cross directorates and specialties. There were signs of movement to a process-based mode of working at interdirectorate level. Process managers in the surgical directorate started to meet regularly with representatives of operating theatres to evaluate and plan the utilization of theatre resources. Managers within the A&E department were working more closely with those in the medical directorate to improve the functioning of patient assessment units and manage the flow of emergency patients through the hospital. At an operational level, a group of process managers drawn from a range of specialties and directorates met on a regular basis to address issues around the processes of entry, admission, and discharge of emergency patients. Within orthopaedics, a 'Process Link Group' was formed in 1996. This group was a multi-professional group that met on a weekly basis to analyse and improve the care process for orthopaedic patients. Chaired by a process manager within orthopaedics, meetings of the Process Link Group involved representatives of the A&E department and operating theatres as well as clinicians in the specialty of orthopaedics.

There is evidence of both continuity and change in the personnel occupying senior positions within the hospital. Occupants of key senior management positions within the Trust such as chairman, chief executive, medical director, directors of finance, nursing and human resources, and the reengineering programme leader were unchanged over the period of the study. However, there was considerable turnover of clinical directors and clinical heads of service within the hospital. Alongside the cadre of newly appointed process directors and process managers these changes represent a complete turnover of clinical and managerial personnel within the senior to middle management positions of the hospital (although their replacements come from the same occupational groupings). Whilst turnover is not necessarily attributable to reengineering, selection decisions appear to have been influenced by reengineering. Senior managers and clinicians instrumental in processes of appointment suggested that the reengineering intervention contributed to their developing a different view of the leadership required by LRI. They believed that an alternative view of leadership influenced processes of replacement, recruitment, and succession at clinical director, head of service, and the former business manager levels. During 1997 the purpose and composition of some of the highest-level decision-making forums, such as the Hospital Executive, were reconstituted to improve managerial and clinical interaction within strategic and operational decision processes.

Processes of educational, training, and management development also changed. Notably, a leadership development programme accompanied changes in personnel and roles at senior and middle levels of the organization. The programme was directed at the top stratum of managers from clinical and managerial backgrounds, for instance, clinical directors, executive directors, process directors, process managers, and heads of service. The programme lasted for three days and was attended by approximately twenty people at any one time. By August 1997, seventy-two individuals had attended the programme. Plans were in place to open the programme up to individuals within the LRI aspiring to these roles. A feature of the programme was the attempt to broaden individuals' perspective about other personnel, processes, and activities within the hospital. The hospital's Centre for Best Practice also provided training and education in patient process redesign. New educational processes, such as the leadership development programme, brought clinicians and managers together to address change from the perspective of the whole hospital. In terms of support amongst clinical leaders within LRI at operational and strategic levels LRI is apparently better conditioned for process redesign that it was at the outset of the programme. There is evidence of a new cadre of organizational leaders, both clinical and managerial, having been identified as seemingly more open and prepared for process-based change than perhaps their predecessors were in the period of 1994 and 1996 (Hackman and Wageman 1995).

Empirical work in late 1997/early 1998 amongst the majority of clinical directors, business managers, and heads of service within LRI revealed some cynicism and scepticism about the tangible effects of reengineering to date. However, permeating the above views on a consistent basis was an argument that reengineering continued to be a catalyst for change. The catalytic qualities of reengineering seemingly related to perceptions that reengineering had encouraged people to think about change, provided energy and momentum for change, legitimized change, and created an environment to try to change practices. Whilst overt manifestations of reengineering such as the laboratories, reengineering committees, management consultants, and culturally alien language of 'baselining', 'reengineering', and 'roll-out' were viewed cynically within LRI, the idea of change through process redesign seemed enduring:

the word reengineering turned people off but the principle of looking at what you do and better ways of organizing is a good one. It has led people to question. (Consultant and clinical director, September 1997)

In practice many of the process innovations studied in detail in Chapter 6 were sustained and continued to develop over the period of field study. The work in the specialty of orthopaedics redesigning processes of care for musculo-skeletal patients was an ongoing process with strong clinical and managerial support. As the authors left the site, two more consultants were reported to be developing menstrual clinics. Newer change initiatives and ideas were emerging alongside these older more established process interventions. There were signs that LRI had learned from the experience of the past few years and was trying to develop an approach to process redesign that was more coherent across specialty and directorate boundaries. Learning from earlier innovations that started at specialty and directorate level was being transferred and proving useful to ongoing momentum for patient process redesign within LRI, the implications of which promised to transcend particular specialties and directorates. Within the specialty of orthopaedics new processes were developed related to the discharge of patients and development of collaborative notes amongst carers on the wards. Learning from these initiatives was being discussed in forums outside orthopaedics for possible wider implementation within the Trust.

Ongoing patient process redesign work related to a clearer demarcation between 'emergency' and 'elective' care processes. The care of patients admitted as emergencies represents a large and increasing component of the total work of the LRI. Some of the early work of the emergency entry laboratory and some recent work within the medical directorate exposed problems for the hospital related to the process of emergency admission. Work was ongoing to better manage processes by which increasing numbers of emergency patients were being admitted, treated, and discharged. Standard reengineering methodologies such as 'process-mapping' were being used by clinical and managerial representatives from a range of specialties and directorates to better understand the increasing demands that 'emergency patients' make on the hospital at different times of the year, and how demands may be best met. Both early work of the emergency entry laboratory about the 'flow' and 'placement' of emergency patients around the hospital and the operation of assessment units were contributing to an emerging corporate approach for managing emergency care within LRI. Learning from the process and effects of some of the earlier attempts at process redesign was informing a more corporate-wide view at Hospital Executive level of the approach to the provision of elective care. Improved testing processes, and the spread of pre-operative assessment practices (discussed in detail in the cases of reengineering elective surgery in ENT and gynaecology) were contributing to changing practices of admission into hospital for elective surgery.

The period of the reengineering exposed a highly contentious relationship between the area known as operating theatres and surgical specialties. Problems emerged about: the availability of operating theatres; the locus of control of operating theatres; and the transportation and flow of patients between theatres and the wards before and after operation. In 1997, problems were exacerbated by budget overspends in operating theatres. Though surgical services and operating theatres were managed through different clinical directorates attempts were being made to improve the interface between surgical specialties and operating theatres. There appeared to have been a marked improvement in the utilization of operating theatres in recent years. Information about the utilization of operating theatres was more widely disseminated between theatres and surgical specialties than was previously the case. The introduction of a process management structure across surgical specialties during 1996 and 1997, alongside changes in the internal organization and management of theatres, contributed to ongoing attempts to improve patient processes between surgical specialties and operating theatres. After November 1997, managerial responsibility for surgical services and theatre processes rested within the remit of the surgical process director. Operationally, process managers from a range of surgical specialties began to meet representatives from operating theatres on a weekly basis to look at the utilization of operating theatre time and plan operating lists.

7.2.2   *The survival of clinical directorates and specialties as an example of structuration*

Though noteworthy, the changes reviewed above and in the preceding chapter do not constitute evidence of organizational transformation. Whilst it was never articulated by senior management that a restructuring of directorates was a prerequisite for reengineering, a proposal developed by senior management in 1996 to reconfigure clinical directorates within LRI did not materialize. The configuration of clinical directorates and clinical specialties that existed prior to reengineering was largely undisturbed. Directorates have survived as a basic form of organization within LRI. Indeed, not only did directorates and specialties survive, they considerably shaped the process and impact of service redesign in LRI. As reported in Chapter 5, process redesign occurred within the framework of specialties and clinical directorates that existed prior to reengineering. One may interpret the adaptation of the reengineering methodology to suit the circumstances of directorates as a sign of a robust and successful defence of existing organizing arrangements by both managers and clinicians at directorate and specialty levels of organization. The devolution of responsibility for reengineering to managers at these levels further embedded the capability of managers and clinicians operating at these levels to address change on their own terms. Subsequently, process management was in fact being developed within an existing framework of functionally inclined organizing arrangements. Rather than being guided by a core process logic, process redesign and process management were in practice framed and constrained by a structure that reinforced processes of managerial differentiation, clinical specialization, and work jurisdictions.

By contrast with the all-encompassing ambition at the outset of the reengineering intervention, changes to organizational and patient processes can be assessed as patchy and uneven across specialties and groups of patients. It is difficult to relate much of the change activity that occurred to generic core processes identified early in the reengineering programme and reported in Chapter 5. A great deal of patient process reengineering was concentrated on particular patient groups within particular clinical specialties. The mobilization of process redesign tended to follow imperatives at the levels of a particular patient group, clinical directorate, clinical specialty, or even medical consultant rather than some overarching logic associated with predefined sets of core processes. A consequence was that the process of reengineering and many of the effects were confined to particular patient groups, particular clinical specialties, or even particular medical consultants. The considerable variation in the rate and pace of reengineering across the clinical specialties and directorates of LRI was both a product and process of a limited realization of reengineering ambition to make changes to generic processes that crossed specialty and directorate boundaries. A principle of reengineering is that changes need to be made at the work interfaces. However, a feature of the reengineering intervention within LRI, especially in relation to emergency and elective care processes, is that making change across the interfaces of existing specialties and clinical directorates proved a slow and difficult process.

Whilst it would be misleading to suggest reengineering simply created a collection of low-level, discrete, incoherent projects there is a lack of compelling evidence of interconnected and coherent process redesign across LRI as a health care system. Some reengineering initiatives transcend directorate and specialties levels of organization and have a more generic application within LRI. The effective clinic concept represented a major reengineering initiative that achieved a Trust-wide implementation. A new and redesigned testing facility, the Balmoral Test Centre, was accessed by a number of specialties. The redesign of clinical support services such as pathology, radiology, and pharmacy had implications for large numbers of patients receiving treatment across a wide range of specialties. However, the reengineering programme within LRI had trouble in creating, through process redesign, multiple, interconnected changes across LRI as a health care system.

Whilst reengineering sought to redesign all patient services, in practice it touched only some services. Furthermore, cases in Chapter 6 revealed that those that were touched were not radically changed or transformed. Relatedly the numbers of patients who experience a redesigned service were relatively low, especially those admitted to LRI as emergencies or for elective surgery (Bowns and McNulty 1999).

Over the period of study, the adoption and impact of reengineering was observed to vary enormously across clinical specialties and directorates within LRI. Obstetrics and gynaecology was one directorate where reengineering resources and ideas contributed to service change for a relatively large number of patients, both inpatients and outpatients. By comparison, the use of reengineering resources and related ideas was much more limited in some other directorates and specialties and hence confined to smaller numbers of patients. It is revealed below how the grouping of specialties and services located within the medical directorate displayed very differing rates of adoption and impact of reengineering.

The considerable variation in the rate and pace of reengineering across clinical specialties and directorates of LRI contributed to the impact of process redesign in one part of the LRI health care system being limited by a lack of change in another part of the hospital or by other agencies located outside the hospital. This was a general weakness of the impact of reengineering within LRI. The case studies of the care process for patients admitted for ENT surgery and with a fractured neck of femur are illustrative of this problem. The effects of redesigning the care of orthopaedic patients were limited by a lack of change in aspects of the care process under the jurisdiction of the A&E department and social services. Whilst services such as pathology and radiology were redesigned and potentially impacted of patient processes that flowed across the hospital, senior managers and clinicians in both radiology and pathology remained sanguine about the magnitude of changes to these services. There remained for these managers a large gap between 'theories' and 'visions' of reengineered radiology and pathology services and current practice. They also questioned whether the mechanisms and processes were in place at specialty level to exploit changes and improvements made to these services. The creation of the menstrual clinic is one example whereby improvements in histology facilitated the design and practice of a new clinic. Developing greater coherence of process redesign across specialties directorates was a major feature of ongoing process redesign work within LRI toward the end of the period of fieldwork. However, in the context of clinical specialties and clinical directorates, process redesign continued to run the risk of being framed and constrained by conditions of clinical specialization and work differentiation. Such conditions seemingly enhanced the possibility for incoherence and a lack of interconnectedness within patient processes that flowed across specialties and directorates of the hospital.

This uneasy coexistence of a process and functional approach to organizing is further explored with reference to the role of the medical directorate within the reengineering programme. From autumn 1995, responsibility for reengineering was increasingly devolved to the pre-existing directorates. Up to that point, medicine had been seen as a laggard in reengineering terms. However, along with obstetrics and gynaecology, medicine can also be seen as a 'high-change capability' directorate. With devolution and some new appointments, a higher level of commitment to reengineering became evident at directorate level which energized and supported change at the level of the clinical setting (such as gastroenterology). The medical directorate quickly emerged as a powerful intermediate tier shaping the reengineering implementation process within medicine. Although there were important attempts to improve traditional patterns of interdirectorate working, it should be noted that the formal boundaries of the directorate and its clinical specialties remained largely unchanged through the reengineering experiment.

7.3 Reengineering within the medical directorate

7.3.1 *History and context of the medical directorate*

As of 1995, the medical directorate was the largest directorate in the hospital, containing 319 beds on 14 wards, employing 670 staff, and with an annual budget of about £14 m. It comprised a core integrated medicine service along with a number of defined services and specialties (namely rheumatology, neurology, clinical haematology, dermatology, genito-urinary medicine, physiotherapy and occupational therapy, rehabilitation, diabetic medicine, dietetics, infectious diseases, and clinical pharmacology). An innovative medical admissions ward had been set up in 1992 to control the flow of patients into the directorate from A&E. Patients were initially assessed on this ward, and then placed on the appropriate ward for further treatment. The directorate also exhibited a strong academic orientation and some of the heads of service were professors in the Medical School and ran large research groups.

In 1995, the management structure consisted of a part-time clinical director (a dermatologist), a business manager, a senior nurse, and an accountant. Beneath the clinical director stood an associate clinical director (a gastroenterologist) and a group of clinical heads of service for each specialty. The team was seen as proactive, change oriented, and with a strong internal identity:

medicine has a tradition of a much greater sense of identity and organization—whereas surgery does not have that for a whole host of reasons. It is interesting when looking at the unevenness between medicine and surgery and their constituent parts that the absence within surgery of such a well-defined set of management arrangements has its influence . . . (Management respondent, April 1996)

In late 1995, a new directorate business manager came in (from a reengineering background) and the senior nurse post disappeared in summer 1996, as it did across the hospital. A strong and effective partnership emerged between the business manager and the clinical director that provided a focus for joint leadership. A new cadre of specialty process managers (the terminology was important and signalled a deliberate difference from the terminology used in other directorates) was appointed in 1995 and 1996 to strengthen middle management. The clinical director also quietly replaced many of the clinical heads of service in 1996, to bring in clinicians with a stronger management orientation.

7.3.2   Chronology of reengineering within the medical directorate

7.3.2.1   Summary chronology
The phasing of reengineering within medicine can be described in the following terms:

- phase 1: ad hoc innovation, 1992–4;
- phase 2: low impact, 1994–5;
- phase 3: development of a directorate infrastructure and realigning the strategy, autumn 1995–spring 1996;
- phase 4: slow roll-out and gradually increasing acceptance, spring 1996–autumn 1996;
- phase 5: delegation to operational management and an enhanced focus on interdirectorate working, autumn 1996–autumn 1997.

7.3.2.2   *Phase 1: ad hoc innovation, 1992–4*

Before the start of the formal reengineering programme, two pockets of internally driven innovation had already emerged within the medical directorate. The first was the new medical admissions ward with a 'fast track' down to A&E, created on the move into a 'greenfield' site in a new wing of the hospital. This could be seen as an early intuitive attempt to engage in process redesign in order to manage constant patient bombardment.

The second experiment was the single-visit neurology clinic, which was funded as one of a set of quality initiatives by the Regional Health Authority. The clinical director for medicine was a neurologist and helped lead this project. It was later seen as successful because it was based on radical rather than incremental redesign. However, these principles were not widely adopted by other neurologists. Radical process redesign remained confined to these two bridgeheads within the directorate at this stage.

7.3.2.3   *Phase 2: initial low impact, 1994–5*

With the creation of central reengineering labs, there was an early focus on reengineering patient visit and diagnostic test processes. There was an important early pharmacy project in medicine (changes to testing roles and role broadening for pharmacy staff) and the Effective Clinic Work had been successful in some medical directorate outpatients settings (such as gastroenterology). However, most interventions were targeted at other directorates, especially surgery, A&E, and gynaecology.

The patient visit lab reported moves (January 1995) to create prototype pilots of four reengineered settings in medicine (backpain centre; chest pain centre; hypertension centre; endoscopy) as the first attempt to break out of the 1992 bridgehead confined to neurology. The proposals took a long time to move forward. A stress on the need for greater directorate-level ownership—including by medicine—developed at the corporate centre. By autumn 1995, it was becoming apparent that the in-patient work within medicine had as yet hardly been touched.

Changing this pattern of low impact was a key task for the supporters of reengineering. Some important changes of cast began to appear within the medical directorate. In January 1995, a new clinical director (dermatologist) came in post; the previous clinical director (neurologist) was seconded to work in reengineering. However, there was evidence that process thinking had failed to diffuse into the medical directorate. A key internal Directorate Strategy Paper (July 1995) drawn up by directorate managers proposed a directorate reorganization which focused on the need for clinical specialty development (rather than reengineering), led by clinical development criteria. Many clinicians and managers in the directorate were committed to this pre-existing change agenda. It proposed 'specialty manager' roles to augment operational management (rather than 'process managers').

This document was seen by reengineers as entirely devoid of process thinking. Precisely because the directorate had strong management and internal change capacity, it was seen as untouchable, with reengineering effort being diverted into surgery and ENT. Within medicine, much of the management effort was being soaked up by a massive operational management agenda (contracts; financial management; management development).

In July 1995, the medical directorate team was asked to present to the Reengineering Management Group. The medical directorate was now perceived centrally as a laggard and as a candidate for more extensive piloting work. The first meetings began between medicine and reengineering about high-level baselining and patient segmentation. Analysis went beyond the very early Effective Clinic work.

In autumn 1995, a shift of responsibility to the directorates was being considered but with reporting to the corporate centre. Medicine was asked to report early, given the corporate intention to start reengineering patient processes within the medical directorate. Significantly, a new business manager was appointed in medicine, with a background in reengineering. As of October 1995, 'there was nothing to see or actually be involved in' (reengineer) within the medical directorate. An alliance between the new clinical director and new business manager emerged as an important joint focus, supported by an increased interest from the corporate centre.

7.3.2.4   *Phase 3: development of a directorate infrastructure and realigning the strategy, autumn 1995–spring 1996*

In October 1995, devolution to all directorates took place and as a consequence two reengineers were specifically relocated into the medical directorate. In this phase, there was a slow roll-out of reengineering directly within the medical directorate. However, there was increasing effort placed on developing clinical and managerial leadership within the directorate that later facilitated the spread of reengineering ideas. Appointments to key managerial posts started. The original directorate strategy based on specialty development was allowed to fail, as it did when it went to the corporate centre for approval. A new strategy—more aligned with reengineering thinking—then emerged within the directorate, associated with the new managerial personnel.

In October 1995, an important directorate strategy paper was written by the new business manager which was still heavily influenced by the prior work that had gone on in the medical directorate before reengineering. The paper attempted to define the approach to be taken within the directorate. It tried to reconcile the reengineering programme with the continuing development of specialty-based teams. Pilots were identified in four areas (dermatology/rheumatology; gastroenterology; neurology; and integrated medicine). The programme was widely defined to cover all specialties, potential interfaces, and emergency and elective patient processes. A timetable for roll-out was proposed.

High-level baselining of patient processes led by the two seconded reengineers then started, identifying significant delays and duplication. 'Specialty process managers' (all ex-nursing staff who had developed a broader career path) were appointed to the pilot areas, which were seen as self-contained and promising. They were expected to act as internal change agents, linking in to directorate strategy as well as securing change in their own clinical settings. The word 'reengineering' was not used within the directorate, however, as their term, 'specialty development' was preferred. The directorate vision sought to combine a pre-existing specialty focus with a novel process redesign focus. Early reengineering projects started to move forward and increase in number. A corporate review in early 1996 listed seventeen active projects within medicine.

In early 1996, the initial directorate strategy paper based on a specialty team development model was endorsed by the Directorate Board and then went to the Trust Directors' Group. It proposed to set up nine specialty teams working to a continuous improvement (rather than radical process redesign) model. It was rejected at Trust level for having 'too much old language in it' and for proposing idiosyncratic management posts. Because of this dispute, there were delays in the appointment of further specialty process managers. After this decisive rejection of the old strategy by the centre, the directorate strategy was reshaped. A new paper was presented in April 1996 that marked the formal acceptance of process-based thinking: 'the primary focus is on the Medical Directorate with the end to end medical patient process vision.' There was an attempt to produce a coherent framework for the directorate as a whole and to ensure that energy was not dissipated within isolated projects.

7.3.2.5 *Phase 4: slow roll-out and gradually increasing acceptance, spring–autumn 1996*

By this stage, the directorate strategy had been formally realigned to incorporate a reengineering perspective. There was some evidence of diffusion of reengineering ideas and interventions across different clinical settings within the directorate and of increasing levels of clinical acceptance. This included the introduction of new roles (nurse endoscopist; clinical pharmacist) and a number of symptom-specific and single-visit clinics. Impact was still patchy, and many nursing staff remained critical of reengineering. There were continuing attempts to build up the clinical and managerial leadership needed to progress the reengineering agenda further, with the appointment of a new group of heads of service. Despite some corporate proposals to merge directorates, they remain unchanged as an important unit of organization.

The new strategy was welcomed by the corporate centre as a fresh start for reengineering within medicine. Approval for the other process manager posts was granted. The scope and ambition of reengineering interventions increased within medicine, and some were held up as role models by the centre (e.g. gastroenterology). The centre's paper on organizational redesign (May 1996) proposed a process-based mode of organization at hospital level, with medicine to merge with A&E. Although this merger did not take place, the effective handling of emergency pressures during the winter months depended on effective collaboration between the medical directorate and A&E and this interface emerged as a key priority for work.

In autumn 1996, the second tranche of process managers came into post, attached to specific clinical settings (cardiovascular, haematology, and diabetes). The directorate pushed to improve internal management capacity to ensure that interdependent specialties were communicating effectively. Directorate boundaries remained the same, but there were attempts made to improve links with A&E through some new appointments. The directorate 'time-out' late in the year included a large number of presentations by settings using standard reengineering templates, with support from at least some clinicians.

At the same time, other strategic issues beyond reengineering resurfaced. The Medical Directorate Board met to consider the possible implications for the directorate of an Acute Services Review being led by the Health Authority. The 'hands off' internal market period was ending. It was envisaged that this could lead to important service reconfiguration and rationalization that would severely affect the directorate.

7.3.2.6   *Phase 5: Delegation to operational management and an
          enhanced focus on interdirectorate working, autumn
          1996–autumn 1997*

In this period, responsibility for detailed process redesign work was increasingly undertaken by the expanded cadre of operational managers, with the senior managers in the directorate concentrating on more strategic issues (such as building external networks). Some settings (such as diabetes) began to 'come on stream' for the first time. There were many new appointments to heads of service roles, in an attempt to deepen the inherited clinical leadership capacity where there had been a very mixed level of interest in management in general and reengineering in particular.

While formal directorate boundaries survived, there was increased emphasis on improved interdirectorate working in this phase, notably with A&E where a number of important initiatives were undertaken in order to cope with pressure on beds in the winter months. Many of the patients admitted to A&E (for example, with influenza) would be routed up to the medical wards. In autumn 1997, Emergency Working Groups were appointed to ensure close collaboration between the two directorates in respect of the anticipated winter pressures. The business manager's title was significantly strengthened to that of directorate 'process director', with a specific remit to encourage interdirectorate working (especially with A&E) rather than internal operational management. Active clinical planning also took place, informed by the principles but not by the language of reengineering. Good cooperation was achieved with key managers in A&E, although some A&E clinicians remained sceptical and perhaps wary of interventions from the large and powerful medical directorate. Teams from A&E and medicine were being pulled out for joint 'time-outs' for the first time. There was a growth in joint working, training, and development, and some new joint posts between the two directorates. However, the formal directorate boundaries remained in place.

There was evidence of increased ownership of patient process thinking from some managerially minded clinicians, but also continuing resistance from many nurses. The term 'reengineering' fell into disuse while some of the core concepts associated with it survived. As of late 1997, the impact of reengineering appeared to be very variable across the different clinical settings contained within medicine, with gastroenterology and a couple of other settings in the 'high-impact' grouping. There was also a subgroup of 'low-impact' settings where in reality little work had been done.

## 7.4	Review of the impact of reengineering across clinical settings within the medical directorate

This section gives an overview of the reported impact of reengineering across the various clinical settings contained within the medical directorate, presented in a rough spectrum from high to low impact.

Gastroenterology has been reviewed in detail in Chapter 6 and was seen as a high-impact clinical setting within the directorate.

Diabetes demonstrated an increasingly high level of impact, after a slow start. A process manager was appointed from outside, and the head of service role also changed with a young consultant coming into post. There was a grouping of three consultants who were keen to develop their clinical practice. There were large outpatient clinics serving a long-term caseload that required good organization.

Reengineering was originally here seen as a 'dirty word' or as treating patients like 'a mince pie factory'. However, careful management and simplification of the patient process is of practical benefit to clinicians here. A single-visit clinic was introduced in diabetes, although it benefited only small numbers of patients. The consultants were beginning to move in this direction anyway, but were facilitated by the templates provided by reengineering.

By 1997, the consultants were enthusiastic, using 'time-outs' to review services and further changes in outpatients were planned. There was less activity in ward-based settings and nurses on the ward were understaffed and overworked, and less enthusiastic. There were good links with Vascular Surgery (Foot Clinic) that were further encouraged by reengineering.

Emergency medicine. In 1996 a new head of service role was created within the medical directorate with a brief to cross conventional boundaries between the medical admissions ward and A&E, and also other medical wards. The role also involved the review of the junior medical rota to ensure that staff resources were used to optimal effect across the directorate. While process redesign ideas survived, the techniques of reengineering had been lost. Reengineering was seen as 'having come and gone', with key clinical staff not having been involved widely in the programme and not using reengineering templates. Yet, these staff were taking process redesign ideas forward with the withdrawal of the management consultants from the site. Arguments for redesign were couched in much more clinical language and reengineering templates had vanished. There were good links reported with the process manager in A&E, but there were still some difficulties with some of the A&E consultants in terms of an agreed way of working. Discharge into social care remained an enduring blockage, with sometimes social workers being scapegoated by medical staff for being unable to effect rapid discharge.

Cardiovascular services. This was a highly complex setting with about 100 beds, including the coronary care unit. There is a strong academic presence in the service, supported by a dedicated process manager. The head of service role had been sharpened. The impact of process redesign ideas was assessed here as 'moderate to high', and had been felt most fully in the outpatient settings where there developed a single-visit hypertension clinic. This was consistent with a pre-existing clinical pattern of development. Blood test and ECG services were better organized and integrated and it was easier to give GPs information.

There was also extensive process redesign in the acute and general medical clinics, involving better use of junior medical staff. By late 1997, the clinics were entering a period of consolidation after very rapid change. Ward settings came on stream later but plans for future work were reported in 1997. There developed greater awareness of the need to build links with other services, such as A&E.

Rheumatology was a setting where there was a shared process manager, so managerial time has been thinly spread. A mixed pattern was evident with a high impact of process design ideas in certain outpatient clinics; with lower impact elsewhere. The head of service had tried to implement some reengineering style ideas in his own practice previously, such as reduction in waiting times and an individualized appointment system. He had seen these ideas as 'commonsensical', although he had found it difficult to make such changes on his own, and had been empowered by the arrival of the reengineering programme that had enjoyed consistent support at the top of the hospital.

A new clinic coordinator role was introduced. There was a single-visit clinic for back pain, although this applied only to certain subgroups of patients. There were major changes in outpatient settings, leading to increased patient flow and reduced waiting times. There was an increase in day-cases on the ward, in line with pre-existing clinical developments. There was nurse resistance to process management ideas and roles. There were relatively few changes to the generally favourable pattern of interspecialty relations (key medical specialties were co-located nearby and worked well together) except with pathology (which started to turn X-rays around the same afternoon).

Haemotology. By late 1997, developments were finally starting to happen but after a very slow start. Process thinking was welcomed by those responsible for management in this setting as a powerful and exciting tool which reinforced what they were trying to do anyway (such as set up a multi-team Bone Marrow Transplant service). However, there were important obstacles to change in what was a complex and difficult setting.

The large group of sixty MLSOs was anxious and concerned about possible automation and job losses, blaming reengineering. Nurses were unsettled by rumours sweeping around that reengineering was a 'job taker'. The body of five consultants showed a sharp variation in their attitudes to process thinking, were divided into separate subgroups, and revealed no real change to ingrained habits and perceptions.

Dermatology. This setting was thinly resourced both in terms of head of service time and process manager time. This was seen as a low-impact setting with few concrete process redesign interventions apparent. Such innovation as there was (pigmented lesion clinic) was seen as driven by a pre-existing agenda for clinical development. Nurses were concerned about skill dilution imposed on them as part of reengineering (the downskilling of chaperoning roles; the clinic sister retired and was not replaced). The five consultants displayed very varied attitudes to reengineering. Although the clinical director for medicine was a dermatologist, he could not simply impose his will on the other consultants.

There was an early visit from a reengineer to examine a dermatological outpatient clinic for a week. Some clinicians argued that there was within dermatology such variation in diagnosis and treatment that it was impossible to create any clear patient pathways. Process redesign in pathology had been helpful to the dermatologists in getting test results back more quickly.

Neurology. This specialty can be seen as a major disappointment in reengineering terms. It had, after all, been the site for a very early single-visit clinic (Project Sigma, discussed in Chapter 5), which had received extensive external recognition. One of the first process managers was also appointed to neurology; so that there was a dedicated managerial resource available to progress further change.

However, clinical leadership and consultant support was seen as very variable. Some of the consultants appeared disengaged from managerial thinking, especially after the original neurological champion had been seconded out of the setting and into the reengineering programme. The single-visit clinic was maintained by a successor consultant, but at a lower level. It was a valuable service which reengineering had helped pull together, but was applicable to only small groups of patients. It had a higher profile externally than internally. Some in the setting saw it more as a propaganda vehicle than as a major service improvement.

However, there were improvements in the organization of outpatient clinics. The Effective Clinic programme was well received, and the new clinic coordinators made a big difference. There was nurse resistance, due to decreases in staffing levels that were blamed on reengineering. Some high-quality nurses went off to reengineering and were removed from the clinical arena. There were few other projects or changes in the handling of key interfaces, although there were plans for future work.

Genito-urinary medicine. As an outpatient setting it was both physically and culturally separate from the rest of the hospital. There were special and indeed legal requirements, for instance, to ensure the confidentiality of patient records. The consultants worked well together as a team, but were relatively conservative in relation to management issues. GUM was allocated a shared process manager (a first wave appointment) but the post-holder spent relatively little time there, given the high workload elsewhere. Nurses were very anxious about staff cuts and delayering (they had lost their sister post).

GUM was reported as a low-impact setting, with very few reengineering interventions apparent. While the consultants tried to extend opening hours to manage overcrowded clinics, these developments were medical rather than reengineering led. Clinic coordinator roles had not been introduced and a traditional pattern of staffing maintained. Important links to other settings (infectious diseases, dermatology, and the Women's Hospital) were stable and had not been reengineered.

7.5 Reengineering the medical directorate: a thematic overview

Following this chronology, the following analytic themes apparent within the medical directorate case study are explored within this analytic overview: slow development and patchy impact; gradually turning it around; obstacles to reengineering interdirectorate and interorganizational patient processes; the role of the intermediate tier; survival and reproduction of the old structures amid the new.

7.5.1　*Slow development and patchy impact*

Reengineering had in a sense been invented within the neurology single-visit clinic, which was of course a clinical setting located within the medical directorate. This was an interesting and high-profile experiment, but one suitable for a relatively contained patient segment. So, neurology is an interesting example to cite, as even here commitment was very dependent on a single clinical product champion and slow to diffuse out to other consultants in the group or other settings within neurology. As of 1995, reengineering was seen by some as a prophet without honour in its own land within medicine. As one reengineer put it (April 1996): 'the fundamental failure of reengineering within the medical directorate is that you mention the word and they turn their nose up ... ' In some quarters, reengineering was seen as the word that dare not speak its name. Broad internal ownership was slow to develop within the medical directorate, certainly beyond the specialist subgroup of seconded reengineers and managers. Reengineering never managed to diffuse in any substantive way into a subgroup of medical directorate specialties at all during the period of study and many medical and nursing staff remained disengaged throughout.

The slow pace of development reflected a feeling that initially reengineering was not 'sold' well to the clinicians and nurses, particularly in the early labs phase. The external consultancy support was seen as strong on analytics, but weaker in handling behaviours and the management of change. While there was corporate learning from early mistakes, it proved difficult to recover from them as negative stereotypes about reengineering quickly consolidated. The language system and templates associated with reengineering were perceived as cold and alien, provoking rejection from clinicians and recourse to language games:

they wanted to stamp their own identity on it. They wanted it to be theirs, they wanted to show that they can think, they did not want the reengineers to teach them the use of overhead slides, 'that is an overhead *transparency*', people refusing to use the word 'slide' because it was the jargon of reengineering, umpteen other things like that. (Reengineer, August 1996)

The more intellectual tone (some critics said intellectual arrogance) of the directorate was here evident in the physicians' reluctance to accept 'off the shelf' templates or management jargon without critical scrutiny. The contractual regime set up as part of the internal market that the directorate faced was based on block contracts so that the incentive to achieve higher throughput and designated activity increases was small.

As well as these important subjective and process-based factors, it was also argued that many patient processes within medicine (when compared with ENT) were objectively of a more indeterminate nature than presupposed within the reengineering model. It was therefore difficult to apply core reengineering ideas of patient segmentation and pathways to such complex patient groupings. It should be recalled that the clinical in-patient workload within the directorate was 90 per cent of an emergency nature (often routed through A&E) and the elective component small. Important areas such as integrated medicine were difficult to segment into clear patient groupings. Diagnosis was not always easy within medicine and indeed diagnosis was a key clinical skill for physicians. Many patients in the directorate (e.g. the elderly) could present with multiple pathologies that required multiple interventions rather than a single pathway.

So there were important limitations to the applicability of reengineering ideas given the nature of the clinical workload undertaken within medicine. On the other hand, there were still some well-defined areas (such as outpatient clinics for chronic conditions) where reengineering thinking fitted well. There were also a number of clinically led attempts to develop care pathways (such as gastrointestinal bleeds presenting at A&E) apparent.

So how should one characterize the relationship between the reengineering programme and the two main professional groups (doctors and nurses) within the medical directorate? The physicians were of course the dominant professional group historically within the directorate. There were virtually no examples of imposed reengineering change onto core clinical practices within the medical directorate. Rather reengineering ideas were adopted where they chimed with a pre-existing clinical agenda (as in rheumatology). Clinical support was in the early phases confined to a few key individuals, so that impact was highly variable even within a group of consultants (including neurology). Heads of service had a key role in trying to shift and reshape clinical opinion, but consultants in some specialties appeared to display fixed and negative views about management in general and reengineering in particular that were difficult to influence.

Nursing was a larger professional group, but less powerful and more likely to see itself as a change victim in respect of reengineering ideas. There was evidence of continuing resistance from many nursing staff, often in a covert rather than overt form, to reengineering ideas in the medical directorate. Nurses often saw themselves as powerless, and as unable to respond to the technical and esoteric language of reengineering.

Withdrawal, apathy, covert resistance, and reliance on informal rather than formal mechanisms of communication ('the gossip chain and Chinese whispers') may be typical patterns of behaviour exhibited by such powerless groups. Local and informal networks were used to resist the cosmopolitan and formalized world of reengineering where front-stage compliance from nurses masked backstage hostility. As one nurse put it:

I used to have a chuckle to a nurse who had done reengineering . . . I had worked with her when she was a G grade in outpatients and both our sons had swimming lessons at the same time and she would sit there and say 'have you been to any meetings?' I would tell her what had been happening and she used to say 'if only they knew what we were thinking, they are not fooling you at all, are they?' And I would say 'no.' I sit there because it is the done thing and it is good on my CV to say that I have done process-mapping at some point. I have had an interview recently and I was able to spout all the jargon and say how good the things are that have come out of it . . . (Nurse in medicine, August 1996)

Many nurses saw reengineering as a 'job taker', as stripping out traditional ward manager posts and thus delayering nurse middle management. In particular, the loss of the senior nurse post in the directorate in late 1996 provoked a wave of anxiety: 'the time when Medicine really started to shake was when their senior nursing post went' (Trust executive director, July 1996). It was also reported that many of the MLSOs were reengineering resistant, associated with fears about job security and the contracting out of their service.

7.5.2 *Gradually turning it round*

This picture of early disappointment and low impact changed somewhat with the passage of time and the introduction of a directorate-led approach. By late 1996 and into 1997, there was gradually increasing awareness and acceptance of reengineering as a potentially useful tool among a subgroup of managerially minded doctors:

awareness of what you can achieve with it is increasing. Familiarity and comfortableness with the concepts is increasing quite markedly, certainly among the senior medical staff. Only some of the nurses have come to terms with it yet . . . at the very beginning, it would have been far better to have gone bottom up than top down, and also the central part of the organization did not change and adapt while it was telling everyone else to change and adapt. (Clinical manager, November 1996)

'Roll-out' was at last happening as a critical mass of projects began to develop beyond the often cited gastroenterology example.

Why did this shift take place? The appointment of the new business manager represented an important change of personnel, as she had a reengineering background but was now clearly located within the directorate and also personally seen as approachable, sensible, and able to deliver practical benefits by a growing number of clinicians. She also shrewdly waited for the old directorate strategy to fail when it went to the corporate centre, as this cleared the way for a fresh approach. Secondly, medicine may have been fortunate in not being the recipient of intensive reengineering interventions in the labs phase. This avoided the early mistakes of imposed and externally led change apparent in some other settings and provided some organizational learning to inform this second cycle of activity.

But perhaps a price was paid for devolution to the directorate and a slow fostering of internal ownership in terms of loss of pace, attack, and ambition:

I would say that they (i.e. the medical reengineers) did belong to the directorate . . . they did not have the more focused lab atmosphere and the deadlines were not so stringent. (Reengineer, August 1996)

Many of the reengineering interventions were acceptable to clinicians only if they incorporated aspects of their own internal change agendas, and reengineering was not able or willing to impose changes on physicians. The underlying power bases did not then shift radically. Within nursing, there were two sub-areas where commitment levels to reengineering were higher than among the mass of nurses. The first was a small group of younger, more managerially minded nurses who had made the transition into the new process manager posts as a way of broadening their careers. There were also particular wards or settings where nurse opinion had been turned round through a particularly well-judged intervention, which may have reduced paperwork or brought in training and development opportunities.

7.5.3 *Obstacles to reengineering interdirectorate and inter-organizational patient processes*

Early proposals to merge the medical and the A&E directorates were not in the end implemented and the directorates survived as the basic mode of organization throughout the period of the study. However, the stress apparent by 1997 on improving joint working across conventional agency and directorate boundaries was noticeable. There was much more active coordination with the A&E department, in part driven by the need to respond to winter beds pressures. Senior management in the directorate increasingly concentrated on these lateral tasks, delegating internal operational management to middle management. It was also reported that there was better joint working with oncology. There were still limits to these improvements in interdirectorate working. Even with the A&E department, there was some continuing niggling issues as both directorates clung on to their independent identities and sometimes stereotyped the other. These issues included the nature of the triage system in A&E and the ability of the junior medical staff from medicine to work within A&E; and also a job title used within medicine (head of emergency medicine) to which some A&E consultants took exception.

There were more intractable problems of ensuring coordinated working with some important external agencies that were difficult to address from a reengineering perspective. These outside agencies included the ambulance service, community health services (both were organized as separate NHS Trusts with their own budgets and governance structures), and social services (delivered and financed through local government and not the NHS) which delivered or financed social care support or residential care.

In the medical directorate, a very large number of patients were elderly, with potentially long-term social care needs as well as acute medical needs. Speedy and appropriate discharge from an acute medical bed back into the community or residential care was then a fundamental step in the care pathway. Without effective arrangements for such discharge, the problem of 'bed-blocking' jeopardized throughput on the medical wards. These external agency boundaries remained stable throughout the period of fieldwork. The boundary with social services in particular remained both of major importance and problematic and will be considered here in some depth.

The view was taken within an experimental discharge project launched on one medical ward that it was easier to identify internal causes of delay to discharge before moving on to the external agencies. This project included the speeding up of referrals from hospital staff to the ward-attached social worker as the first step in simplifying the process. New forms were designed to speed up the process that were eventually accepted. Relations at this field level with ward-attached hospital social workers were often good, as they were often valued members of multi-disciplinary teams. This was however a micro-solution to a macro-problem and some important general policy-level differences between the hospital and the Social Services Department (SSD) were observable, particularly in relation to assessment for long-term residential care (the home help and meals on wheels services were easier to arrange). The hospital was sometimes seen as increasing the emphasis on speedy discharge and as adopting a narrow bottom-line orientation which did not always take account of the fact that relocation into residential care was a major life event for an elderly person which needed to be handled sensitively.

Within the SSD, policy guidelines included the time scale within which social workers could be expected to complete and implement the conclusions of a complex assessment. These guidelines were not necessarily time specific as it depended on whether the client was jointly seen as having attained the optimal health status that is possible in a health care setting. From that date, the SSD defined target was up to twenty working days to secure a place in a residential or nursing home.

Other policy or organizational developments apparent in the course of the study made this hospital/SSD interface even more problematic. The SSD financial system was completely separate from NHS financing, and was under financial pressure as the demand for community care increased but expenditure levels were capped by central government. The move to a purchaser/provider split within social care in the early 1990s also increased transaction costs and lengthened time scales, as there was a move from in-house providers to external providers. Social care purchasers had an increased and time-consuming role in negotiating care packages and prices and could not 'command' in-house provision. Finally, local government reorganization in the mid-1990s meant a move from one SSD to two SSDs (one in the city and one in the county), with different directors, policies, and perhaps even political leadership, increasing the complexity of liaison from the point of view of the hospital. The prospect of accelerating discharge or reengineering the inter-organizational care pathway remained remote in the face of these continuing obstacles.

7.5.4   *The role and capacity of the intermediate tier*

This case study is of particular interest as it is located at the intermediate directorate level. This tier was shown to exert a powerful shaping influence in the implementation of the reengineering programme in relation to the various clinical settings contained within medicine. Indeed, the corporate centre was highly reliant upon it as a mechanism for 'getting into' a self-confident and self-contained directorate. While the intermediate tier had increasingly to report upwards to the corporate centre and so did not have full autonomy, nevertheless it enjoyed considerable discretion in shaping the reengineering implementation strategy within medicine. For example, important directorate-wide analytic and strategy papers were produced and debated, for example, at special working parties or directorate 'time-outs'. The directorate also played a crucial role in selecting and supporting the original clinical settings (such as gastroenterology) within early reengineering interventions.

At directorate level, the clinical director, accountant, and business manager roles remained during the course of fieldwork (with the last being significantly strengthened), but the traditional senior nurse role disappeared here, as in the rest of the hospital. The dyadic relationship between the clinical director and the business manager created an effective alliance for pushing reengineering forward.

The directorate played an important indirect role as well in building up capacity to support an ambitious reengineering agenda. An important human resource role of the directorate was to strengthen further the middle management capacity apparent within the clinical settings, as without a dedicated management resource it was difficult to provide the focus for sustained reengineering efforts at local level. The appointment of process managers represented an important development in middle management capacity, with many of them coming from a nursing background but going on to broaden their careers. Many clinicians were comfortable with these appointments and grateful that process managers were able to deal with operational issues that might otherwise come to them.

As in the other cases, the presence of clinical change champions (as in the early neurology case and then gastroenterology) was another key factor at supporting change at the level of the clinical setting. Internal change agents were more evident and influential than external change agents such as the management consultants. A well-developed partnership between a process manager and a committed head of service was potentially a powerful force for pushing forward reengineering. Selecting and supporting clinical change leaders was another important human resource role undertaken at directorate level, and it was noticeable that many heads of service appointments changed in 1996 and 1997 in an effort to increase the managerial capacity and commitment level of this key linking group.

7.5.5 Concluding remarks: the survival and reproduction of the old amid the new

The case illustrates empirically once more the limits to a strategy of organizational transformation and 'blank sheet' process redesign as evident within the medical directorate. The new process-based organization that was supposed to emerge in reality continued to be profoundly influenced and shaped by the old, functionally organized hospital. Let us consider the question of structure first. The old functional structure (directorate and service boundaries) largely survived the challenge presented by process-based thinking and remained as the formal principle for the organization of clinical work. Indeed, the functionally based intermediate tier (that is the directorate) increasingly took on an important implementation role with the dissolution of the central labs.

Secondly, there is the question of the extent of change to key decision-making systems. The directorate continued to shape important decision-making systems, such as strategy development; budgetary allocation and control; and human resource strategy. While there was a genuine attempt to improve lateral working across traditional directorate boundaries, this proved to be of a partial and incremental (rather than radical) character. It also proved highly problematic to reengineer inter-organizational patient flows, even though these were of major importance to the medical directorate (given the high numbers of elderly patients who might remain in acute beds for social rather than medical reasons). The relationship with social care agencies proved difficult to influence, with the time period for social worker assessment for long-term residential care proving a major issue of contention.

This pattern of partial impact was also evident because reengineering conflicted with an internally generated and clinically rooted sense of strategy. Reengineering did not enter into a strategic void but encountered a prior commitment to a strategy of clinical specialty development. The directorate's strategy combined for some time the different principles of specialty development and process thinking within a hybrid mode. This clinically focused strategy for specialty development conflicted with a purely process-based model and led to disputes about the appropriate mode of organizing:

Reengineering was something that they did not really want in here. Reengineering was not a word that you said here, there was in tandem a reorganization going on around specialties which was not really about the process, it was about developing clinical specialties. (Management respondent, July 1996)

Some changes (such as the broadening of nurse roles) were consistent with both strategies, so that it was difficult to attribute cause and effect.

A third indicator is the extent of change to personnel. Successful organizational transformation might also be associated with major changes in personnel, and the formation of new power groups. However, there were few radical disturbances to the composition of personnel in the directorate. External change agents (such as the management consultants) had a highly contained and time-limited presence within the directorate. Once they had withdrawn, the use of reengineering techniques and templates eroded (although broader process redesign ideas lived on). Internal change agents (the specialty process managers) were largely nurses by original profession, and they were precisely because of this background seen as able to persuade some of the physicians to shift their attitudes. The physicians remained the dominant group throughout the period of the study and often remained working within the hospital for very long periods (longer than most managers). The physicians retained their control over the key clinical director and heads of service roles. It is true that many heads of service were replaced, but it was still by other physicians.

A fourth factor is the extent of cognitive reorientation apparent. Physicians' prior socialization experiences and embedded cognitive models remained largely in place, although some interventions such as the Leadership Development programme may have provided an additional managerial knowledge base. There is insufficient evidence of radical change within the directorate along these indicators to warrant the view that there has been a successful organizational transformation.

Moving down to the level of the clinical setting within the medical directorate, the overview provided in this chapter confirms the picture of very patchy impact, with a wide range of experiences apparent. There was a subgroup of high-impact settings; but also a subgroup of low-impact settings. Common themes evident across many of the clinical settings include the very partial level of physician ownership of reengineering; continuing nurse resistance; and the inability of reengineer to impose change against the wishes of the clinicians. It was when reengineering chimed with a pre-existing clinically defined agenda that process redesign was more likely to happen, but this led to a loss of 'purity' within process redesign.

It is concluded that the underlying organization of clinical work within the medical directorate displayed important elements of stability throughout the period of the study. The functional structures and associated decision-making systems proved to have considerable staying power at both directorate and setting level. Looking outside the hospital, the wider regulatory and institutional environment in which physicians operated did not shift radically and indeed by the mid-1990s it was clear that the introduction of the internal market was not going to have the very sharp impact that initially had seemed possible. The prospect of a radical and sustained 'external shock', which might deinstitutionalize the established order, therefore receded during the course of the programme.

Physicians remained the dominant occupational group within the directorate, albeit with management as a secondary group but one that was of rising importance (Alford 1975) both in terms of general management and a subgroup of clinical managerial hybrids. Physicians were still able to define limits to the impact of the reengineering programme, particularly when it began to threaten the organization of core clinical work. Moreover, managers were aware of this continuing physician dominance and therefore framed their interventions so as to construct 'win win' situations in terms of underlying interests and also to be persuasive at an interpersonal level.

8

Limits to Organizational Transformation: Explaining Local Variation within a Change Programme

In Chapter 5 reengineering was presented as a programmatic change strategy through which senior management sought rapid hospital transformation. Evidence presented in preceding chapters suggests that whilst reengineering effected some change in the organization of the hospital and provision of patient services, it did not have the anticipated transformational effect when assessed against either qualitative measures employed in this analysis (Ferlie et al. 1996) or quantitative measures (Bowns and McNulty 1999). Whilst the intended strategy of reengineering was radical and revolutionary in method and ambition respectively, the emergent strategy of reengineering proved to be more evolutionary and convergent in both overall approach and impact. In short, second order change rhetoric gave way to first order impact. Why, in practice, did reengineering develop into a more evolutionary as opposed to revolutionary strategy for change, uneven and variable in its impact across LRI, more convergent with than divergent from pre-existing organizational arrangements and conditions? Explaining these key observations with attention to micro- and more macro-levels of analysis is a prime concern of both this and the remaining chapters of the monograph.

The above assessment of impact is based on a model of organizational transformation developed by Ferlie et al. (1996) not previously applied at the level of the single organization. A critical indicator of transformation employed within the model is integrated change spanning a depth and breadth of the organization. However, a key observation that informs our overall assessment of impact in this case is one of variation in the rate and pace of reengineering across clinical and managerial units of the hospital. Preceding chapters reveal how reengineering was highly contested and markedly variable in progress and effects across many clinical settings of the hospital. By deeper examination of variation this chapter is able to shed further light on why an intended programme of organizational transformation, in this case, became a process itself transformed by the conditions of programme development and implementation (Child 1997; Brass and Burkhardt 1993; Giddens 1984).

Identification and explanation of variation in this case has a more general theoretical and empirical relevance for scholars and practitioners of change and organizational transformation. There are some notable studies of differential change at industry or sector level (Ferlie et al. 1996; Pettigrew and Whipp 1991) but few studies explain variation in the rate and pace of change within the same setting where the content of change is broadly similar. The variation observed arose out of a research process inclined to longitudinal study of change spanning multiple organizational levels and settings. The finding of variation in the rate and pace of change across different parts of the hospital lends weight to scepticism about excessive assumptions of linearity and uniformity within commentary about change and transformation. Study findings stand against a stylized and exaggerated imagery of organizational change and transformation proceeding as a planned, linear process unfolding at a uniform rate and pace across the organization. Rather, the image of change presented so far is more one of multiple processes at multiple levels, containing patterns of both change regression and progression, upward and downward spirals of momentum, plural interpretations and actions by individuals and groups, and mixed effects.

The above empirical scenario is analysed in this chapter with particular attention to dynamics operating at the micro, hospital level of analysis. Comparative analysis across clinical settings, using data initially presented in preceding chapters, especially Chapter 6, further helps to expose and explain variation in progress and fate of reengineering at the local level. Inductive analysis of data has yielded some higher-level pattern recognition that is used here to discuss both strengths and weaknesses of the programmatic approach to reengineering adopted within LRI and the complexity of patient process redesign in practice. A model is developed that directs attention to the possibilities and problems of patient process redesign in practice. By exposing these dynamics, the model has some predictive potential concerning the redesign of organization and patient processes in and around health care contexts. More generally, this discussion elaborates on key themes raised at the outset of the monograph related to the limits of organizational transformation in public and highly professionalized settings which are further developed in Chapters 9 and 10.

8.1   Strengths and weaknesses of the Reengineering programme

Chapter 2 observed the role of managerial agency in organizational change and transformation. Classical BPR prescription, with its heavily prescribed change methodology was portrayed as a radical transformation strategy that presents a stark contrast to accounts of transformation whereby change agents engage in long-term and somewhat open-ended processes of influencing and conditioning organizations for change. Data presented in Chapter 5 reveal that over the period August 1994 to May 1996, senior management adhered to classic BPR prescription (Hammer and Champy 1993) by adopting a programmatic change strategy (Pettigrew 1998). This entailed a major investment of organizational time and human and financial resources in reengineering as a pre-existing technology for change. Management consultants were appointed as external change agents. Internal change agents were appointed using staff seconded from their operational, clinical, and managerial roles within LRI. Internal and external change agents were located in specially created reengineering laboratories to work together to redesign a number of organizational processes. A set of governance arrangements was created for the programme. Plans were made whereby a sequence of core processes would be reengineered by May 1996.

The suggestion arising out of Chapters 2 and 3 that BPR was a high-risk transformation strategy is borne out by the overall assessment of impact. The approach to reengineering within LRI displayed some of the reported strengths of programmatic change efforts (Pettigrew 1998). Unlike reports of many change programmes reengineering did not flounder or falter due to a lack of top management support and commitment. From the outset, some senior managers and clinicians championed reengineering and sustained top management support for reengineering over time. A cadre of personnel in some of the highest clinical and managerial positions within LRI continued to champion reengineering and process redesign over the period of study, ensuring that organizational attention to reengineering was maintained. Operationally, reengineers within laboratories and then later those within the Centre for Best Practice helped to generate and sustain a continued energy and momentum for process redesign within LRI. Reengineering did not wither due to senior management disinterest, apathy, or loss of energy. Indeed, patient process redesign was being practised as the fieldwork of this study concluded. Given this level of sustained top management support why has reengineering not achieved the anticipated level of impact?

Notwithstanding some other institutional and organizational dynamics discussed later in this chapter and Chapter 9 that one can argue were not conducive to reengineering or process organizations, empirical data presented in the preceding chapters reveal signs and symptoms of previously acknowledged weaknesses of programmatic change efforts (Pettigrew 1998). Some of these weaknesses appear as mistakes and miscalculations directly associated with the approach and actions of reengineers. Other weaknesses appear as unintended consequences of the organization, management, and conduct of the programmatic approach adopted. In effect, these weaknesses undermined the credibility and legitimacy of the reengineering programme within LRI, generated a degree of apathy and resistance within LRI toward reengineering, and enabled the reengineering agenda to be shaped considerably by clinical directorates and specialties. These weaknesses and related effects to do with the ambition of the programme, reengineering laboratories, involvement of managers, and contribution of management consultants are discussed below.

8.1.1 *Ambition*

In a context of intensifying cost and service quality improvement pressures upon the hospital the initial level of ambition which stated that the programme would transform LRI within two years appears to have been informed by at least three factors. First, initial aspirations and objectives were consistent with the message and advice of reengineering gurus to address change radically and quickly (Hammer and Champy 1993): the logic of the argument being that people need to think big and think radically to realize the dramatic promise of reengineering. Second, attaining financial support of the NHS Executive and local purchasers perhaps required the hospital to commit to dramatic results. Third, after an initial exercise in process redesign in an outpatient clinic in 1992 reengineering champions believed that the lessons and positive effects of this work could be 'rolled out' to accomplish a more generic impact across the breadth and depth of the hospital. In time, initial ambitions and expectations were modified as senior managers and reengineers realized the full magnitude of the task they had started and the progress made.

In terms of generating support for reengineering the initial ambition was a double-edged sword. For some the grand ambition and the hospital's appearance as an innovator in its field proved attractive and energizing. For others, the very public statements of ambition generated tensions and problems within the process of reengineering and undermined support for reengineering within LRI. In practice, reengineering quickly became a change programme caught between the rhetoric of transformation and realism of what could be achieved. Reengineers expressed, albeit privately, feeling torn between a pressure to be seen to be ambitious in thinking about change, and their own thoughts and experience about what was achievable. Reengineers reported feeling enormous pressure to commit to 'stretch targets' and 'deliverables' for areas and services already experiencing operational problems of staffing shortages and contract underperformance. The programme often gave the impression of trying to do too much too soon. The pressure on reengineers to set targets quickly and achieve 'quick hits' encouraged action at the expense of learning and reflection. The case study of A&E is not an isolated example of an instance when reengineers were criticized within the hospital for being in a 'rush to pilot' and adopting a 'short-term' approach.

The public impression management associated with reengineering as a national pilot cannot be ignored in explaining the above perceptions and actions. Reengineers were expected to report, regularly, 'reengineering deliverables' (that is, results, anticipated and actual) to the Reengineering Steering Group and external agents. Post-March 1995, reengineers were observed expending great time and effort presenting reports to reengineering committees and the wider NHS community. To many within the organization these presentations and events often appeared little more than exercises in creating an impression of progress. Indeed, the phenomenon of positive impression management became more evident as the programme slipped against its own initial targets.

Among the corpus of managerial and clinical staff within the hospital, ambition and objectives appeared to generate cynicism about reengineering, rather than interest and enthusiasm. Some managers and staff responsible for services at an operational level and knowledgeable of pressures of budgets, contracts, and staffing problems regarded reengineering ambition as fantasy. Others who were prepared to engage more readily with the ambition and participate in reengineering in the hope that they may solve long-standing problems of departments and services often reported being quickly disappointed by process redesign solutions which they perceived as either misguided or short-term. The purpose and ambition of the programme was challenged by some senior clinicians as being based on narrow and limited experience of early process redesign in outpatient services and clinical support services. The credibility of plans and aspirations for reengineering more complex emergency and elective processes was especially doubted as based on experience and learning from reengineering services to groups of patients in confined and relatively predictable work settings such as outpatient clinics.

8.1.2 *Reengineering laboratories*

Chapter 5 reported two generations of reengineering laboratories over the period of study containing individuals from both within LRI and outside LRI (management consultants). In the course of study, laboratories were observed as busy places in which great energy and effort were expended on analysing and redesigning processes. However, in terms of progressing change the reengineering laboratories were flawed concepts in a number of respects. First, for many people within LRI they informed perceptions that reengineering was an exclusive and pompous initiative. The creation of laboratories populated by a group of individuals labelled by senior management as 'the brightest and best' (senior manager, March 1995) generated some animosity and resentment within LRI. The laboratories symbolized reengineering, at least in the early phases, as an elitist and exclusive approach to change. The methodologies and associated language employed within the laboratories, such as 'baselining', 'quick hits', and 'roll-out' further distinguished and distanced the group of reengineers from the mass of people within the hospital who were working processes that this perceived select group of reengineers were apparently intent on redesigning. Certainly, in the phase of the programme up to autumn 1995 many business managers and clinicians at operational level reported being 'turned off' by the language and style of the programme.

The composition of laboratories was perceived by many clinicians to be deficient in terms of expertise, status, and knowledge. Whilst some business managers, clerks, nurses, and professionals allied to medicine were seconded to work full time within laboratories, with two exceptions, doctors did not suspend clinical practice to become full-time members of the laboratories. Those within the laboratories therefore expended a lot of effort trying to engage doctors in the work of the laboratories. The difficulty was exacerbated when post-March 1995 the programme embarked on emergency and in-patient elective services. The programme was almost entirely reliant on informal means to secure medical involvement and interest in the programme. Members of laboratories used their own personal networks to persuade doctors to become involved, for example in the case of ENT. However, on the whole the approach of the programme to generating 'clinical champions' to lead change was unsystematic and piecemeal. By the summer of 1995, management consultants and reengineers were expressing concern that an inadequate numbers of clinicians were engaged in the programme.

Compositional weaknesses within laboratories often led to criticisms by clinicians, especially doctors, that those within laboratories had insufficient experience and knowledge of specialties to redesign services. This argument proved to be one basis on which doctors were able to challenge, undermine, and regulate reengineers' efforts to progress change within clinical domains. Perceived gaps in the knowledge and experience of reengineers about a particular specialty provided individuals at specialty level with clinical grounds to argue against, undermine, and slow down attempts at process redesign. For their part, reengineers did experience difficulties and express self-doubt about their ability to challenge the thoughts and working practices of individuals, especially doctors, whom they perceived as having a higher status within the organization. Ultimately, managers and clinicians at directorate and specialty levels were successful in arguing that the generic core processes could not be redesigned and then 'rolled out' across specialties.

Third, a second generation of reengineering laboratories was created in March 1995 to support reengineering the core processes of patient visit, patient stay, emergency entry, and clinical support services. The organization and work of these laboratories quickly became difficult as reengineers experienced that clinical support was proving difficult to mobilize and focus using a generic set of core organizational processes. Rather change activity became more organized around the imperatives of clinical directorates, specialties, and patient groups rather than core processes. Laboratories struggled to accommodate the change for a number of reasons. Tailoring process redesign to different specialties, patient groups, and consultants is a much more complex task than redesigning a small number of general core processes and then rolling them out across specialties and directorates. Laboratories did not have the resources to support this customized approach to reengineering evenly across the organization. Also, the organization of each laboratory around a core process, for example, the emergency entry laboratory as distinct from the patient visit laboratory meant that collectively laboratories were not organized to cope with interdependency within patient processes. In private, several members of the various laboratories criticized the work of the four laboratories formed after March 1995 as incoherent and duplicating. By the summer of 1995, those charged with managing the reengineering programme became increasingly concerned to integrate the plethora of change projects being unleashed within LRI. The integration and coherence of process redesign initiatives across specialties and directorates remained a major concern amongst some senior members of the Trust up to the point fieldwork ended in 1998.

8.1.3 *Problematic involvement of middle managers*

In summer 1995, an informal meeting of senior reengineers and management consultants was observed. The meeting was set up to 'discuss the next phase of the reengineering programme' (management consultant, August 1995). A number of issues were discussed at the meeting related to the 'current state of the programme' (management consultant, August 1995) including a perceived lack of progress reengineering surgical and medical services and the need to focus efforts in the light of reducing resources for reengineering. Within the meeting argument centred on shifting responsibility for implementing reengineering from centralized laboratories to clinical directorates. In the course of discussion, business managers were identified as 'future project leaders' (reengineer, August 1995). Over the months that followed, responsibility for reengineering was indeed shifted to business managers and clinical directors.

However, antecedent conditions of the shift made the handover of reengineering responsibility problematic. Some business managers felt unprepared emotionally and intellectually for this responsibility. Receptivity of a number of business managers to this responsibility was jaundiced by not having been identified as amongst the brightest and the best some months earlier. Perceiving themselves as having been initially marginalized from the work of the reengineering laboratories, some baulked at being told that they were now responsible for it. A widespread reaction of business managers was that reengineers had 'dropped this responsibility' (business manager, January 1996) onto them. Some who had felt ignored and rejected by the reengineering programme up to this point were now being expected to lead change. Furthermore, in some instances the responsibility was perceived as somewhat imposed and punitive. It was indeed observed in forums such as the Reengineering Steering Group and Management Group, that some business managers were being made responsible and accountable for reengineering projects, objectives, and targets that they felt they did not own or necessarily agree with. Furthermore, the onset of process management was threatening to remove their roles. Business managers were being given responsibility for a change initiative the logic of which rendered their 'functional management' role obsolete.

Thus, how business managers reacted to this responsibility in practice varied. Some business managers, for instance in gynaecology, accepted responsibility on behalf of the directorate and used reengineering responsibility to legitimize and progress changes they and colleagues wanted to make. Unsurprisingly, such changes tended to give primacy to the directorate and local clinical agendas rather than the broader reengineering agenda. Other business managers did very little with the reengineering responsibility, seemingly unable or unwilling to manage this added burden of responsibility on top of existing operational responsibilities.

There were unintended consequences of the shift in responsibility. A differential willingness and skill of business managers to reengineer processes at directorate and specialty levels was a contributory factor to the marked variation in rate and pace of change across LRI. Consequently, the mixed practice of reengineering activity at directorate level generated further problems of change coherence across the hospital. Also, the shift of responsibility created greater opportunity for the process of reengineering to reflect various existing directorate and specialty agendas as it 'went into the business' (former reengineering and process manager, December 1996), rather than challenge those agendas. Over time, the shift of responsibility for reengineering to directorate level did generate greater ownership and momentum for change amongst clinicians, managers, and staff at specialty and directorate levels. However, the paradox is that the more momentum for process redesign and ownership of change increased at these levels, the more the reengineering programme became convergent with rather than transforming of existing organizing practices and processes at these levels of LRI. Plurality and paradox was in evidence during this particular change journey (Eisenhardt 2000).

8.1.4 *Use of management consultants*

Two separate firms of management consultants were used by LRI as part of the reengineering programme. The initial firm helped prepare the programme, through involvement in the scoping study in 1994. The second consultancy firm started in the summer of 1994 following the support of the NHS Executive for the programme. The evaluation observed both positive and negative contributions of this second firm of consultants to the progress of reengineering.

The management consultants made a number of important contributions to the reengineering programme. Their appointment symbolized LRI's commitment to reengineering and their presence enabled reengineering to question established norms, conduct, and behaviour within LRI. Their lack of experience and knowledge of hospitals satisfied the guru rhetoric that in a reengineering programme you need a capability to 'think outside the box' and 'develop paradigmatic shifts in thinking'. The management consultants did draw on their experience of reengineering in manufacturing contexts to bring a new perspective to thinking about processes within the hospital. Within LRI, the management consultants were keen to promote concepts of patient segmentation and hospital capacity planning. They contributed in transferring analytical models, change-management tools, and techniques into LRI. The consultants also helped develop skills of process analysis and process-mapping within LRI. They also introduced project management skills and computer literacy into reengineering laboratories. They educated many reengineers within LRI in skills of change management and project management. Their contribution was evident in approaches to patient process redesign described in Chapter 6.

However, the overall lasting impression is that their image, input, and impact were not well regarded within LRI. At the root of the perceived weakness of the management consultants' contribution is something that some initially considered a strength; namely their lack of experience of change in the NHS. Change is an influence process and their perceived lack of experience of and knowledge about hospital processes and associated power relations meant that their analytical contribution was undermined by a naivety about how to manage change in a UK health care context. They were disappointed and disheartened to find a context in which some of the 'usual levers for change' (management consultant, August, 1995)—for example, management information systems, performance management systems, and line managerial responsibility and accountability—were all adjudged by consultants as not operating in the way they expected. This proved to be a problem, as their whole approach appeared premissed on understanding change as a process led by management in a top-down fashion. As a collective it took them some time to realize the limits of managerial power and influence over medical consultants. A senior management consultant offered a most revealing comment in August 1995:

perhaps a lesson will be that we should have involved clinical leadership much earlier . . . it is my first experience of a hospital and it is frustrating when things do not happen quickly and you cannot get the chief executive to go and beat somebody up.

It seemed that by the time the management consultants became attuned to the power dynamics of the hospital their contracted input was decreasing as planned and there were few resources remaining for them to make the impact that they and the hospital envisaged.

8.2   Patient process redesign: organizational, behavioural, and political dynamics

In addition to weaknesses of the programmatic strategy for trans-formation adopted in this case, our assessment of the limited impact of reengineering also needs to attend to micro-complexities of patient process redesign in and around clinical directorates and specialties. Inductive analysis of case-study data presented in Chapter 6 reveals a set of five interconnected organizational and behavioural issues to have impacted on the process and effects of patient process redesign interventions. The factors discussed below and presented in Table 8.1 are labelled: organization, management, and resourcing of the reengin-eering programme; receptive and non-receptive contexts for change; scope and complexity of patient processes; approaches to planned change; and resources. These factors help explain much of the observed variation in the rate and pace of reengineering across clinical services, specialties, and directorates.

8.2.1   *Organization, management, and resourcing of reengineering within LRI*

A differential rate, pace, and impact of reengineering between clinical specialties and clinical directorates within LRI is in part explained in Chapter 5 and above by uneven distribution of reengineering effort and resource across the hospital during critical phases of the reengin-eering programme, devolution of responsibility for reengineering projects to clinical directorates after autumn 1995, and limited central resources to support reengineering after May 1996.

Table 8.1 *Explaining variation in the implementation and impact of process reengineering within LRI*

Organization, management, and resourcing of the reengineering programme	Receptive and non-receptive contexts for change	Scope and complexity of patient processes	Approaches to planned change	Resourcing change
• application of reengineering efforts and resources • devolution of reengineering to clinical specialties and directorates • limited resources for reengineering over time	• perceptions about the determinacy of patient processes • clinical support and leadership • organization and management processes at directorate and speciality levels	• interdependence —clinical —directorate —agency • changing service provider roles, routines, and relationships • work jurisdictions • scarce resources	• internal/external change leadership • clinical champions and championing teams • continuity of change leaders • preparing change intervention —objectives —targets —communication • conducting change interventions —analysis —pilots —language • influencing clinicians especially doctors	• capital investment • skill-mix and training investment • investment in IT

Chapter 5 reveals how initially responsibility for reengineering was located with distinct groups of individuals organized into a number of dedicated reengineering teams reporting to a Reengineering Steering Group. The philosophy of change was top-down and premissed on a belief that a small number of generic core processes could be redesigned and then 'rolled out' throughout the LRI enveloping the mass of activity at clinical service levels. However, empirical data reported in the preceding chapters reports how reengineering efforts and interventions became focused more upon the needs and circumstances of particular groups of patients and clinical specialties rather than a set of generic core processes that could be redesigned and rolled out across specialties and directorates. In effect, what started as a centrally managed programme focused on a limited set of core hospital processes became highly decentralized in its responsibilities and accountabilities, as well as disaggregated and dispersed in its intervention activities. Processes of decentralization, disaggregation, and dispersion of the reengineering programme need to be seen as both a product of and major contributor to the uneven development of the reengineering intervention across LRI over the period of the evaluation.

Though the formal statement of ambition for the programme at March 1995 was one of concurrent change of core processes across LRI, the indeterminacy of core processes (Buchanan 1997) contributed to reengineering laboratories quickly focusing change interventions on particular services and specialties within the hospital. By summer 1995 those within the reengineering laboratories were openly articulating that reengineering interventions needed to be tailored to suit the particular needs and circumstances of patient groups, clinical specialties, and individual clinicians, especially consultants. A disaggregated level of reengineering activity resulted in reengineering interventions becoming relatively more focused on some specialties and patient groups, creating unevenness in terms of the development of reengineering across the clinical specialties and patient processes within the hospital. In an organizational context containing many patient groups and clinical specialties there was, in practice, a limit to the number of specialties and patient services that those within reengineering laboratories could attempt to reengineer, or encourage to reengineer, at any one time. More by default than design on the part of those responsible for reengineering at that time, reengineering resources and effort were applied unevenly within the LRI during the period between March and December 1995. In the period of reengineering up to the end of 1995, more effort and resources were put into reengineering surgical services than medical services. Furthermore, amongst surgical specialties, ENT was a particular focus of reengineering efforts in preference to other specialties.

Uneven development of reengineering within LRI was given fresh impetus by events in autumn 1995 and thereafter. At the meeting between senior management consultants and senior reengineers in August 1995, mentioned previously, discussion about the next phase of the reengineering programme centred on the following issues: slower than expected impact of the programme within the hospital; variation in the impact of reengineering projects across the hospital; the planned decline of dedicated centralized resources available for reengineering; and priorities for the future. Some of the key statements made at this meeting were as follows:

we have got to get into a debate with medicine about what the flippin processes are . . . (Management consultant, August 1995) we have few identified resources for reengineering medicine . . . we are having to start from scratch in medicine. Look how long it has taken to get things done in ophthalmology and ENT. Medicine is much bigger still. (Reengineer, August 1995)

we have not been able to fight battles on all fronts . . . leaving a directorate out will give off terrible signals but to do them all spreads the effort too thinly. The middle ground is to do all but to move some quicker than others. (Management consultant, August 1995).

By the end of August 1995, the prevailing view amongst senior reengineers and management consultants was that the time had come to 'hand over reengineering to the directorates' (management consultant, August 1995). The process of devolving responsibility for reengineering intervention gathered pace during autumn 1995 and coincided with the dissolution of reengineering laboratories. Those who continued to have reengineering responsibilities were expected to work more within the clinical directorates as change agents using reengineering skills and techniques learned over the previous six months.

There is some evidence that the devolution of reengineering responsibility to clinical directorates increased (as hoped for by senior reengineers and management consultants) the momentum for reengineering throughout the whole organization. From autumn 1995, considerably more pressure was applied by senior management to directorates to account to the Reengineering Steering Group and Reengineering Management Group for the progress of reengineering. By November 1995, a senior reengineer reported over 100 reengineering projects across all areas of the hospital. Closer inspection of the data and some projects reveals widely varying stages of project development. The variation was itself a reflection of differential progress between directorates and specialties. Paradoxically, whilst increasing the pressure for change the devolution of responsibility had simultaneously accelerated the already uneven development of reengineering across LRI. Some directorates and specialties were shown to be more able and willing to take responsibility for reengineering projects than others. The medical directorate and the obstetrics and gynaecology directorates were notable by their acceptance of responsibility for reengineering and the formulation of process reengineering interventions in the light of existing directorate and specialty plans. By comparison, less progress had been made in the surgical directorate and theatres and critical care directorate. Over a period covering 1995 and 1996, these directorates gave the appearance of the reengineering change agenda being crowded out by operational and financial problems within these directorates.

For those leading the reengineering programme, the growing number of projects at various stages of development across the breadth of the hospital, allied to the decentralized responsibility for reengineering projects, raised issues of programme coherence, control, performance measurement, and management.

we are starting to ask questions about 'where are the interdependencies between various projects and how are we going to build across the interdependencies' . . . we have a lot of projects . . . now we need to take a top-down approach to pull it all together . . . (Reengineer, March 1996)

The struggle for coherence of both reengineering effort and effect throughout the whole organization proved to be a consistent feature of the programme. Furthermore, after May 1996 it was not possible for resources to be directed to address issues of unevenness. The bulk of the funding acquired specifically for the reengineering programme was spent, as originally intended, between 1994 and May 1996. However, in the context of the whole hospital, the period between May 1994 and May 1996 can be characterized as one of very partial process redesign. The overview of the reengineering programme presented in Chapter 5 reveals momentum for process redesign continued beyond May 1996. However, post-May 1996 it is noticeable that resources were limited to support change where progress was either slow or where investment was needed to achieve full effect of an intervention. It is apparent that some areas of the hospital, for example, the surgical directorate, operating theatres, and the Accident and Emergency department, struggled to absorb and operate a reengineering change agenda whilst coping with operational problems and crises. Some other areas such as pathology required capital investment to fully exploit the effects of the redesign of the service over the previous two years. The lack of available funding specifically for reengineering after May 1996 meant that there was only a small centralized resource remaining to help progress process redesign. This centralized resource consisted of a small group of reengineers and support staff (up to six people) who became members of a 'centre for best practice' created to facilitate ongoing development of process management and process services redesign within LRI.

8.2.2 *Receptive and non-receptive contexts for change*

Cases of patient process redesign studied in Chapter 6 share a temporal and spatial context, having all occurred within Leicester Royal Infirmary at a similar point in time. However, the closer one gets to clinical service settings the more one sees how features of those settings shape the possibilities, processes, and effects of change interventions. The study observed variation in the readiness and preparedness of directorates and specialties to undertake process redesign with parts of the hospital appearing to be more or less receptive contexts for change. Receptivity to patient process redesign within directorate and specialty settings is explained here in relation to: perceived determinacy of patient processes; the presence of clinicians, especially medical consultants willing to lead, support, and sanction redesign interventions; generic processes of organization and management at directorate and specialty levels; and the quality of existing relationships within and between clinical settings. Classic reengineering texts (Hammer and Champy 1993) that promote a blank-sheet mentality to organization change are revealed to be naive as reengineering is seen as imbued and shaped by the associated physical, historical, cultural, and social conditions of change. The argument about receptive and non-receptive contexts for change (Pettigrew, Ferlie, and McKee 1992) is developed below as each of the factors identified above are illustrated with data from case studies.

Health care reengineering involves trying to identify flows and processes of patient activity in, around, and out of the hospital, with a view to predicting, planning, and redesigning those patient flows and processes. In LRI, the perceived level of determinacy of patient processes shaped the formulation, development, and sequencing of reengineering interventions. It is noteworthy that reengineers concentrated on surgical and not medical services in a crucial phase of the programme between March 1995 and autumn 1995. Relative to planned elective surgery, especially of a minor nature, medical conditions are often complex and of an emergency nature. ENT was deliberately chosen as the first reengineering project involving in-patients and surgery because of the perceived level of determinacy of the ENT patient process. Ninety per cent of the work of the ENT specialty was identified as planned and elective as opposed to emergency. Similarly, senior managers and clinicians within the obstetrics and gynaecology directorate focused reengineering interventions on elective gynaecology services rather than maternity services because the latter were seen as clinically more complex, unpredictable, and carrying a higher legal risk. Gastroenterology was one of the first services to be reengineered within the medical directorate because it was a specialty perceived to function as a relatively contained and routine service setting with a discrete range of conditions and processes. Characteristics attributed to the service made it more amenable than, for example, integrated medicine, to the application of standard reengineering methodologies such as patient segmentation and plotting of patient flows. The implication here is that the perceived degree of determinacy of patient process is an issue critical to understanding variation in the pattern and sequence of process reengineering within LRI over the period of study.

The observed pattern of patient process redesign within LRI was also influenced by the identification of clinicians, especially medical consultants, willing to support or lead reengineering interventions. The uneven development of process reengineering is in part explained by the uneven numbers of clinicians across specialties and directorates over the period of the programme that were willing to engage with and champion reengineering interventions. Undoubtedly, some of the earliest reengineering interventions, such as that in ENT, were developed because reengineers identified a clinician or several clinicians willing to support or lead a change intervention. Planned change interventions in ENT, gastroenterology, orthopaedics, and gynaecology demonstrate the critical role of clinicians in leading and supporting change. Conversely, reengineering interventions lagged behind in those areas where there was a failure to cultivate clinical support for change. The attempt to reengineer the care process for patients attending the Accident and Emergency department with minor injuries failed to generate sufficient levels of support amongst doctors in the department and lacked impact as a result.

A large part of the explanation for the willingness of some clinicians to support reengineering interventions, or at least not veto interventions, relates not to their support for reengineering *per se* but their desire to accelerate the progress of agendas, ideas, and strategies for service development. Receptivity of clinicians to reengineering needs to be understood, at least in part, as a function of the broader context in which clinicians operate. In some cases, there was a momentum for change which reengineering was adjudged to complement. Orthopaedic surgeons acknowledged that reengineering came along at a time when their sense of desperation with the trauma orthopaedic service made them receptive to ideas for change. In the specialty of orthopaedics there was already a strategy in place for improving orthopaedic trauma services and reengineering was perceived as complementary to the implementation of the strategy. Patient process redesign in gynaecology proved complementary to long-term national trends in the pattern of clinical services indicating a movement away from a traditional in-patient care model to more outpatient and community-based care.

Within the specialty of gynaecology in 1995/6, care processes that promised to reduce length of stay in hospital were attractive to managers and clinicians because they were able to contribute to making the necessary bed reductions required to support investment in a new women's hospital. Also at that time a sufficient number of senior experienced nurses in gynaecology wanted to extend their role subject to clinical protocol. The nurses were prime movers behind process reengineering in this case. The case study of the menstrual clinic is evidence of reengineering being used to accelerate the interest of some clinicians in clinical audit and evidence-based medicine.

By contrast, the case of minor injuries within the A&E department suggests a set of conditions that proved antithetical to patient process redesign. As the monopoly supplier of A&E services within the county the department faced both an increasing workload and quality imperatives from central government. Patient process redesign coincided with major problems of nurse recruitment and retention. The design of the department did not lend itself to the vision of patient process projected by reengineers. Doctors within the A&E department were not persuaded that reengineering could be a positive force in the department. Consequently, doctors in the department quickly lost faith in the objectives and purpose of the reengineering initiative, perceiving it as adding to, rather than alleviating the problems of the department.

Given the devolution of responsibility for reengineering interventions to directorates after the autumn of 1995 it is no surprise to find that organization and management capability at directorate and specialty levels also shaped the progress and effects of process reengineering. The case of the medical directorate reported in Chapter 7 reveals the directorate to have been a powerful intermediate tier of management between the corporate centre (apex) and clinical specialty level, shaping the response to reengineering within the medical specialties. In the directorates of medicine, and obstetrics and gynaecology, there was a conscious effort by those responsible for managing the directorates to manage the process of reengineering within the directorate. Somewhat paradoxically both of these directorates appear to have benefited from there having been very little reengineering effort expended on the directorates by the time reengineering responsibilities were devolved to directorates. Both of these directorates engaged with reengineering ideas largely on their own terms and within the context of larger strategies of service development for the directorates. Furthermore, these directorates possessed a capability to plan, prepare, and implement change. They, in effect, interpreted the reengineering agenda to make it consistent with strategic direction and operational imperatives at directorate level. In both gynaecology and gastroenterology patient process redesign interventions enjoyed the support and 'blessing' of both senior clinicians and managers at directorate level. Such internal support was important in protecting the intervention from any excessive and counter-productive interference from central reengineering and senior management. These interventions progressed using a team of individuals with managerial and clinical interests from within the directorate and specialties concerned. In both cases, commitment, ownership, and resources for change came from within the directorates and specialties concerned.

The approach to reengineering within the surgical directorate is an interesting contrast to that described above. The surgical directorate contained specialties that were geographically diverse within the hospital, reportedly making internal communication difficult. There was a perception that relative to the medical directorate the surgical directorate consisted of highly individualistic consultants providing a disparate collection of services. For much of the period of this study there was little sense of strategy for the surgical directorate. Whilst in the directorates of gynaecology and medicine, reengineering was addressed through directorate processes and organization this was not the case in surgery. Rather, surgical specialties were the subject of a lot of attention and intervention by reengineers after March 1995. This was a period when reengineers and management consultants were bullish in their approach to process reengineering. It was not apparent that managerial processes within the directorate were significantly shaping reengineering activity. Reengineering of surgical services therefore proceeded seemingly without a guiding or mediating influence of directorate management. Indeed, over the period of the programme it was possible to detect conflicts and tensions between operational pressures on this directorate and related specialties and the reengineering agenda. In an important phase of the reengineering programme between March 1995 and August 1996 senior management within the surgical directorate appeared barely involved in reengineering interventions. They were seemingly more focused on managing operational problems and addressing contractual underperformance than planning and preparing reengineering interventions. As the reengineering programme was moving into the 'clinical heartlands' of the hospital, senior management in the directorate were experiencing reengineering attention as a distracting and unwelcome pressure. When responsibility for reengineering was then devolved to directorates later in the autumn of 1995, it was perceived and received as another burden imposed upon the directorate. Managers at directorate level inherited reengineering projects with what they perceived to be unrealistic targets such as the case of ENT, and of which they had no 'ownership'. It is unsurprising that within the surgical directorate reengineering interventions are adjudged to have made little progress during 1995 and 1996. Across surgical specialties reengineering suffered many false starts and unrealized ambitions. The case of ENT shows that when the 'flagship' project in the specialty of ENT ran into difficulties, directorate management was incapable of contributing to the resolution of the problems. Rather, contractual pressures and financial crises at directorate level contributed to the slow rate and pace of change in ENT. A winter-beds crisis slowed pilots, as did a lack of resources for change once the reengineering laboratories had dissolved.

If processes of organization and management at directorate level shape the progress of reengineering interventions, so do processes at specialty level. In the absence of a strong role for directorates in planning and preparing change, it is imperative that processes of organization and management at specialty level inform the preparation, planning, and progress of change interventions. However, in some cases weaknesses at directorate level were mirrored by weaknesses at specialty level. In the case of ENT problems in the organization and management of the specialty contributed to the problems that this change intervention experienced. Indeed, the subsequent recovery of the momentum for change in ENT is to a large part explained by changes in the organization and management of the specialty through the appointment of a new head of service and process manager. Problems of managing change within the Accident and Emergency directorate reveal a disconnectedness of managerial processes at directorate and specialty levels. By contrast, the cases of reengineering in gastroenterology, and obstetrics and gynaecology, reveal specialty management to be closely linked by both process and personalities to management processes at directorate level and to have been instrumental in progressing change interventions.

Established working relationships within service settings are another important factor to consider in explaining how conditions of the setting for change shaped the progress of change interventions. Reengineering interventions typically involved changes to established roles and routines. The preparedness of people to contemplate and practice changes to roles and routines is influenced by the quality of personal and working relationships between individuals within service settings. Relationships are inextricably part of more general processes of collaboration and competition within and between specialties and directorates. In some cases, established relationships facilitated the progress of the change intervention. The case study of reengineering elective gynae-cology reveals clinicians willing to devolve responsibilities for dis-charging patients to nurses within the specialty subject to medical protocol. The preparedness of consultants to pilot nurses discharging patients from hospital is attributed to the established working relation-ships and 'trust' between the consultants and nurses in question. By contrast, the processes of extending nurses' roles in the Accident and Emergency department proceeded very slowly. Part of the explanation for the slow progress rests in an alleged reluctance of doctors in the department to support an extended role for nurses.

It is not just the history of relationships between clinicians that was important to the progress of reengineering interventions. Relations between clinicians and non-clinicians, especially non-clinical man-agers, shaped the possibilities and progress of patient process redesign. Planned interventions in gastroenterology, gynaecology, and orthopaedics proceeded with joint managerial and clinical leadership. The cases of A&E and ENT were characterized less by clinicians and managers working together to achieve change. Interdirectorate, inter- and intraspecialty relationships are critical to progressing process redesign interventions. There were long-standing tensions between surgical specialties and the central operating department about the control and provision of theatre services. The tensions surfaced and were manifest in the controversies in the ENT case and, to a lesser degree, orthopaedics.

Physical facilities within which services are provided also impacted on the progress of reengineering visions and ideas. The case of A&E shows reengineers' vision for the service was constrained in practice by the physical architecture of the clinical setting. Within the A&E depart-ment, clinicians and managers acknowledged that the physical design of the department has been a factor impeding a radical reengineering of 'patient flows' into and out of the department. In gastroenterology the move towards centralization of clinic facilities on one site was an incentive to change, as was the development of the women's hospital in gynaecology.

The preceding discussion has identified how features relating to the setting for change shape the genesis, development, and impact of change interventions. On a cautionary note, the concept of receptivity to change is in practice dynamic and ambiguous. Comparison between the two interventions in gynaecology is illustrative of the point. The development of the menstrual clinic and the reengineering of elective surgery reveal two reengineering interventions that proceeded within the same group of clinical and nursing staff at the same time, yet with different outcomes in terms of 'roll-out amongst gynaecology consultants'. A reengineered process of elective gynaecological surgery was rolled out from two to nine consultants within six months of a pilot using two consultants. By contrast, the practice of a menstrual clinic had not 'rolled out' beyond initiating two consultants two years after being piloted in March 1996. Clearly, the context for these interventions was not uniformly receptive and additional explanations must be sought for the differential impact of interventions. Our search for additional ingredients to our explanation of the implementation and impact of process reengineering within LRI leads us to examine more closely the nature of the patient process being redesigned.

8.2.3 *Scope and complexity of patient processes*

Discussion of the scope and complexity of patient processes is intended to direct analytical attention to the issue of interdependence within patient processes and how interdependence may affect the progress and effects of planned change interventions. The scope of a patient process differs according to the levels of clinical, directorate, and agency interdependence within a patient process. The complexity of reengineering a patient process differs according to: whether the junctures of interdependence are perceived to be in need of change; whether change challenges established roles and routines of service providers within an existing patient process; and whether conflicts over work jurisdiction (Abbott 1988) and scarce resources are generated by the practice, or even the prospect, of change. Across the case studies, major differences were observed in the relative scope and complexity of the patient processes being reengineered.

Issues of scope and complexity help reveal the inherent social and political nature of process redesign interventions. The more socially and politically complex a process redesign intervention the more difficult it is to realize intended effects. For instance, reengineering the care process for patients admitted with a fractured neck of femur is adjudged a task of high complexity, as the scope of the patient process is broad, incorporating clinical, directorate, and agency inputs and interdependence. Creating change at the junctures of interdependence generated conflicts about work jurisdiction and control of scarce resources. By contrast, reengineering outpatient services in gastroenterology, for example, proved to be a relatively less complex intervention because the scope of the patient process is relatively narrow, with only limited clinical and directorate interdependence. Also, with a limited number of actors involved in the care process, working together in a confined setting, role change was more easily negotiated and introduced. Attempts at changing junctures of clinical (and directorate) interdependence through role change triggered conflicts of jurisdiction between doctors in A&E, nurses in A&E, and doctors in the specialty of orthopaedics. These conflicts impacted considerably on the rate and pace of change in these instances. In effect, each change intervention can be seen to have generated its own set of social and political dynamics that in turn impacted upon the realization of intended effects of redesign interventions. The argument about the scope and complexity of patient processes is developed in more detail using subheadings of interdependence, service provider roles and routines, and jurisdiction.

8.2.3.1 *Interdependence*

Reengineering focuses on changing business processes as opposed to attitudes and values (Buchanan 1997). A technique for reengineering business processes is 'process-mapping'. In all the case studies of reengineering reported process-mapping was used to identify the interdependence of tasks, people, and resources within existing and espoused patient processes. The greater the level of interdependence within a patient process the more control is seen as dispersed across the process, both clinically and managerially. From a change management perspective, the more dispersed the process of control within a patient process the more difficult it is to plan and manage the process of change and create intended effects. The case studies discussed in Chapter 6 highlight three main types of interdependence within patient processes: clinical, directorate, and agency. Associated with each type of interdependence are issues of task performance and the supply of resources—human, material, and financial. The presence of each form of interdependence varies considerably across the case studies of patient process reengineering.

Clinical interdependence relates to the clinical inputs and referral processes that are part of a patient care process. Patient care typically involves members of the medical profession as well as other clinicians such as nurses and members of professions allied to medicine. The level of clinical interdependence varies across the case studies. The care process for patients with a fractured neck of femur contains a relatively greater degree of clinical interdependence than, for example, the care process for patients attending the menstrual clinic or gastroenterology clinic. Patients admitted into LRI with a fractured neck of femur were referred by a doctor in the Accident and Emergency department to an orthopaedic specialist on the ward. They were anaesthetized prior to their operation. The patient care process involved nurses in A&E and on orthopaedic wards. Post-operatively, as part of the process of rehabilitation, patients were referred to an occupational therapist, physiotherapist, and perhaps a social worker. By contrast, the care process for patients attending the Accident and Emergency department with a minor injury contained fewer interdependencies. After an initial consultation with the doctor they were discharged or referred to a nurse in A&E for minor treatment. In some instances patients were referred to an orthopaedic doctor, for example, in fracture clinic following X-ray. The process of care for patients attending outpatient clinics for gastroenterology or menstrual disorders contained, at least in its early phases, relatively limited interdependence. The interdependence within this patient process is related simply to patients undergoing diagnostic tests whilst attending the clinic.

Directorate interdependence is revealed in a number of case studies. Patients admitted into hospital requiring surgery access a service that flowed across several specialties and clinical directorates. For example, the ENT specialty was part of the surgical directorate. A patient's admission for surgery required the patient to be referred to an anaesthetist prior to entering the operating theatre. This example of clinical interdependence is also an example of directorate interdependence as the coordination of anaesthetists and responsibility for the provision of operating theatres were tasks within the remit of the theatres and critical care directorate, not the surgical directorate. Similarly, the care process for patients admitted with a fractured neck of femur crossed the orthopaedic trauma and Accident and Emergency directorate, as well as the theatres and critical care directorate.

Agency interdependence is evident when the care process requires professional inputs and resources outside the institutional control of the LRI. Excepting the interdependence resulting from referral by a general practitioner to a hospital consultant, only one of the case studies reported in Chapter 6 reveals a reengineering process involving agency interdependence. The process of discharging patients admitted with a fractured neck of femur required collaboration between the hospital and social services. With some notable exceptions, reengineering of patient processes has tended to be confined to the care processes within LRI. Links with GPs and external agencies have not been subject to reengineering.

8.2.3.2   *Service provider roles and routines*

The complexity of patient process redesign as a change intervention is also a function of the extent to which existing clinician roles and routines are challenged. Interventions reported in Chapter 6 all required some change in service provider roles and routines to achieve the intended effects. Routine is defined as a regular or customary way of doing things. Role refers to the part played by a person in a particular social setting. However, the magnitude of the change to roles and routines varies across the cases. The magnitude of the variation is itself connected to interdependence within the particular patient process being reengineered.

The case of the menstrual disorders clinic is unique among the patient process redesign interventions studied, being the only one that explicitly sought to change clinical practice. Other cases show reengineering interventions to have had some small impact on doctors' clinical practices, roles, and routines. Nurses were the clinical group whose roles and routines appear most changed by reengineering interventions. Many of the new roles established because of reengineering involved change to nursing roles. For some nurses reengineering initiatives led to an extension of their role. Nurses in the A&E department began to order X-rays and issue minor treatments at triage for patients with minor injuries. The intervention in elective gynaecology devolved responsibility for discharging patients to each consultant's primary nurse. Nurses were able to discharge some patients from hospital after gynaecological surgery and visit them at home immediately after the operations. Both the interventions in elective gynaecology and elective ENT introduced the practice of 'pre-clerking'. Consultants, along with nurses and other professional colleagues assess and prepare patients for surgery in a clinic several days before admission into hospital. Within gastroenterology experienced nurses developed a role as nurse endoscopists with responsibility, under consultant supervision and clinical guidelines, for their own patients. The case study within orthopaedics reveals nurses in A&E ordering X-rays for patients admitted with a suspected fractured neck of femur and being more involved in planning the process of discharging patients from hospital. A reconfiguration of orthopaedic wards saw nurses organized into consultant-based rather than ward-based teams. Shift patterns also altered.

However, it would be mistaken to present a view that reengineering extended the roles of nurses across the board. A large proportion of nurses did not have their role extended though they may have been affected by the changes made to the organization and management of the nursing function within the Trust following reengineering. For some nurses the introduction of 'process management' structures contributed to a downgrading of position. Consequently, there were very diverse perceptions of reengineering amongst nurses within the Trust. There were perceptions that some nurses benefited from reengineering through role extension and promotion, whilst the majority did not benefit, with some losing their jobs or experiencing demotion. The variable impact of reengineering on the corpus of nurses within LRI is another component of the explanation for variation in the rate and pace of change.

The preceding discussion has identified that patient process reengineering required changes to established roles and routines of clinicians. Achieving change in roles and routines is a critical aspect of the complexity of change interventions because changes to roles and routine challenge established existing patterns of control over work processes. The degree of controversy associated with changes to roles and routines varies across the cases. Change of responsibilities between doctors and nurses in the case of elective gynaecology proved relatively uncontentious. By contrast, shifting responsibilities for the ordering and assessment of X-rays within A&E was highly contentious. Role change in the case of ENT also proved controversial and subject to difficult disputes between operating theatres and reengineers. The menstrual clinic was a clinically controversial innovation among gynaecology consultants. To help understand the contentious nature of changes to established roles, routines, and junctures of interdependence it is useful to use the concept of 'jurisdiction'.

8.2.3.3 *Jurisdictions*

Abbott defines jurisdiction as 'the simple claim to control certain kinds of work' (Abbott 1988: 64). Abbott suggests that jurisdictions contain claims to classify a problem (diagnosis), reason about it (inference), and take action on it (treatment). The implication of Abbott is that professionalized organizations are subject to disputes about who is qualified to perform, control, and supervise clinical work. Empirical data from this study suggest that reengineering generated a number of jurisdictional conflicts that adversely impacted on the realization of intended effects of reengineering interventions.

The menstrual clinic sought to radically challenge processes of diagnosis inference and treatment. Explanation for the slow roll-out of the menstrual clinic beyond the two gynaecology consultants who piloted the clinic in March 1996 lies with consultant resistance to attempts at standardizing clinical practice. Slow progress of the two change interventions affecting Accident and Emergency services (minor injuries and fractured neck of femur) is in part explained by a reluctance of A&E doctors to devolve responsibilities within the care process to nurses, radiographers, and orthopaedic specialists. These attempts at changing junctures of clinical (and directorate) interdependence through role change triggered conflicts of jurisdiction between doctors in A&E, nurses in A&E, and doctors in the specialty of orthopaedics. Comments below indicate that the conflicts can be related to control over processes of diagnosis and treatment for certain groups of patients. Also, that conflict needs to be understood in the context of a deeper, long-standing competitive relationship between the specialty of orthopaedics and the A&E department.

the nurses would like to X-ray above the elbow and above the knee . . . you would only ever be looking at minor injuries but you would then be getting into the realms of the nurse making a diagnosis. (Nurse manager, A&E department, September 1997)

A&E consultants finally agreed to nurses ordering X-rays below the knee and elbow. Initially they came out with a number of clinical issues to suggest that we would not be giving optimum care to the patient . . . they were not issues just delaying tactics. (Doctor, orthopaedics, December 1996)

In the case of the care process for patients admitted with a fractured neck of femur, A&E doctors did not support plans to shift the responsibility for reviewing X-rays of patients admitted with a fractured neck of femur to radiographers and other doctors on the ward.

We have still not been able to get over radiographers reviewing X-rays. The A&E medical staff are against this one because it threatens their professional standing. They start saying 'well why do you need doctors at all in that case if radiographers and nurses can do the job'. It is difficult to persuade them on that one. They also feel there is a risk to patient care if that happens. Personally, I feel that we could get patients reviewed by a doctor on the acute ward in a shorter time than they see the A&E doctor. (Orthopaedic doctor, December 1996)

Underlying these disputes was a deeper level of competition between the area of A&E and the specialty of orthopaedics over responsibility and control of the large group of patients attending A&E with musculoskeletal injuries.

Orthopaedics integrate closely with the A&E department, 99% of our patients come through A&E and we have always felt that we would like what some of my colleagues crudely call control over it. But I think really what we are looking for is a more integrated service. I think A&E consultants see that as a threat. It is perceived that we would be taking over control of their patients. I perceive it more as a partnership though many of my colleagues would like to take over the care of their patients. (Orthopaedic consultant, December 1996)

Controversies about extending the role of nurses in the Accident and Emergency department contrast with the extension of nurse roles in the cases of gastroenterology and elective gynaecology. In these cases, doctors supported the extension of nurse's roles to cover processes of discharging patients. In gastroenterology nurse endoscopists developed their own lists of patients, assessed patients, oversaw recovery, and gave health education and advice.

Not all the jurisdictional conflicts and issues involved doctors. Progress reengineering the care process for patients admitted with a fractured neck of femur was regulated by a need to create agreement among nurses and therapy professionals for new processes of assessing patients' rehabilitation needs and discharging patients. Creating greater interdisciplinary team working on orthopaedic wards and introducing new procedures within the care process challenged existing patterns of influence and control over processes of patient rehabilitation assessment and discharge between nurses and those members of professionalized occupations allied to medicine working on orthopaedics wards.

The key people in rehabilitation are occupational therapists, physiotherapists, social workers, and nurses. There are lots of issues with them and we have had to work closely with them looking at issues of professional boundaries and the way they work together . . . we have had a big problem with occupational therapy due to professional boundaries and the fact that OT's role has expanded over the years. They have built up an enormous role for themselves that they cannot now deliver. Yet, they have a lot of control on the assessment and discharge process that we have to look at . . . (Process manager, September 1996)

The case study of ENT reveals controversies related to both clinical and directorate jurisdiction. The reengineering vision of the process by which patients receive elective surgery implied change at some important junctures of clinical and directorate interdependence within the care process. Clinically, there are a number of important inputs into the care process involving ENT doctors, ENT nurses, anaesthetists, and recovery nurses within operating theatres. Organizationally, these inputs and resources were controlled within two clinical directorates. ENT services were managed within the surgical directorate whilst the resource of operating theatres along with clinical inputs of anaesthetists and recovery nurses were organized within the theatres and critical care directorate. Reengineers' plan that ENT nurses should take responsibility for the total process of patient care including recovery of patients after operation proved to be very controversial. The ambition proceeded only as far as some training for ENT in recovery skills as the change was perceived as a challenge to the work jurisdiction and job security of nursing staff responsible for recovering patients in operating theatre. The intended change never progressed to becoming established practice as recovery nurses preserved their role in recovering ENT patients after operation and the theatres directorate maintained control over staff working in the theatres area. The conflict generated contributed to the slow pace and impact of process reengineering in this case. This dispute represented a conflict about who treats (recovers) patients after operation and which directorate controlled the clinical inputs within the care process. Issues central to this dispute were widespread within the hospital as it endeavoured to develop process management whilst still operating centralized management of services such as operating theatres.

8.2.4 *Approaches to planned change*

The fourth component of Table 8.1 is presented to argue that the approach to planned change is also an important factor to consider when accounting for the process and outcome of change interventions. Across the case studies there are marked differences in the impact of patient process interventions. A finding of this study is that the progress of planned change interventions designed to reengineer patient services was greatly influenced by the level of support, cooperation, and resistance for the intervention amongst clinicians, especially medical consultants. Data presented below show how some approaches to change fostered support and ownership of the change intervention amongst clinicians responsible for the patient process whilst other approaches to change mobilized opposition to process reengineering. By approaches to planned change we mean not simply the application of particular analytical tools and techniques for change but rather the processes of leading, communicating, preparing, and influencing change.

The case studies of A&E and ENT reveal patient process redesign to have been led, at least initially, by people (reengineers) from outside those specialties. By contrast case studies of medicine, gastroenterology, and the menstrual clinic were 'internally led' with prime movers of change in these cases being individuals already working within these specialties and patient processes. The cases about fractured neck of femur and gynaecological surgery reveal a mixture of internal and external change agents working within the process of change. In these case studies, interventions were internally led with external support.

Across the cases, difference can be observed in terms of whether the prime movers of patient process redesign are clinicians, managers, or reengineers. The menstrual clinic was an intervention largely led by clinicians. Prime movers behind the reengineering of elective surgery in gynaecology were a number of senior experienced nurses within gynaecology. Change interventions in orthopaedics and gastroenterology proceeded on the basis of joint leadership by managers and clinicians. The prime movers behind the intervention to reengineer the care process for patients attending the A&E department with minor injuries were initially reengineers and later managers within the department.

Processes of leading change may also operate from a narrow or wide base of support. Reengineering elective ENT surgery proceeded, at least initially, on the basis of a relationship between a reengineer and a single clinician. Relatively, this was a narrow base of leadership as compared to the cases of orthopaedics and elective gynaecology. These interventions were broader based in the sense that a wider range of individuals, clinical, managerial, and reengineers, operating at different levels of LRI, were scripted into the change process at early stages within the intervention.

A differential ability to sustain leadership of an intervention over time is also apparent across case studies. The leadership of the intervention in ENT underwent numerous changes of leadership personnel over the period of the intervention. By contrast, the interventions in gynaecology, medicine, and orthopaedics benefited from continuity of personnel leading these interventions over time. Quality and continuity of leadership appear critical to the progress of change especially when the scope and complexity of change is high and progress can only be made over relatively long time frames.

Major differences were also observed across the cases in terms of preparing change interventions, communicating change, and influencing people to change. Within A&E reengineering came to be regarded by staff with the department as unwelcome, disruptive, and intrusive. On the other hand, reengineering methods and resources were welcomed as useful contributors to desired change in the specialty of gastroenterology. The A&E department was subjected to a lot of analysis by reengineers and there is evidence that reengineering 'pilots' disrupted day-to-day working within this area of the hospital. One pilot was infamous amongst doctors and nurses for the 'chaos' caused within the department. Indeed, after this it proved difficult for reengineering personnel to recover credibility within the department. In other cases, such as gastroenterology and gynaecology, processes of 'baselining', 'process-mapping', and 'piloting' were applied in ways that did not generate the same levels of resistance and antagonism amongst clinicians as they continued their day-to-day work.

Means and methods of communication differ across the case studies. Some interventions were characterized by a reliance on formal, group-based methods of communication. Others used a greater level of informal communication. It is the mix of approaches to communication that seems to be significant here in terms of progressing change. The case study about reengineering elective surgery in gynaecology illustrates the effectiveness of regular, planned formal communication with a wide group of stakeholders within the care process complemented by almost daily one-to-one, informal communication, focused on persuading clinicians to engage and pilot change interventions. In the cases of A&E and ENT, communication by reengineers about patient process redesign interventions was perceived by clinicians more as a fait accompli than consultation. Language used (often by reengineering and management consultants) in relation to interventions such as 'reengineering', 'roll-out', 'quick hits' alienated individuals rather than enthused them. It is interesting that the case of medicine reveals a conscious rejection of such language in deliberations and conversations about change.

Some approaches to change were more confrontational than others. Within ENT and A&E visions of reengineered care processes were perceived as threatening to the roles and responsibilities of some individuals and groups. In these cases, perceptions of the threat intensified as these change interventions proceeded to generate overt conflict between individuals, specialties, and directorates. By contrast, interventions in gynaecology and orthopaedics proceeded with less overt conflict. In both cases, individuals leading the change recognized the need to avoid unnecessary conflict amongst individuals and groups involved in the care process.

Change interventions are also distinguished by the extent to which individuals and groups were able to 'customize' (Pettigrew 1998) interventions to accommodate preferred objectives and approaches to change. The interventions in A&E and ENT suffered from being developed at a time when the reengineers in the laboratories and management consultants were acting in a particularly bullish and zealot-like fashion.

Across the hospital, their behaviour was widely perceived as an example of reengineering imposing objectives, targets, and change methodologies on the rest of the organization. In earlier phases of the reengineering programme many clinicians and managers at directorate and specialty level were antagonized by what they perceived as imposition of a 'one best way' approach by reengineers. Case studies about the medical directorate, gynaecology, orthopaedics, gastroenterology, and latterly ENT support the more general observation that the energy for change and momentum of change throughout the hospital increased when individuals at these levels felt more able to adopt, adapt, and customize reengineering ideas and resources to suit local circumstances and purposes.

As a summary of the preceding discussion, Table 8.2 suggests that interventions with relatively high impact displayed the following approaches to change: leadership of change within the specialty or directorate; clinical ownership and support for change; low or non-existent clinical resistance to change; support for change both politically and materially beyond the immediate clinical setting; partnerships of clinicians and managers leading change; objectives of change that incorporate professional development, service development, or service problem-solving. Cost and activity-related objectives alone are unlikely to create sufficient incentives for clinicians to reengineer patient processes. It is necessary to construct a team of people working within the patient process to champion process change. Formal and informal communication methods that are genuinely consultative are also required. At clinical service level, processes of persuasion that are informal, and based on one-to-one communication with doctors, are critical to the effectiveness of influence strategies. The cases of elective gynaecology, gastroenterology, medicine, and orthopaedics exhibit many of these features. On the other hand features of the process of change associated with slow rate and pace of change in patient process level include: externally led change; a narrow base of change leadership including reliance on a single clinical champion; insufficient clinical–managerial partnerships prepared to champion change; unsophisticated preparation of the process, content, and context of the intervention due to imposition of intervention objectives, culturally alien language, disruptive, and intrusive change methods; poor consultation with stakeholders within the process; and an approach to change that is perceived as confrontational. The discussion below illustrates points made above using more detailed comparative data from case studies reported in Chapter 6.

Table 8.2 *Approach to planned change: positive and negative factors*

Factors with a positive impact on the pace, progress, and impact of change	Factors with a negative impact on the pace, progress, and impact of change
Internal leadership of change;	Externally led change;
Clinical ownership and support for change;	Narrow base of change leadership including reliance on a single clinical champion;
Weak clinical resistance to change;	
External support for change both politically and materially;	No clinical–managerial partnerships;
Partnerships of clinicians and managers leading change;	Unsophisticated preparation of the process, content, and context of the intervention due to imposition of intervention objectives;
Objectives of change that incorporate professional development, service development, or service problem-solving;	Culturally alien language; Disruptive and intrusive change methods;
Formal and informal communication processes	Poor consultation with stakeholders within the process; Approach to change that is unnecessarily confrontational

The timing of the interventions in ENT and A&E coincided with the formation of the reengineering laboratories in March 1995. In these cases, reengineers and management consultants located outside the specialties led the change intervention, providing much of the energy and impetus for change. In so doing, they failed to generate a necessary level of support for change amongst the body of clinicians involved in the respective patient processes being reengineered to achieve the intended effects.

one of the management consultants came here first to soften me up on a one-to-one basis . . . we had meetings, good meetings, they gave each of the consultants things to do. But it was driven by them rather than us. (Doctor 1 in Accident and Emergency department, December 1996)

Though we got involved in reengineering and made suggestions the overriding thing was that it was a group of people making decisions who were apart from A&E . . . Our suggestions were not taken seriously because I always thought that they were not what they wanted . . . they were not enthusiastic about ideas. (Doctor 2, Accident and Emergency department, December 1996)

In terms of clinical support for change, the change interventions in A&E made a poor start and proceeded on a spiral of decline thereafter. Amongst senior clinicians within the A&E department the change intervention was perceived as a 'paper exercise' and focused on 'a quick fix' rather than on 'solving the real problems of the department'. In the cases of ENT and A&E performance targets were set for each of the interventions by reengineers and lodged with the Reengineering Steering Group. These targets were not 'owned' by the clinicians who worked within the change process. In the case of A&E the targets were judged to conflict with targets set by the British Association of Emergency Medicine. Techniques used to analyse patient processes were judged 'intrusive' and approaches to piloting changes to patient processes were viewed to have caused disruption to the daily work of the department. Reengineers involved in that analysis and piloting of patients process later acknowledged that the department was subject to many pilots and staff felt 'piloted to death'. Some within the department charged reengineers with conducting a 'rush to pilot', in spite of clinical opposition and work pressures on the department.

Single queue was not piloted at a good time, they were low on staff, low on morale. Non-qualified nurses were being introduced which was contentious and it did not have the backing of people. (Reengineer, May 1996)

. . . we tried the concept of the single queue, even though we knew it would not work. It became clear that we did not have enough cubicles to operate the system . . . the trial was stopped after a few hours because the waiting time [in the A&E department] quadrupled and all hell broke loose . . . we told them [reengineering] that it would happen . . . but it was felt by reengineering to be a good idea . . . (Doctor in Accident and Emergency department, December 1996)

Unlike the interventions in A&E, the change intervention in ENT started with the involvement of a senior consultant willing to lead change. However, despite the formation of a 'working party to take forward change', change was progressed on the basis of a narrow alliance between a senior reengineer and the single consultant 'champion'. However, after a 'successful' pilot the change intervention floundered for more than one year. At the point that reengineering sought to 'roll out' the piloted patient process amongst other consultants within the specialty, the fragility of the narrow alliance of reengineering and a single consultant was revealed. The credibility of the pilot exercise was undermined when it became widely viewed that the pilot had not used a representative case-mix. ENT consultants resisted 'roll out', pointing to the restricted case-mix used in the pilot and the 'lack of consultation'. Further development of the intervention met with overt resistance of nurses and anaesthetists in the theatres directorate who felt nursing posts were threatened by plans within the new process for ENT nurses to take

responsibility for recovering patients after their operation. The consultant who had led the pilot began to doubt the motives of reengineers, perceiving that undue emphasis was being given to patient throughput. His
enthusiasm to continue piloting the new patient process was further
dampened by antagonism amongst nursing and clinical colleagues and
a perception that senior management were reluctant to make the capital
investment needed to facilitate patient admission into hospital. At this
point, the clinical champion alledgedly refused to further pilot the new
patient process, and over the subsequent months that followed, it was
apparent that the approach to this change intervention had failed to
secure a strong base of support amongst clinicians working across the
care process.

My gut feeling was that there was not a lot of ownership from the working side
of the project, from the nursing side. They felt we had devolved this project to
them and 'roll-out' is the time we pulled back . . . (Former reengineer on
the project)

We really did not develop ownership [of the project] as well as we ought. They
did not see it as their project, they did not see the value in terms of quality and
care and what they could actually achieve as a team. (Former reengineer on
the project)

It was presented as a fait accompli—'you in theatres will do this'. (Manager in
theatres)

The one-time flagship reengineering project floundered for nearly a
year before changes in the management of the specialty provided fresh
impetus for the intervention. By this time, the reengineering laboratories had been dismantled and the management consultants had left
the organization. The development of the new elective process in ENT
became an intervention led by a broader group of people inside the
specialty rather than by people outside the specialty. As an approach to
change the case is instructive in revealing that the identification of a
clinical champion for change is not a sufficient condition of success of a
planned change intervention.

  The approach to reengineering elective gynaecology is in stark contrast to the approach to change used in ENT. The essence of the
approach to change in elective gynaecology is captured by constant use
of words and phrases such as: 'bottom-up change rather than top-down
change', 'internal ownership', 'use of internal rather than external
change agents', 'maximum communication, maximum participation'
and 'intensive one-to-one communication with consultants'. The
process and impact of the intervention reveals the words and phrases

were supported by actions. It was perhaps fortunate that the start of reengineering interventions in gynaecology coincided with the devolution of responsibility for reengineering projects to the directorates. From the outset of the intervention there was a shared view held by senior clinicians and managers at specialty and directorate levels that change interventions would be 'directorate led rather than reengineering led'. By contrast to ENT, the intervention was prepared and promoted by a corpus of clinicians, managers, and nurses at both directorate and specialty levels. Initial analysis of stakeholders' opinions, the creation of a reengineering communication strategy, and the formation of a reengineering steering group with representation of key stakeholders represent good examples of preparation for change. This preparation was viewed as a critical part of the process of creating 'ownership' of both the objectives and process of the change intervention amongst clinicians and managers responsible for the process being reengineered. By contrast to the ENT case which was, at least initially, characterized by a restricted and individual leadership base, here was a change intervention constructed from the outset on the basis of a championing team rather than a single individual.

we very much thought about how we were going to implement things. Who did we need to get on board and for how long. How we were going to roll it out, what was our strategy for rolling it out. (Manager, obstetrics and gynaecology directorate, January 1996)

The approach to progressing the change intervention on a daily basis revealed skilful 'customization' of reengineering ideas (Pettigrew 1998) and expertise to suit local circumstances. Within the directorate, reengineering expertise was welcomed. However, people with reengineering expertise were used (with their agreement) in ways that created and promoted internal ownership of the change by nurses and doctors within gynaecology. A partnership of two 'internal change agents'—a reengineer and a respected senior nurse from within the directorate—was instrumental in the process of driving the change intervention forward on a daily basis. These internal change agents were located together in a room next to the wards rather than on some distant reengineering laboratory. There was a conscious attempt to ensure that approaches of baselining and process-mapping were applied in ways that were appropriate to specialty working arrangements and circumstances.

There were intensive efforts put into 'selling the project' to individual consultants. The efforts were broad based in the sense that they involved more than one person. In this case, the business manager of the directorate, the two internal change agents, and primary nurses all communicated with clinicians about the change intervention. Communication efforts were informal and individualized as well as formal. In addition to formal project meetings (which consultants often had difficulty attending), the two internal change agents, the business manager, and primary nurses all recognized the need to communicate with consultants informally, often out of normal working hours, on a one-to-one basis in order to persuade them to support the change, or at least not resist it. Impersonal methods of communication such as memorandums, newsletters, and minutes of project group meetings were regarded as less effective processes of communication.

You cannot make them [the consultants] toe the line. You have to make it good for them to toe the line. It is about getting solutions to their problems that are also solutions to yours. That is a one-to-one thing, it is not a meetings thing. (Manager, obstetrics and gynaecology directorate, January 1996)

we used the primary nurses to persuade the consultants on a number of issues . . . they have quite a lot of influence with consultants. (Manager, obstetrics and gynaecology directorate, January 1996)

one of the nurses persuaded the consultant to pilot [the new process] because she wanted to go out into the community, she wanted continuity of care. . . . peer persuasion. If the nurses were happy, he would be happy. (Internal change agent, August 1996)

Taking place six months after the ENT experience those leading the change intervention recognized a need to avoid the conflict generated by a similar intervention in ENT. In the case of gynaecology, the change intervention proceeded without triggering the conflicts of jurisdiction evident in ENT and A&E. Much effort went into satisfying concerns that anaesthetists may have had about the new elective process in gynaecology. A decision was taken not to attempt to introduce nurses from the gynaecology wards into operating theatres to perform the task of recovering patients.

By contrast to the cases of ENT and A&E, the process of piloting proved an effective methodology for advancing change in gynaecology. The pilot was seen as progressing an idea that clinicians wanted to progress without causing major disruption to existing work processes. The pilot proceeded using two consultants rather than one, as was the case in ENT. This dual involvement gave greater political support and credibility to both the process and results of the pilot. Unlike the case of ENT, the pilot was not pre-empted or followed by public statements of 'roll-out' or ambitious performance targets that could be interpreted in a controversial way by key organizational actors.

They [the consultants] came, they saw it work and said, 'I want it too please'. (Consultant gynaecologist, July 1996)

Some of the nurses thought it was a silly idea but the two teams that led it were enthusiastic and motivated. They worked at the clinical protocols and were really committed to making it work. The consultants were also. Having made it work within the pilot with nurses who have credibility—the others knew it worked. Similarly, the pilot was with the right doctors. When it was such a success with the two teams it was harder for other consultants to say 'we will not do this' . . . (Primary nurse, March 1998)

the next step after the pilot—if it is successful—is to ask other consultants whether they want to participate and get it introduced through them opting into it. Rather than us saying, 'right we will roll this out among everybody' . . . (Manager, obstetrics and gynaecology directorate, September 1996)

The initiatives in gynaecology and ENT were similar initiatives in terms of the scope and complexity of the patient process and possibility for conflicts of jurisdiction. However the differences in both the level of conflict generated by the two initiatives and their progress over time suggest the approach to planned change is an important factor to consider when accounting for the process and outcome of change.

As in the case of elective gynaecology, the process redesign intervention in orthopaedics benefited from a change process that was led and owned by clinicians within the specialty. The intervention was based on the support of a wider group of people rather than a single clinician. The change intervention represented a fusing of clinical and reengineering agendas. The intervention within orthopaedics started at the same time as that within A&E but proceeded to develop in a starkly contrasting way. Unlike in A&E, reengineering ideas and personnel were seen by doctors as a resource to be utilized to address certain problems within the specialty. Also, reengineering was not perceived as being 'imposed' by people who were perceived by clinicians as failing to understand the problems of the specialty.

. . . if you asked them 'why they allowed themselves to be subjected to this?' I think they will say somebody gave time to them and they dedicated time back. So it was reciprocal, giving and taking and the fact that people came up with ideas that we tried and experimented. (Reengineer, November 1996)

There was wide consultation within our directorate. It was very much a consultative process rather than reengineering being done to us. (Orthopaedic consultant, December 1996)

Piloting was seen as an effective methodology for introducing change. It is noteworthy that pilots occurred without causing major disruption to the day-to-day operations of the specialty:

> we will move forward by piloting because we find piloting a very useful way of bringing in the change programme. Often people do not realize that the pilot has occurred. Therefore you can go back to people and say 'well we have done this for a month and there has not been a problem, so should this continue' . . . piloting is critical. If you move forward with a pilot that works people do accept it. (Orthopaedic consultant, December 1996)

In summary, this discussion of the approach to change covers a cocktail of factors related to concepts of leadership, communication, preparation of change, and influence. The importance of the approach to change to the progress and fate of interventions is inextricably linked with some of the other factors discussed within the model. For instance, change interventions of broad scope and high complexity, involving non-receptive contexts for change, are a greater test of the approach to change than interventions of low complexity in a receptive context.

8.2.5 *Resources*

Classic reengineering texts (Hammer and Champy 1993) suggest that reengineering releases resources and cost savings through the elimination of waste and duplicity within existing organizational practices and processes. The hospital's original reengineering proposals stated that over a short time period the programme would be cost saving. Cost savings of a great magnitude proved more difficult to achieve than anticipated at the outset of the reengineering programme (Bowns and McNulty 1999). At clinical service levels the rate and pace of process reengineering interventions was regulated, and often slowed, by the need for additional investment in capital, staffing levels, or training needs. Many of the initiatives reported here required investment in staffing, capital, or training to progress. Not always was such investment possible. The implication of this finding is that patient process reengineering may actually require resources over and above existing levels.

Reengineering encountered and generated controversies over resources that have impacted adversely on the progress of planned change interventions. The rate and pace of change was slowed considerably in both ENT and gastroenterology by the need for capital investment. In the case of Accident and Emergency, it became recognized that radical change to the 'flow' of patients around the department was limited by its physical structure and layout and major capital investment was required to make radical change. The Balmoral Test Centre, a much publicized reengineering success story, required capital investment. Implementation of a redesigned pathology service requires considerable capital investment, which in the period of this study was not made available. Turning the reengineering vision for the care process for patients attending the A&E department with minor injuries into practice was impeded by a shortage of nurses in triage to administer treatments and order X-rays. Additional nursing resources were only attained some eighteen months after the initial piloting of nurses ordering X-rays and administering minor treatments. The extension of nursing roles in the A&E department and specialty of ENT required investment in nurse training. The redesigned process of care for patients admitted with a fractured neck of femur was judged by those within LRI to have been impeded by a lack of resources within the care process. In part explanations of why a reengineering intervention did not have the anticipated impact on service quality measures, such as patient length of stay, include references to a shortage of operating theatre time and discharge delays related to the availability of resources for rehabilitating patients and discharging patients from hospital.

By contrast, other reengineering interventions benefited from extra resources not directly related to the reengineering programme. Within orthopaedics reengineering helped accelerate change already set in motion by additional resources provided as part of the orthopaedic trauma strategy for the locality. Improvements in waiting times and activity in ENT cannot be adequately explained without reference to a recent increase in the number of ENT doctors to deal specifically with waiting list demand. Interventions in gastroenterology and gynaecology benefited from the appointment of process managers and secondment of internal change agents, respectively. Not all areas of the hospital were able to obtain additional dedicated resources to progress change interventions.

8.2.6   *Concluding remarks*

To summarize, this particular reengineering programme is judged to have resulted in some change but mostly continuity, as the process and outcomes of reengineering were more convergent with than divergent from preceding organization processes and outputs. Using an inductive analytical approach to data analysis this chapter has sought to explain this assessment of the limits to organizational transformation in this case by in-depth analysis of strengths and weaknesses of the programmatic approach to reengineering adopted within LRI and the complexity of process redesign in practice.

Reflecting the contextually sensitive nature of change we have been careful at this point in the monograph to develop a detailed empirical account of reengineering, covering the context of development and implementation, as well as actions of managers and clinicians. Our empirical attention provides a robust and detailed account of change in this instance that further informs an organizational change literature that often skates over the richness and nuances of organizational dynamics in conveying an impression of uniform change processes in and around organizations. We support the move within change theorizing that seeks greater attention to notions of ambiguity, unintended consequences, contradiction, plural interests, and outcomes (Eisenhardt 2000).

The theoretical proposition in Chapter 2 that reengineering would prove to be context sensitive is supported by empirical evidence. The process that advocates of reengineering believed would deliver organizational transformation was transformed by conditions of reengineering development and implementation (Child 1987; Giddens 1984). Scepticism is rightly justified towards reengineering gurus' metaphorical emphasis on starting transformation from a blank page (Grint and Case 2000; Hammer and Champy 1993). This large acute hospital presented a difficult set of conditions in which to attempt transformation via reengineering. In this setting, change across clinical and managerial domains was regulated by resilient negotiated orders and associated power relations. Competitive processes over resources and work jurisdictions (Abbott 1988) involving managers and clinicians allied to a tension between functional and process principles of organizing represented major challenges to the importation and implementation of reengineering into hospital contexts.

The pattern of clinical specialties and clinical directorates within LRI resembled a 'mosaic' of groups differentiated by functional tasks, employment status, occupational specialization, each capable of pursuing sectional goals and interests (Greenwood and Hinings 1996). Specialty formation and configurations of clinical directorates within LRI are artefacts of organization politics in that they represent hard-won gains of previous battles for managerial and clinical jurisdiction. It is unsurprising that such settlements were not being given up lightly. Witness the controversies within LRI, described in earlier case studies of ENT and A&E, about the control of operating theatres and the role of A&E in process organization. Such power battles and jurisdictional disputes played out at specialty and directorate levels symbolize the plural and ambiguous interpretations of reengineering and process principles. Clearly, some individuals and groups perceived reengineering as a threat to their existing position and power whilst others saw an opportunity to change their position and extend their power and influence. The spectre of winners and losers was never far away from actions and reactions, and was part of a dynamic that ultimately regulated and redirected the anticipated path and progress of reengineering. Reengineering is inextricably linked to organizational politics. The difficulty of trying to transform existing organizing processes and arrangements is not simply a task of changing business processes. Transformation also involves changing existing structural forms with the associated values and interests.

At this point we are reminded about the importance of not over-privileging matters of micro-change management and implementation in accounting for the impact of reengineering in this case. The micro-dynamics revealed by this chapter send out a very powerful message that change can indeed be regulated or enabled by phenomena at the micro-level. However, such micro-observations need to be related to meso- and macro-levels of organizations. It is too simplistic to see these forces of resistance to change as solely rooted within the confines of a single hospital. The next chapters develop this explanation of reproduction rather than transformation linking the problems of the change programme and complexity of process redesign to wider organizational and institutional dynamics in health and public sectors.

9

Dynamics of Programmed Transformation and Reproduction

9.1 Introduction

Building upon the preceding inductive account of change dynamics at hospital level this chapter represents a higher-level analytic endeavour which aims both to link the substantive study findings to other accounts of programmatic change in health care contexts and engage with wider theoretical debate about radical organizational change. The study's key empirical conclusion that radical change ambition resulted in convergent change demands that the chapter revisit dynamics of transformation and reproduction in organizations. This is the main purpose of the chapter. In pursuit of this purpose, the chapter seeks to complete the progression within the empirical component of the monograph from in-depth empirical description and analysis to wider theoretical explanation and generalization. This chapter further utilizes the empirical material in preceding chapters as it moves to a higher level of analysis and draws out some of the more general empirical and theoretical observations emerging from this case. The organization and argument of the chapter proceed as follows.

First, the chapter relates the findings of this study to the wider research evidence about change programmes in health care settings. Overall, empirical findings at the corporate level are considered against other substantive findings of change programmes in health care contexts. Do other studies confirm, modify, or reject the findings coming out of this single case study? A sample of studies about BPR and TQM reviewed in the chapter show the observation of limited and patchy change in this case to be highly consistent with a wider body of empirical literature about programmatic change strategies in health care contexts.

Explaining the limited impact of change programmes in UK health care moves us to our second key concern in the chapter—namely understanding processes of transformation and reproduction in and around organizations. The thrust of the remainder of the chapter is therefore to build on the commentary in the preceding chapter to further understand the wider organizational and institutional dynamics that shaped process and impact of reengineering in this case. Developing this study's contribution to contemporary scholarly enquiry into the possibilities, problems, and processes of organizational change and transformation in professional service contexts, study findings and explanatory concepts are linked to theoretical developments previewed in Chapters 2 and 3, such as strategic choice (Child 1997, 1972), neo-institutional theory (Greenwood and Hinings 1996), new organizational forms (Denison 1997) and sedimented organizational conditions (Brock, Powell, and Hinings 1999; Cooper et al. 1996).

Specifically, the second half of the chapter utilizes Greenwood and Hinings's (1996) model of radical change. Previewed in Chapter 2, it combines many developments in change theorizing, not least the concern for action and context and avoidance of the polemic of agency and environmental determinism that has blighted understanding of organizational change processes. The timing, circumstances, and objectives of the study did not lend themselves to a strict archetype approach to change as advocated by Greenwood and Hinings's model. However, our adoption of an alternative approach to archetype analysis for assessing the impact of reengineering in this case does not preclude our more limited use of the model for explaining our assessment of the impact of reengineering in this case. This study and the model share assumptions of organizations as plural and politicized entities, and of change processes as non-linear and uncertain in their processes and effects.

Responding directly to a call for more empirical applications of the model (Greenwood and Hinings 1996), the integration of our data with this theoretical model provides a novel empirical account that confirms the explanatory power of the model and extends some of the theoretical constructs and relations at the heart of the model. Notwithstanding our observation of change presented in Chapters 6 and 7, our explanation of the reproduction rather than reengineering of organization process and performance appeals to institutional explanations of change without falling into the trap of institutional determinism (Whittington 1992). Through the model we continue in the vein of preceding chapters by attending to the mix of institutional and organizational dynamics. In so doing, the chapter deepens insight into key concepts and relations implied by the model. The ambiguous relation between market and institutional dynamics and organizational change is confirmed as reengineering is seen to have first gathered momentum and then been checked by agents' enactment of institutional and organizational conditions. Greenwood and Hinings (1996) observe radical change as needing a 'capacity for action'. By attending to reengineering resources and ideas as central to the 'capacity for action' in this instance we are able to engage the model with the phenomenon of programmatic change strategies (Pettigrew 1998).

Following on the discussion of strengths and weaknesses of the reengineering programme in Chapter 8, Chapter 9 further theorizes why reengineering was insufficient for the task of transforming the hospital. Reproduction of organizing arrangements and processes confirms the importance of local power dynamics in accounting for the hospital's failure in this case to move from the prospect to the reality of transformation. One particularly noteworthy feature of the power dynamics in this case is that of managers and professionals finding common ground in preserving existing arrangements. This is an unusual combination as it is widely observed that professionals and managers do not typically share common values or interests. The unlikely collaboration in this case is understood using the theorized conflict between process and functional organizational arrangements (Denison 1997). The preservation of functionally inclined organizing arrangements—in this case clinical directorates and specialties—by managers and clinicians confirms the structuration thesis that change and transformation initiatives are shaped and indeed transformed by the very conditions and dynamics they are meant to transform.

Towards the end of the chapter discussion proceeds beyond the above model of radical change to engage with wider debate about authoritative change processes in organizations, sedimented organizational conditions, and diffusion of managerial technologies across sectors. Further doubt is cast on conceptualizations of change in professionalized contexts that rely on assumptions of top-down and authoritative change leadership (Hinings, Brown, and Greenwood 1991). Whilst acknowledging the possibilities for strategic choice by senior managers the study casts further doubt on the ability of senior managers to wholly manipulate and control organizational change processes. The unforeseen actions of managers and clinicians in defending existing organizing arrangements is used to link debate about restructuring in professional service contexts and the development of process modes of organizing more closely linked than in previous literature (Pettigrew and Fenton 2000; Brock, Powell, and Hinings 1999; Denison 1997). Following the counter-intuitive reactions and collaborations of professionals and middle managers in this case in defence of specialty and directorate arrangements it is suggested that organizational sedimentation appears more durable than initially theorized and an important condition to take account of in understanding the prospect of further change in professionalized service organizations. Finally, the chapter challenges the thesis of relatively unproblematic diffusion of managerial technologies for change across sectors. In this case of health care the institutional and organizational dynamics observed over time suggest some major differences in the conditions of private sector and public organizations that limited the diffusion of reengineering in this case. This point is made as a precursor to a fuller consideration in Chapter 10 of the prospects for process organization in UK public services.

9.2   Related studies on change programmes within health care organizations

This empirical account suggests that reengineering-inspired change within the health care organization studied was of too contained and slow moving a nature to be seen as an 'organizational transformation'. A blank sheet mentality to process redesign gradually became enmeshed in existing work practices, power relations, and leadership processes. This study was based on only one hospital, albeit of a number of settings nested within that hospital and so needs to be tested against other studies. Is the finding of contained impact broadly supported by other studies or is it an isolated finding?

Buchanan's (1997) analysis of reengineering within the surgical directorate of an acute hospital in the UK argues that there was not the 'blank sheet and fresh start' impact that was hoped for because as a change methodology it was highly contextually inappropriate. Reengineering was badly adapted to the decision-making processes apparent in a highly politicized organization such as a hospital. Different professional groups and segments continued to defend their own territories and jurisdictions, with the retention of autonomy advanced as a guiding principle. Reengineering was subject to many different interpretations, especially as it overestimated the extent to which patient trails could be readily established and core processes proved to be somewhat indeterminate.

Willcocks, Currie, and Jackson's (1997) study of the introduction of reengineering in four public sector settings includes an acute teaching hospital. The study is particularly interested in the development of information systems needed to underpin reengineering. It paints a picture of slow roll-out, some clinician support, caution from many of the nurses, and a shortage of time and resources to support the development of new IT systems. Again, it is concluded that the political, cultural, and human resource aspects of change are crucial in this context. In spite of the long time scales implied, it is argued that support has to be built up gradually among professionals, as this is the only way in which change will 'stick'.

Packwood, Pollitt, and Roberts's (1998) evaluation of the impact of reengineering in an acute teaching hospital is perhaps the nearest comparator to our own study. It also takes the form of an intensive case study of a single hospital. This Trust was located in London where there was (early 1990s) a perception that an internal market could quickly develop which would threaten the whole viability of the organization (although these market forces were later damped down). This assumed crisis was also a way of generating clinical staff support for the change programme at that stage. A reengineering-inspired programme labelled 'Transforming Healthcare Delivery' was reportedly introduced to lead to a 'step change' in performance. As in the case of LRI, Packwood, Pollitt, and Roberts (1998) find a shift from an initial desire to transform the whole system to securing change of more manageable proportions. Process redesign ideas achieved highly variable levels of impact and appeared more successful in settings that were coherent and integrated, rather than those with many interests, many objectives, and many interfaces with other services. The study concludes that it proved extremely difficult to transform an organization like a teaching hospital quickly. Senior management also found it difficult to sustain the time commitment needed by the change programme over a considerable period of time.

Findings of TQM programmes are also relevant. Whilst some writers pointedly distinguish BPR from total quality management (Hammer and Champy 1993), the shared process ideals of TQM and BPR were noted in Chapter 2 (Denison 1997) as was the relationship in practice between TQM and BPR ideas (Keleman, Forrester, and Hassard 2000). Some core findings of earlier TQM evaluations undertaken within health care settings echo many of the themes apparent in this case and the wider BPR literature, most notably that the impact of many TQM change programmes has been mixed and mostly disappointing to advocates.

Joss and Kogan's (1995) evaluation of the impact of early TQM projects funded by the Department of Health within the NHS in the early 1990s produced a number of findings of wider significance. Case studies were used to compare a group of eight pilot site adopters of TQM inside and outside the NHS, including two comparators in recently privatized industries. Interestingly, they found a lower level of impact in the NHS than the private sector comparators, partly because the work context was more complex, and because the level of resourcing for TQM programmes was much lower. NHS programmes were poorly resourced—especially in the area of education and training—and vulnerable to collapse once the special central monies had run out, given the lack of internal ownership. Large acute hospital settings could be seen as particularly problematic sites for intervention. There was a marked degree of variation apparent within the NHS sites, with a subgroup of high-learning, high-change sites emerging. In the weaker sites there was little evidence of an overall framework for quality and little sign of any dialogue between the top and bottom of the organization (despite such a dialogue being advocated in TQM change theory). The presence of an explicit structure for TQM implementation was helpful, as was a dedicated TQM manager. In many sites, top management showed a lack of commitment to TQM, there was minimal involvement from senior or junior medical staff, and very weak shifts from providers' definitions of quality to consumers' definitions of quality.

The theme of lower impact within public sector organizations is also apparent in Morgan and Murgatroyd's (1997) review of the experience of TQM in UK public sector agencies. It is argued that a combination of factors, including the lack of customers or markets, resistance to change, lack of incentives to adopt TQM, and the unwillingness of politicians to take risks associated with the empowerment of front line staff all blunted the impact of TQM ideas within public sector settings.

Some interesting international studies are also available which expand our knowledge base beyond the relatively small number of studies available in the UK. Such corporate change programmes have been widely adopted within the American health care sector. Arndt and Bigelow's literature review (1995) of the impact of TQM programmes within American health care argues that initial promises are often not fulfilled and that the assumptions underlying TQM are often incompatible with the mission or core activities of hospitals, even in this more market-led system. Arndt and Bigelow (1998) later developed this line of enquiry to cover the literature that was available on BPR interventions within health care organizations. They view that this literature is mostly of an anecdotal or prescriptive nature with little high-quality evaluative work apparent. Speculatively, Arndt and Bigelow (1998) argue that many of the same underlying conditions inhibited the impact of BPR and TQM programmes. Hospitals are seen as adopting BPR on the grounds of legitimacy rather than efficiency, as it would improve a hospital's reputation for being 'leading edge'. Also, hospitals may claim adherence to the principles of BPR without really enacting them, or even trying to enact them beyond a strategy of 'impression management'. This would predict that a wave of early enthusiasm for BPR would rapidly be succeeded by disillusion and rejection. Arndt and Bigelow (1998) advance a variant of an institutionalist perspective which implies that BPR adopters implement reengineering programmes in a superficial and non-resource-intensive manner, dropping them as soon as an ever newer managerial fashion is apparent.

Shortell, Bennett, and Byck's (1998) review of a set of American studies into the impact of continuous quality improvement (CQI) approaches within health care organizations concludes that there was evidence of 'pockets of improvement' but no evidence had as yet emerged of an organizational wide impact on quality. They suggested that CQI was likely to achieve its potential when it was integrated into a more systematic and organizational wide approach (which in some ways BPR represents). Another American study (Gerowitz 1998) of management teams within American health care organizations concludes that TQM/CQI interventions are related neither to performance levels nor to cultural change.

Walston, Kimberly, and Burns (1999) use a survey instrument to explore the extent to which reengineering has been implemented within American health care and its consequences for a hospital's cost profile. Sixty per cent of CEOs surveyed reported that reengineering had been implemented in the previous five years, showing a much more rapid diffusion path in the American than in the UK system. Walston, Kimberly, and Burns (1999) report variation in impact on cost profile, depending on whether or not a more sophisticated change strategy is apparent. Their overall finding is that reengineering alone is not sufficient to improve the relative cost-competitive position of a hospital, indeed by itself reengineering appeared to increase hospital costs relative to competitors. This finding reminds us of the considerable investment in monetary and staff time required by the reengineering programme in our case-study site (Bowns and McNulty 1999). A similar recent Canadian study (Wager and Rondeau 1998) reports that many health care organizations have initiated a TQM programme but are unable to report significant performance enhancements, especially where there was no deep internal commitment to quality as a guiding value.

Some scholars argue that public sector organizations remain radically distinct from firms so that models and tools appropriate for firms are inappropriate for public agencies. Drawing on a tradition of theorizing about the distinctive nature of public sector agencies (Wilson 1987), Kaboolian's (2000) theoretical review of the growth of quality programmes within American public sector organizations argues that they are likely to be useful only in a subset of public organizations with specific characteristics. These are likely to be those public organizations which are most 'firm-like' in their nature, displaying characteristics such as: a united range of supportive stakeholders; a market-like environment; clear tasks and goals; measurable outcomes; and ability to link rewards to performance. Attention is also drawn to strong lines of upward accountability to politicians—who supply mandates and resources—as an enduring feature of public sector agencies. It is argued that the widespread diffusion of quality programmes within American public sector agencies should not be seen as an unambiguous efficiency gain, but rather may have been adopted for legitimacy reasons, for the purposes of 'impression managing' relations with politicians, or as a sense-making device for managers facing volatile and complex sets of tasks. Kaboolian also calls for more systematic evidence in relation to the empirical impact of quality programmes within public sector agencies.

This is one such study and its empirical findings of patchy and contained impact of a BPR change programme within a health care organization are highly consistent with the wider body of empirical literature. What makes the results of this study particularly interesting is that the results are reported from a site that in some ways can be seen as 'leading edge' and a more receptive context than many of the settings studied. Relative to weaknesses observed in other change programmes there was substantial investment in BPR as a national pilot site, sustained top-level support, a systemic framework, and a specialist implementation infrastructure available. Without these features the level of likely impact might be thought to be even lower. Clearly much analysis and prescription about change in professional service settings is only scratching the surface and there are more complex dynamics at play in effective 'successful change'.

To summarize, in spite of the confident rhetoric that accompanies most programmatic change strategies the research base suggests caution about the possibilities of effecting organization change and transformation. In the light of the preceding evidence, the transformational rhetoric of reengineering is out of step with experience of managerially inspired change in UK health care organizations. Study findings are consistent with findings of decades of government-inspired reform designed to promote better organization and management (Harrison and Pollitt 1994). The history of reform in the NHS suggests that realizing intended effects of planned change in hospitals cannot be assumed especially when it is managerially inspired change within clinical domains. It seems incredible that dramatic change in hospital processes and performance can be achieved in the time scales advocated by classical reengineering literature and initially anticipated in LRI. Similar to other management ideas and concepts imported into the NHS during the 1980s and 1990s, such as general management and total quality management, the process and fate of reengineering within LRI has been shaped by features of the setting within which it is being introduced. The inductive model in the preceding chapter helps capture some of the complex dynamics of radical process redesign within hospitals associated with the politicized nature of health care, professionalism, medical autonomy, and limits to managerial power and influence. This chapter now seeks to delve into this complexity further by applying data from this study to Greenwood and Hinings's (1996) generic theory of radical organizational change.

9.3 Reengineering and a theory of radical change

This study has subjected the hype of transformation and reengineering to particular scrutiny. Our finding of convergent change reminds us that within the burgeoning literature on organizational transformation, institutional theory, somewhat soberly, highlights processes of reproduction rather than change in and around organizations. However, as revealed in Chapter 2, institutional explanations for organizational stability and inertia are subject to criticism on the grounds of institutional determinism (Whittington 1992). From the outset of the study our approach to understanding reengineering as a transformation project has heeded recent developments in theorizing which point to explanations of change that attend to an interaction of context and action (Pettigrew 1987; Child and Smith 1987). Therefore to further generalize about the key empirical finding that radical change ambitions of senior management pursued through reengineering led to convergent rather than transformational change, the study engages with recent theoretical developments which point to the need to explain change processes by attending to a mix of organizational dynamics and institutional dynamics (Greenwood and Hinings 1996).

Greenwood and Hinings's (1996) theory of radical change posits a set of interconnected dynamics necessary to accomplish radical or transformatory change. As revealed in Chapter 2, the theory underlying the model is that radical change or transformation requires an interacting set of precipitating and enabling dynamics, some 'exogenous', for instance, market and institutional forces, and some 'endogenous', for instance, internal interests, values, power dependencies, and capacity for action. Specifically, it is proposed that radical change follows 'group dissatisfaction' with existing organizing arrangements coupled with a 'value commitment' ('competitive' or 'reformative') to alternative organizing arrangements. These dynamics create a pressure for organizational change the intensity of which is related to wider market and institutional pressures for change and stability. For radical change, such precipitating dynamics need to be accompanied by enabling dynamics of supportive 'power dependencies' and 'capacity for action'. Radical change requires those in positions of power to favour proposed change. Institutional and market pressures may shift power dependencies in favour of an alternative template but radical change will only result if the 'dominant coalition' recognizes the weakness of the existing organizing template and is aware of potential alternatives. Capacity for action, a second enabling dynamic of radical change, refers to an ability to manage change to an alternative template. It is a function of understanding the new conceptual destination, being able to manage how to get there, and having skills and competencies required to function in that new destination (Greenwood and Hinings 1996).

Believing the model to be an important recent development in change theory we are curious at this point to see whether the above theory of radical change helps explain the overall judgement at the corporate level that convergent rather than radical or transformatory change materialized in this case of reengineering. Specifically responding to Greenwood and Hinings's (1996) call for developments in understanding of radical change, we therefore offer the following integration of data of this study with their more generic theoretical model of radical change. The manner in which we present and apply our data to the model enables us to comment directly on theoretical propositions contained in the model, associated concepts, and wider related debates as we proceed through the remainder of the chapter.

By way of introduction it is important to reiterate that the study has not up to this point used the archetype approach to assess and explain transformation, preferring to focus more on actions and their consequences rather than underlying meanings and interpretative schema of professionals (Ferlie et al. 1996). However, other features of the study are consistent with the model. The theory's attention to intra- and extra-organizational dynamics is complementary to this study's interest in a more subtle understanding of context and action outlined in Chapter 2. Our assumptions about the nature of change and organizations reported in Chapters 2 and 3 are consistent with those that underlie the model. Also, a contextualist, processual longitudinal methodology has yielded data amenable to addressing the organizational and extra-organizational dynamics that lie at the heart of the model.

9.3.1   *Possibilities for transformation: enabling and precipitating dynamics*

A critical question in the change literature concerns how radical organizational change occurs (Oliver 1992; Greenwood and Hinings 1996). Analysis of how the hospital emerged as an innovator in its sector is revealing about why radical change, or at least the prospect of radical change, may emerge at the level of the single organization. The commentary below confirms previously theorized conditions of radical change (Greenwood and Hinings 1996). A mixture of institutional and agency forces inspired reengineering as a challenge to the existing organizational form and process within the hospital. Other hospitals responded to a similar institutional context without adopting reengineering. This suggests that the adoption of reengineering as a radical change strategy lies in the interpretation and mediation of institutional and organizational pressures by members of hospital senior management. The case therefore reveals the power of managerial agency to utilize resources (Whittington 1992), whilst subject to normative and coercive pressures and prone to mimetic conduct. Reengineering as an organizing and change methodology came from beyond the institutional field of health care. Amongst the senior management cadre who championed reengineering one can observe many of the theorized influences for 'normative fragmentation' (Oliver 1992). Most notably these include perceptions of increased performance exposure, experience of operating at the boundary of medicine and management, and an ability to utilize ideas as 'resources' accessed through personal development programmes (Whittington 1992).

Chapter 3 observed the sector of UK health care to be a mature, plural, politicized institutional field subject to heightened challenge and change throughout the 1980s and 1990s. Health care policy in these most recent times reveals policy-makers' dissatisfaction with the ability of NHS institutions to meet public expenditure levels and public expectations. Progressively, policy changes have presented a more radical challenge to clinical and administrative practice culminating in the combination of markets and managers as central ideas of the new public management in the early to mid-1990s. Recent policy change reveals a health sector more subject to importation of private sector approaches to organizing and managing health care than ever before. NHS Trusts and markets represent institutionally derived templates promoted by a policy process laced with coercive, normative, and mimetic attributes and couched in a rhetoric of decentralization, devolved managerial responsibility, and market freedoms.

The NHS internal market and the onset of NHS Trust status proved critical elements in the immediate antecedent conditions that preceded the hospital's reengineering programme. Exemplifying structuration theory (Giddens 1984), the reflexive nature of the organizational and environmental relationship is demonstrated as reengineering is seen to have developed as a local response to new responsibilities and freedoms of NHS Trust status and anticipated market pressures (Child 1997; Giddens 1984). Subject to these institutional pressures, the hospital simultaneously converged with and diverged from its peers within its field. It converged in adopting the NHS Trust form of organization, yet used Trust status as a platform to embark on a distinctive change programme that marked the hospital out as an innovator in its field. The revealed interplay of structure and agency here ensures the case is a good example of how contextual pressures are interpreted and acted upon by organizational actors. Senior managers articulated organizational transformation through reengineering as a necessary response to government policy and pressures of cost control and service quality improvement. Adhering to the model of radical change (Greenwood and Hinings 1996), market and institutional pressures precipitated managerial action to transform the hospital using the ideas and techniques of business process reengineering. A mix of context and action is observed with reengineering being used to build on these contextual precipitators of change as an internal driver of change (Pettigrew 1987; Child and Smith 1987).

Thereafter ideas of business process reengineering, allied to the results of a previous quality improvement initiative (Project Sigma), contributed to senior managers' dissatisfaction with the hospital's ability to meet the simultaneous cost and quality improvement pressures emanating from national policy level and local purchasers. Features of the hospital's wider operating environment were thus mobilized by members of senior management to justify and prepare a

case for radical organizational change to strategic constituencies inside
and outside the hospital. In the contemporary context of markets and
NHS Trusts senior managers championed reengineering as a new
organizing logic and means for organizational effectiveness. Reengineering represented strategic choice and change informed by senior
actors interpretations of a changing operating environment. Such
processes of choice and change were simultaneously a reactive and
proactive response by hospital management who saw the new corporate status of NHS Trust requiring radical change in hospital process
and performance.

Indeed, looking closely at the composition and action of senior managers in the cadre that initially championed reengineering one sees
support for propositions about normative fragmentation and agency
(Greenwood and Hinings 1996; Oliver 1992; Whittington 1992). One
can observe within the managerial cadre who championed reengineering a perception of increased performance pressures emanating from
central government and looming crisis, boundary-spanning roles that
highlighted a need for improving the clinical and managerial interface,
and the ability of managers to access ideas in the wider domain as
'resources' for management and change in local organizational settings. Data presented in Chapter 5 reveal that during 1993 and 1994 a
cadre of individuals in senior management positions developed, each
sufficiently dissatisfied with existing organizing arrangements and
performance to favour the radical prescription of reengineering. Some
individuals were in senior administrative positions, whilst others were
clinicians albeit with senior managerial responsibilities in the hospital.
Within this collective reengineering seemingly tapped and helped
articulate dissatisfaction with existing organizational resources and
performance.

One individual, charged with developing a quality improvement
initiative, used the concept of business process reengineering to make
sense of a very mixed set of results of a previous quality initiative in the
hospital. Reengineering seemingly promised a very different and more
fruitful approach to quality improvement than that previously taken.
Other senior managers in the hospital, seeking to establish organizational legitimacy and vitality in the network of wider organizational
relations, were dissatisfied with the financial resources to do so. For
these individuals, reengineering appealed as an approach to radically
changing the cost structure and quality benchmarks of the hospital. At
board level, some individuals cited their experience of private sector
business practice to express dissatisfaction with hospital performance

and managerial arrangements for securing performance outputs and results. Reengineering apparently offered some of the rationalizing tendencies that they believed existed in the private sector.

Crucially within the coalition of initial supporters and reformers were clinicians who saw the inadequacies of existing service provision arrangements and embraced possibilities for change. One medical consultant publicly reported the impressive results of a recent service quality initiative to be a result of totally reorganizing services for the benefits of patients and not staff. This individual was persuaded that reengineering was a reorganizing logic with a potential to apply this ideal across the whole hospital. The initial impetus and force behind reengineering within the hospital lay with these individuals' interest in and interpretation of reengineering in the light of hospital performance and new institutional pressures. They subsequently mobilized further support and legitimacy for the programme outside the hospital, by securing public endorsement of the programme by reengineering guru Michael Hammer and financial resources from the NHS executive for the hospital to become a national pilot site for reengineering.

It is possible therefore to observe in this account of processes and events associated with health care policy and local managerial action in the early to mid-1990s some initial precipitating and enabling conditions that help explain the initial adoption of reengineering as a radical change strategy. Initial dynamics of interest dissatisfaction and power are apparent at senior management level and informed a capacity for reengineering action manifest in the two-year programmatic change strategy embarked upon by the hospital between 1994 and 1996. How then do we explain the results of the study reported in preceding chapters and elsewhere (Bowns and McNulty 1999) that reengineering did not result in the radical impact anticipated by its champions? At this point attention turns more to conditions of reproduction than transformation and builds on the discussion in the preceding chapter about the weaknesses of the programmatic change strategy and complexities of process redesign.

9.3.2 *Reproduction: necessary but insufficient conditions*

Notwithstanding the above, the key empirical finding of radical transformation ambition followed by convergent change ultimately directs our attention to the 'reproduction' of existing organizing arrangements and services. The language of reproduction is preferred to that of stability or inertia here, as it is concluded elsewhere that the hospital is not the same organization it was prior to the reengineering programme. Chapters 6 and 7 reveal changes have occurred in organization processes and service provision—though these are presented as occurring mostly within a wider scenario of reproduction of organization and service arrangements that existed prior to reengineering.

Continuing with the theory of radical organizational change by Greenwood and Hinings, reproduction is also explained below as an outcome of institutional and organizational dynamics. Over time, the precipitating and enabling dynamics that enabled the initial introduction of reengineering into the hospital proved necessary but insufficient for reengineering to produce the long-term impact desired by senior hospital managers. These dynamics did not develop sufficiently to produce in a sustained fashion the favourable power dependencies and effective capacity for action necessary to create either an organization-wide 'reformative commitment' or a sufficiently powerful 'competitive commitment' to radical change.

Among the corpus of managers and clinicians within the hospital reengineering failed to generate sufficient dissatisfaction with existing organizational arrangements to mobilize a reformative or competitive value commitment to reengineer the hospital. Actions and their consequences reported in preceding chapters suggest that the value commitment of clinicians and managers at key operating levels of the hospital were more inclined to the preservation of the existing status quo. Overall, many individuals at specialty and directorate levels were apparently defensive or indifferent to reengineering and their responses contributed greatly to reengineering proceeding in a fashion that reinforced rather than reformed existing organizing and clinical service arrangements. The introduction and implementation of reengineering as a managerial technology for organizational transformation was thus mediated through existing organizing arrangements and ended up more preserving than reforming those established organizing arrangements and the associated interests and power relations. As a capacity for action, the change programme proved insufficient for the task of organizational transformation, failing to generate enabling power dependencies and legitimacy to realize senior management's ambitions for the programme.

The theorized conflict between process and functional models of organizing (Denison 1997) helps our understanding of this failure of reengineering to generate sufficient power dependencies and interest dissatisfaction. The conflict was exposed and became more explicit as responsibility for reengineering 'went into the directorates and specialties' (reengineer, 1996). For those leading the reengineering programme there was always a tension between their control of the programme and the need to engender commitment to reengineering interventions at operational levels of the hospital. Responsibility for reengineering was ultimately devolved to operational levels throughout the hospital. This diffusion of responsibility amongst directorates increased the possibilities for directorates and specialties to interpret and apply reengineering to suit local parochial interests and agendas. Specialties and directorates were arrangements that afforded managers and clinicians a position from which to interpret, evaluate, and negotiate the reengineering agenda. Clinicians and managers with directorate and specialty membership in common found a jurisdiction and accompanying set of arrangements to defend, albeit perhaps for different reasons. Managers and clinicians interpreted and acted toward reengineering to control, with some success, the implications of reengineering for the purpose of local agendas and preferences. Through their actions, functional arrangements, such as specialties and clinical directorates, with associated resource patterns and demarcations, were largely preserved and unchallenged. As detailed in Chapter 7, the considerable change activity related to reengineering across and within directorates is adjudged rather uneven, incoherent, and patchy in impact. Cases most revealing of change were those where process redesign was confined to either single services, specialties, or directorates, served to promote a particular clinical agenda, and did not threaten the practice of doctors. It seems that reengineering failed to extend from the initial championing cadre at senior management level throughout the depth and breadth of the hospital in the manner envisaged by reengineering gurus and hospital senior management because it did not fuse with the values and interests amongst the corpus of managers and clinicians performing in the critical operational domains of the hospital.

Evidence of managers and clinicians at directorate and specialty levels finding common ground in defence of existing specialty and directorate arrangements against some of the initial radical ambitions of reengineers is a notable and somewhat counter-intuitive finding of the study. Processes of preservation and reproduction are revealed in those instances when the meaning of reengineering was contested and the identification of core processes effectively challenged as illegitimate and indeterminate (Buchanan 1997). Differing from some normative transformation texts, we suggest that such weaknesses in the capacity for action are not simply problems of inadequate communication and change leadership processes. Rather, the failure of reengineering to generate a competitive or reformative value commitment in Greenwood and Hinings's (1996) terms suggests not satisfaction with existing arrangements but low incentive to change on the part of managers and clinicians in the direction suggested by reengineers.

Reengineering did not mobilize sufficient dissatisfaction with existing arrangements and commitment to a new organizing logic to overarch or replace value commitments manifest in the coexistence of clinical specialties and directorates. The case supports therefore the theorized link between existing interests and convergent change (Greenwood and Hinings 1996). Outside its initial and admittedly dedicated champions, reengineering failed to generate a critical mass of support. Reengineering seemingly failed to be widely perceived as helpful to the operational problems and agendas of managers and clinicians, who were inclined to solutions that were parochial and preserved existing resources and jurisdictions. As the ambition and organization of the reengineering programme were transformed by managers and clinicians operating within specialty and directorate arrangements the reformative spirit implied by BPR as a change technology was weakened, the initial strategic intent dissolved, and the vision of core processes lost. This picture again portrays the importance of interests and politics within processes of change and shows reengineering not to be a neutral technology for change but one that was perceived by managers and clinical professionals to implicate and threaten existing arrangements. Consequently, the practice of reengineering was laced with scepticism and caution and characterized by negotiation and contest. At a general theoretical level, the description and analysis of reengineering in this case confirms the structuration thesis that change initiatives are shaped and can be transformed by the very conditions and dynamics they are supposed to transform (Child 1997; Giddens 1984).

9.4 Limits of authoritative change models in professional settings

For its advocates strategic management in professional service settings appears to be a frustrating challenge. Evidence about the old shaping the new, especially at operational levels of the hospital, identifies the particular difficulties management in this case experienced in changing conditions that influenced the interpretation of situations and regulation of ideas (Denis et al. 1999; Norman 1977). The changing composition and ideology of senior management in professionalized service contexts is noted elsewhere (Brock, Powell, and Hinings 1999; Whittington, McNulty, and Whipp 1994). However, one cannot assume a new strategic management process involving greater power and influence over operational levels. The newly formed strategic management cadre in this case experienced difficulty complementing their exercise of strategic choice with control over the reengineering change process. Senior management experienced problems establishing their vision of a reengineered organization. Core processes proved to be more indeterminate than they initially imagined (Buchanan 1997). In practice, a large gap developed between reengineering ambition at strategic level and action at operational levels (Pettigrew and Whipp 1991).

Having scrutinized the rhetoric and reality of reengineering the case further adds to evidence about the limitations in theory and practice of top-down or authoritative change philosophies in professional service contexts (Hinings, Brown, and Greenwood, 1991). Transformation theorized as a top-down change process is once again unsubstantiated in practice. Within these times when corporate management systems are reportedly strengthening within professional service contexts the case reveals the possibilities for senior management to exercise strategic choice but not necessarily organizational control. The complex link between change ambition, intention, and effects is confirmed (Pettigrew 1987) as are limits to the managed professional business form (Brock, Powell, and Hinings 1999). Management's ability to fully engineer and control change cannot be assumed. Findings of the study confirm the indifference and resistance that planned, programmed, top-down change strategies may face, not just from clinical professionals in this case, but also other managers. Reengineering is revealed as an idea and rhetoric for change undermined by its contextual insensitivity and overconfident assumptions about managerial agency.

The study lends further support to those who view the organizational change literature as glossing over power relations. Classical and incremental revisionist accounts of business process reengineering are confirmed as excessively agency centred and overconfident in their view of the ability of senior managers to conceive of and execute change in a planned top-down manner. Some of the key conditions or variables supposed by normative texts of transformation were in place. Reengineering was a piece of agency and strategic choice on the part of a senior management coalition. Investment was made in reengineering, a capacity for action was created, and top management commitment sustained. However, senior management in this context was not necessarily the 'dominant coalition' (Child 1972). Whilst reengineering represented strategic choice on the part of hospital management, the practice of securing the implementation and impact of reengineering lay outside the scope of senior managerial control. Top management support for change in this case proved a necessary but insufficient condition for organizational change and transformation. Classic reengineering methodology reflects a top-down model of change management based on assumptions of clear line management and relatively uncontested managerial control. In hospitals, such conditions do not apply and as such, the methodology is flawed and ill-suited to the practical challenges of transforming organization performance. The evidence of change in this highly professionalized setting reveals the limits of top management power and the capacity for social and organizational practices to be reproduced even during supposed periods of transformation of professionalized sectors and organizations (Brock, Powell, and Hinings 1999).

Over time, professionals have shown themselves not to be passive recipients of managerially and policy inspired change. Rather, they possess high levels of knowledge, skill, and other power resources to adopt and adapt change imperatives in the light of their preferences and interests. Such has been the case here, with the organization and practice of clinical work proving resistant to the particular rationalizing logic of reengineering. In relation to the redesign or reengineering of clinical work, senior management has been shown to have little power to direct or impose change. Rather, at operational levels of hospitals much real power remains with a loose coalition of clinicians engaged in incremental development of their own service largely on their own terms and conditions. Changes observed in the approach to reengineering within LRI over the period of this study acknowledge that the progress of change is mediated greatly by clinical and managerial actors located in the operational domain. The experience of reengineering at LRI confirms that where service change is at stake, it is unlikely that sufficient energy and momentum for change can be generated either by top management or other 'external' change agents such as consultants operating from outside these domains. Indeed, such attempts may have the contrary effect.

Relations between clinicians also affected the process and possibilities for change. Values of clinical specialization and differentiation are embedded within work processes and organizing arrangements of hospitals. As well as cooperation between clinicians, structure and action are processes laced with professional competition over scarce resources and work jurisdiction (Abbott 1988). There exists inter- and intra-profession competition (Drazin 1990) on a daily basis for the right to control work processes which in reengineering terms make up only a small part of a core process. These competitive conditions contribute to the development and maintenance of episodic and fragmented views of patient processes at service delivery levels and enduring conflicts of jurisdiction within patient process redesign interventions. It is well known that senior management in professional service contexts experience difficulty establishing hierarchical control and that inhibits their ability to communicate and cascade change ambitions to operational levels. This case shows that when change ambition implies a shift from functional to process organization, the problem of vertical control and coherence is compounded by the problem of establishing functional coherence. Creating a process-inspired professional service organization is not simply a test of the quality of manager–professional relations. It is also a test of inter- and intra-professional collaboration and underlying service ethos. Large slices of the BPR literature have little to say about problems of resistance, conflict, and competing values. All in all, this study adds weight to the evidence that is sceptical about BPR and more generally the possibilities for programmatic strategies to effect Big Bang transformational change in professional service contexts.

9.5   Stable sedimentation

At this point, the analysis is able to engage and extend the theoretical debate about sedimentation within organizational change processes (Brock, Powell, and Hinings 1999; Cooper et al. 1996). In Chapters 2 and 3 contemporary analyses of professional services contexts such as law, accountancy, and health identify the presence of sedimented organizational conditions where diverse sets of beliefs and values are embedded in dynamic organization structures and processes. In the specific instance of health care, it is argued that within the formal institutions and structures of the NHS a market and managerial based archetype developed during the 1990s alongside a professional archetype (Kitchener 1999). At the local level, such sedimentation may be seen as manifest in highly differentiated organizing arrangements of clinical specialties and clinical directorates. One may also interpret this coexistence of organizing principles as evidence of an existing 'competitive value commitment' between organizational and occupational principles with the latter infused with values of professional specialization and jurisdiction, and the former infused with values of resource management and control.

Somewhat counter-intuitively, we have seen in this case, as expressed through the actions of clinicians and managers, that these existing functional organization arrangements have been defended in preference to alternative organizing arrangements more reflective of the core process logic associated with reengineering. During the period of reengineering there was portrayed more of what Greenwood and Hinings (1996) describe as a 'commitment to the status quo' or 'indifferent commitment' to reengineering and process-based organization with the result that these two design templates of directorates and specialties have proved to be mutually reinforcing and durable throughout the period of reengineering. The unexpected patterns of collaboration and cooperation evident between managers and clinicians in defence of existing directorate and specialty arrangements suggest that sedimented conditions in this case contributed to managers and professionals preserving functionally inclined arrangements and jurisdictions in preference to process inclined arrangements. The suggestion here is that the sedimented arrangements observable within this UK hospital displayed some unexpected 'functional' coherence that helps to explain why clinicians and managers were able to 'fend off' the prospect of process-based organizing arrangements.

The resilience of these sedimented arrangements is of theoretical and practical significance for several reasons. First sedimented conditions have previously been theorized as schizoid and insecure forms (Hinings and Greenwood 1988; Cooper et al. 1996). Second, sedimented conditions in health care (Kitchener 1999) exhibit an unforeseen coherence supportive of functional rather than process organization. Third, the unlikely collaboration between managers and professionals found in this instance suggests that managerial–professional relations are more nuanced and contingent than some earlier literature suggests (Watson 1995; Harrison and Pollitt 1994).

Early archetype theory (Hinings and Greenwood 1988) suggests that organizations tend to archetype coherence and hybrid or sedimented forms are theorized as insecure and unstable arrangements. The findings of this study call for further questioning of the presumed limits to the stability and durability of sedimented conditions in organizations. We have presented evidence of managers and clinicians at directorate and specialty levels finding common ground in defence of existing specialty and directorate arrangements against some of the initial radical ambitions of reengineers. This is an important finding of the study and points to an alternative scenario of a stable negotiated order developing amidst sedimented arrangements. The unexpected pattern of clinico-managerial relations based on the managers and professionals working alongside each other in clinical directorate and specialty arrangements meant that the prospect of process organization has been managed and mediated through pre-existing functional structural arrangements. Not only did reengineers intent on transformation have to engage with a diffuse and powerful clinical community, they also had to negotiate with a diffuse and powerful cadre of middle managers, who often acted in consort with clinicians to protect existing specialty and directorate arrangements. In LRI, many individuals both clinical and managerial did not support the change agenda being set for them by reengineers and management consultants and saw fit to challenge, with some success, the objectives and logic of proposed changes. A major challenge to core process redesign was the argument by managers and clinicians within directorates and specialties that hospitals have hundreds, if not thousands, of processes and product lines, because of the vast array of patient conditions that need to be treated. This line of argument proved a very effective rhetorical defence of directorate and specialty practice against imposition of change from outside the specialty and directorate. In practice, the handful of core processes devised by the reengineering teams proved insufficiently robust at the redesign stage. Much subsequent change activity was led from specialty and directorate levels, reflecting imperatives at these levels rather than the logic of core process redesign.

Therefore emerging from this explanation of differential and patchy impact is the finding that managers and professionals have acted in ways that supported the preservation of existing 'functional' organizing arrangements at the expense of new process-based ways of organizing. In view of the historical differences in value position attributed to professional and managerial relations, this is an unlikely and unanticipated source of enduring coherence (Watson 1995).

So sedimented conditions (Kitchener 1999) may exhibit an unforeseen coherence that contributes to organizational reproduction. Our conclusion is out of step with presently received theoretical hypotheses about the insecurity and unstable nature of sedimentation. In this case of reengineering, sedimented conditions proved to be durable and were perpetuated through the actions and reactions of clinicians and managers. At a more general theoretical level, the implication of our analysis is that a sedimented organization may exhibit greater stability than often assumed: it may display conditions of a stable negotiated order as much as an insecure and fragile state. We encountered some interesting and novel patterns of collaboration and competition involving managers and professionals in defence of sedimented organizing arrangements. They suggest that research and debate about sedimentation needs to progress beyond a concern simply with explaining the creation of sedimented conditions as an outcome of institutional pressures for change, to an interest in understanding sedimentation as a critical condition of dynamic professional service contexts that shapes the process and possibilities of further organizational change.

9.6 Sectoral diffusion

In the field of UK health care, the hospital acquired innovator status through its reengineering efforts. The case itself has proved to be a high-profile one in its sector—having achieved national pilot site status. The empirical observation of senior management acceptance and importation of an organizing concept from outside the institutional sector relates the study to wider debate about the diffusion of managerial technologies for change within and between sectors. Through BPR, Hammer and Champy (1993) exemplify arguments for the generic quality and diffusion of certain organization and managerial technologies. Those who adopt a contextualist stance to organizational change are much more cautious and liable to point to the distinctiveness of organizational contexts. For this study, a pertinent example of this latter stance is offered by those who make a strong case for distinctive conditions of public services and reject notions of unproblematic diffusion of private sector-based ideas and techniques for organizing and managing public services (Wilson 1987; Kaboolian 2000). By applying our data to the conceptual model of Greenwood and Hinings (1996), we are further able to reveal a very mixed, though on the whole resistant, set of dynamics for reengineering and process modes of organizing. In short, senior management imported reengineering as a recipe for organizational success only to see its transformatory ambition and process principles rejected by clinicians and managers within the organization. It is suggested below that while the convergence thesis may have some basis in the developments of the new public management, other sectoral and local level dynamics suggest conditions that are not analogous to private sector contexts and more suggestive of an enduring public/private divergence.

The case reminds us that the relations between organizations and their wider environment are mediated by agents and characterized by ambiguity and inconsistency. The above commentary reveals over the period of study an ambiguous and volatile relationship between the wider institutional and organizational context and reengineering-inspired change in this case. In keeping with Greenwood and Hinings (1996) we concur that the problem of championing and mobilizing support for change in this instance cannot be seen as divorced from institutional, organizational, and market dynamics. The preceding commentary observes how institutional forces shaped the adoption, process, and fate of reengineering. Over the period of study, reengineering is seen as having been initially facilitated then undermined by forces operating at local and more macro-levels.

On the one hand reengineering was partly born out of institutional change with managers using newly introduced organizing forms of NHS trusts and internal markets to mobilize their ideas and support for reengineering. Initial adoption of reengineering by the hospital suggested convergence between public and private sector operations. BPR entered the discourse of management in this hospital and the wider health care community as local managers introduced and publicly proclaimed it as a recipe for radical performance improvement. Changing policy and economic imperatives in and around the UK health sector helped create the case for reengineering at local level. The manner of adoption and implementation further exemplified an attempt to import in full the idea of BPR from industrial, manufacturing contexts of the USA to a public service setting in the UK.

Thereafter the expected challenge that reengineering would make to the process and performance of the hospital did not materialize. Over time, institutional forces did not prove to be uniform and consistent in precipitating and enabling reengineering. Rather, over the period of study, some institutional conditions, albeit mediated by the managers and professionals, served to contradict process organization ideals (Denison 1997) and a reengineered vision of the hospital. Subsequent dampening of quasi-markets in health care, intensifying specialization in the division of medical labour and local differentiation of management, proved less conducive to reengineering in this case.

The radical nature of health policy reduced in the mid- to late 1990s as market pressures were reeled back in. Denison (1997) theorizes market conditions as a critical condition of process organization. More locally, reengineering floundered within highly differentiated, embedded, functionally inclined arrangements for managing and delivering professional services. Furthermore, processes of specialization and differentiation within medicine and management appear to be intensifying within overall processes of health care organization and provision. Clinical directorates are key managerial arrangements in hospitals that are functionally inclined and informed by a desire to develop stronger performance management processes in hierarchical contexts.

Following on this last point a concern to announce the post-bureaucratic age and emergence of process-based organization may be somewhat premature in the health sector. The case confirms functionally inclined specialization and bureaucratization as enduring organizational processes. The conclusion that the old shaped the new in this case challenges the empirical validity of claims that organizational innovation and transformation occur as a quantum leap from one state to another. This assessment of more continuity than change supports those who are suspicious of claims that we live in a world of discontinuous change whereby traditional organizational forms are simply being replaced by new organizational forms (Pettigrew and Fenton 2000). In this particular professional service context, traditional bureaucratic, functional arrangements proved enduring with some modest incorporation of new process-inclined organization form.

The above points serve as an important precursor to Chapter 10. In the next chapter, we turn our thoughts to recent developments in public policy and the prospects for change at the sectoral level of health care. Parallels are observed between the rhetoric of reengineering and championing personnel in this case and subsequent developments in NHS policy (Cm 4818, 2000). It would seem that policy-makers are now challenging managers and clinicians to display a determination to secure efficiency and quality gains through greater integration and collaboration across boundaries of health care institutions. In the light of evidence from this case, the rhetoric and prospects of integration and collaboration within current public and health care policy demands further attention.

9.7   Concluding remarks

To summarize, the study has been concerned with attempts by senior managers within a hospital to reengineer organizing processes and performance in the light of changing imperatives and demands at local and national level. Reengineering is one of the most controversial managerial technologies for change of recent times. It reflects an approach to change whereby ideas are imported by local managers and practitioners and driven from the top of the organization. It is also seen as contributing to an emergent and novel 'process' paradigm of organizing (Denison 1997). As a basis for developing the study's broader theoretical and empirical contribution, we observed in Chapters 2 and 3 some serious reservations about many accounts of reengineering pointing to doubtful assumptions about the nature of organizations and associated processes of change and leadership. In short, too many accounts of reengineering and change more generally are restricted in their usefulness to either theoreticians or practitioners through their concern to simplify the complexity of change for the sake of prescribing. Such an approach does no favours to either practitioner or scholarly communities. In seeking to engage the findings of the study with a plurality of interested communities, spanning academe to health care practice, we have sought to lace our analysis of the implementation and impact of a major reengineering change programme in this case with a balance of description, analysis, and explanation. To do so we have consciously sought to develop our understanding and approach to reporting a much heralded contemporary management phenomenon, with a conscious recognition of recent developments within wider change theorizing. One of the most notable points made in Chapter 2 is that informing the considerable interest and effort to understand organizational change is a rejection of extreme positions of either determinism and voluntarism in change processes in favour of analyses which attend to intra- and inter-organization dynamics, including agency.

Reengineering has been presented as a strategic choice through which senior management within the hospital sought to transform hospital process and performance. Our findings of unrealized aspirations on the part of senior management in this instance are consistent with results of other studies of change programmes in health care contexts. In a substantive sense, an empirical contribution of the study is that it adds to a stock of knowledge about the possibilities and problems of managing change programmes. The broader theoretical contribution is that the case continues to promote and deepen interest in the interaction between context and agency in trying to understand change processes in and around organizations. The change literature in its broadest sense remains populated by some very directive- and leadership-centred views of change. The study reminds us again of the importance of recognizing the importance of agency at the highest levels of organizations but not over-privileging such agency, either in terms of its practical significance or explanatory relevance. Programmatic strategies for change such as reengineering offer alternative ways of accomplishing change leadership. However, the theoretical schema employed in this study confirms that programmatic change strategies and activities, such as visioning change, communicating change, and leading change, are just part of a much more complex dynamic that renders highly uncertain the possibilities for planned, programmed organizational transformation over reproduction of organizing arrangements and processes.

10

Process-Based Organizations in the UK Public Services? Prospects for the Future

10.1 Introduction

In this final chapter, we move back to a health and indeed public sector-wide level of analysis. Following the presentation of case-based material in earlier chapters, we now consider the possible relationship between the emergent process-based organization and the broader New Public Management movement already discussed. A key question is: do these two developments complement or indeed contradict each other?

Chapter 3 argued that the NPM movement is a public sector-wide change process of real breadth and depth, rather than a superficial managerial fad as sometimes assumed. It was also argued that the UK could be seen as a 'high-impact' site for NPM ideas. Within the UK public sector, the health care subsector is itself 'high impact' in terms of the early and sustained introduction of NPM style reform efforts. The new NPM archetype could be seen as substantially embedded here by the late 1990s (Ferlie et al. 1996), although we considered that further evidence was still needed about the extent of change in the most fundamental cultural and ideological spheres.

This chapter will first update this earlier analysis of the UK NPM movement and in particular consider the implications of the advent of a Labour government in 1997 for the organization and management of UK public services. The NPM was initially associated with radical right governments in the 1980s and 1990s. So is it a paradigm whose time has now gone or has it survived into the new political climate? We revisit the early definition of the NPM movement advanced in Chapter 3 ('markets plus managers') and distinguish in more detail between four different subtypes. We consider whether there is evidence of a shift to any one of these subtypes during the late 1990s. The chapter develops an initial assessment of the impact of New Labour on the organization and management of the public services. We suggest that any shifts in direction are too mixed and ambiguous to have any major deinstitutionalizing effect on an embedded NPM archetype.

The chapter then considers the extent to which the fundamental conditions needed for a process-based model of organization 'fit' within current public service organizations. Many NPM-inspired reforms have strengthened vertical lines of authority and reporting, and paradoxically make the move to lateral forms of organization more problematic. We suggest there may be some major contradictions between NPM style modes of organizing and that of the lateral organization that help explain why the case-study site was unable to achieve an organizational transformation.

10.2   The evolution of the UK NPM movement in the late 1990s

The NPM movement was originally defined in Chapter 3 as representing the introduction of 'markets and managers' within public service organizations. This definition marks a contrast to the professionalized bureaucratic mode previously dominant within hospitals. There has been a significant shift towards a more managed form within the UK hospital sector (Kitchener 1999), although we agree with Kitchener that the evidence of change is as yet partial. However, the widespread introduction of clinical directorate structures represents an important development and a new form of authority relations. Despite these structural shifts, clinicians appear so far to have retained substantial control over their day-to-day working practice.

There may be some tension between these two high-level NPM style organizing principles of 'markets and managers': the evolving principles of NPM may not be internally consistent. Market-based organizations may foster an entrepreneurial style; highly managed organizations may fit better with a 'command and control' style. Market-based organizations in such areas as externalized public services (e.g. in the utility and transport sectors) may be directed by a founding entrepreneur rather than a public service salariat. So, a typology of NPM subtypes is needed to reflect variation along these two basic dimensions. In earlier work, Ferlie et al. (1996) argued that four NPM subtypes could be distinguished. A contest was evident between these four models and the degree of influence achieved in the field waxed and waned over time. Here we briefly recapitulate their properties.

10.2.1 NPM 1: the efficiency drive

This was the earliest NPM model to emerge, dominant throughout the 1980s, but coming under challenge in the 1990s. It represented an attempt to make the public sector more 'businesslike', led by crude notions of efficiency. Key themes included:

- an increased attention to financial control; a strong concern with value for money and efficiency gains; 'getting more from less'; a strengthening of the finance function; more elaborate cost and information systems;
- a stronger general managerial spine; management by hierarchy; a 'command and control' mode of working; clear target-setting and monitoring of performance; a shift of power to senior management;
- an extension of audit and benchmarking systems; the growth of regulatory bodies;
- a move to individualized labour market contracts for senior managers;
- a reduction in the self-regulating power of the professions; 'getting professionals into management';
- new forms of corporate governance with marginalization of elected representatives and trade unionists; moves to a board of directors model with a shift of power to the strategic apex of the organization.

While there were experiments with market forces (such as income generation efforts) and less bureaucratic forms of management, they were of secondary importance within this model. This model is high on line management and low on market mindedness. We characterized the driver for this model as the new Thatcherite political economy of the 1980s. The public sector was here seen as bloated, wasteful, over-bureaucratic, and underperforming so that general management and other change levers were introduced to 'turn it round'. NPM Model 1 can be seen as emphasizing vertical reporting lines and as highly unreceptive to 'process-based' modes of organizing which stress lateral links (Denison 1997).

10.2.2 NPM 2: Downsizing and decentralization

Ferlie et al. (1996) suggested that NPM 2 could be seen in the mid-1990s as of increasing significance, undermining and contradicting earlier changes brought about by NPM 1. This model replicates the growth of 'post-Fordist' forms within the public sector (Hoggett 1991). Fordist enterprises—and their analogue in the public sector, the Welfare State agencies—are highly bureaucratized, with a hierarchy of offices, rules, and regulations, and a small range of standard products. 'Post-Fordist forms' are by contrast characterized by a search for flexibility and the unbundling of vertically integrated forms of organization. Large organizations are typically downsizing, delayering, contracting functions out, and splitting up internally into more autonomous business units. Very similar trends may be evident in public sector as well as private sector settings, and we argued that this model was of rising importance in the early 1990s with the decline of the early NPM Model 1. The 1990 reforms to the health care system embodied many of these NPM Model 2 ideas, with the construction of a quasi-market and the creation of local provider organizations with greater operational autonomy. NPM 2 can be seen as high on marketization but low on management. Key themes of Model 2 include:

- the growth of elaborated and developed quasi-markets; the eclipse of planning as a vehicle for allocating resources within the public sector; a split between purchasers and providers;
- a move from management by hierarchy to management by contract; the emergence of looser forms of contract management; more loosely coupled (and critics said fragmented) local organizations;
- a split between a small strategic core and a large operational periphery; market testing and contracting out of non-strategic functions;
- delayering and downsizing of staffs; moves to flatter organizational structures;
- in terms of management styles, a move from the 'command and control' styles associated with NPM Model 1 to alternative styles such as network-based organizations or management by influence;
- an attempt to move away from standardized forms of service to greater flexibility and variety.

NPM Model 2 can be seen as potentially fitting well with the core ideas of process-based management (Denison 1997), with its emphasis on networks, joint production, and also its market and customer value creation inspired ethos.

10.2.3 *NPM 3: in search of excellence*

NPM 3 is most obviously associated with the 'excellence' stream of management literature of the 1980s, influential through best-selling texts (Deal and Kennedy 1982; Peters and Waterman 1982). It represents the application to the public services of 'soft' management theory such as the human relations school of management with its strong emphasis on organizational culture. It rejects the highly rationalistic approach of NPM 1 and instead highlights the role of values, culture, rites, and symbols in shaping how people actually behave at work. There is a strong interest in how organizations manage change and innovation. It is relatively low on marketization but high on 'soft' approaches to management.

In turn, NPM Model 3 can be subdivided into *bottom-up* and *top-down* approaches. The bottom-up approach has been articulated through the 'learning organization' movement (Senge 1990; Pedler, Burgoyne, and Boydell 1991) and stress on local 'product champions' in stimulating innovation. These models do not necessarily accord top management a privileged role in the change process, indeed their role may be to foster and orchestrate energy for change held at the local level. There are links with 'empowerment programmes' which have attempted to reduce the field's over-dependency on the top tiers.

However, *a top-down form* of NPM 3 is also evident. This would include a use of charismatic or transformational (rather than merely transactional leaders); the introduction of planned culture change programmes, and attempts to shift the collective culture of an organization in a desired manner. The leadership style is highly personalized, coming from a newly appointed senior manager who attempts to inspire the organization with a personal vision. This approach may involve symbolic management. Such approaches may be particularly appealing to top management in a turnaround situation. So, NPM 3 can be characterized by the following themes:

- in its bottom-up form, an emphasis on organizational development and learning; organizational culture is used as a normative 'glue' rather than performance management systems; top-down backing for bottom-up product champions; radical decentralization with performance judged by results;
- in its top-down form, explicit attempts to manage culture change; projection of a top-down vision; charismatic forms of top-down leadership; more intensive corporate training programmes; use of mission statements, logos, uniforms, speech codes, and other forms of symbolic management; an explicit communications strategy; a more assertive and strategic Human Resource Management function.

NPM 3 might be thought to be broadly neutral in relation to its stance towards process redesign efforts, although a top-down version may be seen as a moderate facilitator of top-down corporate change programmes.

10.2.4 *NPM 4: public service orientation*

Ferlie et al. (1996) saw this model in the mid-1990s as the least well developed and still to reveal its potential. It represented a fusion of private and public sector management ideas, re-energizing public sector managers by outlining a distinct public service mission (Osborne and Gaebler 1992), but one compatible with good practice transferred in from the private sector. The Public Service Orientation (Ranson and Stewart 1994) model is a good example of this genre, taking 'soft' management ideas from the private sector but applying them in a distinctively public sector context. This subtype can be seen as low both on 'markets' and on 'management', especially in its conventional upwards-facing form. It represents a defensive adaptation and restatement of position by thinkers committed to the distinctive value base of public sector organizations. Key themes include:

- a major concern with quality including TQM approaches; a value-driven approach based on a concern to achieve excellence in public services;
- reflection of user (rather than customer) concerns and values in the public management process; reliance on user voice rather than customer exit as the main mode of feedback; a concept of citizenship; also a reinvigoration of 'downwards facing' modes of public accountability to local citizens;
- a desire to shift power from appointed to elected local bodies; scepticism as to the role of markets in public services;
- stress on the development of societal learning over and above the efficient delivery of local services;
- a continuing set of distinctive public service tasks and values; management of the distinctive politics of collective provision; public participation and accountability as legitimate concerns of management in the public domain.

NPM 4 is cautious as to the applicability of private sector models such as BPR within public sector settings, arguing that these organizations instead retain many distinctive features (Kaboolian 2000).

Ferlie et al. (1996) presented work drawing on NHS fieldwork undertaken in 1990–3. It concluded that the earlier dominance of NPM Model 1 was in decline and that there were signs of a shift to NPM Model 2 (which could create a more receptive context for process redesign ideas). Another observation was that there was increasing organizational diversity within the newly created and decentralized provider units (NHS Trusts). These organizations displayed strong ideologies of organizational autonomy and were developing their own managerial personalities. In one case study, there was an explicit attempt to shift to an NPM 3 mode, led by a new CEO who had previously been the HRM director and had experimented then with these novel approaches. This argument for increasing diversity contradicted the assumptions of population ecology or institutional theory (Di Maggio and Powell 1983; Hannan and Freeman 1988) that a field would tend towards isomorphism.

How do these early observations stand up when tested against the later picture revealed here? Are ideology, policy, and managerial practice still NPM orthodox or have radical new approaches appeared? If the NPM is still embedded, which variant appears to be currently in favour?

10.3 Key changes since the mid-1990s: some evidence and speculation

1995–7: the decline of the internal market and shift back to 'command and control'. What have been the major shifts in the organization and management of health services since the mid-1990s? The first argument is that the internal market had far less effect than we originally anticipated (Ferlie et al. 1996). Mays, Mulligan, and Goodwin's (2000) review of the literature on the NHS internal market suggested it had little direct effect. Their explanation of limited impact was that market forces were never really unleashed by the policy system. Over time, the management component of the 'managed market' became more powerful and the market component weaker. Government controlled competition between providers to avoid politically sensitive closures (for example, creating a special review in London which effectively suspended the operation of market forces there). With the partial exception of GP Fundholding, the NHS remained dominated by central directives and bureaucratic incentives. Although the empirical evidence in relation to the behaviour of NHS Trusts was poor, few of their original goals seem to have been met. There was little supply-side competition and a series of bilateral monopolies (between large providers and the macro-purchasers) emerged. In the end, Trusts enjoyed fewer operational freedoms than promised, as their access to new sources of capital was constrained and national pay bargaining was largely maintained.

Crilly's (2000) research on the objectives of NHS Trusts drew attention to the failure to allow for market exit which essentially neutralized the operation of market forces. Local Conservative politicians became increasingly anxious about the market forces they had themselves unleashed and lobbied to prevent the possible closure of hospitals in their own constituencies. Hard budgetary constraints became soft as hospital deficits were bailed out. Crilly's (2000) case study of a first-wave Trust is a story of an organization which started off displaying a radical and entrepreneurial mode of management, but these initial characteristics were eroded as market forces were damped down. This literature is consistent with a retreat nationally as well as locally from NPM 2 to NPM 1, even before the change of political control in 1997.

1997–2001: the arrival of New Labour: how to assess its impact? The NPM movement emerged within a period (1979–97) dominated by radical right governments, yet in 1997 a New Labour government was elected with a big majority. How significant was this change of political direction for the organization and management of public services? Here we present some argument, mainly of a theoretical rather than an empirical nature at this stage, and drawing on institutionalist theory, in order to enable us to address this problem.

The institutionalist perspective (Di Maggio and Powell 1983; Zucker 1983, 1987) within organizational theory assumes that organizations tend towards similar designs and activities across a whole field. Inertia is much more common than change. The work activities undertaken within such fields are stable, enduring, and change resistant. Alternative ways of working are difficult to conceive, let alone adopt. Pressure for continued isomorphism comes from external agents such as the State, the professions, and knowledge carriers such as management consultants. These forces are especially strong within the public sector, which combines a dependence on State finance, powerful professional groups, and a heavy use of management consultancy.

Given these constraints, how does radical change ever take place within public sector organizations? Hinings and Greenwood (1988) argued that organizations tend towards coherent deep patterns or 'archetypes' which consist of three distinct but interrelated components: the formal structure; systems of decision-making; and underlying interpretive schemas (which include such elements as core values, beliefs, and ideology). For there to be a successful transition, simultaneous and reinforcing change is needed along all three dimensions, and especially within the ideological sphere. Such archetypical transition ('a successful reorientation') is rare and difficult, but it is possible on occasion to overcome the high inertia levels within institutionalized orders. However, high and sustained energy levels are needed to break down an embedded archetype.

10.3.1 *The NPM archetype: four drivers*

Within much of the UK public sector, we suggest that we have already seen a transition from a public administration archetype to an embedded NPM archetype. The question now is whether the NPM archetype will reproduce itself within the new political conditions, or whether there may be sources of 'deinstitutionalization' (Oliver 1992) that lead to entropy of the archetype and perhaps the emergence of a successor archetype (such as the lateral organization). The initial archetype transition to the NPM was driven by the coincidence of four fundamental drivers, of which change in the political economy represents only one (albeit an important one).

First, and within the political economy, the growth of the middle class and the taxpayers' revolt against the large public sectors characteristic of social democratic states have indeed acted as a powerful driver for downsizing, a performance orientation, and more 'businesslike' techniques. Social democratic parties have converged on the template established by the New Right, with a fear of traditional 'tax and spend' positions. The reduction of social costs has been a key political priority and enables a reduction in taxation levels to politically acceptable levels. These political and ideological changes can be seen as an important driver within the UK in the 1980s and 1990s with the development of the new Thatcherite political economy of the public sector.

There are other factors to consider. Secondly, there is the decline of deference towards traditional sources of authority, including public sector professionals such as teachers and doctors. There is growing customer mindedness displayed by increasingly affluent and educated consumers within public services as in their private consumption. Such consumers have far more experience of service industries (hotels; restaurants) than their parents, and expect choice, access, and variety. The 'money rich but time poor' (such as urban professionals) will exit to the private sector if public services cannot provide ready access.

Thirdly, and within the division of elite labour, there has been a dramatic and sustained rise of the management function, knowledge, and discourse (that is a managerialization process) comparable only to the rise of the legal and medical professions in the mid-nineteenth century. Key generic management concepts (e.g. quality improvement, governance) have been newly adopted within health policy (Cm 4818, 2000). Managerial control and language could replace the professional-ized control and language historically dominant within health care, at least at the level of formal policy. This managerialization process seems to have been especially prominent in the UK public sector, with the rapid growth of management as a function. This compares, for instance, with the German model of the *Rechtstaat* (Pollitt and Bouckaert 2000) where judicial and administrative forms of authority are more important than managerial forms.

Fourthly, and within the sphere of managerial technology, new forms of performance management (Hoggett 1996) have been made possible by rapid technical advances in new IT systems. We see the cre-ation of increasingly sophisticated databases which can be used for external audit, performance review, and benchmarking. Performance management has also been strengthened by changes in the HRM func-tion with the growth of contract-based employment.

Of these four drivers, only the first is related to the conventional sphere of the political economy (and that weakly so as many social democratic parties such as New Labour have moved to the right in order to recapture tax averse voters and now accept much of the NPM agenda). Therefore our first proposition is:

> Proposition 1: a political transition from a neo-liberal to a 'reformed' social democratic regime such as New Labour will not by itself produce the sustained political leadership needed to deinstitutionalize an embedded NPM archetype.

A radical and sustained change in the political regime might in theory (Oliver 1992) open up a further archetype transition. The move to the NPM archetype in the 1980s and 1990 was associated with a strong 'reformative commitment' (Hinings and Greenwood 1988) from the new Conservative regime, although other reinforcing drivers can also be detected. This suggests that archetype transition is more likely where there is a strong and coherent reformative ideology that claims to make a radical break with the failed old ways. High-impact change is also more likely *either* when aligned with similar pressures from the professions *or* (more likely) associated with an assault on the auton-omy of the professions to remove them as an independent force.

We need to question whether further fundamental change is occurring in the three 'non-political' drivers identified. At first glance, it seems unlikely that informatization, managerialization, and the decline of deference have been reversed as long-term social processes since 1997, indeed they may continue to reproduce themselves technologically and socially within the new period. The call for public services to be 'user based' and for a reduction in the power of public sector professionals is as strong as ever. The magnification of scandals involving poor professional performance has been evident since 1997, and mobilizes public concern about the ineffectiveness of traditional forms of professional self-regulation. IT systems continue to be used to produce ever more sophisticated forms of performance management and benchmarking. While the managerial numbers of the top tiers in the NHS are reduced, their core function (performance management) continues to expand.

The ideological domain is an important one in archetype change and can be seen as even more fundamental than changes to formal structures and systems. The experience of the 1980s suggests that archetype transition within the public services is more likely where there is a strong and coherent reformative ideology, which legitimates the claims of a radical break with failed old ways, particularly when this ideology is espoused by leading power centres. So, it is necessary to consider the extent to which there has been a major shift in underlying political ideology in respect of the organization and management of public services.

It is still too early to make a final assessment of the impact of New Labour on the underlying organization and management of public services, as changes in practice (and even more fundamentally in ruling values) proceed over a long time span. At the time of writing (May 2001), we are coming to the end of the first term of Labour government, so that some kind of interim assessment is now appropriate. In order to do this, there are three levels of analysis that can be usefully separated out. The first level relates to declared expressions of political ideology and rhetoric specifically in relation to the organization and management of public services. The second relates to formal policy statements that have been made which pronounce on the structure and decision-making systems of public services. The third and deepest level relates to changing managerial practices and beliefs within service settings and this is the most difficult (yet important) area of assessment.

10.3.2 *Weak reformative ideology*

Has the arrival of the New Labour regime been associated with the emergence of a strong and coherent alternative value system that might plausibly challenge the institutionalized NPM belief system? Political parties often seek to mobilize support, provide collective rationales, and ensure coherence across actions through the promotion

of distinctive political ideologies, which blend normative and empirical arguments. Is it possible within the realm of New Labour theory to
spot a new archetype of laterally based public organizations? An initial
observation is that New Labour is an 'ideology light' movement. It
seeks to be inclusive, to put together broad coalitions and place a high
premium on the possession of technical expertise as well as political
ideology (hence its stress in technically based approaches such as
'Evidence-Based Policy'). It appears to lack the strong set of mobilizing
ideas associated with the NPM of the 1980s, notably the fundamental
work on public choice theory, transactions costs, and principal agent
theory provided by the New Right. However, two high-level works of
political ideology provide further evidence about whether there is
strong political commitment to the creation of laterally based organizations within the public sector.

10.3.2.1   *Giddens's* The Third Way

One of the most sophisticated expressions of the 'Third Way' ideology
seen as underpinning the New Labour government has surely been
provided in Giddens's (1997) *The Third Way: The Renewal of Social
Democracy*. The full title suggests that Giddens is trying to achieve the
ideological renewal of social democracy rather than its repudiation.
Within a very broad work of synthesis, Giddens necessarily touches on
the specific question of the organization and management of the public
sector only briefly.

Within this analysis, a number of the New Right's criticisms of the old
public sector are accepted and there is certainly no desire to return to the
public sector of the 1970s. However, an analysis of the text suggests two
very different potential models so that one can perhaps distinguish
between Giddens One and Giddens Two. Giddens One argues that
democracy needs to be deepened and broadened, with governments
acting in partnership with agencies in civil society so as to combat civic
decline. The retention of high levels of autonomy and self-organization
will be important if these agencies are not to be swamped by distorting
State power. Established traditions of participative planning and community development can be complemented by experiments in direct
democracy (such as citizens' juries). The fostering of active civil society
is an important task for the State, with support for 'bottom-up' politics
of community renewal. This implies a greater role in service provision
by non-profit organizations; more localized distribution channels; and
the public sector should work to develop the capacities of local communities. While there is no sustained discussion of the professions, they

might be seen as autonomous, self-regulating, knowledgeable, and publicly orientated groupings that can contribute to civic renewal, independently of government. This model of the Democratic State stresses the basic values of democracy, participation, and localized rather than efficiency, productivity, and performance management. This model has some similarities with NPM Model 4, but may go even further and represent a post-NPM alternative.

There is however a second model (Giddens 1997: 74–5) which centres on administrative efficiency as a way of rebuilding public sector legitimacy. Giddens Two argues that the restructuring of government should be based on the principle of 'getting more from less', understood not so much as radical downsizing as a way of delivering improved value. Governments should not have recourse to the construction of quasi-markets at every opportunity, but the use of generic management tools (such as target controls, effective auditing, flexible decision structures, and increased employee involvement) could increase performance. While there is a retreat from the market mindedness of the 1980s (the New Right has failed as much as the Old Left), this approach is much more NPM orthodox and can be seen as a mix between NPM Models 1 and 3. In neither account, however, is there an elaborated 'process-based perspective' applied to public service organizations.

10.3.2.2 *Leadbetter* Living on Thin Air

Primarily interested and involved in economic (rather than social) policy-making, Leadbetter (2000) argues that the need to build a knowledge-based economy requires the reform and 'modernization' (a key New Labour word) of many UK institutions. Manufacturing and routine service industries will give way to post-material, intangible (or 'thin air') industries based on knowledge and creativity (such as software, management consulting, or the media). Within the knowledge society, ideas, intelligence, and branding become the key yet intangible factors of production. Leadbetter argues that this central idea provides a more exciting vision than that provided by the ideology of the Third Way which in practice led to a continuation of pro-market policies, slightly rebalanced by attempts to strengthen social institutions.

The public sector is seen as an important part of the knowledge-based economy as there are many areas in which markets fail and where there is a need for the provision of public goods. There is an explicit repudiation of the New Right's claim that public sector services are necessarily poor quality services. Some of the public sector 'brands' (such as the NHS and BBC) have higher public reputations than most

UK private sector firms and are a vital part of the new economy. Leadbetter further argues that market-driven reforms of the 1980s (as in the NHS) had little effect except for the creation of more jobs for managers and administrators and should be repudiated. Yet, he accepts that the public sector needs to be very different from its predecessor in the 1970s (in our terms that there should be no return to the public administration template).

Public sector organizations are seen by Leadbetter as change resistant and poor at innovation. There are continuing political limits on 'tax and spend' policies that have to be recognized and which mean that other ways have to be found to increase productivity within the public sector. However, in order to fulfil its full potential, knowledge-based society needs to be inclusive and not dominated by an elite class of 'symbolic analysts'. Here is a democratic model of the knowledge society: 'scientists and other specialists cannot simply lay down the law to trusting consumers. Ideas have to be explained and justified' (Leadbetter 2000: 238). The public sector provides a strong basis for socially inclusive institutions, and the NHS would be a good example of social inclusion in action. This policy position leads to a preference for the redirection of social spending from social security into social investment (in areas such as education and training) to create generalized forms of social capital, as seen within the realm of practical politics within welfare reform programmes. It also suggests that public institutions (such as the NHS) which can command the confidence of middle class as well as working class consumers play a strategic 'binding' role.

In his analysis of how the public sector could be revitalized, Leadbetter stresses the role of a new breed of managers, such as 'turnaround headmasters' in failing schools, who seek to secure more value from the public assets that they are stewards of: 'the public sector does not need more restructuring or rationalization: it needs reviving and renewing'. There is a need for a more entrepreneurial and creative orientation to develop innovative public services. Leadbetter recognizes that the empowering of public sector innovators is difficult as traditional vertically organized accountability mechanisms stress the virtues of predictability and standardization.

His key principles of public sector renewal include a policy 'to invest systematically in the creation of new services and the dissemination of new ideas, especially those which combine different departments' (2000: 244). There is a strand of thinking which emphasizes connections between traditionally free standing public sector organizations consistent with process-based thinking. However, the main burden of his analysis centres on a 'knowledge based management' perspective: innovation, creativity, human capital, and social entrepreneurship rather than 'joined up government'. Nor does his analysis merely stress managerial efficiency but also the question of political renewal: public sector organizations are highly political, and rightly so (more consistent with a NPM Model 4 perspective).

These two important works of theory do not argue for 'joined up government' as a central intellectual platform nor more indirectly for a shift towards NPM Model 2 ('downsizing and decentralization') which is the subtype most consistent with process-based organizations. They seek to justify a retreat from that position, which is now identified with the fragmenting excesses of the New Right in the 1980s and 1990s.

> Proposition 2: New Labour's ideological base is too weak and ambiguous to act as a force which could effectively sustain an archetype shift to process-based organizations.

10.4 Major statements of proclaimed policy in relation to the organization and management of the public services

This section moves down from the ideological sphere to examine three important statements of declared policy in relation to the organization and management of the public services produced by the Labour government since 1997. This constitutes the second level of analysis. These strategic texts are interrogated to locate any statements about the preferred form of public service organizations. Documents from two (rather different) central departments are considered before moving onto the recent statement of health care strategy announced by the Department of Health.

Cm 4011 (1998), *Modern Public Services for Britain*, represents the outcome from the early Treasury-led Comprehensive Spending Review. The primary management style apparent in the text reflects a strong orientation to performance management and vertical reporting and can be seen as NPM 1 orthodox. Each department (including of course the Department of Health) has signed up to a public service agreement in return for resources. For example (p. 17) 'delivery' was to be assured by such measures as: close monitoring of each department's public service agreement; regular reporting on progress towards each department's targets; reviews to deliver against tight time scales and maintain pressure on departments to secure further service improvements. Within the NHS, for example, a performance target of 3 per cent a year for value for money improvements was set. Performance is to be tightly monitored centrally to ensure that the periphery 'delivers'.

A secondary theme was 'joined up government', ensuring that different agencies worked together to tackle complex issues (an approach more consistent with process-based thinking). Six reviews were carried out on a cross-departmental basis, for example, the cross-departmental review of illegal drugs which brought together the criminal justice system, health, and education agencies. Joint budgets were introduced in a small number of areas such as asylum support. In other areas, joint working was to be encouraged. In the example of drugs, the anti-drugs strategy should integrate activity across agency boundaries through partnerships and coordinate joint action locally through Drug Action Teams. The policy areas in which there were significant moves to 'joined up government' remained of a contained nature.

By contrast, the Cabinet Office's text (Cm 4310, 1999, *Modernising Government*) placed more emphasis on institution-building and less on purely financial criteria such as value for money. It also contains some important and critical reflections on the NPM. This text argued that the 1980s and 1990s had been characterized by an excessive concern for management efficiency and that too little attention had been accorded to the development of an effective policy process. Laterally, many complex policy areas required work across conventional boundaries, either between different central departments or between central and local government. Vertically, the split between the small strategic core and large operational periphery characteristic of the Next Steps agency model had led to a lack of involvement from front-line staff. 'Joined up government' was identified as one key objective of a reformed policy-making process, along with an outcome orientation, a shift towards evidence-based policy-making and a learning organization, and a more futuristic and outwards looking orientation. This text is more supportive of process-based models of organization, reflecting its preference for 'joined up government'.

Which of these two different texts is likely to have more influence? A major facilitator of the rise of the NPM in the 1980s was that public sector reform was not contained as a technical issue for the Cabinet Office but engaged the attention of the Prime Minister. Public sector reform was seen as a truly strategic issue politically. It appears that the reform of the machinery of government has remained much lower down the corporate agenda during the first Labour government, with no fewer than three ministers filling the Cabinet Office post within four years. Given this relatively weak political leadership, one presumption is that power has drifted to the Treasury, with its highly NPM orthodox approach.

Within health care, Cm 4818 (2000) represents a key text that sets out the long-term strategy to 'modernize' the NHS. This is a centrally produced document that outlines a global strategy for the whole of the NHS. The 'vision' is one of (p. 17) 'fast and convenient care delivered to a consistently high standard. Services will be available when people require them, tailored to their individual needs.' Considerable sums of new public money are being made available to effect the transition. This vision implies better working across organizational boundaries, for example, with a new service (NHS Direct) being introduced to launch a 'one-stop shop' and easy point of access. Process redesign efforts are commended (although the term BPR is not used), and are to be diffused more widely through the establishment of a new central body (the 'Modernization Agency').

However, other sections of the document indicate the growth of 'command and control' or performance management systems. National systems of audit, regulation, and standard-setting are to be much expanded, with the introduction of central agencies (another new central body: the Commission for Health Improvement), National Service Frameworks, and new systems of single organization-based clinical governance. The national Performance Assessment Framework is to be expanded from Health Authorities to include individual hospitals and primary care organizations. Autonomy is to be 'earned' on the basis of this Performance Assessment Framework through a 'traffic lights system' with health care providers classified into 'green', 'yellow', or 'red'. There are to be increased levels of central intervention in the case of the 'red' organizations and Trusts will clearly want to take actions to avoid being classified as 'red'. The intent to achieve accelerating rates of change has also led to the imposition of highly ambitious national change targets that managers are expected to deliver locally.

This review of key post-1997 policy statements indicates that there is some evidence of a declared intent to move towards 'joined up government' and laterally based organizations, a theme championed in particular by the Cabinet Office. We suggest however that this is a subordinate theme when seen in the round. The Treasury appears to demonstrate a performance management orientation and to have access to a greater range of levers to influence the big spending departments such as Health. The *NHS Plan* suggests that within the substantive domain of health policy top-down and target-driven approaches will characterize the dominant implementation strategy. The policy system

seems to be reverting to a new variant of NPM Model 1, in which traditional levers of direct managerial control are increasingly complemented by new audit and quality assurance systems (Power 1997).

> Proposition 3: the dominant post-1997 policy in relation to health
> care is essentially NPM 1 orthodox and unlikely to support an
> archetype shift to laterally based organizations.

10.5   Empirical observations from the case-study site

We now consider the results from the case-study site which provide
at least some local empirical data. The fieldwork for the present study
took place in a later period (1995–8) and usefully updates our early
interpretation (Ferlie et al. 1996). The newly created NHS Trusts were in
the early 1990s given enhanced operational freedoms, including the
freedom to experiment with new forms of organization and management. Indeed, LRI's bold decision to introduce an ambitious BPR programme was seen as a leading example nationally of this increased
capacity to engage in organizational experimentation.

Shortly after being accorded NHS Trust status, LRI can be seen as
developing a style of working influenced by both NPM 2 and 3 (in its
top-down variant) both of which sought to get away from NPM 1. The
exogenous driver for the adoption of NPM 1 was the anticipated effect
within Leicester of the internal market. There was in 1994/5 an expectation that strong market forces would develop in the city, putting intense
pressure on the hospital to become more competitive. The city represented a 'health system' that was ideally placed to develop a quasi-
market, with three co-located acute hospitals. The introduction of BPR
was defended on the basis that the hospital's competitive environment
would become much harsher and that proactive action needed to be
taken. The prospect of the internal market triggered major internal
organizational change in that new functions emerged in the hospital
(such as marketing and service contracts), picking up market intelligence. Some of the clinical services keenest to embrace process redesign
were those facing strongest competitive pressures, for example, needing to get waiting times down for micro-purchasers (GP Fundholders).

However, from about 1995 onwards, market forces were progressively damped down by the macro-purchaser (the Health Authority)
that acted to 'manage the market'. The macro-purchaser effected
changes in its contract portfolio to stabilize major providers and prevent

market exit, which would have been politically difficult. Budgets were 'softer' than they initially appeared. The macro-purchaser soon had recourse to planning as a non-market-based means of service rationalization between the three hospitals. By the late 1990s, the 'excursion' towards NPM 2 was being damped down locally as well as nationally (Mays, Mulligan, and Goodwin 2000) by the revival of NPM 1 based models of planning.

There had also been an internally generated drive to NPM 3 in the BPR programme. It was largely top-down in nature, with the corporate centre launching a planned change programme which the clinical settings were to 'buy into'. The programme was 'top led but bottom fed': there was a projection of a top-down vision, but the corporate centre also sought to empower change champions at local level to deliver this vision. There were NPM 3 orthodox symptoms as: an explicit communications strategy; an attempted increase in change management capability; more interest in the use of education and training programmes to consolidate knowledge and skill bases; the emergence of a new special language by the change group. External change agents such as management consultants were used to import new ideas and challenge taken for granted assumptions.

There were limits to the impact of NPM 3. Top management remained stable and dominated by internal appointments and there was no external manager brought in to 'turn the organization around' through the projection of a radical new vision. The managerial leadership style remained transactional rather than charismatic in nature. The management consultants brought in were not able to produce 'frame-breaking' change, as the old order proved resilient. There were limits to the extent to which clinical and nursing staff 'bought into' the reengineering vision, despite the communications and management of change strategies. The hospital (like all hospitals) had to meet the performance targets being elaborated nationally, which became more demanding as time went on and which placed constraints on local managerial autonomy. The transition to an NPM 3 within the hospital remained of a partial nature, although it showed more staying power than the abortive excursion to NPM 2. We conclude that there were some shifts in the style of organization and management apparent in the case-study site in the mid-1990s, although they were partial and difficult to sustain. Our early proposition based on a review of LRI case data is:

Proposition 4: Despite the presence of interesting organizational experiments, the NPM 1 orthodox performance management style is likely to remain dominant over the long run within managerial practice in the NHS.

Our overall assertion is that vertically based principles of organizing are likely to remain important and indeed dominant within the NHS and perhaps other UK public services.

10.6 Process-based models of organizing and the new public management: contradictory rather than complementary?

In our study, reengineering has been presented as one exemplar of a process approach to organizing. These ideas have had some increased influence in the world of UK public policy, albeit coexisting with a dominant performance management model. What is the relationship between these process-based ideas and those of the New Public Management which we argue have also remained influential?

Increasingly, it is recognized that processes of change may involve paradoxes (Eisenhardt 2000). Our study suggests that many public service organizations are likely to encounter a tension between process and functional principles of organizing. A juxtaposition of these two sets of principles is evident empirically in the case-study site. On the one hand, functional organizing principles promoted over the last decade have strengthened the specialty and directorate as a mode of organizing within health care. On the other hand, process principles promoting lateral integration and collaboration have also emerged. The tension between these two sets of principles poses considerable management challenges. In the case-study site, for instance, the ambition held by reengineers to move from a directorate-based to process-based mode of organizing was not achieved.

There is little other evidence as to how 'boundary shifting' reforms have affected professionalized organizations such as hospitals (but for an exception see Denis et al. 1999). We found in our study that securing change across the boundaries of clinical specialties and directorates has been a difficult and often frustrating task for process reformers. Our study observed the failure of reengineers to establish a set of core processes as legitimate constructs to facilitate corporate change. The decision to devolve responsibility for implementing reengineering to the clinical directorates often did not result in significant change to professional practices. Yet, Kitchener (1999) reports that some 70 per cent of UK hospitals are now organized around directorates and specialties as a result of earlier NPM style reforms. This newly strengthened functionally based pattern of organization may well make the introduction of process-based approaches difficult. Intensified performance management also operates through vertical lines and strengthens functionally based patterns of reporting.

In addition, long-term processes towards medical specialization and differentiation are continuing and the exogenous pressure which could have been placed on the system by the quasi-market and assertive customers has been removed. There is little in the way of customer pressure to force 'joined up services'. This combination of factors suggests caution about the prospects of process-based modes of organizing emerging as a new dominant logic within UK hospitals and spawning new patterns of professional collaboration and integrated services.

Interventions designed to change patterns of clinical care still need to generate a critical mass of clinical support and to overcome active or even passive resistance from clinicians. An important part of the influence process for those leading process redesign efforts is to deal with the criticisms of doctors, whether real or latent, publicly or privately expressed. As Denis et al. (1999) argue, this requires an appreciation of the nature of professional collaboration, its underlying dynamics and power relations, and creating incentives for professionals to engage in more collaborative forms of change. Our study provides some support for their contention that change strategies need to be tied to professional incentive structures and 'naturally occurring' interactions to be effective.

Countering Mintzberg's view of the individualistic nature of professional work, Denis et al. (1999) observed professional collaboration to be a natural feature within hospitals, at least in the Canadian ones they studied. Professional collaboration developed within 'emergent operating units', which evolve from below and which may not even be represented on a formal organization chart. There are mixed implications arising from this pattern for attempts to integrate clinical work. On the one hand, this suggests that different professional subgroups can learn to work together. Against this, this model reminds us of the continuing dominance of doctors within the provision of health care. This dominance is reaffirmed when external actors (managers, reengineers, and management consultants) intervene from outside and there remain severe limits to the exercise of managerial power. Paradoxically, the pre-NPM model of organically developing professional networks may be better able to support laterally based modes of working than reformed NPM organizations where vertical reporting has developed much more strongly.

Our study suggests some uncomfortable lessons for policy and management. The present policy aspiration of greater integration clashes with the set of functional arrangements such as clinical directorates which have been strengthened considerably over the last decade, initially to get the NHS ready for the quasi-market experiment but more recently as a device for strengthening the top-down accountability and performance management of the NHS as a whole. There is a rich seam of irony here: previous public sector reforms originally launched in the name of better management may now be proving antithetical to the new policy model of process-based management.

10.7 Final remarks and challenges for the future

Our overall interpretation of the impact of the BPR programme within the case-study site is a nuanced one: there were some pockets of change, but no organizational transformation. Change was patchy, difficult, and took much longer than originally expected. Clinicians and to a lesser extent nurses remained key stakeholder groups with the power to block or adapt change. There were no examples of process change imposed on clinicians found in our study: instead, consent had to be won. There were some interesting attempts to move away from conventional management styles but these proved difficult to sustain over long periods of time and there was regression to more conventional ways of managing.

What might the future hold? Given the equivocal results from evaluation, there may well not be a rapid 'roll-out' of BPR in the UK health care system as the Department of Health acts as a gatekeeper in a way which is not possible in the more decentralized American health care system. However, there is continuing policy interest in the broader notion of 'process redesign' (Cm 4818, 2000), with 'Breakthrough Collaboratives' and 'managed networks' emerging as models of choice within the next iteration. There may therefore be further cycles of attempts to move towards a more process-based mode of organizing. Some basic questions remain to be explored. First, how do powerful professional groups react to such changes? Do they retain the power to block or shape them? Secondly, how can process-based models be constructed within the public services given the continuing absence of 'customers' or even empowered consumer proxies? Thirdly, and perhaps most fundamentally of all, are all these process-based models associated with an organizational 'counter-culture' which in the end lacks the power to challenge dominant, vertically led, and performance-managed modes of organization? In what sense, for example, can the currently fashionable concept of a 'managed network' really be enacted? Behind the veil of process rhetoric, are we in reality seeing a reversion to NPM Model 1 as the dominant organizational form within the UK public sector? That implies the continuing presence of strong vertical lines and reporting systems which will overwhelm a few process-based experiments. Organizational research will have an important role in commenting on these major and enduring public policy issues.

References

ABBOTT, A. (1988), *The System of Professions: An Essay on the Division of Expert Labour*. London: University of Chicago Press.

—— (1992), 'From Causes to Events: Notes on Narrative Positivism', *Sociological Methods and Research*, 20: 428–55.

ABRAHAMSON, E. (1991), 'Managerial Fads and Fashions', *Academy of Management Review*, 16/3: 586–612.

—— (1996), 'Management Fashion', *Academy of Management Review*, 21/1: 254–85.

ACKROYD, S. (1996), 'Organization Contra Organizations: Professions and Organizational Change in the UK', *Organization Studies*, 17/4: 599–621.

ALFORD, A. (1975), *Health Care Politics*. London: University of Chicago Press.

ALTHEIDE, D. L., and JOHNSON, J. M. (1994), 'Criteria for Assessing Interpretive Validity in Qualitative Research', in N. Denzin and Y. Lincoln (eds.), *Handbook of Qualitative Research*. London: Sage, 485–99.

ARGYRIS, C. (1999), *On Organizational Learning*. Oxford: Basil Blackwell.

ARNDT, M., and BIGELOW, B. (1995), 'The Implementation of TQM in Hospitals: How Good is the Fit?', *Health Care Management Review*, 20/4: 7–14.

—— —— (1998), 'Reengineering: Déjà Vu All Over Again', *Health Care Management Review*, 23/3: 58–66.

BACHRACH, P., and BARATZ, M. (1970), *Power and Poverty*. London: Oxford University Press.

BARLEY, S. R. (1986), 'Technology as an Occasion for Structuring: Evidence from Observations of CT Scanners and the Social Order of Radiology Departments', *Administrative Science Quarterly*, 31: 78–108.

—— (1990a), 'Images of Imaging: Notes on Doing Longitudinal Fieldwork', *Organization Science*, 1/3: 220–47.

—— (1990b), 'The Alignment of Technology and Structure through Roles and Networks', *Administrative Science Quarterly*, 35: 61–103.

—— and TOLBERT, P. S. (1997), 'Institutionalization and Structuration: Studying the Links between Action and Institution', *Organization Studies*, 18/1: 93–117.

BARZELAY, M. (1992), *Breaking through Bureaucracy*. Berkeley and Los Angeles: University of California Press.

BAUM, J. C. (1996), 'Organizational Ecology', in H. Clegg, C. Hardy, and W. Nord (eds.), *Handbook of Organizational Studies*. London: Sage, 77–114.

BECKER, H. S., and GEER, B. (1982), 'Participant Observation: The Analysis of Qualitative Field Data', in R. D. Burgess (ed.), *Field Research: A Sourcebook and Field Manual*. London: Allen Unwin, 239–50.

—— —— HUGHES, E., and STRAUSS, A. (1961), *Boys in White: Student Culture in a Medical School*. Chicago: University of Chicago Press.

BECKERT, J. (1999), 'Agency, Entrepreneurs, and Institutional Change: The Role of Strategic Choice and Institutionalised Practices in Organizations', *Organization Studies*, 20/5: 777–99.

BECKHARD, R., and HARRIS, R. (1987), *Organizational Transitions*. Wokingham: Addison Wesley.

BEER, M., EISENSTAT, R., and SPECTOR, B. (1990), *The Critical Path to Corporate Renewal*. Boston: Harvard Business School Press.

BELMONT, R. W., and MURRAY, R. J. (1993) 'Getting Ready for Strategic Change', *Information Systems Management*, Summer: 23–9.

BERO, L., GRILLI, R., GRIMSHAW, J., HARVEY, E., OXMAN, A., and THOMSON, M. A. (1998), 'Getting Research Findings into Practice: Closing the Gap between Research and Practice—An Overview of Systematic Reviews of Interventions to Promote the Implementation of Research Findings', *British Medical Journal*, 317: 465–8.

BLUMENTHAL, B., and HASPESLAGH, P. (1994), 'Towards a Definition of Corporate Transformation', *Sloan Management Review*, Spring: 101–6.

BOWLING, A. (1997), *Research Methods in Health*. Buckingham: Open University Press.

BOWNS, I., and McNULTY, T. (1999), "Reengineering LRI": An Independent Evaluation of Implementation and Impact', University of Sheffield, www.shef.ac.uk/~scharr/lri

—— THOMAS, K., COLEMAN, P., KNOWLES, E., and NICHOLL, J. (1998), 'Interim Report on a Study of Services for Patients with Fractured Neck of Femur, Comparing Changes over Time at Leicester Royal Infirmary'. University of Sheffield (ScHARR).

BRASS, D. J., and BURKHARDT, M. G. (1993), 'Potential Power and Power Use: An Investigation of Structure and Behaviour', *Academy of Management Journal*, 36/3: 441–70.

BRAVERMAN, R. (1974), *Labor and Monopoly Capital*. New York: Monthly Review Press.

BROADBENT, J., DIETRICH, M., and ROBERTS, J. (1997), *The End of the Professions?* London: Routledge.

BROCK, D., POWELL, M., and HININGS, C. R. (1999) (eds.), *Restructuring the Professional Organization*. London: Routledge.

BRYMAN, A. (1989), *Research Methods and Organizational Studies*. London: Routledge.

—— and BURGESS, R. (1995), *Analysing Qualitative Data*. London: Routledge.

BUCHANAN, D. (1997), 'The Limitations and Opportunities of BPR in a Politicised Organizational Climate', *Human Relations*, 50/1: 51–72.

BURKE, G., and PEPPARD, J. (1995), *Examining Business Process Reengineering*. London: Kogan Page.

BURRELL, G. (1996), 'Hard Times for the Salariat?', in H. Scarborough (ed.), *The Management of Expertise*. London: Macmillan.

—— and MORGAN, G. (1979), *Sociological Paradigms and Organizational Analysis*. London: Heinemann.

CARON, J. R., JARVENPAA, S. L., and STODDARD, D. (1994), 'Business Reengineering at CIGNA Corporation: Experiences and Lessons Learned from the First Five Years', *MIS Quarterly*, Sept.: 233–50.

CARONNA, C., and SCOTT, W. R. (1999), 'Institutional Effects on Organizational Governance and Conformity: The Case of Kaiser Permanente and the US Health Care Field', in D. Brock, M. Powell, and C. R. Hinings (eds.), *Restructuring the Professional Organization*. London: Routledge, 68–86.

CHILD, J. (1972), 'Organization Structure, Environment and Performance: The Role of Strategic Choice', *Sociology*, 6: 1–22.

—— (1997), 'Strategic Choice in the Analysis of Action, Structure, Organizations and Environment: Retrospect and Prospect', *Organization Studies*, 18/1: 43–76.

—— and SMITH, C. (1987), 'The Context and Process of Organizational Transformation: Cadbury Limited in Its Sector', *Journal of Management Studies*, 24/6: 565–93.

CLARKE, J., and NEWMAN, J. (1997), *The Managerial State*. London: Sage.

CLEGG, S., HARDY, C., and NORD, W. (1996) (eds.), *Handbook of Organizational Studies*. London: Sage.

Cm 4011 (1998), *Modern Public Services for Britain: Comprehensive Spending Review*. London: HMSO.

Cm 4310 (1999), *Modernising Government*. London: HMSO.

Cm 4818 (2000), *The NHS Plan*. London: HMSO.

COOKE, B. (1999), 'Writing the Left out of Management Theory: The Historiography of the Management of Change', *Organization*, 6/1: 81–105.

COOPER, D., HININGS, C. R., GREENWOOD, R., and BROWN, J. L. (1996), 'Sedimentation and Transformation in Organizational Change: The Case of Canadian Law Firms', *Organizational Studies*, 17/4: 623–47.

CRILLY, T. (2000), 'The Objectives of NHS Trusts', Ph.D. Thesis, London School of Economics.

DAHL, R. (1961), *Who Governs? Democracy and Power in an American City*. New Haven: Yale University Press.

DALE, M. W. (1994), 'The Reengineering Route to Business Transformation', *Journal of Strategic Change*, 3: 3–19.

DAVENPORT, T. H. (1993), *Process Innovation: Reengineering Work through Information Technology*. Cambridge, Mass.: Harvard Business School Press.

—— and SHORT, J. E. (1990), 'The New Industrial Engineering: Information Technology and Business Process Redesign', *Sloan Management Review*, Summer: 11–27.

—— and STODDARD, D. B. (1994), 'Reengineering Business Change in Mythic Proportions?', *MIS Quarterly*, June: 121–7.

DEAL, T. E., and KENNEDY, A. A. (1982), *Corporate Cultures: The Rites and Rituals of Corporate Life*. Reading, Mass.: Addison Wesley.

DENIS, J. L., LANGLEY, A., and CAZALE, L. (1996), 'Leadership and Strategic Change under Conditions of Ambiguity', *Organizational Studies*, 17/4: 673–99.

—— LAMOTHE, L., LANGLEY, A., and VALETTE, A. (1999), 'The Struggle to Redefine Boundaries in Health Care Systems', in D. Brock, M. Powell, and C. R. Hinings (eds.), *Restructuring the Professional Organization*. London: Routledge: 105–30.

DENISON, D. R. (1997), 'Towards a Process Based Theory of Organizational Design: Can Organizations Be Designed around Value-Chains and Networks?', in *Advances in Strategic Management*, 14, Greenwich, Conn.: JAI Press, 1–44.

DENZIN, N., and LINCOLN, Y. (1994) (eds.), *Handbook of Qualitative Research*. London: Sage.

DI MAGGIO, P., and POWELL, W. (1983), 'The Iron Cage Revisited: Institutional Isomorphism and Collective Rationality in Organizational Fields', *American Sociological Review*, 48:147–60.

DIXON, J. R., ARNOLD, P., HEINEKE, J., KIM, J. S., and MULLIGAN, P. (1994), 'Business Process Reengineering: Improving in New Strategic Directions', *California Management Review*, Summer: 93–108.

DJELIC, M.-L., and AINAMO, A. (1999), 'The Coevolution of New Organizational Forms in the Fashion Industry: A Historical and Comparative Study of France, Italy and the United States', *Organization Science*, 10/5: 622–37.

DONALDSON, L., (1996), 'The Normal Science of Structural Contingency Theory', in H. Clegg, C. Hardy, and W. Nord (eds.), *Handbook of Organizational Studies*. London: Sage, 57–76.

DRAZIN, R. (1990), 'Professionals and Innovation: Structural Functional Versus Radical Structural Perspectives', *Journal of Management Studies*, 27/3: 245–63.

DU GAY, P. (2000), *In Praise of Bureaucracy*. London: Sage.

DUNLEAVY, P., and HOOD, C. (1994), 'From Old Public Administration to New Public Management', *Public Money and Management*, July/Sept.: 9–16.

DUNPHY, D., and STACE, D. (1988), 'Transformational and Coercive Strategies for Planned Organizational Change: Beyond the OD Model', *Organizational Studies*, 9/3: 317–34.

EDEN, C., and HUXHAM, C. (1996), 'Action Research for the Study of Organizations', in H. Clegg, C. Hardy, and W. Nord (eds.), *Handbook of Organizational Studies*. London: Sage, 526–42.

EISENHARDT, K. (1989), 'Building Theories from Case Study Research', *Academy of Management Review*, 14: 532–50.

—— (2000), 'Paradox, Spirals, Ambivalence: The New Language of Change and Pluralism', *Academy of Management Review*, 25/4: 703–5.

—— and BOURGEOIS, J. L. (1988), 'Politics of Strategic Decision Making in "High Velocity" Environments: Towards a Mid-range Theory', *Academy of Management Journal*, 31/4: 737–70.

ELSTON, M. (1991), 'The Politics of Professional Power: Medicine in a Changing Health Service', in J. Gabe, M. Calman, and M. Bury (eds.), *The Sociology of the Health Service*. London: Routledge, 58–88.

EXWORTHY, M., and HALFORD, S. (1999), *Professionals and the New Managerialism in the Public Sector*. Buckingham: Open University Press.

FERLIE, E. (2000*a*), 'Quasi Strategy: Strategic Management in the Contemporary Public Sector', in A. Pettigrew, H. Thomas, and R. Whittington (eds.), *Sage Handbook of Strategy and Management*. London: Sage.

—— (2000*b*), 'Organizational Studies and Health Services Research', Imperial College: School of Management.

—— and FITZGERALD, L. (2000), 'The Sustainability of the NPM Paradigm in the UK: An Institutionalist Perspective', Presentation at the Academy of Management Conference, Toronto, August.

—— and MCNULTY, T. (1997), '"Going to Market": Changing Patterns in the Organization and Character of Process Research', *Scandinavian Journal of Management*, 13/4: 367–87.

—— ASHBURNER, L., FITZGERALD, L., and PETTIGREW, A. (1996), *The New Public Management in Action*. Oxford: Oxford University Press.

FINCHAM, R. (2000), 'Management as Magic: Reengineering and the Search for Business Salvation', in D. Knights and H. Willmott (eds.), *The Reengineering Revolution: Critical Studies of Corporate Change*. London: Sage, 174–91.

FITZGERALD, L. (1994), 'Moving Clinicians into Management: A Professional Challenge or a Threat?', *Journal of Management in Medicine*, 8/6: 32–44.

—— and FERLIE, E. (2000), 'Professionals: Back to the Future?', *Human Relations*, 53/5: 713–38.

—— —— WOOD, M., and HAWKINS, C. (1999), 'Interactive Forces and Their Differential Effects: Innovation and Change in Health Care', All Academy Symposium Paper, American Academy of Management Conference, Chicago, August.

FLYNN, R. (1992), *Structures of Control in Health Management*. London: Routledge.

FREIDSON, E. (1970), *Professional Dominance: The Social Structure of Medical Care*. New York: Atherton Press.

—— (1994), *Professionalism Reborn*. Cambridge: Polity Press.

GEROWITZ, M. (1998), 'Do TQM Interventions Change Management Culture? Findings and Implications', *Quality Management in Health Care*, 6/3: 1–11.

GIDDENS, A. (1979), *Central Problems in Social Theory*. London: Macmillan.

—— (1984), *The Constitution of Society*. Cambridge: Polity Press.

—— (1993), 'Structuration Theory: Past, Present and Future', in C. Bryant and C. and D. Jary (eds.), *Giddens Theory of Structuration*. London: Routledge.

—— (1997), *The Third Way: The Renewal of Social Democracy*. Cambridge: Polity Press.

GLASER, B., and STRAUSS, A. (1967), *The Discovery of Grounded Theory*. New York: Aldine.

GOFFMAN, E. (1961), *Asylums*. New York: Doubleday.

GRANOVETTER, M. (1985), 'Economic Action and Social Structures: The Problem of Embeddedness', *American Journal of Sociology*, 91/3: 481–510.

GREENWOOD, R., and HININGS, C. R. (1993), 'Understanding Strategic Change: The Contribution of Archetypes', *Academy of Management Journal*, 36: 1052–81.

—— —— (1996), 'Understanding Radical Organizational Change: Bringing Together the Old and the New Institutionalism', *Academy of Management Review*, 21/4:1022–54.

—— —— and BROWN, J. (1990), 'P2 Form Strategic Management: Corporate Practices in Professional Partnerships', *Academy of Management Journal*, 33/4: 725–55.

GREINER, L., and BARNES, L. (1970), 'Organization Change and Development', in G. Dalton, P. Lawrence, and L. Greiner (eds.), *Organization Change and Development*. Homewood, Ill.: Irwin Dorsey.

GREY, C., and MITEV, N. (1995), 'Reengineering Organizations: A Critical Appraisal', *Personnel Review*, 24/1: 6–18.

GRIFFITHS, R. (1983), *Report of NHS Management Enquiry*. London: HMSO.

GRINT, K. (1994), 'Reengineering History: Social Resonances and Business Process Reengineering', *Organization*, 1/1: 179–201.

—— and CASE, P. (2000), 'Now Where Were We? BPR Lotus-Eaters and Corporate Amnesia', in D. Knights and H. Willmott (eds.), *The Reengineering Revolution: Critical Studies of Corporate Change*. London: Sage, 26–49.

—— and WILLCOX, L. (1995), 'Business Process Reengineering in Theory and Practice: Business Paradise Regained', *New Technology, Work and Employment*, 10/2: 99–109.

HACKMAN, J. R., and WAGEMAN, R. (1995), 'Total Quality Management: Empirical, Conceptual and Practical Issues', *Administrative Science Quarterly*, 40: 309–42.

HALL, G., ROSENTHAL, J., and WADE, J. (1993), 'How to Make Reengineering Really Work'. *Harvard Business Review*, Nov./Dec.: 119–31.

HAMMER, M. (1990), 'Reengineering Work: Don't Automate, Obliterate'. *Harvard Business Review*, 68 (July–Aug.): 104–12.

—— (1996), *Beyond Reengineering*. London: Harper Collins Business.

—— and CHAMPY, J. (1993), *Reengineering the Corporation: A Manifesto for Business Revolution*. New York: Harper Collins.

HANNAN, M. T., and FREEMAN, J. (1988), *Organizational Ecology*. Cambridge, Mass.: Harvard University Press.

HARDY, C., and CLEGG, S. (1996), 'Some Dare Call It Power', in S. Clegg, C. Hardy, and W. Nord (eds.), *Handbook of Organization Studies*. London: Sage.

HARRISON, S., and POLLITT, C. (1994), *Controlling Health Professionals*. Buckingham: Open University Press.

—— HUNTER, D., MARNOCH, G., and POLLITT, C. (1992), *Just Managing: Power and Culture in the NHS*. Basingstoke: Macmillan.

HAUG, M. (1973), 'Deprofessionalisation: An Alternative Hypothesis for the Future', *Sociological Review Monograph*, 20: 195–211.

HAWORTH, J. (1997), 'Review of Services for Older People with Fractured Neck of Femur', Summary Report. District Audit, 1995/6. Leicester Royal Infirmary.

HEYGATE, R. (1993), 'Immoderate Redesign', *McKinsey Quarterly*, 1: 73–87.

—— (1994), 'Being Intelligent about "Intelligent" Technology', *McKinsey Quarterly*, 4: 137–47.

HININGS, C. R. (1997), 'Reflections on Processual Research', *Scandinavian Journal of Management*, 13/4: 493–503.

—— and GREENWOOD, R. (1988), *The Dynamics of Strategic Change*. Oxford: Basil Blackwell.

—— BROWN, J. L., and GREENWOOD, R. (1991), 'Change in an Autonomous Professional Organization', *Journal of Management Studies*, 28/4: 375–93.

—— GREENWOOD, R., and COOPER, D. (1999), 'The Dynamics of Change in Large Accounting Firms', in D. Brock, M. Powell, and C. R. Hinings (eds.), *Restructuring the Professional Organization*. London: Routledge, 131–53.

HOFF, T. J., and MCCAFFREY, D. (1996), 'Adapting, Resisting and Negotiating: How Physicians Cope with Organizational and Economic Change', *Work and Occupations*, 23/2: 165–89.

HOGGETT, P. (1996), 'New Modes of Control in the Public Service', *Public Administration*, 74/1: 9–32.

—— (1991), 'A New Management in the Public Sector?', *Policy and Politics*, 19/4: 243–56.

HONIGMAN, J. J. (1982), 'Sampling in Ethnographic Fieldwork', in R. D. Burgess (ed.), *Field Research: A Sourcebook and Field Manual*. London: Allen Unwin, 79–90.

HOOD, C. (1991), 'A Public Management for All Seasons?', *Public Administration*, 69 (Spring): 3–19.

—— (1995), 'The New Public Management in the 1980s: Variations on a Theme', *Accounting, Organization and Society*, 20, 2/3: 93–110.

HOUSE, R., ROUSSEAU, D., and THOMAS-HUNT, M. (1995), 'The Meso Paradigm', in L. L. Cummings and B. M. Staw (eds.), *Research in Organizational Behaviour*. Greenwich, Conn.: JAI Press, 17, 71–114.

HUNG, S. C., and WHITTINGTON, R. (1997), 'Strategies and Institutions: A Pluralistic Account of Strategies in the Taiwanese Computer Industry', *Organization Studies*, 18/4: 551–76.

JOHNSON, G. (1987), *Strategic Change and the Management Process*. Oxford: Basil Blackwell.

JOSS, R., and KOGAN, M. (1995), *Advancing Quality: TQM in the NHS*. Buckingham: Open University Press.

KABOOLIAN, L. (2000), 'Quality Comes to the Public Sector', in R. Cole and W. R. Scott (eds.), *The Quality Movement and Organization Theory*. London: Sage.

KEEN, J., and PACKWOOD, T. (2000), 'Using Case Studies in Health Services and Policy Research', in C. Pope and N. Mays (eds.), *Qualitative Research in Health Care*. London: BMJ Press, 50–8.

KELEMAN, M., FORRESTER, P., and HASSARD, J. (2000), 'BPR and TQM: Divergence and Convergence?', in D. Knights and H. Willmott (eds.), *The Reengineering Revolution: Critical Studies of Corporate Change*. London: Sage, 154–73.

KIRKPATRICK. I. (1999), 'Managers or Colleagues?: The Changing Nature of Intra Professional Relationships within UK Public Services', *Public Management*, 1/4: 489–510.

KITCHENER, M. (1999), ' "All Fur Coat and No Knickers": Contemporary Organizational Change in UK Hospitals', in D. Brock, M. Powell, and C. R. Hinings (eds.), *Restructuring the Professional Organization*. London: Routledge, 183–99.

KLEIN, K. J., TOSI, H., and CANNELLA, A. A. (1999), 'Multi Level Theory Building: Benefits, Barriers and New Developments', *Academy of Management Review*, 24/2: 243–8.

KLEIN, R. (2000), 'From Evidence Based Medicine to Evidence Based Policy?', *Journal of Health Services Research and Policy*, 5/2: 65–6.

KNIGHTS, D., and MCCABE, D. (1999), ' "Are There No Limits to Authority?": TQM and Organizational Power', *Organization Studies*, 20/2: 197–224.

—— and WILLMOTT, H. (2000) (eds.), *The Reengineering Revolution: Critical Studies in Corporate Change*. London: Sage.

KUHN, T. S. (1962), *The Structure of Scientific Revolutions*. London: University of Chicago Press.

LANGLEY, A. (1999), 'Strategies for Theorising from Process Data', *Academy of Management Review*, 24/4: 691–710.

LEADBETTER, C. (2000), *Living on Thin Air*. London: Penguin.

LEVY, A. (1986), 'Second Order Planned Change: Definition and Conceptualisation', *Organizational Dynamics*, Summer: 5–20.

LEWIN, A. Y., and VOLBERDA, H. W. (1999), 'Prolegomena on Coevolution: A Framework for Research on Strategy and New Organizational Forms', *Organization Science*, 10/5: 519–34.

LINDBLOM, C. E. (1959), 'The Science of Muddling through', *Public Administration Review*, 19: 79–88.

LRI NHS Trust (1994*a*), *The Strategic Direction*. Leicester Royal Infirmary NHS Trust, March.

—— (1994*b*), *Reengineering the Healthcare Process: Programme Initiation Document*. Leicester Royal Infirmary NHS Trust, January.

—— (1994*c*), *Reengineering the Healthcare Process: Report of Scoping Study*. Leicester Royal Infirmary NHS Trust, July.

—— (1995), *Reengineering the Healthcare Process: Full Report*. Leicester Royal Infirmary NHS Trust, January.

—— (1996), *Reengineering the Healthcare Process: Achieving Results*. Leicester Royal Infirmary NHS Trust, March.

—— (1997), *Evaluating Outcomes of the Leicester Royal Infirmary Re-engineering Programme*. Leicester Royal Infirmary NHS Trust, August.

LYNN, L. (1998), 'The New Public Management: How to Turn a Theme into a Legacy', *Public Administration Review*, 58/3: 231–7.

MCCABE, D., and KNIGHTS, D. (2000), 'Such Stuff as Dreams Are Made on: BPR up against the Wall of Functionalism, Hierarchy and Specialisation', in

D. Knights and H. Willmott (eds.), *The Reengineering Revolution: Critical Studies of Corporate Change*. London: Sage, 63–87.

MCNULTY, T., and FERLIE, E. (1998), 'Reengineering LRI: An Independent Evaluation of Processes of Implementation and Impact', University of Warwick Business School: Centre for Corporate Strategy and Change.

—— WHITTINGTON, R., and WHIPP, R. (1996), 'Practices and Market-Control: Work Experiences of Doctors, Scientists and Engineers', in J. Leopold, I. Glover, and M. Hughes (eds.), *Beyond Reason: The National Health Service and the Limits of Management*. Avebury: Aldershot.

MARK, A., and DOPSON, S. (1999), *Organizational Behaviour in Health Care*. London: Macmillan.

MAYS, N., and POPE, C. (1995), 'Rigour and Qualitative Research', *British Medical Journal*, 311: 444–6.

—— MULLIGAN, J.-A., and GOODWIN, N. (2000), 'The British Quasi Market in Health Care: A Review of the Evidence', *Journal of Health Services and Policy*, 5/1: 49–58.

MEYER, J., and ROWAN, B. (1977), 'Institutionalised Organizations: Formal Structure as Myth and Ceremony', *American Journal of Sociology*, 83: 340–63.

MILES, M. B. (1979), 'Qualitative Data as an Attractive Nuisance: The Problem of Analysis', *Administrative Science Quarterly*, 24/4: 590–601.

MINTZBERG, H. (1979), *The Structuring of Organizations: A Synthesis of the Research*. Englewood Cliffs, NJ: Prentice Hall.

—— (1989), *Mintzberg on Management*. New York: Free Press.

—— and WATERS, J. A. (1985), 'Of Strategies, Deliberate and Emergent', *Strategic Management Journal*, 6: 257–72.

MONTGOMERY, K. (1990), 'A Prospective Look at the Specialty of Medical Management', *Work and Occupations*, 17/2: 178–98.

MOORE, M. (1995), *Creating Public Value: Strategic Management in Government*. Cambridge, Mass.: Harvard University Press.

MORGAN, G. (1993), 'Organizations as Political Systems', in C. Mabey and B. Mayon-White (eds.), *Managing Change*. London: Paul Chapman Publishing.

—— and MURGATROYD, S. (1997), *TQM in the Public Sector*. Buckingham: Open University Press.

MOSS KANTER, R. (1977), *Men and Women of the Corporation*. New York: Basic Books.

MUMFORD, E. (1972), *Job Satsifaction: A Study of Computer Specialists*. Harlow: Longman.

MURPHY, E., DINGWALL, R., GREATBATCH, D., PARKER, S., and WATSON, P. (1998), 'Qualitative Research Methods in Health Technology Assessment: A Review of the Literature', Health Technology Assessment 2/16: University of Southampton: NCCHTA.

NADLER, D., and TUSHMAN, M. (1990), 'Beyond the Charismatic Leader: Leadership and Organizational Change', *California Management Review*, 31/10: 77–97.

NHS Centre for Reviews and Dissemination (1996), *Undertaking Systematic Reviews of Research on Effectiveness: CRD Guidelines*. University of York: CRD.

NORMAN, R. (1977), *Management for Growth*. London: Wiley.

OAKLEY, A. (2000), *Experiments in Knowing*. Cambridge: Polity Press.

OLIVER, C. (1992), 'The Antecedents of Deinstitutionalisation', *Organizational Studies*, 13: 563–88.

—— and MONTGOMERY, K. (2000), 'Creating a Hybrid Organizational Form from Parental Blueprints: The Emergence and Evolution of Knowledge Firms', *Human Relations*, 53/1: 33–56.

OSBORNE, D., and GAEBLER, T. (1992), *Reinventing Government: How the Entrepreneurial Spirit is Transforming the Public Sector*. Reading, Mass.: Addison Wesley.

OTTOWAY, R. (1976), 'A Change Strategy to Implement New Norms, New Styles and a New Environment in the Work Organization', *Personnel Review*, 5/1: 13–18.

OVRETVEIT, J. (1997), 'Towards Evidence Based Management Technologies in Health Care', Paper presented at the Second European Forum on Quality in Health Care, Paris, April.

PACKWOOD, T., POLLITT, C., and ROBERTS, S. (1998), 'Good Medicine: A Case Study of BPR in a Hospital', *Policy and Politics*, 26/4: 401–15.

PARKIN, F. (1979), *Marxism and Class Theory*. New York: Columbia University Press.

PARTIN, J. J. (1973), *Current Perspectives in Organization Development*. Reading, Mass.: Addison-Wesley.

PAWSON, R., and TILLEY, N. (1997), *Realistic Evaluation*. London: Sage.

PEDLER, M., BURGOYNE, J., and BOYDELL, T. (1991), *The Learning Company*. London: McGraw Hill.

PENTLAND, B. (1999), 'Building Process Theory with Narrative: From Description to Explanation', *Academy of Management Review*, 24/4: 711–24.

PEPPARD, J., and ROWLAND, P. (1995), *The Essence of Business Process Reengineering*. London: Prentice Hall.

PETERS, T., and WATERMAN, R. (1982), *In Search of Excellence*. New York: Harper and Row.

PETTIGREW, A. (1985), *The Awakening Giant*. Oxford: Basil Blackwell.

—— (1987), 'Context and Action in the Transformation of the Firm', *Journal of Management Studies*, 24: 649–70.

—— (1990), 'Longitudinal Field Research on Change: Theory and Practice', *Organization Science*, 1/3: 267–92.

—— (1997), 'What is Processual Analysis?', *Scandinavian Journal of Management*, 13/4: 337–48.

—— (1998), 'Success and Failure in Corporate Transformation Initiatives', in R. D. Galliers and W. R. J. Baets (eds.), *Information Technology and Organizational Transformation*. Chichester: John Wiley.

—— and FENTON, E. (2000), *The Innovating Organization*. London: Sage.

PETTIGREW, A. and McNULTY, T. (1995), 'Power and Influence in and around the Boardroom', *Human Relations*, 46/8: 845–72.

—— —— (1998), 'Sources and Uses of Power in the Boardroom', *European Journal of Work and Organizational Psychology*, 7/2: 197–214.

—— and WHIPP, R. (1991), *Managing for Competitive Success*. Oxford: Basil Blackwell.

—— FERLIE, E., and McKEE, L. (1992), *Shaping Strategic Change*. London: Sage.

POLLITT, C. (1990), *The New Managerialism and the Public Services*. Oxford: Basil Blackwell.

—— and BOUCKAERT, G. (2000), *Public Management Reform: A Comparative Analysis*, Oxford: Oxford University Press.

POLSBY, N. (1963), *Community Power and Political Theory*. New Haven: Yale University Press.

POPE, C., and MAYS, N. (1995), 'Reaching the Parts Other Methods Cannot Reach: An Introduction to Qualitative Methods and HSR', *British Medical Journal*, 311: 109–12.

—— —— (2000) (eds.), *Qualitative Research in Health Care*. London: BMJ Press, 2nd edition.

POWER, M. (1997), *The Audit Society: Rituals of Verification*. Oxford: Oxford University Press.

PRESSMAN, J., and WILDAVSKY, A. (1973), *Implementation*. Berkeley and Los Angeles: University of California Press.

QUINN, J. B. (1980), *Strategies for Change: Logical Incrementalism*. Homewood, Ill.: Irwin.

RANSON, S., and STEWART, J. (1994), *Management for the Public Domain*. London: Macmillan.

REASON, P. (1988), *Human Enquiry in Action*. London: Sage.

ROMANELLI, E., and TUSHMAN, M. (1994), 'Organizational Transformation as Punctuated Equilibrium: An Empirical Test', *Academy of Management Journal*, 37/5: 1141–66.

ROSEN, R. (2000), 'Applying Research to Health Care Policy and Practice: Medical and Managerial Views on Effectiveness and the Role of Research', *Journal of Health Services Research and Policy*, 5/2: 103–8.

SCALLY, G., and DONALDSON, L. (1998), 'Clinical Governance and the Drive for Quality Improvement in the New NHS', *British Medical Journal*, 317: 61–5.

SCHEIN, E. (1985), *Organizational Culture and Leadership*. San Francisco: Jossey Bass.

SCOTT POOLE, M., VAN DE VEN, A., DOOLEY, K., and HOLMES, M. E. (2000), *Organizational Change and Innovation Processes: Theory and Methods for Research*. Oxford: Oxford University Press.

SENGE, P. (1990), *The Fifth Discipline*. New York: Doubleday.

SHORTELL, S., BENNETT, C., and BYCK, G. (1998), 'Assessing the Impact of CQI on Clinical Practice: What Will It Take to Accelerate Progress'?, *Milbank Quarterly*, 76/4: 593–624.

—— GILLIES, R., ANDERSON, D., ERICKSON, K. M., and MITCHELL, J. (1995), *Remaking Health Care in America*. San Francisco: Jossey Bass.

STABLEIN, R. (1996), 'Data in Organizational Studies', in H. Clegg, C. Hardy, and W. Nord (eds.), *Handbook of Organizational Studies*. London: Sage, 509–23.

STARKEY, K. (1996), (ed.), *How Organizations Learn*. London: International Thomson Business Press.

STEWART, R. (1999), 'Foreword', in A. Mark and S. Dopson (eds.), *Organizational Behaviour in Health Care*. London: Macmillan, pp. ix–xi.

STOCKING, B. (1985), *Initiative and Inertia in the NHS*. London: Nuffield Provincial Hospitals Trust.

STRAUSS, A., SCHATZMAN, L., EHRLICH, D., BUCHER, R., and SABSHIN, M. (1963), 'The Hospital and Its Negotiated Order', in E. Freidson (ed.), *The Hospital in Modern Society*. London: Collier Macmillan, 147–69.

SUSMAN, G., and EVERED, R. (1978), 'An Assessment of the Scientific Merits of Action Research', *Administrative Science Quarterly*, 23: 582–603.

TAYLOR, J. A. (1995), 'Don't Obliterate, Informate!: BPR for the Information Age', *New Technology, Work and Employment*, 10/2: 82–8.

TENG, J. T. C., GROVER, V., and FIEDLER, K. (1994), 'Business Process Reengineering: Charting a Strategic Path for the Information Age', *California Management Review*, Spring: 9–31.

THACKRAY, R. (1993), 'Fads, Fixes and Fictions', *Management Today*, June: 40–2.

THOMAS, K., COLEMAN, P., KNOWLES, E., and BOWNS, I. (1998), 'Reengineering the Care Process for Patients Attending Leicester Royal Infirmary with Minor Injuries: The Impact on Patient Satisfaction and Waiting Times'. University of Sheffield, School of Health and Related Research, Medical Care Research Unit.

THORNE, M. (1997), 'Being a Clinical Director: First among Equals or Just a Go between?', *Health Services Management Research*, 10/4: 205–16.

TICHY, N., and ULRICH, R. (1984), 'Revitalising Organizations: The Leadership Role', in J. Kimberly and J. B. Quinn (eds.), *Managing Organizational Transitions*, Homewood, Ill.: Irwin.

TURNER, B. A. (1988), 'Connoisseurship on the Study of Organizational Cultures', in R. Burgess (ed.), *Doing Research in Organizations*. London: Routledge.

TUSHMAN, M., and ROMANELLI, E. (1985), 'Organization Evolution: A Metamorphosis Model of Convergence and Reorientation', in L. L. Cummings and B. Staw (eds.), *Research in Organization Behaviour*. Greenwich, Conn.: JAI Press.

VAN DE VEN, A. (1992), 'Suggestions for Studying Strategy Research: A Research Note', *Strategic Management Journal*, 13: 169–88.

—— and SCOTT POOLE, M. (1995), 'Explaining Development and Change in Organizations', *Academy of Management Review*, 20/3: 510–40.

—— POLLEY, D., GARUD, R., and VENKATARAMAN, S. (1999), *The Innovation Journey*. Oxford: Oxford University Press.

VANKANTRAMAN, N. (1991), 'Information Technology and the Network Form', in M. S. Scott Martin (ed.), *The Corporation of the 1990s: Information Technology and Organizational Transformation*. Oxford: Oxford University Press.

WAGER, T., and RONDEAU, K. (1998), 'Total Quality Commitment and Performance in Canadian Health Care Organizations', *International Journal of Health Care Quality Assurance*, 11/4: i–vii.

WALSTON, S., BURNS, L., and KIMBERLY, J. (1999), *Does Reengineering Really Work?*. Ithaca, NY: Cornell University Press.

—— KIMBERLY, J., and BURNS, L. R. (1999), *Following Fads or Economic Needs: Adopting Reengineering in Hospitals*. Philadelphia: Wharton School.

WATSON, T. J. (1995), *Sociology, Work and Industry*. London: Routledge, 3rd edition.

WHITLEY, R. (1989), 'Knowledge and Practice in the Management and Policy Sciences', Manchester Business School, Working Paper 174, Manchester.

WHITTINGTON, R. (1992), 'Puttting Giddens into Action: Social Systems and Managerial Agency', *Journal of Management Studies*, 29: 693–712.

—— MCNULTY, T., and WHIPP, R. (1994), 'Market Driven Change in Professional Services: Problems and Processes', *Journal of Management Studies*, 31/6: 831–45.

WILLCOCKS, L., CURRIE, W., and JACKSON, S. (1997), 'In Pursuit of the Reengineering Agenda in Public Administration', *Public Administration*, 75/4: 617–50.

WILLMOTT, H. (1984), 'Images and Ideals of Managerial Work: A Critical Examination of Conceptual and Empirical accounts', *Journal of Management Studies*, 21/3: 350–67.

—— (1995), 'The Odd Couple? Reengineering Business Processes, Managing Human Relations', *New Technology, Work and Employment*, 10/2: 89–98.

—— (1997), 'Rethinking Management and Managerial work: Capitalism, Control and Subjectivity', *Human Relations*, 50/11: 1329–59.

WILSON, J. Q. (1987), *Bureaucracies: What Government Agencies Do and Why They Do It*. New York: Basic Books.

YIN, R. K. (1989), *Case Study Research: Design and Methods*. Beverly Hills, Calif.: Sage.

ZUCKER, L. (1983), 'Organizations as Institutions', in S. B. Bacharach (ed.), *Research into the Sociology of Organizations*. Greenwich, Conn.: JAI Press.

—— (1987), 'Institutional Theories of Organization', *Annual Review of Sociology*, 13: 443–64.

Index